LEGACY
OF THE GODS

This edition first published in 2011 by Hampton Roads Publishing
Company, Inc.
Copyright © 2010, 2011 Freddy Silva

Cover and book design by Freddy Silva.
Front and back cover photos by Freddy Silva.

*Whilst every effort has been made to ensure the use of quoted text and images
have been credited correctly, sometimes errors can occur. If any authors or pho-
tographers feel this to be the case, please contact the author, and the necessary
corrections will be made in future printings.*

Hampton Roads Publishing Company, Inc.
Charlottesville, VA 92206

www.redwheelweiser.com

ISBN: 978-1-57174-667-2

Library of Congress Cataloging-in-Publication Data available upon
request

10 9 8 7 6 5 4 3 2 1
MAL

Printed in USA.

LEGACY
OF THE GODS

THE ORIGIN OF PLACES OF POWER
AND THE QUEST TO TRANSFORM
THE HUMAN SOUL

FREDDY SILVA

HAMPTON ROADS

in memory of

JOHN MICHELL

and

HAMISH MILLER

TWO GIANTS

who

WALKED

AHEAD OF MEN.

ACKNOWLEDGMENTS

Some people need to be thanked, some want to be thanked, some need to be spanked. Starting with the editor Maggie Marullo.

Marilee Marrinan, for the little morsels of inspired insights which opened big halls of research.

Martin Page, a *big* thank you for donating much-needed photos for this self-financed project. It improved the words-to-pictures ratio.

To the various friends and colleagues who allowed me to use their work: Paul Broadhurst, Robin Heath, Dr. Masaaki Kimura, John Martineau, Kevin Ruane, Ba Russell. IOU a pint of 'research'.

Santha Faiia for permission to use her photo of Yonaguni.

The various individuals who provided images to Creative Commons and allowed them to be shared.

Wendy, your friendship has kept me sane. You have been a great gift.

John Michell, wherever you are I hope this work does you proud.

Habib Koite, Marcio Faraco and Roine Stolt. Your music keeps me illuminated well beyond bedtime.

And to the tens of thousands of fans out there who've supported me through thick and thin, particularly thin, for despite my earlier book, which was a best-seller published in four languages, I still ended up driving an eighteen-year old car. I look forward to an improvement this time!

This one is for you.

CONTENTS

Our Legacy Bequeathed by Gods. *p.10*

ACT I

1. A Long Memory of Places of Power. *p.17*

Sourcing the earth force; original landscape temples; spirit roads and other invisible paths; sacred mountains as doorways; the nature of paradise.

2. The Mystery of the Three Steps of Vishnu. *p.33*

The three faces of the gods; what really happened in Eden; the orderly alignment of sacred mountains; the geometry of Siva.

3. Navels of the Earth, Places of the Gods. *p.43*

Where kingship descends from the sky; sacred centers; Innu-Heliopolis and the primordial mounds; the inherent power of navel stones; the legitimate source of divinity .

4. Cities of Knowledge. *p.57*

What happened at Tiwanaku; temples with older roots; the Golden Age; places of the First Occasion; mirrors of the heavens; Giza at 10,500 BC; appearing and disappearing craftsmen; where humans are transformed into bright stars.

5. Here Comes The Flood. *p.73*

Tales of lost lands and submerged temples; dating the great flood; recurring flood myths; more than one Noah.

6. Seven Sages. *p.85*

Giant people bearing great wisdom; traditions of levitating stones; the Followers of Horus; networks of adepts; seeding the knowledge for the future.

7. Builders of the Grid. *p.101*

Resurrecting the former world of the gods; strategic positioning of sacred sites; a universe in number; codes inside myths; the precessional cycle and other stellar mechanics; the global alignment of temples.

8. Kingdoms of Conscience. *p.121*

The law of correspondences; the raising of great stones; sacred engineering at Avebury; telluric lines across Europe; expansion of the grid; the mystery of Stonehenge's elbow; the New Zealand-Galicia ley. And back.

ACT II

9. A Very Personal Odyssey. *p.155*

Interacting with the invisible at places of power.

The Seven Principles of Sacred Space:

10. Principle One: Water. *p.167*

11. Principle Two: Electromagnetics. *p.177*

12. Principle Three: Sacred Measure. *p.195*

13. Principle Four: Stone. *p.201*

14. Principle Five: Sacred Geometry. *p.207*

15. Principle Six: Orientation. *p219*

16. Principle Seven: The Human Key. *p.229*

ACT III

17. The Rise and Fall of the Temple. *p.239*

The on-going cycles of humanity; falling asteroids and changing climates; temple-building in overdrive; collapse of culture; Akhenaten strikes against corruption; the cult of blood; abuse of energy and the power of tyrants; Alexander the Great and the resurgence of Light; the decapitation of the divine feminine.

18. Return of the Invisibles. *p.259*

From knowledge to liberty; the great Catholic impostor; the big Templar secret; what was inside the Ark; rise of the Great Work; emergence of the Gothic; a college of invisibles; the return of the gods; the deliberate debunking of crop circles.

19. 108 Degrees of Wisdom. *p.283*

The renewal of the soul; empowerment as a threat; emergence of the brotherhood in modern times; the knowledge as a capital.

References. *p.290*

Image credits. *p.306*

Index. *p.311*

Alexandria, yesterday.

0

OUR LEGACY BEQUEATHED BY GODS.

Written traditions such as the Edfu *Building Texts* inform us how groups of sages and creator gods embarked on temple-building programs at carefully chosen locations in the aftermath of a global flood.[1] These temples represent some of the most awe-inspiring structures on Earth, and many have survived at least 11,000 years of abject politics, weather and warfare. Clearly, whoever created such durable structures meant to do so for posterity, perhaps so that the principles upon which they were founded would serve future generations.

Or perhaps they would remind future generations of the principles they'd abandoned.

These "gods" are often described as people of enormous stature, or having unusual physical characteristics, literally and metaphorically. But physical beings nevertheless.

Super-men, perhaps.

Left: Sunrise pilgrim at Stonehenge, England

In the land of Sumer, a god of giant stature once gave men "an insight into letters and sciences, and every kind of art. He taught them to construct houses, to found temples, to compile laws, and explained to them the principles of geometrical knowledge... so universal were his instructions, nothing has been added materially by way of improvements."[2] Tales of traveling gods escaping a global deluge underscore the myths in practically every culture, and they regularly appear in groups of seven.

In the Indian *Vedas* seven sages are said to have come from an island, "the home of the primeval ones" destroyed in a great flood. The few survivors became "builder gods, the lords of light." With them came the principle of maintaining indefinitely a society in perfect balance with itself and with the universe through earthly and cosmic balance.[3] The same tradition appears in Egyptian texts, which refer to seven sages arriving from an island that was swallowed up in the waters of an earth-destroying flood to establish sacred mounds along the Nile that served as foundations for future temples. An identical situation exists in the myths of Easter Island.

This priesthood, for lack of a better noun, was dedicated to the preservation and transmission to the future of a body of spiritual knowledge from the remote past. The cities and temples from which the gods emerged and then recreated were no ordinary places; as with Siva, the god of wisdom, they ruled *jnana puri*, literally "the city of knowledge."

Evidence of this intent is imprinted in the very fabric of the structures they left behind, as a hundred years of analysis of sacred sites now reveals knowledge of advanced geometry, the mathematics of the Earth's Precessional Cycles, solar, lunar and stellar alignments, and so forth.

And yet their true function is far and beyond that of Universal encyclopedias. Though we may live in a modern and largely cynical society, there is hardly a person who will dispute the fact that we are immersed in times of turbulence, where change is the only constant. There is the uneasy realization that we have lost our faith in the world around us and lost sight of fundamental principles. We are disconnected from some primal source with whom we once felt comfortable, and which served to restore our umbilical resonance with worlds that cannot be seen or touched. Even though we are experiencing the ills of disconnection, lying all around us in plain view are the means through which ancient cultures once maintained themselves in balance for thousands of years.

They are called temples.

Pyramids, stone circles, menhirs, dolmens, sanctuaries and mounds. Regardless of their shape and size, they all were built by faceless experts from forgotten ages to the same end: to be mirrors of the heavens so that ordinary men and women may be transformed into gods.[4] As the Egyptian builder gods once stated, "Whosoever shall make a copy thereof, and shall know it upon earth, it shall act as a magical protector for him in heaven and in earth, unfailingly and regularly and eternally." [5]

Texts discovered at Nag Hammadi stipulate how leading away from such spiritual places caused people to die not knowing the truth, never understanding the Source or why they are here, deceived by darkness and ignorance.[6] And darkness and ignorance aren't just the prisons of modern society, they are lead curtains that threaten to obscure the light which groups of enlightened individuals have championed to re-establish for the past 4000 years. All we need do is rediscover the special places marked for us on the face of the Earth by beings of great stature whose aim was to maintain an unbroken chain of self-help centers in the face of potential chaos. To do this it is necessary to understand the motivation behind the temple-builders, the principles behind their temples and how they work.

This book is not a general saunter through famous temples and sacred sites around the world. There are many books that already delve into such territory and they do it admirably. This is a unique insight, a behind-the-scenes look into the mind and soul of temple-building: why these "special chosen locations" are so; how ordinary landscapes were transformed into places of power; and the seven principles that master craftsmen combined to transform mere stones and subtle forces into sacred environments. Theirs was an art of manipulating natural laws, and inside their creations the veil between worlds isn't just perceptibly thin, your senses of awareness are acutely enhanced so as to be capable of perceiving them.

This knowledge has appeared sporadically and haphazardly, but to the best of my knowledge, has never been published in whole. It once formed the cornerstone of subtle energy teachings in ancient Mysteries Schools.

Few lay people have been privy to this information, and there is very good reason for this. Because temples are living organisms that amplify the human potential, the laws that govern them have been used and misused throughout history. Enlightened rulers, sages and pharaohs once were entrusted with the keys to the temple, and used these sacred places for the improvement of humanity – to 'transform base metal into gold', to coin the alchemical metaphor. In time they were usurped by a false priesthood, who in turn were supplanted by corrupted Caesars and Catholic Popes. Irresponsible people driven by ego such as tyrants, despots, dark Freemasons and Nazis have sought to apply this knowledge to bring about the subjugation of entire nations.

Because just like stone, human intent, properly channeled, can become a very powerful weapon.

The secrets of the temple have been quietly handed down among esoteric societies such as the Cathars, Bogomils and Manicheists, later to be rediscovered by the Knights Templar during their excavations of the Temple of Solomon in Jerusalem.

The majority of these sects died horrifically at the hands of the despot Philip IV and Pope Clement V. Rather than give up timeless secrets, they took them to the grave.

It is now time for the lost knowledge of temple-building to resurface. Like any sacred space, the idea behind this book is to let you enter as an initiate and re-emerge an adept.

Far from being dead and forgotten, ancient temples are as alive as the day they were built, and anyone who has visited Stonehenge or Saqqara, not as a tourist but as a pilgrim, understands this. Temples are first seen, and then felt. And it is through that feeling that the soul of the Universe extends its pen and inscribes the clay tablet that is Man.

The gods did not build temples for the benefit of one culture or creed. They designed these heirlooms to last as a legacy for all races unborn, an insurance policy for times which they foresaw as dangerous to the proper conduct of human life.

They built temples for our common wealth.

Uragh stone circle, Ireland. The vision of a very tall woman is often seen here.

ACT I

The Giant of Manio, Carnac. And a potentially future giant.

1

A Long Memory of Places of Power.

Touching the untouchable.

One of the rare good things that came out of the Spanish genocide otherwise known as La Conquista was a written account of the creation myth of the Quiche´ Maya. Like other distinguished cultures before them, great emphasis was placed on committing to memory the laws, history, astronomy, sacred knowledge, events, and other vital information pertaining to their collective wisdom. As with the ancient Egyptians or the Hopi, valuable knowledge was transmitted orally from generation to generation. It was an art held in great esteem, and a privilege entrusted to a few, responsible individuals. But in 1701 it was the Dominican Friar Francisco Ximénez's turn to hear the oral history of the Quiche´ Maya and immortalize it in paper. The timing couldn't have been better, for the tribe had been practically eradicated from this mortal coil either by Spanish swords or the diseases of the savages wielding them.

Of all the interesting things about this corpus named *Popul Vuh*, two items in particular stand out. First, its depiction of life during a "Golden Age" before a catastrophic global flood swept the Earth sounds remarkably like most gnostic texts compiled by other civilizations with whom the Quiche Maya supposedly had never interacted. Second, it describes how the "First Men" possessed clairvoyant ability: "Endowed with intelligence, they saw and instantly they could see far; they succeeded in seeing, they succeeded in knowing all that there is in the world. The things hidden in the distance they saw without first having to move… they were formidable men." [1]

It seems that our remote ancestors were highly attuned to nature and applied their ability accordingly. Indeed many cultures who share close contact with the land have always been attributed with the power of natural divination. Celtic cultures – and later the Druids – as well as the Bushmen of the Kalahari, were not just highly intuitive, but also telepathic.[2] This natural-born ability enabled them to see the unseen and touch the untouchable.

Besides being more attuned to their surroundings they also understood the origin of what they felt, and why it was there. The Hopi creation myth describes how life on Earth came into being, and although its symbology is unique to that culture, its metaphors bear an uncanny similarity to other religious texts. In their legend, one of the first people created by the Source is sent to the South Pole with a drum where he hears the heartbeat of the Earth. As he beats a rhythm in sympathetic harmony, a surge of life energy is directed into the center of Gaia, sending streams of life force up to the surface whereupon Earth becomes abundant with life. However, some places became significantly more abundant with this energy. The Hopi called them "the spots of the fawn," [3] and over time they would become sacred places.

Indeed, there has always been a sense among shamanist traditions that certain locations – particularly mountains – are repositories of a vital life force more concentrated than surrounding geographical locations. They are thresholds into a non-

The spirit road at Teotihuacan.

ordinary reality, places where the worlds of the material and the spirit convergence and the ancestors offer advice.

The ancients appreciated that human beings are, first and foremost, individuals, and that their journey towards spiritual enlightenment is an individual act where success is based on persistence, patience and perseverance. The hazards along this road are plenty and the distractions immense. Therefore, a little help on the journey has always been sought. And as far back as even the Aborigines can remember, we have sought places on the land where the veil between worlds is thinnest. Ancient traditions describe these as resident places of the spirits – what western scholars interpreted to be 'gods'. They are power places that help enlighten the individual and where the greater good of the community is served. And contrary to our modern perception of power as a monetary or political tool, they are repositories of energy, insofar as they provide a more direct connection with an astral reference library and with the Great Spirit that flows through life.

The ways and roads of the spirit.

Like the force that drives mammals to migrate along invisible roads century after century, the peoples of the land were drawn to specific hotspots, and if they lived far from these special places they utilized a network of hidden highways that led them there. Native tribes of Bolivia and the American southwest refer to them as *spirit roads*; in Ireland they are the *fairy paths*, in China the *Lung Mei*. The compacting of the earth by millions of pilgrim feet walking them over the course of thousands of years has even transformed some of these once occult roads into visible footpaths. In the area around Chaco Canyon, New Mexico, these old straight tracks are described in Navajo lores as tunnels along which the Anasazi could invisibly travel; in Britain you can still walk hundreds of such paths called *dod lanes*, a term handed down from the early Saxon *deada waeg*, the "path of the dead." This is also one of the names of the Via Sacra ("sacred way") connecting the pyramid complex at Teotihuacan, which goes by a second name, the "Way of the Stars."

Other celebrated spirit roads are those of the Australian Aboriginal tribes, whose own oral tradition, the *altjurunga* ("dreamtime") recalls events that took place over a million years ago.[4] Thankfully, Aboriginal tribes are still with us, and it is from them that we get a sense of what it feels like to tune-in to the land. And why.

To say these people live among featureless terrain is an understatement, and yet the hardy inhabitants of the Outback are able to find their way around by sensing invisible lines of force. They call them *djalkiri*, "footprints of the ancestors." [5] When a tribesman walks across a spirit road, if he or she is attentive, they will hear the resonance imprinted by those who walked before. In a way, the invisible *djalkiri* behave like strips of magnetic cassette tape, recording the song of every individual. This led them to be described by westerners as *songlines*, but more accurately the

Aborigines describe the spirit roads as *dreaming tracks*.[7] They are imprinted with lore and ritual beyond living memory, a permanent record of events, enabling the Aborigines to walk hundreds of miles while listening to a data-stream. And just like modern-day cloud computing, the information can be accessed on-demand.

These spirit roads lead to spiritually important places despite the latter being physically separated by hundreds of miles. That makes them all the more important, especially when so many energy hotspots tend to be unobtrusive and possess no redeeming features, at least to the ignorant eye. But there is no doubt that the spirit roads guide the Aborigines to an intended destination. The thing is, when they are used to figure out directions to distant non-sacred places, the margin of error is as high as 67%, but when using sacred sites as destinations the errors are less than 3%.[7] Talk about magnetic attraction!

This implies that the primary use of these pathways is shamanic rather than orientational. Magician-shamans called *Karadji* – sometimes referred to as "Men of High Degree" – have long used such pathways to locate energy nodes, and to transmit information telepathically and receive it in the form of visions.[8] The same folklore surrounds pre-Bronze Age hill forts in Britain, the flat-topped earthen enclosures erroneously labeled as fortifications, where telepathy and communication with other levels of reality was conducted right up into the era of the Druids.[9] In fact, telepathy is enhanced thousands of times at sacred sites dating to the Neolithic era.[10] And just like the Aboriginal places of power, all such sacred sites are connected by a network of spirit roads.

The energy nodes and their effect on the individual are not restricted to ancient people or modern shaman. Anyone attuned to the environment is able to open a doorway of communication at these focal spots, and that can lead to an intimate experience with the spirit of place. Mountaineers are just such a type. Although the concentration demanded of them requires intense mental clarity and total left-brain engagement, at certain moments a climber's bond with the rock can become a religious experience. One such occasion occurred to Maurice Herzog while climbing the Annapurna in Nepal, a holy mountain named for the Goddess of Fertility: "I had the strangest and most vivid impressions such as I had never before known in the mountains… all sense of exertion was gone, as though there was no longer any gravity… I had never seen such complete transparency, and I was living in a world of crystal. Sounds were indistinct. The atmosphere like cotton wool. An astonishing happiness welled up in me, but I could not define it. An enormous gulf was between me and the world. This was a different universe… we were overstepping a boundary."[11]

That Hertzog experienced this transcendental moment on a mountain deemed sacred by local people is not unusual to those who understand such places and their effects; the fact that such a right-brain revelation occurred in a place with a 40% fatality rate for climbers – making this the most dangerous mountain in the world – is what gives credence to his shamanic experience.

In some cultures, natural power places are marked with petroglyphs, notably in the American southwest, the Sahara and Australia, and particularly where landscape temples have been in continuous use for millennia as hotspots for vision quests, as well as healing. They are often some of the most serene places on Earth, where the sky and the earth seem limitless and in balanced proportion to one another.

They are also unique in that they are located at unusual electromagnetic or gravitational hotspots. Every dawn, the Earth is subjected to a rise in the solar wind, which intensifies the planet's geomagnetic field; at night this field weakens, then picks up at dawn and the cycle repeats *ad infinitum*. But there are places on the land where the geomagnetic field interacts with another force, and the effect intensifies. In physics it is called a *telluric current*; ancient people call it a spirit road. These subtle lines of force tend to travel better along soil with a high content of metal and water, and possibly quartz. Drier, less metallic ground conducts telluric currents minimally. Where a boundary between these two types of land occurs, the telluric current crossing it either reinforces or weakens the daily fluctuations of the geomagnetic field.[12] This

Petroglyphs mark a magnetic hotspot and temple. Arizona

generates a hotspot called a *conductivity discontinuity*, and even though ancient people did not own magnetometers, they were able to locate them long before science built machines that proved them right.

The Sioux call this energy *skan*, and when concentrated at power places it is claimed to influence the mind, creativity, as well as elevate personal power in the form of spiritual attuning. In essence, the energy raises one's resonance, and contact with multiple power places builds up a kind of numinous state of mind. Chinese Taoist beliefs agree on this experience, and state that the proper relationship with China's five sacred mountains awakens the "Great Man" within. It is a belief that is culturally shared throughout the world and forms the basis of pilgrimage.

Though the people who originally discovered, used, honored and reinforced the power places are long gone, their tradition lives in the rituals of native cultures around the world, such as the Aborigines and the tribes of North America, and to some extent the latter-day practitioners of Druidism and Hinduism. Regardless of whether they visit sacred caves, mounds or mountains, devotees continue this practice to acquire the numinous energy of place, and in correctly harnessing this power they are able to receive visions. Or they serve others by re-directing the energy into a distant place or person, as a Karuk shaman explains: "A medicine man must go to the mountain or some other power center to pray for his people. I connect with the power and shoot it straight down from the mountaintop into the sacred dance. It is like a beam of light or electricity. It will make the healing more powerful... and I ask the spirits from the mountain to come down and dance with us in the ceremony as our ancestors originally did in the beginning." [13]

Jesus did precisely the same as a way of strengthening his power to heal people. [14]

Invisible roads leading somewhere.

What the spirit roads share in common, from Britain to Bolivia, is that they all connect hundreds of energy hotspots, a good number of which are sacred mountains.

One has to wonder how and why some mountains ever became sacred. Did some force or entity present itself in a way that was vastly different to the surrounding land? James Swan, a professor of anthropology, explains that "a place becomes sacred ultimately to us when it is perceived as somehow able to energize within us those feelings and concepts we associate with the spiritual dimensions of life."[15] Thus, a perceptual reality commonly experienced and reinforced by people of similar purpose over long spans of time serves to mark the location as sacred.

There is no doubt that some places on Earth are more powerful than others. A large body of scientific evidence shows that energy concentrates and behaves differently at certain geographic locales. And ancient places of veneration, without exception, always reference areas of geomagnetic anomalies, even gravity anomalies.[16] So, if such places strike us as powerful, it is probably because they are. Humans, after all, are sensitive to their surroundings and were undoubtedly more so thousands of

Hsuan-k'ung Ssu, seemingly defying gravity.

years ago when they did not have to contend with a morass of electronic devices, and the signal-to-noise ratio was far stronger. A difference in the local magnetic field of just a few gammas is enough to be sensed by people, and anomalies at sacred sites register far stronger.

Atomically speaking, a mountain is nothing more than a vast accumulation of energy. In all nature, form follows function. And form, or matter, is simply energy made concrete: atoms, molecules and electrons spinning, resonating and bonding together. If we expand this, landforms can be regarded as manifestations of an inherent energy; a mountain range may be the result of a physical collision between tectonic plates, but those plates are the result of the movement of energy within the Earth, which itself is a ball of solidified atoms and molecules. Thus, in a manner of speaking, a mountain is a repository of considerable life force, it is one of the bigger "spots of the fawn."

Taktsang Dzong, Tibet

Sacred mountains, then, can be seen as landscape temples made by nature and later identified as such by human beings.

And if they are a kind of temple, then they may be doorways to an ineffable threshold of awareness, as a shaman of the Tewa people hints: "Whatever life's challenges you may face, remember always to look to the mountaintop; in so doing you look to greatness."[17] Such sage advice is probably an echo of the legendary actions of gods and gurus who in remote times sought out specific locations on specific mountains, often following arduous journeys. Such as the legend of a Tibetan tutelary deity named Padmasambhava, who is said to have flown some 300 miles from Tibet to Bhutan, on the back of a tiger, to consecrate a cave on the side of a mountain. His motivation for the stupendous journey was to "tame a local tiger," an old euphemism for securing or anchoring telluric or earth energies so as to create an energy hotspot or node. Padmasambhava's flight obviously succeeded, for a prominent monastery named Taktsang Dzong (Tiger's Nest), was later built on the edge of the mountain.

Certainly when one looks at some of these monasteries one has to ask what kind of revelation prompted these endeavors that look like architectural experiments in anti-gravity? Delicate structures built on vertiginous cliffs and meandering ridges are found from China to Greece, one of the most wonderous examples being the wooden temple of Hsuan-k'ung Ssu, the "Temple Hanging in Air," built on the side of one of China's most sacred mountains, Heng Shan, where indeed it has defied gravity since 491 AD. From a distance it actually looks as though it is floating in mid-air, overlooking the curiously-named stream, the Brook of the Gods.

Clearly these sites were not located and then built upon on a whim, and the numerous legends of gods chasing some type of force offers a window into the underlying motivation.

Windows into paradise.

The mountain, both as a symbol and metaphor, occupies a central position in the human psyche. Perhaps the best known example throughout eastern religious lore is Mount Meru or Sumeru, for it represents at the same time an allegorical structure of the universe, as well as the highest spiritual achievement sought by adepts in the physical, spiritual and metaphysical cosmology of Hindus, Buddhists and Jains. The roots of Jainism, in particular, are as old as mountains themselves, and its influence is noted in many other religions. Interestingly, these faiths share similar spiritual philosophies: the practice of self-effort in progressing the soul towards divine consciousness through non-violence, and the conquering of inner struggles (commonly known as the seven deadly sins). To overcome such conditions, devotees have traditionally sourced the energy of places of power, such as making pilgrimage to sacred mountains, where meditation and integration with the spirit of place helps a person disentangle from such negative limitations as fear, anger, envy, and so forth. And once enlightenment is reached, one attains a state of bliss. Or as many of us prefer to call it, we reach paradise.

Mt. Meru in Bhutanese art.

'Paradise' originates from the word *pairidaeza* in Avestan – the sacred language of Zoroastrianism – and literally means "a walled enclosure."

A Jain who has mastered discipline over the physical world and achieved the state of godliness is called a *Jina*. As this word traveled west it became the Arabic *Djinn*, along with its derivative *Allah-Djinn*, and finally, the Latin *genius* – a kind of tutelary spirit, like one's personal guardian angel. By the 17th century it appears as *genie*, later to be known in the West as *Aladdin*.

Back in the days when Asia Minor was Assyria, this *Djinn* was a supernatural

Mt. Kailas. Abode of Siva and sacred to over a billion people.

being. And rightly so, since the root *j-n-n* means "hidden;" it is also the root of *jannah*, the Islamic concept of paradise. Its derivative in Portuguese – a language brimming with Arabic – is *janela*, "a window, an opening in a wall."

In other words, paradise is a hidden space that is demarcated and separate from the ordinary and troublesome world. And if we follow this dizzying etymological trail, it seems we can get into this 'walled enclosure' through 'an opening in the wall'.

Paradise is, admittedly, what every living human being strives for, be it in the now or in the afterlife. Could a sacred mountain be a window into such a place?

It might just be. We already know that such places are energetically active, and electromagnetic energy, properly guided, does influence the human body to a degree that it alters brainwaves, causing heightened states of consciousness.[18] The allegorical Mount Meru's earthly counterpart is Mount Kailas, a 22,000-foot high granite cube that tapers into a pyramid-shaped summit, which is approached by pilgrims walking a path resembling an ever-decreasing spiral. Pilgrims to Mecca perform the same ritual around the cubic Ka'ba ("spirit-body") as do pilgrims to Ireland's holiest sacred mountain, the pyramidal Cruach Phádraig. Like perambulating a labyrinth, the need to walk in slowly decreasing orbits induces oneness between mind, body, spirit, and God – it creates a shamanic experience that leads to a blissful state of oneness with all levels of creation.

That is paradise.

Meru/Kailas' position both as an explanatory model of cosmology and path of spiritual revelation finds its way into later Christian beliefs. If we examine one of the New Testament's most important characters, Mary, it is stated that the mother of Jesus came out of Egypt. That may be so, but her origins and association with the

*The Divine Mother and child.
From top left: in Babylon; Mary and
Jesus; Indrani, Hindu goddess;
Isis and Horus.*

sacred landscape are far older than the official Gospel traditions. Like Meru, she may be an archetype through which one may find salvation – paradise.

Mary was 'Beloved of God', wore a veil, and traditional icons pose her seated with the infant Jesus on her lap. The same applies to the Egyptian goddess of creation, Isis, who was 'Beloved of God', wore a veil and is identically posed with the infant Horus. To all extents and purposes, the two entities are one and the same.

Ancient Egyptians called their land *Ta Mery*, "the land of Mery." Mery is also written *Mr*, and the hieroglyph for *Mr* is a pyramid.[19] Etymologically and symbolically then, *Mr*, Mary, Mery and Meru are interchangeable.

Isis' husband Osiris is the god of the afterlife, a kind of sentinel into the otherworld, if you like. He is often depicted sitting on a throne shaped like a cube – just as Christ is compared to a cube-shaped mountain upon which a tower is erected. Egypt's most enigmatic structures are the pyramids, which emerge from a square base – a flattened cube. Even so, they are but representations of an unusual hill across the river from Thebes called Dehenet, an imposing limestone cube of a mountain whose top is shaped like a pyramid, which was the hotspot chosen by pharaohs as the gateway into the otherworld, for it stands over what is known today as the Valley of the Kings and Queens.

And from this serenest of places their souls departed into paradise.

So far, the thread of the sacred mountain as both a power place and a doorway of communication with the otherworld seem quite tenable. Consider also that the Buddhist monuments of veneration, the *stupas*, are said to represent the primordial

Osiris on his cube throne.

sacred mound – the original manifestation of the essence of a creator god – atop which rests a variation of the pyramidal shape. In their venerations, the Sinhalese people of Sri Lanka, in particular, place a stone cube inside the stupas to represent Mount Meru, the center of the world.[20]

All this symbolism ties the cube and the pyramid with Meru/Mery/Mary. In other words, Mary/Meru represents the spirit of place, the center of the world, the 'Beloved of God'. The geometric representation of this principle is the cube and the pyramid, with Osiris, the god of the afterlife presiding over the entrance to paradise.

Thus the sacred mountain – together with the spirit roads leading to it – is 'a way of the spirit'.

The mountain as a landscape temple.

Classic stupa. Nepal.

Such cultural cross-associations reveal how the concept of the sacred mountain is entwined with divinity and the threshold of the human spirit. It is the window into that walled garden called paradise, a portal into a state of bliss.

For all intents and purposes, the sacred mountain is the ultimate landscape temple, the first sacred site. Even today there is no shortage of them in virtually every country in the world, and the traditions associated with each one, handed down from prehistory, affirm their status in world mythology. India, in particular, has long maintained a relationship with such holy places. By looking at some of the traditions associated with sacred mountains we get a sense of why people would later embark on a worldwide construction boom of temples placed on top of these points of power, or as close as their religious outlook would permit.

In the southern Indian province of Tamil Nadu, the god Siva once descended from the sky as an effulgent column of light. Siva's appearance may have seemed rather brash, but there was very good reason for this behavior. He came with news of an impending catastrophe, and wished to nominate a special location where the sum knowledge of everything would be placed for safe keeping: "When the annihilation of all living beings takes place [by an impending global flood]… all future seeds are certainly deposited there… All the lores, arts, wealth of scriptures, and the Vedas are truthfully well-arranged there." [21]

This was cordially received by the second and third creator gods Vishnu and Brahma, despite the bittersweet news. However, so bright was Siva's light that Brahma and Vishnu beseeched him to turn it down a notch so that mortal men could approach it in comfort, otherwise there would be little use in creating a repository of knowledge that could not be accessed by mortals. Siva mulled this, agreed, and lowered his radiance, which would forever remain in the form of a mountain of fire. The spot is today marked by a pyramidal hill of red stone called Arunachela, also called the Sacred Red Hill. There is no doubt as to its numinous quality today, for at its base lies the 24-acre temple of Arunachaleswara, one of the five most important temples dedicated to Siva in India. The constructed temple is itself directly associated with deity, for Siva also manifested a column of stone on the hill's eastern side, after which Visvakarma, the architect of the Gods, erected the first temple with the phallic symbol of Siva, the *Sivalinga*, housed inside its Holy of Holies (the present-day structure rests on these extremely ancient foundations). [22]

Arunachalaleswara temple, as seen from the sacred hill Arunachela. India.

Arunachela embodies the presence of Siva, or divinity, on Earth. Had this occurred in Egypt, the sacred mound would have embodied the presence of Atum. In North America, such a place of connection between divinity and humanity is Tse´Bit'ai ("rock with wings"), otherwise known as Shiprock. Anyone who has traveled to the Four Corners region of New Mexico and approached this 1800-foot vertical wall of breccia cannot be but moved to tears. It happens to me on every occasion. Although this eroded throat of a 27 million year-old volcano can be seen from over 60 miles across the desert, its enchanting effect is also due to the accumulation of millennia of veneration and prayer at the site, which in turn has concentrated the natural power already present. Not surprisingly, Tse´Bit'ai is located at the heart of land that once was the domain of the Mesolithic native people, the Anasazi. As this legendary tribe died out, the site would play a significant role in Navajo religion, mythology and tradition, and it is still recognized today as 'the place of beginning' for these cultures. One ancestral myth describes how a metal bird flew the people from a distant place, and when they alighted and were safe, the bird descended into the earth and emerged as a protective angel.

Tse´Bit'ai is one of several sacred mountains in the American southwest, each serving distinct functions above and beyond mere places of power. So while this acts as the navel, one hundred and twenty miles due southeast, the pyramidal Tsoodzil (Mt. Taylor), is regarded as the doorway to the spirit world – an exact mirror of the relationship between Giza and Thebes in Egypt.

No matter how the legends describe them, sacred mountains are either homes of gods, portals into paradise or places for illumination: Mt. Olympus in Greece ("the

Tse' Bit'ai, sacred center to the Anasazi and Navajo.

dwelling place of the gods"); Serra de Estrela in Portugal ("place of the bright star"); Nanda Devi in India ("the Goddess of Bliss"). The collection is endless.

In addition to sacred mountains being landscape temples, ambulatories of the gods, and windows into other realities, many traditions also mark them as collection-points for universal scriptures handed down by divine beings to be used at a later date, and often as an insurance policy in the wake of impending upheavals. Like so many creator gods, Siva's primary attribute is *gnosis* – knowledge – which he stores at the hill of Arunachela in the form of the oldest Vedic scriptures, the Vedas, meaning "knowledge." Over in China the five sacred mountains of Buddhism have always been places one attends in the pursuit of knowledge; the same applies to Japan's Mt. Miwa. At Mount Sinai, knowledge in the form of laws is exchanged between God and Moses. And following such interchanges, this knowledge was shared with the people by a priesthood of adepts, shaman or sages.

New Zealand has a sacred mountain that once served as a fully integrated ancient academy. And if you know just how such power places function, it still does. Situated on the backbone of the Southern Alps of the South Island, Kura Tawhiti is a curve of limestone megaliths oriented along the saddle of a mountain named Castle Hill. Some of the stones are 50 feet tall. Despite several trips to this magnificent part of the world I still cannot muster the right superlatives to bestow on this landscape temple – "undiminished clarity" is probably what best describes the sensation. The Dalai

The face of Marotini.

Lama himself was moved enough to name this power place "A Spiritual Center of the Universe."

Kura Tawhiti is described as both "the highest place of learning" and "the meeting place of the gods." Its tradition far precedes that of the Maori, who were relative latecomers to New Zealand around 1300 AD. The creators of this astonishing outdoor classroom were the Waitaha, a race of mythical beings who are described as very tall and fair skinned, sometimes with reddish hair.[23]

Each of the stones at this academy served as an initiation into a specific aspect of gnosis. As the initiate understood and embodied the facets taught, he or she would move along to the next stone, ambling progressively uphill and ever closer to the apex of the mountain, where stands an enigmatic monolith, the embodiment of Marotini, goddess and protective entity of the site. In essence, it is a carbon copy of the story of Siva at Arunachela. This magnetically-charged stone[24] actually resembles the face of a lioness, and it is not unusual for people working with earth energies to afterwards capture on camera the face of a woman emerging from the monolith.

While Kura Tawhiti serves as a seeding place and repository of the knowledge of the gods amid the enchanting land of Aotearoa, like New Mexico and Egypt, the actual doorway to paradise is attributed to a secondary site, the perfect cone volcano Taranaki, which sits on the North Island and which from space looks identical to Japan's Mount Fuji, with whom it shares the attribute, "place of abundant immortality."

Marotini, tutelary goddess of Kura Tawhiti. New Zealand.

To quote the mythologist Joseph Campbell, "The idea of a sacred [place] where the walls and laws of the temporal world dissolve to reveal wonder is apparently as old as the human race." [25] There is little doubt that the recurring theme of the sacred mountain as a navel, seeding place, repository of knowledge, and gateway to the gods – to paradise itself – is a culturally shared idea that is beyond mere conjecture, and dates back into prehistory.

These landscape temples, from mounds to sacred mountains, are intermediary locations between the temporal and the eternal, and represent the temple in its purest form. Their importance in the balanced conduct of human affairs was understood and later acted upon by groups of "wise men." Perhaps it is not by coincidence then, that the builders of Stonehenge took the trouble to seek and quarry its bluestones 140 miles away, at the foot of a mountain in Wales named Cairn Ingli, "the Hill of the Angels."

As we are about to see, landscape temples are indeed receptacles of revelation.

Storm over Kura Tawhiti. Even from four miles away it is impressive.

Vishnu and Siva

2

THE MYSTERY OF THE THREE STEPS OF VISHNU.

"Establish the triangle and the problem is two-thirds solved."

~ Pythagoras

The concept of triadic deity is found throughout world mythology, in which three inter-related creative forces are represented by a central figure or god, along with two supporting entities – such as the Christian God, whose aspect comprises Father-Son-Holy Spirit. This idea of wholeness is personified on an earthly level in the Egyptian ibis-headed god Djehuti (Thoth to the Greeks), who is honored as "thrice great" after he becomes the embodiment of perfection.

Just as with the sacred mountain, the holy trinity is also culturally shared.

In Hindu cosmology the god Siva often appears intertwined with the gods Vishnu and Brahma, all three representing the concept of Trimurti, the three-fold nature of the One divine creative aspect regulating creation, maintenance, and destruction.[1] In the *Rig Veda* there is a recurring theme which involves the unusual behavior of the aforementioned Vishnu – whose role it is to protect humans and restore order to the world – and his often-celebrated act of taking three steps: "I will declare the mighty deeds of Vishnu, of him who measured out the earthly regions… thrice setting down his footstep, widely striding… He within whose three wide-extended paces all living creatures have their habitation… Him who alone with triple step hath measured this common dwelling place, long far extended…" [2]

And further along, Vishnu "strode, widely pacing, with three steppings forth over the realms of the earth for freedom and for life." [3]

Strange behavior indeed for a god.

Vishnu is eventually given the attribute Trivikrama, meaning "of the three steps." Is it possible that Vishnu, the bringer of order to the world, paced out landscape temples in threes? Was he being geometrical, perhaps, positioning them in triangles? But mountains are immovable objects, you can't just put them where you like. And furthermore, why was he doing this "for freedom and for life?"

We know that the landscape temples were designated as repositories of the knowledge of the gods, and that 'imbibing' such knowledge empowered the individual to be free – that is, free from the illusions of the world of matter. Under such conditions any individual is able to live life fully aware, precisely as the *Rig Veda* states. One can't help but envision the parable of Adam and Eve when they lived in paradise, and that apple they ate from the Tree of Knowledge. In the account of Genesis given in the Gnostic gospels of Nag Hammadi, which precede the four canonical gospels selected by the Catholic Church,[4] the serpent appears as the benevolent hero of mankind, and the god portrayed in the story is a shadow of the god of Light: "What did God say to you?" the serpent asked Eve. "Was it, do not eat from the tree of knowledge?"

Eve replied, "He said, not only do not eat from it, but do not touch it lest you die." The serpent reassured her, saying, "Do not be afraid. With death you shall not die; for it was out of jealousy that he said this to you. Rather your eyes shall open and you shall come to be like gods, recognizing evil and good." [5]

The Gnostic writings then describe that once Adam and Eve had eaten of the Tree of Knowledge they experienced enlightenment, precisely as one does, and the knowledge empowered them to discover spiritual transfiguration. All of this is in stark contrast to what many have been traditionally taught. Thanks to the machinations of the Church, the attainment of knowledge gets Adam and Eve booted out of paradise, the apple is labeled forbidden fruit, and worse, the whole episode is presided by a serpent who was doing fine as a symbol of telluric forces until the Church turned it into the devil. And just like that, knowledge becomes evil, and coming into contact with it removes you from that state of bliss.

But "drinking" of this knowledge and applying it was precisely the reason why we sought out places of power on the land, and why gods with benevolent intentions, like Siva, imprinted it at special spots for us to find. As a component of that Trimurti, Vishnu is responsible for the protection of humanity, therefore, whatever is at play here is certainly of great benefit to humanity. So, where do the "three steps" fit into this picture?

A few phrases later in the *Rig Veda*, we are given another cunning piece of information: "He, like a rounded wheel, hath set in swift motion his 90 racing steeds together with the four..."

We are here presented with an instruction concealed in an allegorical tale, which was a time-honored method of preserving ancient – and vital – universal knowledge. Since "90 racing steeds" multiplied by "four" equals 360, this implies the number of degrees in a circumference of a "rounded wheel".[6] Since Vishnu is measuring a sphere called the Earth, and the sphere is a circle in 3-D, would the siting of landscape temples along the surface of the sphere have something to do with Vishnu's three steps? After all, he was also in charge of restoring order to the world.

Very orderly sacred mountains.

When looking at traditions behind sacred mountains, it is striking how so many share common stories and plot lines within certain regions. India, for example, is a vast country, enough to be awarded the status of sub-continent, and yet of all its mountains only a small number are sacred, and out of those, fewer still are associated with legends involving the god of wisdom Siva, who in the *Bhagavad Gita* and *Vishnu Purana* is viewed as an inherent part of Vishnu.

My curiosity for Vishnu's three steps made me wonder whether these were connected in some way to a geodetic-geometric placement of sacred mountains and other nodes of energy associated with the manifestation of divinity. Since mountains are natural and immovable objects, such a probability would be astronomical. Then again, all form follows function, and in the Vedic story of Siva, as with so many others, the essence of a creator god descends as a column of light and is anchored into a mountain or a primordial mound; or the light becomes the mountain itself. With so many myths declaring sacred mountains to be manifestations of the power of a 'creative god', one has to wonder if there is substance to these tales, and that the causative power behind what we perceive as matter is far more sentient than we can comfortably admit.

I decided to put the theory to the test.

My point of focus was Mount Kailas, for obvious reasons: it is the earthly depiction of Mount Meru; it is the abode of Siva; it is a place of "eternal bliss," and it is sacred to five religions. The second choice was the holy hill of Gabbar. Like Kailas it is said to be the origin of the Supreme Cosmic Power of the Universe and of India. It is near the source of the famous Vedic virgin river Sarasvati, and the place where Siva left the heart of his first wife, Sati. The third is Maa Sharda, a conical hill used as a sacred mountain since the Paleolithic era, when Siva, mourning over his deceased wife, dropped her necklace on this hill. Linking all three sites creates a perfect right-angle triangle, to within 1° of error. Considering the longest span of this triangle covers 650 miles, that is an incredible degree of accuracy – especially as we are dealing with three distinct natural features. But I soon discovered this was by no means a one-off coincidence. A pattern of triangular alignments between landscape temples exists around the world.

In China, three Buddhist sacred mountains are associated with Bodhisattvas, *bodhi* meaning "enlightenment" and *sattva* meaning "being." It is also translated as "wisdom-being," a clear reference to the mountain as a repository of the god of knowledge. The three are Wutái Shan, Éméi Shan and Putuó Shan, and together they create an isosceles triangle (in which two sides are of equal length); it is

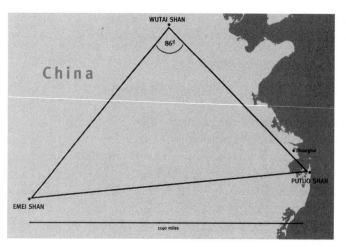

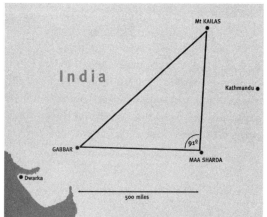

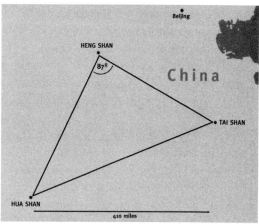

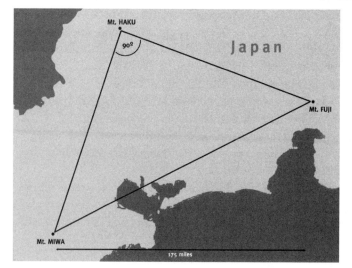

Vishnu's three steps
as applied to
sacred mountains
featuring
similar lores.

also 4º shy of being a perfect right-angle triangle, with its longest span covering an incredible 1,140 miles!

Still in China, I looked at Taoist sacred mountains. Tài Shan is the most holy, having been in use since Palaeolithic times – that is before 10,000 B.C. Huà Shan and Héng Shan have also been in constant use since before records began, and both are claimed to be places of contact with God. These three create a right-angle triangle to within 3º of error, with the longest span stretching 410 miles.

Japan has a similar tradition. Mount Miwa is this island's oldest place of worship, pre-dating history, and is home to the earliest Shinto shrines. Mount Haku is the primary shrine of 2,000 Hakusan shrines; and Mount Fuji is regarded as the supreme incarnation of creation, its sacredness hard-wired into Japanese culture.[7]

These three sacred mountains form a perfect right-angle triangle, with the longest span stretching 175 miles.

By now it was becoming clear that the triple steps of Vishnu in "widely stepped paces" measuring out the earthly regions referred to a geometric-geodetic blueprint of power points.[8] True to his attribute, Vishnu brings order to the world. And this arrangement doesn't just apply to the placement of sites, it is also the order that comes from a balanced mind when interacting with them, which it was hoped would lead to a balanced society. I was curious to see if Vishnu's three steps were simply an eastern revelation or a global pattern, so I applied the process to the Egyptian culture.

No study of Egyptian sacred mounds is complete without reference to the Giza plateau, and there we shall begin. To the ancient Egyptians the hill of Giza was known as *Rostau*, literally "Gateway to the Otherworld." The alignment of the three main pyramids sitting on this hill reflect the belt of Orion as it appeared on the horizon in 10,500 B.C.,[9] and each sits on a primordial mound said to be one of the first manifestations of the wisdom of the gods at the dawn of *Zep Tepi*, "the First Occasion." Later the site would be called Giza, "the embodiment of the place of Isis." As we saw in the previous chapter with Mary, Giza itself has gone through many linguistic permutations, particularly as *Gesa* and *Gesu*, which are linked etymologically and phonetically with *Jesu*, and inevitably *Jesus*.[10] To say this sacred place is important is an understatement!

This plateau of pyramids is linked to an important mountain across the Nile from Luxor which is shaped like a natural pyramid. Called Dehenet, it oversees the Valley of the Kings and Queens. Or, I should say, it was the *reason* why so many pharaohs chose to be buried around or inside this imposing limestone mountain. Its location on a power point and the spirit roads leading to it makes this the Egyptian 'Meru' and the pharaohs' portal into paradise; it is also one of the many reasons why the pyramid was chosen as the shape of power in their land.[11] Which brings us to the third point of this triangle, Sinai – Mount Katherine, to be specific. Like Siva at Arunachala, this is where God spoke with Moses as a pillar of light. Although traditionally regarded as both a Bedouin and early Christian tale, the central character, Moses, was an Egyptian – just to re-affirm the cultural link between the three sites.[12]

The pyramid hill of Dehenet overlooking the Valley of the Kings. And the step pyramid. Saqqara.

These form an isosceles triangle, 310 miles along the longest stretch.

As with Egypt, Celtic Ireland has its own kingly necropolis called Knocknarea. This arresting and freestanding "hill of Destiny" is surrounded by no less than 200 burial mounds, some dating to 7,400 B.C.,[13] including that of Daghdha, father god of the Celts and chief of the mythological magic beings Tuatha Dé Danaan, "the people of the goddess Anne." It is considered a navel of the Earth. As is the hill of Uisneach – the mystical navel of Eire and its geodetic center – where Beltane fires are lit annually on May 3rd. The third point is Cruach Phadraig, the holiest hill in Ireland and dwelling place of Lugh, son of Cian of the Tuatha Dé Danaan, who is often described as a Shining One – a creator god. The word *lugh* is also synonymous with light.

These three sites form a perfect right-angle triangle, with the longest span covering 90 miles.

The Navajo and Anasazi cultures of the American southwest have three sacred mountains associated with creation myths: Tse' Bit'ai and Tsoodzil, both in New Mexico, and Bell Rock in Arizona (sacred to the Sinagua, once part of the Anasazi). All are considered 'navels of the earth'. Tsoodzil resembles a pyramid, Bell Rock a Tibetan bell, a stupa, and when backlit, the classic George Adamski UFO.

The three are connected as a perfect right-angle triangle, with the longest span at 240 miles.

Finally (and I could go on for several pages), in Portugal there exist three near-identical power points, all settled and honored since prehistoric times, all later to become important Templar sites of veneration. They are linked by a right-angle triangle with a 4º margin of error, with the longest span stretching 170 miles.

To the power of three.

It seems that the three steps of Vishnu served a strategic function in establishing the location of natural power places – the umbilical cords between divine knowledge and human enlightenment. But why three steps? Why not four or five?

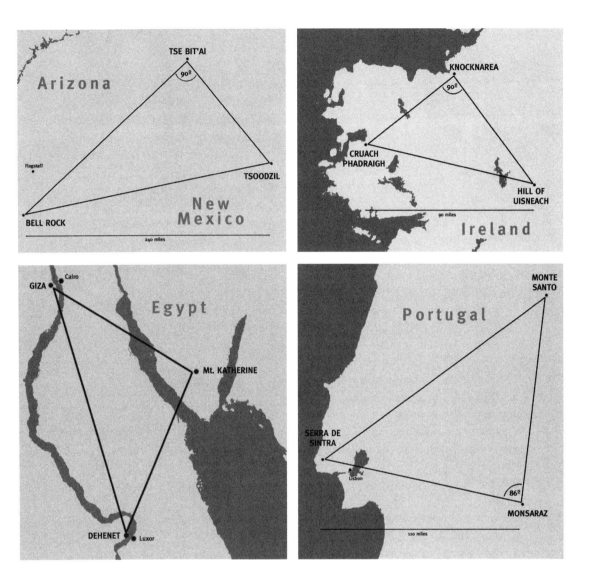

The predominant occupation of the ancients was the observation of nature. By noting the inherent perfection of the universe and then mirroring it, they hoped to bring harmony to mundane life through the creation of forms that were consonant with nature, be it in architecture, art or civil law. The vehicle for transcribing the macrocosm into the microcosm was number, and every number in ancient cosmology has meaning, since it both represents and explains the functions, principles, processes and cycles of nature. One student who graduated from the Egyptian Mysteries Schools of Alexandria expressed this concept well when he declared, "All is number." His name was Pythagoras.

When Vishnu's three steps are expressed two-dimensionally they take on the first form of geometry, the triangle. In innumerable mythologies it is the most important

The pharaoh's apron.

of geometrical shapes because it expresses the relationship of the three-in-one, the divine trinity. The triangle is a reconciling relationship between opposing forces, symbolized by the number two, or dark and light, good and evil, etc. But a third element brings balance through relationship. Egyptologist John Anthony West expresses it succinctly: "Male/female is not a relationship. For there to be a relationship there must be 'love' or at least 'desire'. A sculptor and a block of wood will not produce a statue. The sculptor must have 'inspiration'." [14] The same can be said for the triangular movements of a creator god as he deposited information at energetically-sensitive locations in our physical domain through a beam of light: one, the creative force; two, manifests knowledge; three, for the love of humanity. In this respect Vishnu and Siva (together with Brahma) are all working for and towards the same indivisible whole.

This relationship is depicted in Egyptian art, where the earthly embodiment of the creator gods – the pharaoh, the builder of human-created temples – is regularly depicted in murals wearing what can only be described as an unfeasibly starched apron in the shape of an isosceles triangle.

This triangular understanding between human/earthly/divine was subsequently incorporated into shamanic/religious practice and its search for enlightenment. The most common pose in eastern meditation is the devotee sitting cross-legged with arms touching the knees, making the form of an equilateral triangle. The black robe worn by a Zen Buddhist priest engaged in *Zazen* meditation emphasizes the isosceles triangle form of the priest's body. It is interesting that in their search for inner bliss, such meditational poses mimic the geodetic arrangement of landscape temples – the places of eternal bliss, of paradise – which favor isosceles or right-angle triangles. Like Plato and Pythagoras, the practitioners of Zen equate the triangle with transformation of consciousness, since it symbolizes a method of organization through the joining or mediating of differences. To them the isosceles triangle, above all, embodies the stability of the Absolute Ground of Being of Buddha consciousness.[15] And yet, all of this is but a mirror of natural forces at play: as Aristotle concluded in his study of organic forms, the isosceles triangle is inherent in the gnomic pattern of growth in nature.[16]

Geometry expressed three-dimensionally becomes polyhedral or solid geometry. Thus, a triangle in three-dimensional space becomes a tetrahedron, otherwise known as a triangular pyramid. It is one of the principal Platonic solids as well as the glue of God, because in nature it is the geometry that bonds all molecules. In other words, the tetrahedron is the prime bonding pattern of matter.

What the gods were up to in sacred mountains and other 'navels of the earth' was the imprinting of knowledge, typically via a beam of light, which in the language of science is electromagnetic energy made visible. In an incredible parallel, enlightened physicists looking at subatomic particle dynamics in particle chambers have remarked how particles behave as if they are dancing, leading to comparisons with the dance of Siva, the god of creation, as depicted by early artists.[17] Indeed the comparison may be apt. Statues of the dancing Siva visualize this creator god standing within a flaming circle, two hands and one foot resting on its circumference, the other foot raised and in front, giving the pose a distinct three-dimensional persona. By graphically linking the three limbs touching the circumference, an invisible equilateral triangle is revealed. And extending the lines of construction to meet at Siva's dancing foot in mid-air reveals nature's pyramid, the tetrahedron.

The importance attached to the trinity, first as a symbol and second as the process of creation in equilibrium, is very clear, for it effortlessly describes the framework behind the molecular bond of nature. Its application in the geodetic positioning of the nodes of power by creator gods demonstrates their intent to mirror such fundamental creative processes across the face of the Earth.

The core belief of ancient esoteric practices states that human life should strive to reflect the inherent perfection of natural forces around it, such as the orderly motions of the heavens. This was the "sky-ground dualism" so beloved of the Egyptians, and reflected in their maxim "As Above, So Below," as well as the Gnostic "As Without, So Within." It was then up to the initiate to acquire the knowledge through direct contact and immersion in the processes imprinted at sacred places. As repositories of energy, landscape temples are finely-tuned instruments, they are embodiments of the trinity, whose creative aspect regulates creation, maintenance and destruction. They must be respected if they are to sustain their original function. As every physicist knows, for every action there's a reaction, and the invisible power at sacred places also works on the visible plane. Native elder Grandpa David Monongye explains:

Siva stands on a triangle and reveals the 3-D tetrahedron.

"Anytime human beings interfere with or violate or alter the power center, they are causing a serious imbalance, hence a negative and detrimental reaction can occur." [18]

In essence, the power centers of the land serve the same function as the power centers of the human body in maintaining the whole organism in perfect balance.[19] As such, the act of honoring both establishes and reinforces the circular relationship between the Spirit of place, the human body and the Earth. Perhaps this was the prime reason why we felt motivated to emulate the landscape temples and constructed our very own places of power.

3

Navels of the Earth, Places of the Gods.

Whosoever shall make a copy thereof, and shall know it upon earth, it shall act as a magical protector for him in heaven and in earth, unfailingly, and regularly, and eternally.

~ The Book of What is in the Duat

The Tamil tradition of Arunachala as a repository of a creator god's power and knowledge is ancient, prehistoric even. Arunachala lies in the land of the Dravidian culture, which is at least 10,000 years old; it is the origin of today's Tamil culture. The hill is mentioned in the oldest Tamil sacred literature, the *Tolkappiyam*, which itself refers to an even older work that was based on a library of archaic texts said to have been compiled more than 10,000 years earlier.[1] We are therefore talking about an extremely old scripture spanning unimaginable eons of time, much like the oral traditions of the Aborigines, which have been kept alive through their interactions with the spirit roads. This was a time when "kingship was lowered from heaven,"[2] a "golden age" whose echoes ripple through Quechua Maya myths as well as the *Pyramid Texts* of ancient Egypt.

The hill of Arunachala is the embodiment of Siva and his knowledge, forever a "repository of everything auspicious" and which "exists for the welfare of all."[3] Siva, as we also know, is the god of wisdom and presides over the "city of knowledge." Later he is beseeched to take on the more accessible form of a phallic stone, the *lingam* (a "mark" or "sign"), on the eastern side of the mountain. In the Vedic traditions Siva is also known as Rudra, whose symbol is a pillar, representing all at once a column of

Pilgrims ascending Huà Shan, sacred mountain and navel of the earth. China.

light descending to earth, an umbilical cord rising toward heaven, and a phallic post marking a special spot of fecundity on the land - what the Hopi refer to as "the spots of the fawn." And upon these spots, temples would later be erected to serve as "cities of knowledge," from which sprang entire civilizations.

When the primeval architect of the Vedic gods, Visvakarma, erected a temple around the Siva *lingam* stone, he sparked off a tradition that would still be at play in 1200 B.C. and 3,000 miles away at Petra, Jordan, when the El Deir monastery was sculpted on the side of the hill of Hor. Inside this breathtaking monument stands a cube of stone that is the essence of Dushara, the "lord of the mountain."

The sacred hill that cradles El Deir is named after the Ethiopian magician/god, Hor – a reference to Horus, the Egyptian god of the sky, and in a similar vein to Vishnu, protective god of humanity and sacred places

Legend speaks of another "navel of the earth" that once existed in the kingdom of Kalakh. It was marked by a series of temples dedicated to the triple solar deity Enlil/Ninlil/Ninurta, the focal point of which was a temple assigned to Nabu, the god of knowledge. In time, a new structure was superimposed on the site: a tall, spiral staircase leading to a temple at the summit that the Greeks would refer to as 'the Gate of God', and which we would come to know as the Tower of Babel. In the later Mesopotamian cultures of Sumer, which were sited on relatively flat terrain, the *omphalos* marking the power places took on the form of artificial mountains called *ziggurats*, each built on the foundations of up to sixteen earlier temples. In later times, the same purpose would be realized in structures such as the imposing stepped pyramids of Central America.

In every respect the cube, the omphalos, the Sivalingam and the step pyramid are one and the same markers of a subtle force, where divinity is said to descend and touch the earth.

El Deir, Petra. Carved entirely out of the sandstone hill of Hor.

The idea of power places as navels of the earth is as old as sacred mountains. In fact, quite a number of sacred mountains are accorded this dual designation, their sanctity so unimpeachable that no building is allowed to be erected on them: Mount Kailas in Tibet and Mount Fuji in Japan; the Black Hills of the Sioux of South Dakota and Uluru of the Pitjantjatjara of Australia. Then there are those conical hills or phallic-shaped mountains upon which rest harmoniously designed temples protecting the very energy hotspot, the omphalos or the Sivalingam: Amarnath, Tirupati, Vaishno Devi, Heng Shān, Tài Shān, to name a few.

The quest for the navels of the earth – those "spots of the fawn" – sometimes requires a lot of sleuthing because so many have been integrated into the fabric of modern development, and their roots and importance are often lost upon this new distracted Culture of Twitter. So, unless the answer is placed in front of you in 140 characters or less, many members of today's generation can't be bothered to look. And there's the rub, for these hotspots of self-empowerment once harmonized the pulse of people with the greater world around them. With so many of today's western adolescents not even aware that milk comes from a cow, we are raising a generation that's already become dangerously isolated from the organism upon which it lives.

The Sacred Center.

Iceland is home to Europe's only true high desert, a forbidding and unforgiving place of desolate lava fields and icy crags. And yet there have always been persistent memories as far back as the Viking Sagas that amid this inhospitable terrain lies paradise. Only an eternal optimist could visualize this. And yet by applying an ancient and established method of locating a country's geodetic center it is possible to find the Thingvellir ("Field of the Thing"), the Icelandic version of the omphalos. Despite the grim terrain and climate that circumscribe it, this fissured heart of Iceland (actually the great rift between the North American and Eurasian tectonic plates) was once the site of a meeting mound or *doom ring*, marked by a large rock called the Law Rock – a place of pilgrimage typically undertaken during the summer solstice, the time of year when homage is given to the highest position of the sun in the northern sky. It is the symbolic praising of the ultimate source of Light or God. On such occasions it was the duty of an appointed head of the country – which in Iceland meant an eminent scholar with no executive power – to recite the spiritual laws of the land entirely from memory and remind people of their divine contract with the sacred center. A godly act indeed. Especially as it became the ideal framework for social husbandry for many generations.[4]

The tradition of locating a mound or pillar on the geodetic center of land is found throughout the many islands of the north Atlantic, such as Shetland, Orkney, Islay, and the Faroes. These mounds are still in evidence, many surrounded by lakes, as though portraying the first primordial mounds so regularly mentioned in creation

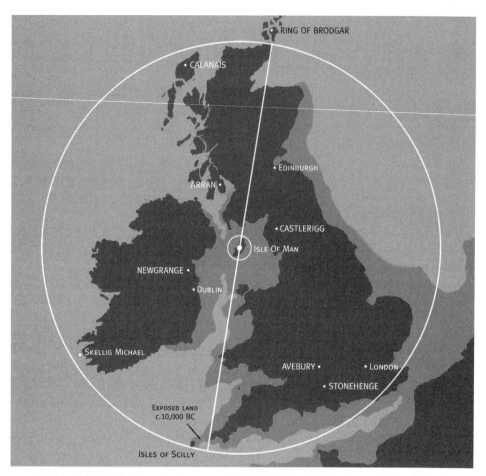

Based on John Michell's work, the center of the Isle of Man is also the omphalos of Britain, especially when the original landmass prior to the rise in sea level is taken into account.

myths. In the case of the Faroe Islands, the navel of the earth is the rock of Tinganes, which not only marks the geodetic center of the island but also divides its main harbor and capital in two. In fact, there has been a running argument for decades as to the wisdom behind locating the island-nation's main harbor on a site that is unprotected and wide open to storms, and only through extensive engineering can it function as a viable port. The answer is that despite its practical defects, the power of the omphalos of Tinganes was felt by its inhabitants as providing balance to the land and to its people, and for no other reason has this spot not only become the capital of the Faroes, but for these Nordic people it is also the navel of the earth.[5]

Sometimes an island becomes the navel of several nations, as is the case with a small piece of real estate in the Irish Sea, midway between Ireland and England, called the Isle of Man. The center of the axis that runs from the northernmost tip of Scotland to the southernmost tip of England passes through this island, making it the omphalos of the British Isles.

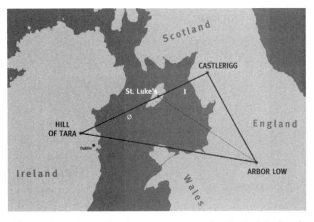

Triangular relationship between stone circles. St. Luke's church marks the Golden Cut along the path.

The national symbol of the Isle of Man is the Triskele, which shares a similar design and ideology with the tri-fold motif of Celtic, Mycenaean and Tibetan Dzogchen traditions, all of which reflect the tri-fold nature of a creator god. Like the attainment of paradise associated with other navel places, the center of the Isle of Man has similarly been known as a place of enchantment. Its history is ancient, and right up to the Roman occupation it was a renowned center of Druidic Mysteries Schools, with a college based at Kirk Michael – "the church of Michael" – where the sons of Celtic and Scottish nobles were sent to learn ancient knowledge. The center of the geodetic axis of the British Isles is located here on a lone hill, on whose slope stands a mound with a pole, the omphalos of Man, and it too served as the traditional assembly and ritual point of the island.[6]

That a small island should lie at the geodetic center of a cluster of nations is an incredible achievement in itself. But what is truly astonishing is that the calculation appears to have been made by including the land off the south-western tip of Britain which now lies submerged beneath the swirling waters of the Atlantic Ocean. This land, together with Brittany, was once connected to mainland Britain and formed the mythical kingdom of Lyonesse, but fell to the waters of a swiftly rising sea around 9500 B.C. All that remains of this kingdom are the tiny Isles of Scilly, which today lie 24 miles off the chiselled coast of Cornwall.[7]

Taking this into consideration, if my calculation is correct, it implies that the original sitting of the navel mound on the Isle of Man took place over 11,000 years ago. Although the mound and its pole are no longer used for their intended purpose, this site is nevertheless presided by a church dedicated to St. Luke, a name derived from the Celtic Lugh, the ancient god of light. And the best way to approach the mound is via an ancient track named the Royal Way, what in other cultures could be called a spirit road. The mound beside the church of St. Luke plays a second role as a geodetic marker. A perfect right-angle triangle connects the stone circles of

The triple spiral, symbol of the three faces of God and the flow of energy in nature, is found from Ireland to Korea. Center: The symbol of the Isle of Man.

Castlerigg and Arbor Low in England to the circles and mounds comprising the Hill of Tara in Ireland, all three sites being contemporaries of each other. When divided by the Golden Ratio – nature's mathematical harmonic – the sacred mound on the Isle of Man represents the golden cut along the northern line of this triangle.

In the previous chapter we encountered the navel of Ireland, the 600-foot high hill of Uisneach, and how it forms part of a sacred triangle with two other of Eire's landscape temples. The land of Eire is perhaps the richest in Europe in terms of legends and mythology, oral and written, especially as its first character, Cessair, is said to have been a daughter of the biblical Noah, thereby anchoring Celtic cosmology to around the time of the great flood. This seems to fit the bill, since it is claimed that she populated Ireland with fifty other women and three men (talk about having your work cut out for you) at the time of a great deluge.[8] Afterwards, the magical beings Tuatha Dé Danaan arrive on the scene by 'travelling through the air'; their queen-goddess Ériu would subsequently lend the country its traditional name.

Whoever measured and marked the hill of Uisneach, both as geodetic center and navel of Ireland is not known, but the myths and traditions do state that the gods once walked certain paths and created specific landmarks – echoes of Aboriginal spirit roads connecting with places of power. If one chooses to find the physical omphalos of Ireland, like the Sivalingam in India, it is marked by a volcanic, free-standing pillar of rock on the side of the hill. This legendary location is reputably a place of ancient revelation and pilgrimage, in the same tradition as Arunachala – as the manifestation and repository of knowledge of a god – served as a focal point. Protected by terrain that is hard to access, the weathered and cracked sixteen-foot tall outcrop of stone is called Ail na Mírenn ("the Stone of Divisions"); it is located in the ancient county of Midhe, meaning "middle," and it was considered the pillar by which a perfect social order was maintained. Beneath it lies the tomb of the proprietary spirit of Ireland, the queen-goddess Ériu, Eire's most popular female saint. Brighid, a Triple Goddess of the Tuatha dé Danaan, also took her vows here.[9]

A lone obelisk marks the site of the once formidable Innu-Heliopolis.

There is little doubt that a relationship exists between navels of the earth as power places, the dispensing of wisdom, the maintenance of balance among people, and the dispensation of laws, both spiritual and mundane. These sacred centers set the example, and from them, cultures flourished all around. It worked like spokes on a well-balanced wheel for countless generations. One place that encapsulates all the qualities associated with a navel place is Innu (also spelled Annu), later named by the Greeks as Heliopolis.

Innu, the navel of the earth.

The influence of Innu as an ancient academy cannot be stated enough: the foundations of an Egyptian temple ritual rests upon it,[10] as did the original Templar and Freemasonic movements (I am referring here to those orders who used the knowledge for *right* action, not the power-hungry lunatics who distorted it later). The history of Innu/Heliopolis emerges like layers peeling off a proverbial onion. By the time Pharaoh Senusret I built a temple to Amun-Ra at Innu circa 1920 B.C. the site was already considered ancient beyond recollection.[11] Ironically, one of the two red granite obelisks he erected at the site is all that remains to mark Innu as a sacred place, for now it is just a tiny spec of a park cut off from the rest of the Giza complex by a bustling Cairo suburb like a prison wall. The modern pilgrim will be forgiven for disbelieving that in its early days Innu was the foremost academy-city replete with obelisks as far as the eye could see.

Innu actually means "place of pillars" and is considered to be the oldest site in Egypt, one estimate placing its founding long before 4000 B.C.[12] Even this date feels conservative in light of the description given in the *Pyramid Texts* – that long before a physical temple was established, Innu was the site of the original Primeval Mound.

As written in the *Pyramid Texts*, the essence of the god Atum first impregnates the site: "…before Heliopolis had been founded that I might be therein." [13] Once established, his energy physically manifests as a primeval mound. The Egyptians believed in the divinization of the physical form of the original creators, and that their embodiment became divine in the sacred mounds of the Earth.[14] Since the mound of Atum at Innu is also his dwelling place, the mound was considered a divine being, from which the four elements of the physical world poured forth.[15]

Benben stone.

On top of the mound there appears a special stone: "O Atum… when you came into being you rose as a High Hill, you shone as the Benben stone…" [16] As with the Sivalingam, it is a stone that "descended from heaven" reputedly shaped like a cone or pyramid.[17] This pillar is subsequently protected within a temple, in an open courtyard: "…you shone as the Benben stone in the Het Benben, the Temple of the Phoenix." [18] This temple is then sanctified by an earthly creator god, typically Ptah, and the site falls under his tutelage. The Primeval Mound, the central stone, and its encompassing temple then becomes a source of initiation and knowledge, but only to those who have the patience and integrity to undertake the journey into *gnosis*: "These are they who are outside Het Benben… They see Ra with their eyes and they enter into his secret teachings… I protect my hidden things in Het Benben." [19]

As for the earthly god Ptah, he subsequently becomes the personification of the mound and its omphalos, the rock of the temple. The name Ptah, of course, is the root of Petra ("rock"), and in later times another temple would be carved out of the rock at Petra in Jordan, which itself housed an omphalos. The sacred mound is re-enacted physically and metaphorically throughout history. In the Bible, Jesus entrusts the 'building' of his church to Peter, meaning "rock": "…you are Peter; and upon this rock I will build my church, and the gates of hell shall not prevail against it. And I will give you the keys of the kingdom of heaven. And whatsoever you shall bind upon earth, it shall be bound also in heaven: and whatsoever you shall loose upon earth, it shall be loosed also in heaven." [20] In this illuminating quote we see blatant references to the worldwide foundations of the temple: how it stands as a force against corruption ("the gates of hell"); that it offers the potential to take the initiate into a state of paradise ("the kingdom of heaven"); and its mediating role in sky-ground dualism ("on earth as in heaven").

Asterisks and obelisks.

As symbolic images go, the mound of Atum and the pyramid-shaped Benben are interchangeable. And in the design of the Benben is reflected the threefold nature of divinity and its two-dimensional geometry, the triangle. Thus, the Benben becomes a

A field of obelisks at Aksum, Ethiopia.

metaphor of the essence of the creator god on a place of power. As more primordial mounds and navels were consecrated across the face of the Earth, each site was marked by a standing stone. In Egypt these took on the shape of obelisks, atop of which a Benben would be fitted as a capstone and plated with electrum, a highly-conductive alloy mixed from two-thirds gold to one-third silver.

Although Heliopolis' light is now much diminished, a mirror of its former glory can still be seen in the field of obelisks at Aksum in Ethiopia, one of which stands 108-feet tall and weighs 520 tons. The obelisk as an omphalos marking a primordial navel of the earth – a power point – is enshrined in the Celtic *men-hir* ("upright stone"). These phallic stones are particularly memorable in the region of Carnac, what today is the province of Brittany, France. Chief among these are the 30-foot tall Dol-de-Bretagne, weighting-in at a deft 140 tons, and the now recumbent 65-foot, 300-ton cyclopean menhir of Er Grah ("The Fairy Stone"), which once could be seen by ships 7 miles out at sea! [21]

Carnac is the most prolific place in the world for mounds, dolmens, menhirs, and standing stones and is often described as a navel of the world. One of its alignments of stones at Menec consists of eleven rows of megaliths stretching for 3,822 feet by 330 feet. Indeed the expanse of over 3,000 prehistoric structures can only be properly appreciated from the air. With each of its enclosures designed for individual purposes, it was a true "city of knowledge" during Neolithic, and possibly Mesolithic times, just as Innu/Heliopolis was the center of the ancient Mysteries Schools of Egypt – just as Aksum is claimed to be the resting place of a curious box of cedar, topped with two gold cherubim protecting the laws of God, and called the Ark of the Covenant.[22]

On a less conspicuous, but equally important scale is a tiny Pacific island whose most famous inhabitants are gigantic statues made of volcanic tuff bearing proud faces and eyes staring at the sky, hence their name Mata-Ki-Te- Rani "eyes looking at heaven." We are of course in Easter Island, whose ancient name Te-Pito-O-Te-Henua means "the navel of the world." [23] And there is indeed an actual navel place, located near the town of Anakena and called Ahu-Te-Pito-Kura, the "golden navel." [24] It is a circular stone enclosure inside which rest a set of what looks like geometrically-arranged super-size cannonballs: four aligned to the

The golden navel, Easter Island.

cardinal directions with the fifth, and largest, in the center. They are said to have been brought to Easter Island by a creator god named Atu Motua ("Father Lord"), who brought civilization and laws and knowledge from a land called Hiva, which legend states was submerged during a violent upheaval of the earth in prehistoric times.[25]

As for the navel stones themselves, these have magnetic properties, and traditions state how they were used by magician-priests for *mana*, "magic" (similar to the Egyptian magic *hekau*), to help concentrate their mental powers while they made the giant statues move silently through the air and position them according to some geodetic plan.[26]

Once again there is this recurring suggestion of a form of energy inherent at the navels of the earth capable of empowering ordinary people and magnifying their god-given potential, what medieval alchemists described as "turning base metal into gold." The transmutation of ordinary being into extraordinary human. This transfiguration into a mirror image of God required training, discipline, and indoctrination into the Mysteries, and when successful, its adepts became an example to others, thereby helping to raise the level of awareness and in turn maintaining societies in balance for thousands of years. That was the intent from the moment the sacred mounds were created.

The abundance of worldwide sacred sites associated with an omphalos, a lingam, a mound or navel is striking. When we take into account their accelerated destruction over the past 800 years and look at what remains, it is still an impressive endeavor. At these locales the phallic masculine inseminates the earth and the umbilical feminine receives this nourishment in the form of knowledge. It is as primal a symbol of the Sacred Marriage as you can get. These places of the gods are of uncountable age, often accompanied by rich traditions associated with creation, knowledge, spiritual truth and power. It is stated in ancient texts from Teotihuacan to Giza to southern India that by traversing these *axis mundi* one can bring back knowledge from the otherworld, and a person or place subtended by this meeting between spirit and matter in turn becomes a repository of that knowledge. The symbolism repeats cross-culturally, from the *Sagas* of Odin and the Yggdrasil Tree, to the Tree of Knowledge in the Garden of Eden, to the story of Jacob's ladder – even Jack and the Beanstalk. They also tend to be nodes from which entire civilizations emerged, bound by a set of cosmic laws directing them to live a harmonious life which, if adhered to, could be maintained indefinitely.[27] As the late antiquarian pioneer John Michell summarized, "traditional cosmologies describe a centered universe in which the principle of order is ultimately paramount. Their social product is a cosmologically ordered form of civilization whose central symbol is the world-pole penetrating the earth."[28]

The omphalos at Delos and a Roman coin. Regardless of shape the standing stone has always been associated with the serpent, symbol of the earth's procreative energy.

Here it is possible to draw parallels between the navels of the earth and the navel of the body – not a huge leap considering we emanate from the soil. The navel marks the center of the human body, but it is also the point of entry of information, disguised as subtle energy, into its electromagnetic circuitry.[29] The phrase "a gut feeling" that so describes the moment one receives information from the surrounding landscape probably derives from this interaction. And just as our navels were initially connected to a source of physical nourishment via the umbilical cord, so the terrestrial omphalos connects us to an invisible source for spiritual sustenance.

The pharaoh Akhenaten understood this concept very well. During his period of kingship he moved the traditional capital from Thebes – which by his time had fallen under control of a corrupted priesthood – and founded the new sacred center at Akhetaten, which actually marks the geodetic center of Egypt. As an adept of the Mysteries Schools, Akhenaten allowed himself to be a channel of *maat*, meaning truth, justice and the perfect order of the cosmos. Free from the misguided idolatry that had come to prevail at Thebes, he sought to do what previous enlightened rulers had done since the days of the primordial mound at Heliopolis: to bring the law and order of heaven to bear on human affairs, to facilitate enlightenment and bring the potential of paradise ever closer to the individual and communal body.

That a certain numinous telluric power is present at these places of the gods is beyond doubt, as scientists armed with expensive magnetometers have found; [30] and as centuries of dowsing have shown, these sacred sites also tend to display a balance of positive and negatively-charged electromagnetic energies. Part of the effect is reflected in the form of the stone pillar itself, as John Michell explains, "Authority at the navel of the earth is upheld by the omphalos rock, which retains the heat of the sun; while the lunar principle is active in the waters that rise beneath the rock, drawn by the moon and corresponding to the dimension of the mind below consciousness." [31] If this assumption is correct then the stone's intended purpose as a mediating agent between earth and sky is true to its function.

The lingam/omphalos stone is a physical marker of the only legitimate source of divine law on earth. It is such a primordial image that it survives into our era. When newly-appointed kings or lawgivers proclaimed their divine right in front of an audience, they would stand on a geodetic navel of the earth, or sat on a stone with associations to divinity, which served to empower their rule or bestow the same unchallengeable force to the monarch's words that were traditionally associated with the rock. The image was then reinforced by the sceptre the ruler held in his hand.[32]

Whole cultures were based on the simple truth that the navel of the world is a central pillar of interaction with the divine, its laws and knowledge, and they granted these sacred centers the appropriate reverence. Even Chinese emperors made it a practice to attend places of power, such as the sacred mountain Tài Shan, to restore well-being to their empire.[33]

Conversely, it was also realized that misuse or loss of connection with the omphalos would precipitate a fall of the tribe, and a cursory look at ancient pharaohs and Caesars who used these temples to claim power purely for egotistical ends shows just how quickly the plot was lost. One of the oldest inhabited cities on Earth is Susa. Dating to 7000 B.C., this proto-Pythagorean city of mathematics and philosophy was once the capital of the Elamite Empire, described as "the great holy city, abode of the gods, seat of their mysteries." [34] It was the seat of Nin-Ana, the "lady of the sky," and home to a tomb surmounted with a conical stone and said to be the resting place of the biblical King David.

Its fame and sanctity grew accordingly. Yet by 330 B.C. the true function of its temple had been lost. Once the divine power of this navel of the earth was aggrandized by the priesthood, it began attracting the appetite of despots who, after waves of plundering the city and mistakenly seeking a material face in the power of the temple, Susa fell and became but a whisper of its former glory.

Such a turn of events in the lifespan of a sacred place is common to so many other navels of the earth, such as the city of Solymna, today's Jerusalem.[35] The stunning Al-Aqsa Mosque sits on a temple that Herod rebuilt; it was a renovation of the initiatory Temple of Solomon (*sol-amun*, the solar deity), which was founded on ancient Egyptian principles yet resting on cyclopean foundation stones indicating a place of remote, possibly Neolithic age. All these rest atop the *Eben Shetiyah* (the Benben), literally "a foundation stone of the Earth," said to be the first object created by God.[36] Layers upon layers of sanctity and age. And yet despite such lofty origins, Jerusalem too has become perennially subjected to the baser qualities of men.

Philosophers such as Plato warned of the consequences of stepping away from the sacred center and the imbalance it brings upon society and the individual. In both *Laws* and *Timaeus*, Plato illustrates the ideal city-state as one anchored by a central, sacred omphalos, out of which radiates twelve lines, with the land and its people defined by specific numerical and geometric codes. There are multiple layers of cosmology encoded in Plato's writings,[37] and in this respect his work and intent are no different to that of the creator gods and their landscape temples and lingams, or the architects who implemented their plans. Plato even notes that the locating of the omphalos is always attended to by specialists within a special priesthood.

One Australian tribe, the Arunta, are a dramatic example of what occurs when contact with the divine is lost. They carried around with them their interpretation of the lingam in the shape of a trunk of the gum tree. For them it acted like a dowsing rod, offering divination and direction. One day the limb broke, the tribe became disorientated, lost their focus, and after wandering aimlessly through the featureless Outback, they lay down as a tribe on the ground and died. While undoubtedly a true story, the central illustration of this tale is metaphoric, in that once contact with the divine is broken, people become detached from the landscape and life loses its direction and purpose.

As Mircea Eliade wrote, "Once contact with the transcendent is lost, existence in the world ceases to be possible." [38]

First, a navel of the earth, then a hermitage dedicated to archangel Michael. Roche, Cornwall.

Moving towards monumentalism.

As we have already learned, we are rich with myths and traditions of landscape temples as places touched by a concentrated telluric force and frequented by gods. It therefore stands to reason that synthesizing the processes at work in these portals and creating carbon copies at other locations would serve humanity in the same manner.

We do not know exactly when human-constructed temples began, yet at some point they did, and as close to the original navel of power as was permitted. These temples became microcosms of a macrocosm,[39] protectors of the navel of power and a reminder of the sacrality of the site. When the essence of Siva manifested as a phallic pillar on the eastern side of Arunachala, the architect Visvakarma erected a temple around it and "became like a god." The deeds of this man of geometry and number would subsequently be re-enacted throughout the ages, most notably by the architect and High Priest of Heliopolis, Imhotep, who brought the pyramid form to Egypt and added the step pyramid to the temple complex at Saqqara. He then becomes a god. These and many other acts originated from a "Golden Age," when men of great stature were moved by an unshakable duty to the divine, to create temples as cities of knowledge, what the Hindu call *Jnana Puri.*

Tiwanaku, c.1923. Bolivia.

4

CITIES OF KNOWLEDGE.

"There are a number of texts and traditions which hint that the monuments may have been used directly as instruments of the knowledge. They are spoken of as places in which the initiate might be 'transformed into a god' or into a bright star."

~ Graham Hancock, in *Heaven's Mirror*

"I asked the natives whether these edifices were built in the time of the Inca. They laughed at the question, affirming that they were made long before the Inca… that they had heard from their forebears that everything to be seen there appeared suddenly in the course of a single night." [1]

Thus reads the eyewitness account by Pedro Cieza de León when he came across a temple two miles above sea level, on the Altiplano of Bolivia. In reading his diary it is clear he struggled for adjectives while attempting to describe what lay in front of him. The year was 1549.

Nearly 500 years later and the problem of finding adjectives persists at the megalithic temple complex of Tiwanaku, or to be more precise, what looters and treasure hunters have left of it. And yet what remains still leaves an indelible mark on even the most obstinate of minds.

Tiwanaku is the oldest sacred site found to date. Its survival after 17,000 years is a powerful testament to the skill and knowledge of its creators, and proof that it was built with longevity in mind: an immortal temple that would survive well into our age. Perhaps they possessed the foresight to teach future generations how to

maintain a culture in balance for thousands of years, simply by observing, studying and following universal laws.

Everything about this temple complex is incongruous with its surroundings. Let's begin at the beginning: the site is composed of various ceremonial structures; a stepped pyramid, semi-subterranean courtyards, an underground chamber, and docks capable of handling a hundred large vessels. One particular block of stone from which the pier was fashioned weighs an estimated 440 tons.[2] All of this sits on a lake 170 miles from the ocean, approximately 12,500 feet above sea level and is as inaccessible from civilization as one can be.

Its primary, and possibly oldest part, is the courtyard within the Temple of Kalasasaya, meaning "Place of the Upright Standing Stones," [3] which indeed it is. There are approximately 99 upright megaliths, some as much as 15 feet high, arranged in a rectangle 421 feet by 389 feet, the size of a small stadium;[4] three pillars resembling lingams stand in the center. The enclosure was partly rebuilt in 1960, yet the quality and precision of the 20th century craftsmanship is visibly disgraced by the original work. And yet we are led to believe this metropolis was all the work of primitive people. Which brings us to the main point: exactly how old *is* this temple?

Orthodox archaeologists have rested on Carbon-14 dating of virgin soil to shoe-horn the temple complex into an acceptable, orthodox, historical time-frame of 300 A.D. Excavated pottery shards show signs of local human activity around 1500 B.C. While there is no doubt that these tests are correct, the dating of the top layer of soil only proves the time of a *final* habitation, not the date of original construction.

To confound things, it's a well-established fact that virtually all ancient temples rest upon the foundations of far older sites. The temple of the Sumerian god of wisdom Enki, at Eridu, was once considered to be no older than 2600 B.C. This conveniently placed it within established biblical parameters, until further digging exposed seventeen more layers of previous temples, at a stroke sliding back the date of original construction to 5000 B.C.[5] The same applies to Stonehenge: four decades ago anyone disagreeing with the established date of 1800 B.C. was considered mad, and yet further digging and improved technology has moved the origin of this most famous of sites to 8000 B.C.[6] (ironically it was the date originally revealed by a number of respected psychics!).

Nothing is as certain as a closed mind, and as far as institutional academics are concerned, no culture could have possibly existed in the Americas that could be in any way superior to that of Europeans. But the evidence indeed proves otherwise.

In the case of Tiwanaku, the different construction methods alone demonstrate that it was built upon over the course of many ages, just like Egyptian temples. The more recent the masonry, the worse – and structurally weaker – the construction, showing how knowledge has not ascended, but *descended* from an older source. Then there is the case of the metal clamps that once held the monoliths together, which bear an uncanny resemblance to those used for identical building purposes around 2600 B.C., and found at Stonehenge and Egyptian sites. These same clamps show signs of having had the metal poured directly into the slots in the stone, implying that a portable smelter

The Gate of the Sun. Tiwanaku.

was used, and considering the type of alloy employed, would have needed to generate temperatures of thousands of degrees Celsius. Such technology was, allegedly, not available at the time.[7]

Honing-in further on the true date of Tiwanaku, around the site are several statues of unusual-looking humanoids surrounded with puzzling, carved images of animals bearing a resemblance to Toxodons, a Pilocene/Pleistocene mammal that became extinct over 16,000 years ago.[8]

Then there is the question of astral alignments. In the ancient world, temples such as Stonehenge, Carnac, the Giza Pyramids, Angkor, Luxor, etc. have been proven beyond reasonable doubt that all were aligned to the extreme rising and setting points of the Sun and/or Moon, to specific stars and even entire constellations.[9] It would be unusual if Tiwanaku proved to be the exception. One clue that proves it isn't is carved on the Gateway of the Sun, one of the temple's most impressive structures. It features a series of iconographs artistically etched into the hard, greenish-grey andesite portal stones. Its central figure represents the solar deity holding a rod in each hand and a head crowned with 19 rays. In the ancient world, numbers were used carefully to express universal laws, yet the numerical value 19 has no direct association with the Sun alone. It does, however, represent the period of years when the motions of the

Sun and Moon synchronize. Called the Metonic Cycle, it occurs every 19 years and allows for precise predictions of eclipses and the design of very accurate solar-lunar calendars. The same calculation device is employed in stone circles such as Stonehenge, and by 3100 B.C. this information was already considered old hat.[10]

One of the most exhaustive investigations into the calendrical functions shown in the reliefs on the Gateway of the Sun concluded that not only was there "nothing like it in the world... this Calendar is also the oldest in the world – nay, that it has actually come down to us from 'another' world." [11]

To understand the relationship between monuments and stars, one needs to be knowledgeable in Archeoastronomy, which one Professor Arthur Posnansky was. And during his forty-eight years of on-site fieldwork at Tiwanaku, Posnansky reached the conclusion that this site was no exception to other temples of great antiquity. In fact, its own antiquity was far older than any other temple on Earth.

Posnansky presumed that an essential component to the layout of the courtyard of Kalasasaya was the alignment of its corner standing stones to the rising and setting of the Sun, particularly at the solstices, throughout its yearly cycle.[12] He took the necessary measurements, correlated them to present conditions, and found the markers to be out-of-true with recent positions of the Sun by as much as 18 minutes. Like any studied astronomer, Posnansky was well aware that the angle of the Earth's axial tilt changes over the course of 41,000 years. Essentially the plane of the Earth's orbit changes relative to the celestial equator, meaning that over time, the Sun sets at different points along the horizon. One consequence of this barely-perceptible movement is that it alters the degree of latitude assigned to the tropics, from 22.1° to 24.5°, over this long period of time. When Posnansky recalibrated the alignments

Eastern gate as seen from the smaller courtyard and its central menhir.

of monoliths in the "Place of the Standing Stones" to coincide with the sunrise and sunset of the solstices, they did so when the axial tilt of the Earth would have been 23º 8' 48".

His work was peer reviewed for three years by a multi-disciplinary group of scientists, who were not so much concerned about fitting temples into convenient historical time-frames as they were on the accuracy of measurement. Posnansky's observations were proved to be correct, and the date of construction for the Kalasasaya was pegged at 15,000 B.C.,[13] proving that Tiwanaku could indeed have been built during the mythical 'golden age', when men were as gods and achieved the seemingly impossible.

In ancient times, the area of Tiwanaku was known as Taypikhala "the stone in the center." [14] Its founder was Kon-Tiki Viracocha, who, like so many other mythical entities around the world, was a regenerative creator god who brought knowledge to the land. 303 miles to the northwest of Tiwanaku lies another site known as Cuzco Cara Urumi ("the uncovered navel stone"), dedicated to Viracocha, and replete with megalithic sites, citadels and purposeful alignments. Its omphalos is virtually all that remains of the sacred temple, which today sits under the Spanish church of Santo Domingo. To the west, on a sandy peninsula in the bay of Paracas, lies another ancient mystery: a 650-foot tall geoglyph representing a stylized 'Tree of Knowledge' carved on a hill, and placed precisely 108º west of the Giza Plateau, and 180º east of the vast temple complex at Angkor in Cambodia;[15] as we shall see later, these alignments are deliberate. The geoglyph also bears a striking resemblance to the constellation *Crux*, the Southern Cross,[16] as it does a triple-pillar of flames perched on a mound – which is reminiscent of the three pillars standing in the courtyard of Kalasasaya,

Megaliths within a more recent wall lining the courtyard of Kalasasaya.

The Tree of Knowledge geodetic marker at Paracas, Peru. 108° west of Giza, 180° east of Angkor.

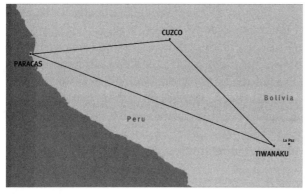

One of Vishnu's triple steps in the Altiplano of South America.

where the ancestors quite clearly observed the skies. This anomalous creation triangulates nicely back to Tiwanaku and the courtyard of Kalasasaya. Three sites sharing common sources, forming an isosceles triangle of precisely 130°, extended across 540 miles.

It's ironic that legends speak of these "cities of knowledge" having been built under the guidance of great men fluent in the arts, astronomy, geometry, laws and letters, and that in modern times it has taken enquiring academics with similar backgrounds to uncover their secrets. What Posnansky accomplished at Tiwanaku, so too did another man of astronomy, geometry, mathematics and the arts, Professor Gerald Hawkins, accomplish at Stonehenge.[17]

In prehistoric times, "cities of knowledge" were erected in accordance with the directions of creator gods such as Siva, Atum and Kon-Tiki Viracocha to protect and promote universal laws. Not only do we have a city of knowledge in Tiwanaku, we also have a sacred landscape planned by ancient surveyors with a passion for creating things on a grand scale that would last many lifetimes. Slowly, these places are coming to the surface of our awareness; others such as Dwarka and Mahabalipuram in India, and Kahnimweiso in Micronesia, now lie well beneath the waves following a catastrophic rise in sea levels around 9600 B.C. (which we'll examine in the next chapter).

While no other record exists of Tiwanaku's full purpose, what remains reveals a complex of great learning: a calendrical site, an astronomical marker, and given the iconography harmonizing solar/masculine and lunar/feminine forces, it is also a temple for the reconciliation of opposites, which was the ultimate purpose behind every place of the gods. There is no doubt that a high degree of knowledge and science was used to create it, just as there is no doubt this knowledge was also taught to others by the sages who once lived in this place of wonder. A sixteenth century account by local Aymara on the origin of Tiwanaku's colossal stone slabs, states "they were carried through the air to the sound of a trumpet." [18]

Places of the First Occasion.

Investigative journalist Graham Hancock has produced a remarkable volume of work proving purposeful relationships between ancient sacred sites and how they were built by those with an expert grasp of universal systems of knowledge. One of his observations concerns the multi-level relationship between Tiwanaku and its attendant Lake Titicaca, and Heliopolis and the Giza plateau 100° to the east.[19]

The primeval mound associated with Tiwanaku lies to the northwest of the temple complex, on a cliff in the Isla del Sol, which from the air resembles the silhouette of an animal emerging from the dark blue water of Lake Titicaca. As it happens, Titicaca means "Cliff of the Lion," [20] also the name traditionally given to the island. It's said to be the place of the "First Time," the primordial mound first created by Kon-Tiki Viracocha through the utterance of a sound. Like Atum and Siva, he represents the threefold nature of a creator god; he was also a solar deity who, as legend has it, also existed in human form.[21]

As we discovered in the previous chapter, Heliopolis was a primordial mound, created by Atum "as a high hill that shone as the Benben stone in the Temple of the Phoenix." [22] And just as Titicaca has its Cliff of the Lion gazing at the eastern sunrise, so another lion sits on a cliff above the river Nile and across from Heliopolis, staring at the same rising sun. In the ancient texts its name is *Shesep Ankh* ("living image of Atum"), or as westerners prefer, the Sphinx.[23] And like Titicaca, it too marks the "Splendid Place of the First Time." [24] Or as the Egyptians called it, *Zep Tepi*.

As with the "navels of the earth," it appears that all major temple complexes are built on or beside primordial mounds – the "spots on the fawn." Like Heliopolis, the site of the historical temples of Edfu, Kom Ombo, Philae, Denderah, Karnak and Luxor are each identified as a "Great Seat of the First Occasion." This was an epoch when the primordial mounds were established along the course of the Nile to serve as foundations of future temples.[25]

These temples are presided by the falcon god Horus. Is it a coincidence, then, that 7,500 miles away in Peru, on a hill overlooking Cuzco ("navel"), sits a massive temple complex erected with cyclopean megaliths called Sacsayhuamán, meaning "place of the satisfied falcon?"

Obviously this concept of a "first occasion" echoes across the world and is associated with places of remote antiquity. So when exactly did *Zep Tepi* occur?

If we recall, temples were designed for the purpose of mirroring images of the essence of a creator god and, by implication, the order of the universe.[26] Acting as "cities of knowledge," they provided guidance in daily ritual and instruction in the proper conduct of human affairs. Or at least that was the intention: that the adepts should teach the laws bound in the temple, thereby extending the education and spiritual experience of ley people and creating a trickle-down effect throughout the population. An early concept of keeping up with the Joneses, so to speak. So far as Egyptian temple life was concerned, this involved the observation of the cyclical and orderly motions of the heavens, as seen in their predilection for sky-ground symbolism. They honored this celestial-terrestrial drama by perpetuating it through myth, allegory and ritual. In a way, they treated the interaction between what was above and below, between mortal life and the spirit world, as a play. Hence, notable humans took on the qualities associated with gods like Isis, Osiris, and Horus, while the gods themselves reflected the essence of specific stellar forces; Ra was the Sun, Djehuti (Thoth) the Moon, Isis was Sirius, Osiris the constellation Orion.

The Egyptians firmly believed the gods of *Zep Tepi* established their earthly kingdom in the triangular region of the Nile Delta, encompassing Giza, Heliopolis, and much later, the site of that great seat of learning, Alexandria. The *Pyramid Texts* in the temple of Edfu make frequent references to the historical temples as "Seats of the First Occasion" at the time of *Zep Tepi*, but stress that the *physical* temples developed much later on from the abstract: first there was the primordial mound, then the consecrated ground, and finally the god's domain.[27] The second text at Edfu, *The Coming of Re to his Mansion*, states the spirit of the Sun (god) finally inhabits a physical structure. This occurred at the start of the sunrise of a new world during pre-diluvial times, long before kingship, long before Pharaonic rule.[28] All future plans of temples, ritual, royal insignia, magical and medical formulae could only be done in accordance with the laws and principles set down at this time.[29] In other words, the laws and guidance set down in primordial times at the "navels of the earth" by the gods were meant to be observed and imitated if a blissful state of affairs was to be maintained. In a way it was their definition of a Garden of Eden.

Nile delta as a pyramid, Giza its Benben.

The principal god in this drama is Osiris, god of the afterlife. According to the *Shakaba Texts*, he was interred "In the House of Sokar… Osiris came into the Earth, at the royal Fortress, to the north of the land to which he had come." [30] Another text, this time inscribed on the stelae standing between the paws of the Sphinx, informs us that the area around Giza is the "Splendid Place of the First Time," and that it rests at the apex of a triangle that is the Nile Delta. In ancient iconography the triangle is often used to represent the primordial mound. Symbolically, then, Giza could be said to stand on the apex of a mound.

The same stelae then informs us that that a large building beside the Sphinx is "the House of Sokar," inside which Osiris will return to the sky. Since Osiris and

Orion reflect each other in sky-ground dualism, this can be interpreted to mean that the spirit of Osiris rejoins the spirit world in the sky at the moment Orion appears as its mirror image.[31] So, when should that occasion have been?

Consistent with sky-ground dualism, the Giza pyramids and the primordial mounds upon which they stand are the mirror image of the belt of the constellation of Orion.[32] All things being equal, there is no reason why the Sphinx should not line up with its own cosmic twin. This enigmatic limestone lion, posing majestically on a cliff, seems to gaze at some feature on the horizon just as we stare at ourselves in the mirror every morning.

PRECESIONAL CYCLE
(wobble of the Pole)
25,920 years

AXIAL TILT
one cycle = 21,600 years

Due to the way the Earth 'wobbles' at the poles, constellations are seen to move, rise and set in different places over a 25,920-year period known as the *Precessional Cycle.* By calculating this rate of movement of the poles it is possible then to watch the constellations dance across the night sky until they find their mirror images frozen on the ground in the shape of temples. At the moment of sunrise on the spring equinox (when night and day are in perfect balance), the monuments of the "Splendid Place of the First Time" are mirrored in the sky: the Sphinx in the constellation of Leo rising above the horizon, and in the south sky, the three pyramids in the belt of Orion.[33] The moment this unique double alignment took place, this moment of the "first occasion," *Zep Tepi,* occurred in 10,500 B.C.[34]

Foundations that go much deeper.

The primary purpose behind the temple was to go on promulgating the knowledge over an enormous span of ages, by which I mean 4,000 years at a stretch. This is an incalculable reach of time by modern standards, particularly as we in this computer age can barely cope with planning a quarter of the year at a time; even a week in the world of e-mail seems like a century. Physical evidence of the multiple layers of structures beneath present temple buildings suggests the original sites were maintained, improved and expanded over the course of thousands of years. Ancient Egyptian traditions assert beyond their 3,000-year recorded history that no site was considered sacred unless it had been built upon the foundations of earlier temples, particularly those connected with *Zep Tepi.*

A temple built during the historic period and superimposed on the foundation of another was determined by a pre-existing entity set in the time of myth, so that this new structure was a concretization of its ancestral predecessor, or as the *Pyramid Texts*

Edfu. The historical temple is dated 237 B.C. but its seat is 10,300 years older.

inform us, "...made like unto that which was made in its plans of the beginning." [35] Thus, the foundation mound of the Great Pyramid at Giza dates to 10,500 B.C, but the additional final courses of outer casing stones over the inner core of the building features shafts that reference specific stars in 2,500 B.C.[36]

The well-preserved Nile temple at Edfu features central structures dating to 237 B.C., yet the inner and outer walls date to 2575 B.C., and it is very likely even they rest on older foundations, for Edfu is also one of the places specifically identified as the creator god's "genuine Great Seat of the First Occasion." [37]

The mysterious underground temple that is the Osirion at Abydos has two ancillary chambers constructed of smaller blocks that are at odds with the cyclopean granite stones used to build the central structure. Even to the casual observer it is clear that the temple was enlarged at a later date, in compliance with the rules set by the creator gods. The inscriptions on the walls of the newer enclosures attribute them to Seti I, a pharaoh of the 13th century B.C, yet they lie outside the original enclosure. Furthermore, there is an engraving bearing the legend "Seti is serviceable to Osiris," [38] an indication that the pharaoh was in employ to the god – in other words the *restorer* of the original temple dedicated to Osiris rather than its original builder. Architecturally, the Osirion has more in common with the same megalithic building style found in the Sphinx temple enclosure.

Likewise, Karnak is an important example of a temple that's been enlarged over the course of different eras. Karnak is at first a confusing mish-mash of directions, angles, passages, avenues and chambers with no apparent cohesion. Yet every element has its intended purpose. Such "cities of knowledge" were typically aligned with astronomical considerations, and since the constellations moved according to the Precessional Cycle, so too did the purpose of the work carried out at the temples in proceeding times, the emphasis shifting with each coming age. This helps de-mystify the wild chronology of Karnak, which ranges from its founding date as a primordial mound c.11,700 B.C. to the historical temple c.3700 B.C.. Across such a large span

The northeast-aligned Osirion at Abydos, today battling a rising water table. The achitecture is practically identical to the Sphinx temple, as is the use of 200-ton monoliths.

of time, because of the tilt of the Earth's axis, focal stars such as Sirius or the rising equinoctial Sun would have aligned with Karnak's processional routes on different dates.[39]

There exists enough published evidence to uphold the notion that foundation dates of ancient sites are far more remote than is conventionally accepted.[40] Additionally, temples on opposite sides of the world share common purposes, ideologies and knowledge that suggest a single point of origin, or several sources with common intent and information all dating to pre-historic epochs. The specialist knowledge of their craftsmen is inherited like a legacy from one generation to the next, and yet they appear and disappear amid the human drama that flirts between order and chaos, then re-emerge mysteriously through some invisible college.

The case of the disappearing, reappearing falcons.

Earlier I had mentioned how the temple/citadel of Sacsayhuamán was the "Place of the satisfied falcon," and interestingly this seemed an unusual attribute for a temple in Peru, since it is a glorification of a site to the Egyptian falcon-god Horus.

The mythological origins of the Egyptian Temple, as enshrined in the *Pyramid Texts*, describe how once the primeval mound was impregnated by the essence of a creator god, a 'perch' was raised on the mound upon which a bird alighted. The site subsequently becomes the *Foundation Ground of the Ruler of the Wing*, the residence of Horus.[41] The falcon-god makes it quite clear there are two different structures involved at two different periods, each belonging to vastly different ages: "They found my house as the work of antiquity, and my sanctuary as the work of the Ancestors." [42]

Sites dedicated to Horus are typically resurrections of earlier sites destroyed in a catastrophe, typically a deluge. In the myth, Horus comes to 'avenge the killing'

Horus. His span covers places well beyond Egypt.

of his father Osiris, implying the destruction and *restoration* of a former world of the creator gods. This binds the legend of Horus with that other most famous of birds, the dove, who returns to the ark with an olive branch following the inundation of the Earth, to show new ground has risen out of the floodwaters.

This would seem to be the case in Cambodia, where a formidable temple complex was built at Angkor by King Suryavarman II in the 12th century – ironically at the same time as Gothic cathedrals appeared, without precedent, across Europe. Like other numinous architects before him, upon completion of this monumental endeavor, he becomes a god. The scale of the Angkor temple complex from the air overwhelms the senses: it consists of over 1,000 temples, sanctuaries, rock carvings and other structures that once formed the hub of an ancient metropolis spreading over an estimated 386 square miles.[43] The entire work is dedicated to Vishnu.

Attempting to describe the main temple of Angkor Wat in a couple of paragraphs is like trying to fit the Pacific into a tea cup. It's like a necklace of intricately-balanced stones floating on rectangular mirror-pools, with layered turrets and filigree bridges, every inch decked with mythical figures performing and describing the endless cycles of creation. Portuguese monk António da Madalena, one of the first westerners to visit in 1586 said, "It is of such extraordinary construction that it is not possible to describe it with a pen, particularly since it is like no other building in the world. It has towers and decoration and all the refinements which the human genius can conceive of." [44] In the mid-19th century, the French naturalist and explorer Henri Mouhot was equally tongue-tied: "One of these temples – a rival to that of Solomon and erected by some ancient Michelangelo – might take an honourable place beside our most beautiful buildings. It is grander than anything left to us by Greece or Rome, and presents a sad contrast to the state of barbarism in which the nation is now plunged."[45]

If you ever wanted to write the story of the universe, had the fortunate opportunity to run out of paper and ink, and were blessed to inscribe it in stone, Angkor would be the result.

In its modern vernacular, Angkor Wat means "city temple," but when broken into vowels it becomes *ankh hor* – literally "Horus lives forever." Yet again we appear to have a misplaced falcon. Could the creator of this Asian masterpiece be telling us he was indoctrinated into the ways of the ancient temple? Was Suryavarman, like Seti I before him at Abydos, a restorer and preserver of a "city of knowledge?"

If you recall, Egyptian mythology conveys that the rebuilding of the temple is allegorical to Horus avenging Seth for the murder of Osiris. If 'Horus lives' at Ankh-hor, then the name of the site informs us of the intent of its creator to re-build a post-diluvial temple, on a site occupied by a previous mansion of the gods, as was the custom. The *Pyramid Texts* are very clear on the importance of a name. The ritual of consecration begins with the ceremony of giving name to the temple, and only through such a procedure can the temple acquire its essential functions and assume its final nature as the dwelling-place of a god. By virtue of this ceremony, the temple was believed to have been brought to life. Should any calamity befall the temple, the residual energy contained in the name was the principal means by which the original nature of the site was transferred to a new building.[46]

This may be the case with Angkor, for like so many other unique temples it just appears mysteriously as if pre-designed and flat-packed out of a cosmic warehouse. An inscription carved on stelae in the Royal Palace of Angkor provides a clue. It states that the Land of Kambu (the original name for Cambodia) is "similar to the sky," re-affirming the sky-ground dualism practiced by ancient Egyptians.[47] An exploration of star maps of the era does not reveal any similarities between the stars and the temple complex during the recorded time of its construction in the 12th century A.D. But if the footprint of Angkor is resting on older foundations, then by the process of

The temple of Angkor Thom, one small part of the city of knowledge that is Angkor.

Ta Phrom, one of the many enclosures of Angkor.

Spherical navel stones. Just as in Easter Island.

precession and by rolling back the night sky across millennia, it is possible to find a mirror-image constellation.

At the moment in 10,500 B.C. when *Zep Tepi* takes place on the Giza plateau – as Orion and Leo find their frozen images reflected on the ground in the pyramids and the Sphinx – the same spring equinox sunrise reveals to the constellation *Draco* its own frozen image: the ground plan of the temples of Angkor.[48] Because of the sheer scale and number of temples, there are also reflections of the prominent stars Deneb in *Cygnus*, Kochab in *Ursa Minor*, and the three stars comprising Corona Borealis, which would not have been visible when their respective temples were built but would, through the effects of precession, have been visible just above the horizon on the spring equinox of 10,500 B.C.[49]

The five central, conical towers of the main Angkor Wat temple suggest to the pilgrim a series of *lingams*; its central sanctuary of Neak Pean ("the entwined serpents") is also shaped like a *lingam* standing on a mound arising out of a pool of 'primordial waters'. A pyramidal structure called The Baphuon Temple covets an actual *Sivalingam*; and the larger temple of Angkor Thom ("The Great City") anciently translated as "Horus Lives Eternally and Is Great," as defined within the *Pyramid Texts*, is an entire omphalos perched atop four gigantic heads arranged like a cube and enclosed within a moat.

Eternal echoes of Mount Meru and Heliopolis abound across continents, cultures, and time.

Far beyond bricks and mortar.

Aside from the visual impact of the sight of Tiwanaku on the eyes of Pedro Cieza de Léon in 1549, it's not unusual that such places should exert a tremendous influence on the pilgrim like a master hypnotist's pass of the hand. Being mirrors of the universe we stare at these temples and see our own image reflected back in stone. It's a commonly-shared experience from generation to generation. It's as though these spaces remain alive, living and breathing, like an organism. This may not seem so far-fetched because the locations chosen by the builder-gods for their "cities of knowledge" are places where planetary electromagnetics behave differently. And being electromagnetic by nature we pick up on these subtleties. The forms of stone and the arrangement thereof serve to amplify the affect.

All across the world, the temples of the gods were designed so that the initiate could be "transformed into a god" or "into a bright star."[50]

Their craftsmen wished to remind us of this someday, lest we forgot. Thus when they built the temples, they also created myths and rituals to preserve the knowledge, so as to survive whatever cataclysm the Earth cared to brew.

Submerged citadel off the Japanese island of Yonaguni.

5

HERE COMES THE FLOOD.

*"…[Djehuti deposited in a sacred place] the secret things of Osiris…
these holy symbols of the cosmic elements… unseen and undiscovered by all
men who shall go to and fro on the plains of this land until the time when
Heaven, grown old, shall beget [humans] worthy of you…"*

~ Kore Kosmou, XXIII

Signs of impending change.

The myths of cities and temples constructed by individuals of great stature exist far and wide, floating around Tiwanaku, Heliopolis, Easter Island, Edfu and Teotihuacan like magnetic mist. The surviving texts of Egypt place the age of the gods in remote, possibly Palaeolithic times: the era of dynastic kings supposedly only began in 3100 B.C. with the Pharaoh Menes, who was considered the first human ruler – that is, a descendent of a pure human bloodline. This was preceded by the era governed by the *Shemsu Hor* ("Followers of Horus"), whose lineage was of divine descent. Prior to this, Egyptian history mentions the "Occasion of the First Time," and we are informed the land was then ruled by the *Neteru* or "gods." [1] This era took place before a massive flood devastated the world.

Advice to initiates of the temple offers a glimpse as to what these supernatural people may have looked like, since the initiates were instructed to "stand up with the Ahau" ("Gods Who Stand Up") who stood 9 cubits tall. That's approximately 15 feet! [2]

By following a trail of clues and the surviving accounts of ancient historians such as Manetho, Heredotus, Solon and Plato, we are offered a picture that prominent temple cities like Innu-Heliopolis are dated to *Zep Tepi*, which evidently took place in 10,500 B.C.[3] In fact, all of the above luminaries learned their craft at said academy as far back as the 6th century B.C., and they praised it as a repository of invaluable knowledge. More importantly, they assert this seat of the knowledge had been maintained for eons: "generations continue to transmit to successive generations these sacred things unchanged: songs, dances, rhythms, rituals, music, painting... all coming from time immemorial when gods governed the earth in the dawn of civilization." [4]

Reading this makes one yearn for this "Golden Age," when life was pursued for higher ideals. Even if everyone did not share this common purpose, there is no doubt the bar was set far higher than it is today in supposedly civilized societies.

Had we been given the choice of incarnating in a period such as 16,000 B.C., the world would have looked a lot different than it does today, for it was the time of the last glacial maximum, when more of the Earth's landmass was exposed. During this period Australia and New Guinea formed a massive continent; the British Isles were joined to each other and to Europe; the Black Sea, the North Sea and the Persian Gulf were dry land; the Mediterranean was a lake, and the Indonesian archipelago and Asia were one.

Southern India was also much more vast and incorporated Sri Lanka, which is now an island. Together they comprised the kingdom of Kumari Kandam, "the Land of the Virgin" [5] – an interesting correspondence to both Mary and the ancient Egyptian land Ta-Mery. As with Heliopolis and Tiwanaku, Kumari Kandam is described in the Tamil texts as a high civilization, part of a "Golden Age," where the pursuit of knowledge was held in the highest esteem and cities of knowledge were created by men of great stature, both

India and the Maldives c.12,400 BC, before the rise in sea level.

physically and mentally, who possessed exquisite skills in temple-building and sacred knowledge that compared them to gods.

But the Palaeolithic world was soon to change, with the Ice Age coming to a close, and ice dams holding back trillions of gallons of water began to collapse. Kumari Kandam, as with many other coastal areas and islands around the globe, fell prey to successive submersions of the land c.16,000 B.C., with more geologic changes following in 14,058 B.C.[6]

Still, there was one more event looming on the distant horizon, and the mere existence of Tamil's sacred texts is evidence of this. The texts survive thanks to three *Sangams* or 'academies' initially set up on the coast of southern India by an enlightened brotherhood to promulgate the knowledge preserved by former academies, all of which are now lost to the sea. The first *Sangam*, reliably dated to 9600 B.C.,[7] was the survivor of four older *Sangams* which had existed prior to the great deluge.[8]

Lost lands, submerged temples.

While the work of the Greek philosopher Plato is highly regarded throughout academic circles, the same circles close rank and flee the room at the point where Plato discusses the drowning by a third, and major upheaval of the Earth of the perfect society of Atlantis, which he claims to have taken place around 9600 B.C. Had Plato existed today he would have been vindicated by geologists and climatologists who, in the last two decades, have agreed that in the period of glacial melting between 16,000 and 9600 B.C., the Earth suffered three abrupt periods of catastrophic flooding that raised the sea level by at least 150 feet – enough to drown thousands of miles of coastline and render once sprawling land into tiny atolls. Today's island nations such as the Açores, Micronesia, and the Maldives would have been formidable landmasses back then, complete with valleys and mountain ranges, and certainly large enough to have been home to the high civilizations claimed to have existed there.

Tamil sacred texts such as the *Skanda Purana* record a similar state of events in and around the Indian sub-continent, and how preparations were made in advance of an inevitable catastrophe, particularly with regard to the preservation of the "knowledge of the gods" at the sacred mountain of Arunachala: "The ground near it is not at all touched by the four oceans that become agitated at the close of the Yuga, and that have the extremities of the worlds submerged in them… all the lores, arts, wealth of scriptures, and the Vedas are truthfully well-arranged there." [9]

With that said, Atlantis, wherever it may now be, was not an isolated event. In fact there are at least twelve identical worldwide legends of great lands swallowed by rapidly encroaching oceans, and with them, the folding of an epic era – the "Golden Age" of the gods. Tamil traditions tell of centers of wisdom and great temples of learning stationed around the coast of present-day India, but lost during a violent swelling of the sea. And there is more than enough physical evidence to validate them. Miles out to sea from the present city of Dwarka lay the stone structures of this original sacred city, once presided by Krishna, an Avatar of Siva/Vishnu, whose foundations rested on the site of a more ancient and sacred city, Kushasthali.[10] In south-eastern India, stone structures belonging to Mahabalipuram ("The city of the giant Bali"), presently lie underwater, along with the Temple of the Seven Pagodas whose golden tips are seen by fishermen during still waters. Similar structures have also been located off the Poompuhur coast.[11] And this is just India.

Several hundred miles to the southwest, in the Maldives, there are staircases submerged 120 feet deep within the ocean, just as there are small pyramids on what little remains of their surface. Prior to the various rising sea levels, this enchanting archipelago of 400 islands was one large landmass which, if still above water today, most definitely would cause commercial shipping routes to be diverted.[12]

On the Micronesian island of Pohnpei ("upon a stone altar"), the pentagonal temple of Nan Madol ("reef of heaven") was built as a mirror image of its sunken counterpart, Kahnimweiso ("city of the gods"). It too now lies beneath 100 feet of ocean water.[13]

In the Mediterranean islands of Malta, structures that once existed on dry land are now two miles out to sea, beneath water that rose abruptly at the close of the Palaeolithic age, around 10,000 B.C.. A substantial prehistoric temple constructed from "rectangular blocks of unbelievable sizes" lies beneath what is today Valletta harbor, wherein up 'till the 16th century could be seen stretching far out to sea. Above, on dry land, the stone blocks outside the temple of Tarxien are artistically carved in a style not only consistent with the same era,[14] but in the same style of art at Tiwanaku in South America, 6500 miles away.

The Sumerian city of Eridu and its temple dedicated to Enki, the god of wisdom, shows evidence of having been violently overwhelmed by mud and debris due to the overwhelming force of rushing water from the Persian Gulf.[15]

Central American traditions describe the origins of the ancestors who constructed the original temple-cities as being very tall and pale-skinned and emerging from a land called Aztlán; a similar word in Central America *atalanticu* means "The place from where our Good Father rests." The stupendous pyramids that pepper this land are generally attributed to the Toltec, although given how archaeological excavations have revealed these structures to be superimposed on layers of earlier construction, it's likely they were added to in later times, as in the case with Egyptian temples. The Maya book of divination *Codex Tro-Cortesianus* appears to support the myths that a violent terrestrial disturbance had sunk an island in the Atlantic, which once extended eastward from the Yucatan peninsula "like a crescent." [16] The deciphering of the Codex places the disappearance of this landmass in the year 9937 B.C. According to Charles-Étienne Brasseur de Bourbourg, the author of these studies, the Codex pinpoints several catastrophes around 10,500 B.C. If correct, it places the events at the same time as *Zep Tepi*, as well as when the ground plans of the monuments at Giza and Angkor were created. Brasseur de Bourbourg also deduced that the Toltecs

Temples sharing a common art style despite being 11,000 miles apart.
Tiwanaku (l), Malta (m) and New Zealand (r).

could have indeed been related to the survivors.[17] Indeed their superior knowledge of astronomy, architecture, mathematics and the arts suggests they belonged to the same tradition of ancient adepts.

The sea level in 10,500 B.C. was significantly lower than it is today and would have exposed a land-bridge linking today's Yucatan with Cuba and the Bahamas. The Yucatan is home to some of the world's most impressive cities of the gods, including Uxmal, Chichen Itza, Tulum, Palenque and Tikal. But in 2001 a team of underwater explorers looking for deep sea oil deposits and sunken ships, and particularly gold-laden Spanish galleons, unexpectedly discovered treasure of a different kind. Sonar signals returning from the bottom of the sea at 2,200 feet suddenly revealed images resembling a vast urban center covering eight square miles, complete with three pyramids, roads, symmetrical stone blocks and anomalous structures reminiscent of Yucatan temple-cities. The images are unnerving because such structures feasibly should not exist at this depth. The team leader's reaction almost sums up the experience: "We were shocked, and frankly, a little frightened. It was as though we should not be seeing what we were seeing. Our first thought was maybe we found some kind of secret military installation." [18]

Frustratingly, no further details have since emerged from the expedition, mostly due to predictable hindrances by the orthodox academic world, and partly because of funding problems. However, rock samples from the area under examination produced two tantalizing points for discussion: firstly, the stones recovered were polished granite, suggesting they were worked by hand, and moved from distant lands, because this part of the Earth is composed entirely of limestone; and secondly, fossils embedded in other samples revealed fauna once common to shallow coastal land.[19]

Possibly the most direct evidence of monolithic temples now sitting underwater lies off the south-eastern coast of Yonaguni, the westernmost island of the Japanese Ryukyu archipelago. Fifteen anomalous structures have so far come to light, some weighing an estimated 200 tons; one feature alone extends 650 feet.[20] These are precisely-cut and sharply-defined slabs of rock resembling all at once Tiwanaku, Sacsayhuamán, Machu Picchu and Stonehenge. Massive steps lead to angular terraces

Yonaguni citadel, ninety feet beneath sea level.

and regular-cut niches; the bulk of the 'citadel' seems to be perfectly aligned to the four cardinal points, just like most pyramids. There is evidence of holes drilled to split the rock, a technique not unknown in ancient quarries. The anomalous features seem connected by an array of narrow roads, and symmetrical trenches occur in places that cannot be accounted for by natural means. The underwater architecture closely resembles the rock-carved tombs on the island; their age is indeterminable, but by their Neolithic style they are believed to be many thousands of years old. The depth of the underwater temple suggests an age prior to 10,000 B.C., when part of this land used to be above water, forming a long and impressive ocean-facing ridge of hills.[21] Professor Masaaki Kimura, who has studied Yonaguni for over twenty years, also strongly suggests that the 'citadel' is triangulated to the island's sacred mountain and a third pinnacle along the coast. If so, it would conform to my earlier hypothesis that ancient sites were in some way triangulated in accordance with the triple steps of Vishnu.

Being advanced astronomers and geometers, it's likely that the builder gods would have foreseen impending astronomical events as well as geological processes taking place on Earth. They definitely were preoccupied with preserving the records and knowledge no matter what presented itself, and built temples to safeguard this precious information. Whether by coincidence or design, the temples at *Zep Tepi* were in the early stages of completion when the Earth's magnetic field flipped 180º.[22] Literally! Uncanny timing to say the least.

There is no doubt that preparations were also taking place for a far greater event, since the *Skanda Purana* comments on them taking place at Arunachala and how in times of change the hill would survive, as would the knowledge deposited there. 3,300 miles away the same preparations were underway in Heliopolis. In the Hermetic corpus of the *Kore Kosmou* ("the Virgin of the World"),[23] the goddess Isis describes how the god of wisdom, Djehuti, "…deposited in a sacred place the secret things of Osiris… these holy symbols of the cosmic elements… unseen and undiscovered by all men who shall go to and fro on the plains of this land until the time when Heaven, grown old, shall beget [humans] worthy of you."

Changing the human race is difficult enough. Preventing the Earth from going about its business is something else.

As it turns out, the flip in the magnetic field was the least of the problems for the guardians of the temples. 700 years later, something far more worrisome would come crashing down.

Crests of many tall waves.

In 1994 the residents of Earth were riveted by a celestial event taking place at a safe distance on Jupiter, as twenty-one fragments from a disintegrating comet hit the surface of the giant planet. One by one they punctured the bands of convulsive clouds which give this orb its peculiar skin. Images of the impact were regularly updated, and for several weeks NASA's website became a Mecca of fascination. But for many people, the awe and wonder was overshadowed by an irrational fear, as if somewhere deep in our collective consciousness the event summoned a memory of a similar situation that happened to us long, long ago.

Something quite large impacted northern Siberia in an area known as the Laptev Sea, near the Liahknov Islands. Millions of trees were uprooted and thousands of bodies of mammoths lay frozen in situ, their flesh so perfectly preserved during recent excavations that at one time it appeared on restaurant menus in Alaska; over 20,000 pairs of ivory tusks were recovered without any signs of decay. Entire mixed herds of bison, bears, horses, wolves and lions were found twisted together with trees and tossed like straw by an overwhelming common force.[24] Some animals were feasting upon meals and stilled in time at the moment of death. An even stranger discovery pointed to the Arctic having been much warmer before this event took place: a 90-foot tree had its fruit and green leaves still preserved in the permafrost.[25] Whatever the cause of catastrophe, it did so in the blink of an eye, and Carbon-14 tests of this well-studied site place the event around 10,000 B.C. [26]

Meanwhile, on the other side of the world, orderly life at Tiwanaku reached an abrupt dénouement. Tremendous seismic movements forced the waters of Lake Titicaca to overflow. Other lakes to the north broke bulwarks, their waters emptied into Titicaca to form a wall of water that overwhelmed everything and everyone in its rampage. Archaeological digs at the site revealed a jumble of human remains tangled with those of fish, pottery and utensils. Stones were mixed with jewels, tools and shells, and megaliths weighing hundreds of tons lay around Tiwanaku, tossed like matchsticks. The event appears to have also occurred around 10,000 B.C.[27]

There's also evidence of this event having consisted of many parts besides a sudden temperature drop and earth tremor. Layers of volcanic ash were deposited all around the world, validating ancient myths of a time when there was "...black, bituminous rain that fell for months." [28] The temperature of the waters of the Atlantic rose 6-10 degrees Celsius, followed by wild and rapid fluctuations in climate. Ice

Blocks of andesite weighing as much as 300 tons were tossed around like matchsticks by the sudden emptying of Lake Titicaca. Temple of Puma Punku at Tiwanaku. Bolivia.

sheets which had taken 40,000 years to develop dissolved within 2,000 years, quickly raising sea levels, and allowing hitherto compressed land to rise abruptly and generate titanic earthquakes.[29]

Mesopotamian traditions are very clear on the subject of a worldwide conflagration. The story was handed down orally for thousands of years, long before it was written on stone as the *Epic of Gilgamesh*. The account reveals the period in question as a time of gods, with Anu being the supreme god of the firmament – a name that resonates throughout Celtic and early European traditions, both as *Anu* and *Ana*, the prevailing god of such tribes as the people of the D*anu*be, the Tuatha de D*ana*an, and so forth. The story describes how the pre-diluvial king Utnapishtim is informed by Ea, protector god of humanity, in the same vein as Vishnu, to build a boat in preparation for a massive flood and stock it with animals, seeds and craftsmen of all trades. The sensible fellow took the advice, and no sooner was the construction of the boat complete when "a black cloud came up from the base of the sky" and "smashed the land like a cup." A flood then overwhelmed the land, accompanied by hurricane force winds and rains thick with mud and debris, for the "people could not be distinguished from the sky." [30] After seven days of cataclysmic hell, it is written that the tempest finally calms down. Gazing upon the complete destruction all around him, Utnapishtim cries, because "all mankind had returned to clay." He then sends a dove to locate dry ground, if any was still available. Eventually the waters do recede and his massive ship runs aground, up onto the side of a mountain.[31]

This story involving a forewarning by a god, the detailed descriptions of an impending turmoil, and the final motif involving a dove (or a similar bird) is identical in other world flood legends featuring the protagonists Noah, Atra-Hasis, Coxcoxtli, Deucalion, Manu, Xisuthros, and Ziusudra, to name a few, for there exist at least 500 comparable flood myths, 86 of which are independent of Hebrew accounts.[32]

The legend of Enoch featured in the *Dead Sea Scrolls* quotes events leading up to the cause of this flood, in which seven stars appeared in the sky as "great burning mountains descending towards Earth." At this time, Enoch is escorted to a mountain by a group of seven beings, who call themselves the Watchers: "…there came forth beings from heaven who were like white men; and four went forth from that place and three with them." These seven beings gave Enoch the ability of foresight so that he may realize the impending flood from the impact of a fragmenting comet: "heaven collapsed and was borne off and fell to the earth. And when it fell to earth I saw how the earth was swallowed up in a great abyss, and mountains were suspended on mountains." [33] Incidentally, the authors of these scrolls found at Qumran called themselves, the Sons of Light.

We shall reconnect with them and the Watchers later.

The *Sibylline Oracles*, originally written around the same time as the *Book of Enoch*, and both part of an oral tradition handed down faithfully through many generations, describe an identical event: "…from heaven a great star shall fall on the dread ocean and burn up the deep sea… there shall be a great conflagration from the sky falling on the earth… and summer shall change to winter in one day." [34]

So, what does science have to say about this event so unanimously shared throughout the world?

Professor of Geology Alexander Tollman compared several flood myths in which the Earth was described as hit by "seven burning suns" before being overwhelmed by floods. He compared these with geological anomalies of molten rock thrown up by impact sites, proving that around 10,000 B.C. the Earth was indeed hit by seven comet fragments, whose impact generated an increase in radioactive Carbon-14, which has been found in fossilized trees dating to that period.[35]

Another impressive study into terrestrial comet impacts concluded that "the environmental data in the flood myths fit remarkably well with the modeling for a large, oceanic comet impact, above the threshold for global catastrophe at or greater than 100 gigatons." [36] The geologic and atmospheric report of the impacts pretty much synchronizes with the description of conditions in the various myths: six or seven days of intense rain and hurricane-force winds, generated and sustained by the air pressure blast wave and the impact plume, not to mention the thick, muddy rain filled with submicron debris generated by the impact itself. The Maya described it as "heavy resin fell from the sky…a black rain began to fall by day and by night." [37]

There is certainly evidence that both animal and human survivors found shelter on tops of mountains as high as 1,430 feet, only to be overwhelmed by advancing water. On the peaks of mountains in France lie the splintered bones of humans violently mixed with that of mammoth, reindeer, carnivores and birds that became extinct shortly thereafter. Whale skeletons and Ice Age marine life can even be found 600 feet above sea level – inland in Vermont! [38]

In short, anyone who chose to incarnate during this period chose poorly.

If a comet or fragments of one collided with the Earth and generated this kind of unparalleled destruction, the soot and particle debris from the event, which according to world legends seems to have blanketed the entire globe, would be sealed in the geologic record as sediment in ice. In 2008 a team of Danish geologists conducting an extensive examination of ice cores in Greenland secured the precise date of the event to 9703 B.C.

Startled by the layer of soot in the ice, they remarked that "the climate shift was so sudden that it is as if a button was pressed." [39]

Plato, it seems, had been right all along when he recorded the date of the final sinking of Atlantis to 9600 B.C.. Arab chroniclers have similarly placed the event around 10,000 B.C., while Coptic traditions place it closer to c10,300 B.C..[40] In any event, the dates are remarkably close to that established by science.

Survivors... shaken and stirred.

It's estimated that from the resulting monumental tsunamis, tectonic plate shifts, disruption of the magnetic field, rise in temperatures and melting of ice, that some 5% of the Earth's surface went underwater as a result of sea levels rising by as much as 150 feet.[41]

Thanks to various individuals forewarned by the gods to build ships and take on-board the necessary provisions to safeguard the future seeds of humanity, people survived and civilization evolved, slowly but surely. Recent excavations at Göbekli Tepe in Turkey have unearthed the earliest post-diluvial temple complex, dating to c9560 B.C.,[42] sited a cautious 1,000 feet up a hill and barely 300 miles from the site of Noah's own ship.

The beauty of myth is that it embalms a truth in a story that can be disseminated from age to age. What is sometimes baffling to us in the modern era is the language in which the stories are written or visualized, and only by taking a step backwards and observing the myth from a wider perspective does it suddenly make sense. As is the case with the allegorical Egyptian creation myth: Osiris and his female consort Isis rule the world in perfect balance. Then Osiris is murdered by his dark brother Seth, who tears him into little pieces. Isis finds Osiris' phallus just in time to become inseminated, gives birth to Horus, who avenges his brother Seth for the murder of his father. In the meantime, Osiris goes on to re-emerge as a beautiful palm tree.

If we now apply this story, albeit highly simplified, to the events surrounding the flood: the sky (Osiris) is in perfect balance with the ground (Isis). Then one day the balance is upset by a global catastrophe, which brings chaos and darkness (Seth).

Naturally, sky and ground become unbalanced and everything falls to pieces (Osiris is torn up). Yet within the chaos of destruction the seeds survive to re-establish new life (Isis finds his phallus and is impregnated), whereupon a new form is born (Horus) that re-establishes the balance of the previous order (avenges Osiris). And with this new order, so the knowledge survives and takes root once more (Osiris sprouts as a palm tree, an omphalos).

As we shall see, each of the world's arks held more than just the seeds of physical survival of the human race. They also contained 'seeds' of another kind – the type that would reconstruct the previous world of the gods and their "cities of knowledge."

For aboard each ark sat seven members of an elite brotherhood.

The still visible hulking mass of Noah's Ark on Mt. Ararat. Quoting Berosi the Chaldean from 290 B.C, the historian Flavius Josephus stated as late as 90 A.D. that, "Its remains are shown there by the inhabitants to this day."

6

SEVEN SAGES.

"And the Elders sat on rough hewn stones within a sacred circle, and held in their hands the sceptral rods of the loud proclaiming heralds, on receiving which they then rose from their seats, and in alternate order gave good judgement."

~ Homer, Illiad, book 18.I.585

The Earth and its organisms flow endlessly in a pentagonal cycle of birth, growth, assimilation, gestation and rebirth. As do ancient monuments, even after the ground upon which they have long stood overwhelms them; just as their founders' renascent ideas, despite the very best intentions of organized religions.

Clearly there were adepts who survived the flood and lived to sow the seeds of new civilizations. The Egyptian temple culture, for one, is proof enough. That it appeared without precedent, as if pre-packaged and re-assembled suggests that its founders already possessed skills, laws and knowledge capable of executing a pre-conceived plan.

The enigmatic moai, staring longingly toward the heavens. Easter Island.

The magnificent seven.

Just like the myth of Jerusalem's Ail-na-Mirenn – today's Temple Mount – the omphalos of Ireland was a place where the great flood first subsided, as was Siva's repository at Arunachala, and so many other primeval mounds of the world. The *Puranas* mention how seven sages visited Arunachala after the flood to collect and dissipate the knowledge; north Indian tradition asserts that Manu and seven sages took refuge in the Himalayas, and after the flood, embarked on reconstructing the area between the Indus and the Ganges while teaching the *Vedas*.

Andean traditions describe the megalithic monument builders as the Huari, a race of white-skinned, bearded giants, the most celebrated of who was a bearded, white-skinned, red-headed god, named Viracocha, who emanated from a boat on Lake Titicaca. Together with seven "shining ones," he set about building the temple complex of Tiwanaku, which then was used as a "navel place" from whence they set out to promulgate the knowledge throughout the Andes.[1]

Just as the *Popul Vuh* represents the oral history of the Quiche' Maya, so the *Codex Vaticanus* records faithfully the very ancient oral traditions of Central America. In one curious passage it states that "in the First Age, giants existed in that country [Mexico]. They relate to one of the seven whom they mention as "having escaped from the deluge… he went to Cholula and there began to build a tower… in order that should a deluge come again he might escape to it." [2] Indeed the pyramid of Cholula still stands, partly because a newer, Spanish church now resides on top of it, and mostly because it's the largest pyramid ever constructed in the world – its volume is greater than that of the great pyramid at Giza.[3] In Nahuatl language it's named *Tlachihualtepetl*, also known as the "artificial mountain." Originally it was named *Acholollan*, meaning "water that falls in the place of flight."

Certainly these builders were physically and intellectually endowed, as one account after another credits these unusual individuals with achieving the seemingly impossible, using techniques that bend the presently-known laws of physics. At the temple complex of Uxmal, the Pyramid of the Magician is said to have been raised in just one night by a man of magical disposition who "whistled and heavy rocks would move into place." [4] Compare this with the traditions of Tiwanaku, in which "the great stones were moved from their quarries of their own accord at the sound of a trumpet… taking up their positions on the site." [5] Similar attributes are common to the creators of Teotihuacan and Stonehenge, as well as the original Egyptian temples, which are described as "speedy at construction." [6]

All this sounds reminiscent of the practice of Egyptian magic *hekau* (the possible origin of the often-misinterpreted hex) with which magicians moved stones with "words of their mouths," just as the Ethiopian Hor magicians carried great stones through the air.

Identical stories involving survivors of the deluge emerging from the oceans and capable of supernatural feats appear throughout Micronesia. On the island of

Pyramid of the Magician. Uxmal, Mexico.

Pohnpei stand 100 artificial islands that comprise the pentagonal citadel of Nan Madol. Within it sits the basalt temple of Nan Dowas and its central pyramid, wherein megalithic foundation stones are said to have been erected by two antediluvian gods who came by boat from a sinking land to the west, and "by their magic spells, one by one, the great masses of stone flew through the air like birds, settling down into their appointed place." [7] Traditionally called Sounhleng, "reef of heaven," it's built as a mirror image of its sunken counterpart, Kahnimweiso Namkhet ("city of the Horizon"). Indeed, undersea ruins of two cities have been discovered here, lying at great depths and complete with standing columns on pedestals rising to 24 feet.[8]

The concept of gods or sages re-emerging from sea-going vessels and other safe havens after a global catastrophe is a recurring theme in myths and traditions maintained by supposedly unconnected cultures. But there are connections, and they're interwoven like the finest Persian carpet.

From the primordial mound at Heliopolis, groups of builder gods, also referred to as seven sages, set about locating other mounds at carefully chosen locations that would act as foundations for future temples, the development of which was intended to bring about "the resurrection of the former world of the gods" following its destruction by a worldwide flood.[9] These Egyptian *Ahau* ("Gods Who Stand Up") were survivors from an island overwhelmed by a catastrophe that "inundated the former mansions of the gods." [10] What's more, these Ahau were described as standing 15 feet tall.[11]

Meanwhile in the Pacific Ocean, the first European explorer to reach the island of Te Pito o Te Henua ("Navel of the World") was Jacob Roggeveen, who did so on Easter Sunday, 1722, hence it's recent, anglicized name of Easter Island. He faithfully recorded the experience along with some of the islanders' traditions; one of them states that the population consisted of two types of races – the Short Ears and the Long Ears. The Short Ears referred to the typical *Homo sapiens*. As for the Long Ears, Roggeveen and his crew had direct experience with them: "In truth, I might say that these savages are as tall and broad in proportion, averaging 12 feet in height. Surprising as it may appear, the tallest men on board our ship could pass between the legs of these children of Goliath without bending their head." [12]

Are we dealing here with the same *Ahau* associated with ancient Egypt?

Apparently, the Long Ears' ancestors were responsible for raising the carved stone effigies that punctuate Easter Island – the enigmatic *moai* ("image"), whose monolithic faces stare longingly at the sky. These magician-builder gods were called *Ma'ori*, meaning "scholar," the full title being *Ma'ori-Ko-Hau-Rongorongo*, "master of special knowledge." [13] According to oral tradition they moved these stone colossi with the use of *mana*, a kind of psychic force where matter yields to the focused intent

Left: Pentagonal citadel of Nan Madol. And right: a Polynesian idol depicting a very tall and slender physique, uncharacteristic for the region.

of a person skilled in the subtle arts.[14] At times they would combine their mana by standing in a circle around a collection of rounded boulders called Ahu Te Pito Kura, "the navel of light,"[15] which still exist today on this island (identical round stones, larger in size can be found near sacred sites in central America, as well as the South Island of New Zealand). Legend states that, by "words of their mouths," the statues were commanded to walk through the air.[16]

Like so many other lands and their flood myths, Easter Island is said to have been part of a larger landmass before a giant cataclysm and a subsequent rise in sea level claimed much of it. Ocean maps validate this to be the case. The natives apparently received survivors from the drowned land of Hiva, and that seven sages, "all illuminated men," carefully surveyed the island before setting up sacred mounds at specific locations; a stepped mound called *ahu* was constructed at their original landing place, upon which seven *moai* were subsequently erected in commemoration of these original seven extraordinary builder gods (*moai* are also present in Teotihuacan and the Marquesas Islands). The masonry style of the *ahu* is identical to that of Andean temples, such as Tiwanaku, and just like said temples, it's built atop much earlier megalithic foundations.[17] *Ahu* are also found under the older *marae* ("sacred place") of other Polynesian islands.

Beside the first *ahu* and its seven *moai*, the builder gods dug a large, rectangular boat grave. Here we see mirror images of Egyptian ritual concerning the sanctification of the sacred mound, for beside the Great Pyramid of Giza, also erected on a primordial mound, there is a deep enclosure that once housed a boat; even linguistically, both cultures share the same words when referring the same processes – the Sun to the Egyptians is *Ra*, just as to Easter Islanders it is *Raa*.

In Egypt, *ahu* is a term describing a supernatural spirit, and its linguistic permutations *akh, akhu, ahu* mean a "being of light," "shining one" or "transfigured spirit." On Easter Island, a "great spirit" is *Aku-Aku*, the essence of which lies embodied in the *moai* who stand forever staring at the stars.

The *tall* magnificent seven.

The Babylonian creator god Uanna is said to have emerged from the Persian Gulf and founded an advanced civilization. He's depicted as either a giant or a man inhabiting the skin of a fish (an analogy to his sea-faring origin), and that he gave to men "an insight into letters and sciences, and every kind of art. He taught them to construct houses, to found temples, to compile laws, and explained to them the principles of geometrical knowledge… he instructed them on everything which could tend to soften manners and humanize mankind. From that time, so universal were his instructions, nothing has been added materially by way of improvement."[18] That such builder gods were described as giants may be an apt indication of their intellectual, and possibly psychic, stature. That would seem the rational way for the modern mind to interpret the legends of unreasonably tall people doing mighty deeds. But could the seven sages have been physical giants too? Even the *Old Testament* recalls how around the time of the flood "there were giants in the earth… and after that sons of God came unto the daughters of men, and bore children to them, the same became mighty men which were of old, men of renown." The Qumran scrolls also qualify these "mighty men" as "giants" who were descended from the pre-diluvial gods.[19] Likewise the Koran refers to the Gibborim ("giants") who inhabited the Near East, and often describe them in the context of remote antiquity and magic, even locating their home in the city of Jericho, "the City of Giants."

Two hundred years of archaeology helps us even further. In Bolivia, after the giant Viracocha and his "shining ones" left Tiwanaku, they traveled to the coastal place called Matarani, which was often used by them as a Pacific port. Traditions assert that from here they were never seen again, disappearing across the ocean in their "magical craft," shortly after bands of humans attacked them, apparently in fear of their size. The legend was finally confirmed when ancient, giant skeletons were unearthed in grave mounds near Matarani. Excavations in Mexico and Peru also produced similar 9-foot tall skeletons buried in ancient mounds or stone-lined graves.

Matarani is a name steeped in Egyptian overtones – Ma'at, goddess of truth, Ra the Sun.[20] Stranger still, the name reappears in New Zealand in a somewhat backwards form as Marotini, the tutelary goddess of the ancient the landscape temple of Kura Tawhiti – set up by its tall, mythical gods, the Waitaha, who came from across the ocean.[21]

Giant lore is most prevalent throughout the British Isles, not just as abstract legends, but in physical proof across the land. Today anyone from central London to Sligo in western Ireland can visit hundreds of Giants Graves – 'long barrow' mounds made from alternating layers of earth and stone, with stone passageways at the front and a profile resembling a Pythagorean triangle. On many occasions during the Victorian Era these mounds were dug up and skeletons measuring between 9- and 12 feet tall exhumed. Most of the descriptions of the digs are accompanied by eyewitness accounts of sudden inclement weather, particularly violent thunderstorms, every time the workmen began disinterring the bodies.[22]

Clearly some sacred things are meant to be left undisturbed.

One exhumed corpse from a Giant's Grave in County Antrim, Ireland, was found fossilized to the point where the skin can still be seen on a photograph in the December 1895 edition of Strand magazine. Alongside the remains of such corpses, rusting armor, axes, and a 7-foot long bow, which was uncovered from another Giant's Grave near Glastonbury, and excellently preserved in its peat soil, have been found. It now rests in nearby Taunton Museum. There are hundreds of such documented cases throughout the British Isles alone, each accompanied by the persistent habit of the bones being sent to high seats of learning, such as the British Museum, and for the evidence to conveniently disappear from public view.[23]

Inside a giant's grave. West Kennett long barrow, England. R: fosilized giant from Co. Antrim.

Native tribes of North America have identical tales of races of giants, particularly the Creek nation, who describe meeting the remnants of giants who'd originally escaped a sinking land in the Atlantic. The Cherokee go so far as to claim much of their traditions were a legacy from a dying race of giants they encountered during their migrations across the Plains and into the Allegheny Mountains. They attribute these people with building many of the great earthworks throughout the Ohio valleys, including the sinuous Serpent Mound. In fact the name Allegheny is a derivation of their name, *Allegewi*. The Cherokee say that during their early history, the *Allegewi* had already become brutish, the remaining strands of a far older and highly civilized race. This is confirmed in Sioux legends, which recount attacks in the central plains by isolated tribes of giants moving out of the mountains of the east.[24] It appears that the incoming nomadic tribes were witnessing the end of a dying race, too few to breed among themselves, and physically too large to breed with human women, leading to hopelessness and the abandonment of civilized behavior. That the last of them did reach California is evidenced by an account in 1833, when soldiers digging a foundation for a powder magazine at Lompock Rancho encountered a stone sarcophagus containing a 12-foot tall human skeleton covered by thin tablets of porphyry – a purple mineral studded with quartz – upon which were engraved a series of symbols resembling a long lost language. In an unusual turn of events, the soldiers actually consulted the Shaman of a local native tribe to seek information on the origin of the skeleton. During a trance, the Shaman stated that the body belonged to an *Allegewi*, whom his ancestors had fought during the tribes' earliest wanderings into California.[25]

As was the case in Europe well into the 1960s, the recent disinterring of these anomalous skeletons would regularly follow the predictable pattern of being shipped off for analysis at the Smithsonian, never to be heard of again.[26] Still, enough published evidence supports the stories.

Whether they are Babylonian *Apkallu*, the Indian Seven Rishis, or the Egyptian seven sages, a fraternity of enlightened people, often of giant stature, survived an unimaginable cataclysm and, fueled by high ideals, ventured to all corners of the world to rebuild the former world of the gods.

The Followers of Horus.

No discussion on rebuilding a system of archaic knowledge could take place without reference to the Egyptian culture. So, that's where we shall go for additional signs of the seven sages.

"The Egyptians believed that in the beginning their land was ruled by a dynasty of great gods, of whom Horus, the son of Isis and Osiris, was the last. He was succeeded by a dynasty of semi-divine beings known as the "followers of Horus", who, in turn gave place to the historical kings of Egypt." [27] Chronologically speaking then, the land the Egyptians once called *Ta-Mery* is first presided by the *Neters* ("creator gods"). In the aftermath of a devastating global flood, their lineage and ideals were continued by the melodiously named *Akhu Shemsu Hor*, the "Shining Ones, those who follow the path of Horus." [28] It is they who take on the responsibilities of kingship until the first fully-human pharaoh, Menes, takes up the mantle of divinely-guided leadership. The Dynastic kings then follow, not all of whom adhered to the spiritual path, and by 1300 B.C., following the era of Akhenaten and his son Tutankhamun, a corrupted priesthood had effectively wrestled control of the temple from the Pharaohs to dominate the religious psyche of the people. But of interest to our inquiry are the aforementioned Akhu Shemsu Hor because, after the floodwaters subsided, like the seven adepts who emerged from Arunachala, it was their charge as high initiates of Heliopolis to re-establish the academy of knowledge founded during the Golden Age of the Neters.

We are dealing here with an elite civilization of enlightened, philosophical and influential individuals to whom the rest of Egypt owes its post-diluvial civilization. As Followers of Horus, one aspect of their responsibility was to teach the passage of the heavens, the precession of the Earth's cycle – the 'wobble' of its axis – and the marking of solar and lunar events. Much of the understanding of stars and numbers would later form the blueprint for the specific alignment of thousands of temples across the Earth. But on a secondary, metaphorical level – and ancient traditions always speak in multiple levels – their instruction was to motivate others towards enlightenment. Horus was, after all, the god of the Sky, and to walk in the footsteps of Horus was to 'reach for the sky' and be bright, like the sun.

An important figure charged with the disbursement of *gnosis* was the ibis-headed god of wisdom, Djehuti, along with his feminine counterpart Seshat, who was similarly the goddess of wisdom, the arts, writing, astronomy and architecture. Possibly the best surviving proof that promulgation of knowledge was the focus behind this 'brotherhood' and the temples they built, lies in the well preserved temple of Edfu, itself the continuation and reflection of a far older, mythical temple. Carved upon its walls are the *Pyramid Texts*. Although but a fragment of a more ancient and complete cosmology, they are nevertheless a faithful "copy of the writings which Thoth made according to the words of the Sages." [29]

The Edfu texts make repeated references to Seven Sages and how they were the only divine beings who knew how temples and sacred places are to be created. Sometimes referred to as the "lords of Light," they initiated construction of the first edifice at the Primeval Mound, a mansion of god described as "speedy of construction" – an attribute also conferred on other temples from Uxmal to Easter Island. [30]

Various traditions state that the knowledge and other important records of such "men of high learning" not only survived the flood, but were also stored in special protective rooms on the building constructed atop the Primordial Mound, namely the Great Pyramid of Giza. Deposited there by the ever-diligent Djehuti, the information would remain protected by a type of Hermetic magic until such time as humans could be entrusted with it. [31] Or at the very least conveyed to people of the highest integrity.

A seat fit for a giant. The Hag's Chair at Loughcrew's 5500-year old passage mound stands over 6 ft. tall, ideal for a person twice the height. Ireland.

Djehuti's own opus, a book titled *Specifications of the Mounds of the Early Primeval Age*, is said to outline the magical formula for temple building and list all the pre-diluvial cult centers, which Djehuti wrote according to the words of the Sages of Mehweret. As far as we know, no lucky turn of the archaeologist's spade has uncovered this tome. It is lost to time.[32] When it does reappear, from the title alone, it will prove a most enlightening read.

Certainly such statements etched on the walls of temples have provided ample inspiration for adventurers over the course of 2,400 years to seek these treasures; even in 400 A.D. the Romans sought underground galleries in the Pyramids they knew had been intended to "prevent the ancient wisdom from being lost in the flood." [33] Much later, a team of Arabs blasted their way into the Great Pyramid out of the same conviction that it held "a profound science" and "knowledge of history and astronomy." Maybe some part of it was discovered, for by the 15th century A.D. the Arabs – and through them the Portuguese – did possess sea maps showing the contours of the South American coastline along with an ice-free continent of Antarctica, a situation which previously occurred between 13,000-9000 B.C.[34]

Whether wisdom/treasure seekers were digging in the right place remains to be seen. Human nature being what it is, people tend to be blinded by the size of things. Personally, I would look where the eye is not so easily fooled, such as the smallest of the three Giza pyramids, the one attributed to Menkaure. It is also the one most dear to Zahi Hawass, Secretary General of the Supreme Council of Egyptian Antiquities, whose composure, contrary to his bombastic media personality, takes on a quiet, almost transcendental quality whenever he speaks of this less prominent edifice.

Another auspicious location may lie near the Sphinx. In 1980 an irrigation company drilling approximately 250-feet to the east of this stone lion inadvertently struck a hard object 50-feet below the surface, which turned out to be particularly hard Aswan granite.[35] This type of stone does not occur naturally anywhere near the Nile Delta. Suddenly, visions of Edgar Cayce's psychic readings indicating a lost Hall of Records beneath the paws of the Sphinx come to mind. Given that in a separate trance reading Cayce dated the flood to c.10,000 B.C. which, as we saw earlier, is a pretty accurate estimate, this seer's body of work should be better respected. It would be another half a century before individuals such as Bauval, Hancock and Steffensen honed-in on the precise date.[36]

But in some form or another, the old knowledge did survive, and probably due to the emphasis placed on committing information to memory. Whether we are talking about *Vedas*, the texts of Djehuti or the oral tradition of Quechua Maya, it was established practice to learn the knowledge by heart. In fact, that much of the archaic rituals and literature of India survive today is due to the supernatural feats of memory practiced by Sadhus and other wise people. Such skills may seem worthless to our computer culture, but back then recital and memory were both admired and celebrated. In his writings concerning the Druids, Julius Caesar remarked that up to 20 years of oral instruction was considered necessary before those who attended the

Mysteries Schools of the Druids were ready for their final initiation.[37] The logic seems reasonable: should the knowledge placed in the temple be destroyed, it will remain invested with the adepts. All they have to do is survive. And all flood myths describe the gods forewarning a few wise men to run to the safety of high ground or take safe passage in arks.

As for writing down information, this has its own drawbacks. As time passes, words change, meanings are skewed, and symbols misappropriated (case in point, the re-working of the noble Hindu swastika by Nazis). By the time the already ancient *Building Texts* were being copied onto the walls of the pyramids of Unas and Pepi I around 3300 B.C., few of the scribes understood the writings in front of their eyes.[38]

Djehuti himself was made aware of the shortcomings of the written word. Shortly after he discovered the art of letters, he sought the counsel of Amun concerning this 'magic' he feels will improve the memorizing of knowledge. Amun's reply is the essence of eloquence: "…now, since you are the father of writing, your affection for it has made you describe its effects as the opposite of what they really are. In fact it will introduce forgetfulness into the soul of those who learn it: they will not practice using their memory, because they will put their trust in writing, which is external and depends on signs that belong to others; instead of trying to remember from the inside completely on their own. You have not discovered a potion for remembering, but for reminding. You provide your students with the appearance of wisdom, not its reality. Your invention will enable them to hear many things, without being properly taught, and they will imagine that they have come to know much, while for the most part they will know nothing." [39]

With the aim of re-promulgating the sacred knowledge inherited from their forefathers, the Seven Sages – whether directly, or via their variants or successors, the Followers of Horus – maintained an unbroken lineage from age to age. According to the *Matsya Purana*, "what the Seven Sages heard from the Sages of the preceding age, they narrated in the next age." [40] As the population grew, so too did the order. We see this in India where groups of Seven Sages were assigned to different regions, much in the way the later order of the Knights Templar grew from nine original knights into a European Order, later to evolve into multi-national movements such as the Freemasons and the Rosicrucians.

Still, the association with the stars remained. Groups of wise men in southern India became associated with the seven stars that comprise Ursa Major, the constellation of the Great Bear – a parallel to Osiris who is associated with the seven primary stars of Orion.[41] As such, these 'separate' traditions can be linked with the northern European spiritual brotherhoods centered on the Arthurian legends – Arthur in Welsh is *arth-wr*, meaning "great bear," and he was likewise associated with Ursa Major.

And although in time the numbers change, the basic principle remains unchanged: twelve knights accorded equal status at a round table and entrusted with restoring the Holy Grail to a besieged kingdom, is a metaphor describing a dedicated group of 'knights in shining armor' – shining ones – on a quest to restore right action to the land. Echoes of this tale abound in Jesus and the twelve apostles, Jason and the Argonauts (a quest for a golden fleece), and to some degree Robin Hood and his twelve merry men (Robin being the 'green man', the symbol of the perennial god of nature, Pan).[42]

The mission of these astronomer-philosophers survived well beyond the fall of Egyptian culture. The Greeks, who were handed the gnostic baton via the Egyptian academy at Alexandria – after Heliopolis had ceased to be – rekindled the concept of the Seven Sages around 620 B.C., in the shape of the *Hoi Sophoí*. According to an account by Socrates, these seven wise men were associated with both Sparta and Delphi: "They all emulated and admired, and were students of Spartan education, and one could tell their wisdom was of this sort by the brief, but memorable remarks they each uttered when they met, and jointly dedicated the first fruits of their wisdom to Apollo in his shrine at Delphi, writing what is on every man's lips: Know thyself."[43]

The oracle of Delphi has been considered a navel of the earth since at least 4000 B.C., and long before temple-building traditions erected a shrine dedicated to Apollo it was a landscape temple consecrated by the god Zeus. According to the playwright Aeschylus, its origins are prehistoric and involved the honoring of Gaia, and during historic times the wisdom and guidance expounded by the Delphic oracle exerted great influence on Greek life, from governmental actions to daily affairs. It's worth mentioning that this sacred site of great antiquity always came under the protection of kings, but when allowed to fall into ruin, whether at the hands of barbarian armies or lunatic rulers such as Nero, the surrounding area became impoverished in tandem with the oracle falling into decay. Tellingly, the power of the site was reinvigorated when rulers contributed significantly towards its restoration, such as during the Flavian dynasty of Rome.

A strong tradition of sages and wise men exists between Delphi and the Egyptian temple complex at Karnak ("The Most Perfect of Places"). Both were dedicated to solar gods (Zeus/Apollo in Greece, Amun/Ra in Egypt); both contained notable examples of *omphaloi*; both were used as places of "distance seeing" or clairvoyance.

Legend states that Karnak is the mother of all oracles, from where all other oracles emanate, and that two doves once flew between Karnak and Delphi, wherein the two temples were used as a means of telepathic communication between each other;[44] the same was practiced between 'hill forts' throughout the British Isles. It seems that in using the oracles, the adepts were tapping into the power of a connected grid so as to amplify the personal ability of the individual. Of course, it also saved time when communicating over lengthy distances. We will touch on more of that later. But why did two doves fly between Karnak and Delphi, a distance of 1,070 miles (a number tantalizingly close to the radius of the Moon)? The dove also makes an appearance as a symbol of communication in the story of Noah who, as Ziusudra, is also the central figure of the Sumerian flood myth, just as he is in *Vedic* texts as

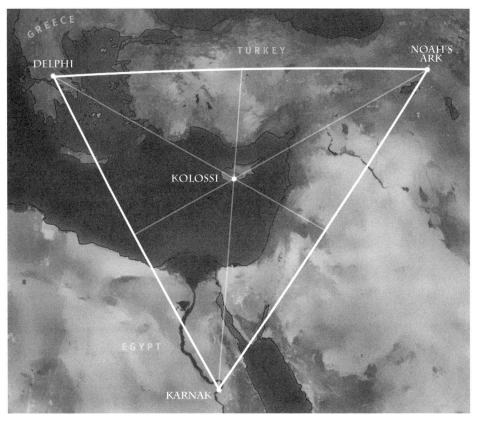

Triple step of Vishnu centered on Kolossi, the Templar castle in Cyprus.

Manu – preserver, father of mankind, and institutor of religious ceremonies. His prodigy call themselves Aryas, meaning "noble," "pure," or "enlightened." [45] In all cases, Manu/Ziusudra/Noah are directly instructed by the gods to build a boat prior to a flood, and are accompanied in the endeavor by Seven Sages (with the notable exception of the Biblical account, which refers to them as members of his family) who, after the deluge, go on to teach wisdom to mankind. In other words, they sow the 'seeds' of civilization. [46]

Since the ancients are so fond of incorporating multiple layers of meaning into one symbol, let's take these connections to another level: Karnak, Delphi and Mt. Ararat (as the reputed location of Noah's ark) [47] all share the same dove symbolism, and all three are connected by a triple step of Vishnu in the shape of a perfect isosceles triangle.

This revelation happened unexpectedly while I was thinking about the dove symbolism. I was astonished by this connection, to say the least, and believed it to be the end of the matter. However, looking at the map and the overlaid 'triple step', I was curious as to what lay at the center of this triangle, which brought me another riddle. The heart of the triangle rests conveniently on the only piece of dry land in that part of the Mediterranean, the island of Cyprus. In fact, the center point rests exactly on the castle of Kolossi, a cube-shaped tower reminiscent of both the Ka'ba – the Islamic navel stone – and the symbol for Mount Meru. In the 13th century, that tower would become the seat of those new sages, the Knights Templar.

Colossal, to say the least. But it also begs the question: was the placement a rebuilding or a continuation of a plan?

The brotherhood of light goes on to reveal itself in Roman times, this time as members of an elite priesthood responsible for locating the sacred center of cities, siting temples and assessing their preferred time of construction. These adepts belonged to the College of Augurs; their counterparts in Greece were the *Oiônistai*. Their work – and name – is still commemorated in the opening of important places, the in-augur-ation.

Further to the north, from Julius Caesar's accounts, we're given a tantalizing insight that the Druids were the continuation of an invisible academy: "Those who would study the subject [the Druidic arts] most thoroughly still travel to Britain to learn it... They discuss and teach youths about the heavenly bodies and their motions, the dimensions of the world and of countries, natural science and the powers of the immortal gods." Although by Julius Caesar's time the Druids were already a mere shadow of their origin – much like the priests of the Aztecs – they still met once a year at the sacred center of Gaul, where today stands the Gothic cathedral of Chartres. Their counterparts in eastern traditions could be said to be practitioners of *feng shui*, who once belonged to the Confucian Board of Rites in China and oversaw social protocol, worship of ancestors and gods, and governed codes of conduct that facilitated civilized behavior; geomancers are descended from identical traditions. In ancient times, these disciplines would be versed in the arts of astronomy, astrology, mathematics, geometry, and geodesy, much as were the priests who founded the oracle at Delphi.[48]

It seems, then, that the Seven Sages and the Akhu Shemsu Hor have been implementing the Great Work while wearing different mantles throughout the ages: the *Organization* of Nag Hammadi, the Gnostics, Bogomils, Manicheists, even the Merchants of Light, in Francis Bacon's New Atlantis – always renewing themselves over time, keeping to a code dedicated to the preservation of gnosis, from architecture, arts, astronomy and astrology, to sacred geometry, numbers, and above all, the application and manipulation of subtle forces by the power of will. As *akhu* they were not merely 'Shining Ones', but also what other meanings of the name imply: bright, excellent, and luminous.[49]

They acted on the knowledge handed down to them to plan a future network of temples, and by their deeds, so they too reached the status of gods: most notably Imhotep, the architect of Saqqara, and Visvakarma, the re-builder of Angkor.

Inscribed on the walls of the present temple of Dendereh, built c.350 B.C. upon earlier foundations, is a statement that the architects of the present temple adhered to "the great plan" exactly as "recorded in ancient writings" handed down from the Followers of Horus.[50] This temple dedicated to Hathor is indeed just that: *Hat-Hor*, "the House of Horus," one of the primeval mounds of the gods.[51]

Barely twenty miles from Dendereh, at Nag Hammadi, the subsequent unearthing of *papyri* containing the Gnostic Gospels reminds us that this 'Organization' built temples "as a representation of the spiritual places," and in doing so, created an antidote against forces of darkness that "…steered the people who followed them into great troubles, by leading them astray with many deceptions. They died not having found the truth and without knowing the God of truth. And thus the whole creation became enslaved forever from the foundations of the world…" [52]

The art of creating temples was serious work involving universal laws and the harnessing of natural forces to create spaces where the veil between worlds is thinner. And part of this practical magic involved a framework whose vestiges can still be seen the world over.

Stones chosen to mark giant's graves bear an uncanny resemblance to faces belonging to the very tall beings excavated at those sites. L: Cumbria; r: Kintraw, Scotland.

Why use a portable piece of stone when a 1100-ton monolith will do. Temple of Baalbek. Lebanon.

7

Builders of the Grid.

"From the relics of the Stone-Age science practiced by the adepts of the ancient world, it appears: first that they recognized the existence of natural forces… and learnt to manipulate them; second, that they gained thereby certain insights into fundamental questions of philosophy, the nature of the universe and the relationship between life and death."

~ John Michell, The New View Over Atlantis

Resurrecting the former world of the gods.

The Edfu *Building Texts* are a source of valuable information regarding the manner in which events unfolded around the time of a catastrophe of nightmare proportions, particularly with regard to the rebuilding of temples. One passage describes the survivor builder gods "entering in that which was in decay" at the opening of this new era, for they found the mansions of the gods reduced to debris.[1] The Egyptians accepted decay as an inherent part of the natural rhythm of life. They also accepted the first temples that ever existed inhabited an era of limited time, as did the life-span of the first generation of gods, the *Neters*. That period spanned some 6,000 years, and all that was accomplished during this period perished in a storm, "an aggression against the island of creation." [2]

After the consecration of the sacred sites, both Egyptian and Vedic texts describe how groups of Seven Sages, divinely-connected beings, and other adepts embarked on works of construction at carefully chosen locations across the world to rebuild a network of power places. With regard to Egypt, they then sailed away, leaving behind the "crew of the Falcon" – the Followers of Horus – to look after the temples while they wandered into the hinterlands to set up additional sites.[3] Looking around the world today, we have indeed inherited an abundant legacy of post-diluvian temples and other places of power. The oldest unearthed temple to-date, Göbekli Tepe in Turkey, an impressive series of eighteen stone circles replete with astronomical alignments and 18-foot carved standing stones, is estimated to have been carefully, but deliberately buried just 140 years after the flood.[4]

As suggested in earlier chapters, the ancient peoples understood the telluric forces of nature. They searched out unique places on the land where electromagnetic energy and gravity behave differently from the norm, and took full advantage of such "spots on the fawn" to reach across the veil and access what Zoroastrians described as *pairi-daeza.*

The adepts memorialized these special places of transformation, then extended the reach of the gods by sourcing the same invisible currents wherever they manifested over the earth, and constructed new temples as mirror images of nature and sky.

A glance at sacred sites far-and-wide, from Stonehenge to Callanish, from Eridu to Sacsayhuamán, shows how substantial cultures evolved around them, demonstrating that despite the incalculable task of rebuilding after the flood, the planning revolved around an energetic 'navel' where order already prevailed. The complexity of thought behind temple designs shows they did not start as rudimentary meeting places either. Astonishing pyramids such as Cholula and Giza, the standing stone rows of Carnac, even the stone circles of Göbekli Tepe, appear suddenly and without antecedent, as if part of a pre-conceived, pre-packaged plan, all designed by people who thoroughly understood how the universe works.

Since one aim of the temple was to help transform the individual "into a god, into a bright star," [5] it seems fair to speculate that under the prevailing circumstances, a resurrection of the previous world of the gods would do no end of good for human morale, to say the least. Sacred texts such as the Qumran Scrolls not only offer advice on the purposeful conduct of life, they also remind us how straying from spiritual places leads people to be deceived by darkness. And with more than enough darkness to go around in the times following the flood, not to mention the need for superior moral examples for the sake of social order in the wake of a mass disaster, the incentive to rebuild the 'cities of knowledge' would probably have ranked high on the list of priorities.

Furthermore, sacred power centers serve the same function as the endocrine glands of the human body.[6] Just like human power centers such as the heart, liver and lungs, they serve to maintain the whole organism in balance. Thus, a temple built as a mirror of the cosmos and situated at an energy node, if correctly used, will serve the

Göbekli Tepe, oldest post-diluvial temple. So far.

human body in the same way – first by influencing the connection of its spirit to the stars, followed by its denser organs in relationship to the environment.

The decision to rebuild a global grid of places of power would also have taken one other important element into account. The worldwide myths clearly point to very large objects falling down from the sky and impacting the Earth with unimaginable force, making the constellations appear out-of-place and the Sun to set in a different location; in fact for several days the Sun did not set at all.[7] Geological analysis has proved beyond a shadow of a doubt that pieces of a disintegrating comet did collide with the Earth, the magnitude of which may have temporarily destabilized its axis, possibly shifting its thin mantle over layers of lubricating magma.

Remember, we are dealing with a formidable impact. By contrast, the 2010 Chilean earthquake alone shifted the Earth's axis by 3 inches, causing the planet's rotation to slow down.[8]

Temple legends describe how many of the power places of great importance – the Great Pyramid of Giza, the Oracle of Delphi, the site of Chartres Cathedral and Temple Mount, for instance – were chosen above underground fissures and streams leading to all parts of the land, by which a vital spirit was terrestrially dispersed. The chthonic mysteries were performed in galleries and chambers below these temples, into which ran metal rods connected to the tips of the buildings, typically a Benben coated in a conducting material such as electron.[9] Just like a lightning rod, it allowed positively-charged electromagnetic energy to be conducted from the atmosphere and into the water veins below the temple and the metals in the rock, making the temple – and its practitioners – an instrument of fusion between the elements above and below: the sacred marriage in sky-ground dualism. With life turned upside down in 9703 B.C., erecting new temples on the crossroads of the Earth's magnetic and gravitational nodes would serve to re-stabilize the planet, enabling it to regain its balance in the cosmic order of things. Following that, balance would be restored to people, and thus, to society.

As above, so below... As within, so without.

If so, such an endeavor would have involved the careful alignment of temples on a global scale.

A left turn into the universe of number.

But first, a small detour.

One of the elements of knowledge taught at ancient Academies and Mysteries schools was the concept of sacred number, and how everything in the universe is accorded a numerical value. The process has the capacity to reduce important concepts such as gods, places, events and tendencies in nature into numbers. It has proved a useful vehicle for storing secret information, especially since it can be transmitted within otherwise innocuous stories and narratives while keeping the information safe from the greedy schemes of abusers and misusers. This art is called *Gematria*. Its practice occurs throughout Greek gnostic texts just as it does in the Qabalah, and was no doubt taught to scholars in Alexandria, and before that, most likely in Innu/Heliopolis.

In Greek Gematria, the name *Jesus* has a value of 888; *Abraxas* – the overarching principle of life – is 365, the same as the number of days in the solar year, as reflected in the number of parts that comprise the human body. The letters of the Hebrew word *life* add up to the numerical value 18, hence why in Jewish custom it is lucky to offer gifts of $18 or multiples thereof – 36, 54, 72, 108, and so on.

One of the most popular examples of Gematria is the numerical value 666, since it makes people see the devil in everything, even if the "number of the beast" merely represents the numerical values of the Sun and the solar deities who personify it, such as Baal and Teitan,[10] and not the cloven hoofed creature of the Catholic Church's fertile machinations. From a scientific point of view, 666 is a reference to the carbon atom, the basis of life on Earth, which comprises 6 neutrons, 6 electrons, 6 protons, thereby reviewing the Bible's specific interpretation of "the number of *a* man" into the more general "number of man." It is quite possible that the misconceptions behind this number date back to the days when Roman emperors were feeding early Christians to the lions. Since the emperor Nero represented the polar opposite of the traits of Jesus Christ, and the name *Neron Caesar* in Hebrew Gematria carries a value of 666, the association stuck. Some Protestant Cabbalists have used this argument against the Church itself, by claiming that the Pope, *I am God on Earth*, also has the value 666.[11] Any Gnostic knows that the numerical value of 666 is neither good nor bad, nor is it representative of any moral quality: it is merely an element in the cosmic scheme of things.

Just as the solar number is represented by 666, so the lunar number is found in 1080, the gematrian value of both *holy spirit* and *spirit of the earth*, what the Chinese refer to as *Ch'i* or *Qi*. It's the composite of the masculine and feminine values represented by Jesus, 888 and Mary, 192. The numerical value of 1080 also happens to be the radius of the Moon in statute miles. This satellite's corresponding mineral is silver which has an atomic weight of 108. The geometric image of the lunar/feminine principle is conveyed in the pentagram, the sides between its angles being 108°. 1080 multiplied by 2 equals 2160, the length of one Great Year – the period in which the Sun traverses one sign of the zodiac. 10800, according to Heraclitus, is the length of years before the destruction of civilization, which climatologists agree as the interval between successive ice ages. 10800 stanzas make up the Rig Veda, and 4 multiplied by 10800 diameters of the moon equals the distance between the Earth and Sun.[12]

These are just a few examples in the world of correspondence.

The brilliant and late English antiquarian John Michell looked into number symbolism in parables, and discovered a series of revelations. Much of the New Testament was written from older sources and brims with hidden codes. One curious story in the last chapter of St. John's Gospel, for example, describes the catching of exactly 153 fish by the apostles. An odd thing, catching exactly 153 fish, and why should anyone care?

Michell observed that the words *fishes* and *net* each have a gematrian value of 1224, and 1224 is 8 multiplied by 153 (ironically, the value of Mary Magdalene). By following the rest of the story, something miraculous emerges. Peter goes fishing on a boat with 6 other apostles; 200 cubits away on the shore, Jesus instructs Peter to cast a net to the right-hand side if he's to be successful at catching the fish. Peter then puts on his father's coat, jumps off and goes ashore, followed behind by 6 apostles in the boat. That's when Peter notices the 153 fish in the net. And yet despite such plenitude "the net was not broken." [13]

Michell broke the story down into numerical values: *Simon Peter* is 1925; as he's the center of the story, Michell took this to represent the circumference of a main circle, whose diameter, 612, translates to *Good Shepherd*, ironically the title Peter inherits upon landing ashore. Next, drawing 6 circles to represent each of the apostles and placing then in the most economical way inside the seventh, an elegant geometric diagram unfolds. A 'net' is then 'cast' to the right of the diagram by placing the compass point on the circumference of the circular 'boat' and drawing an arc of a second, great circle of equal measure, containing a *vesica piscis*, literally "vessel of the fish." The rhombus created within, its width being 612, is divided into 16 squares, each 153 wide – the number of 'fish in the net'. The story of Peter and the fish thus illustrates how a simple parable can be intentionally

The diagram concealed in the parable of Peter and the Fish.

constructed upon an underlying geometry.[14]

Incidentally, the main element of this diagram is called the Flower of Life,[15] an allegory of God creating the world in six days and resting on the seventh; it is also a matrix representing the laws and proportions of the unfolding of creation, such as the division of an embryo; it similarly describes the fundamental forms of space and time.[16] A full version of the diagram is found flash-burned on the cyclopean granite stones of the Osirion temple at Abydos by a method that so far has defied explanation. It is also found engraved throughout many temples and churches around the world, and most prominently on the globes held under the paws of the two lions protecting the entrance to the Temple of Tranquil Longevity - the Forbidden City in China – a symbolism identical to the Sphinx guarding the mansion of Osiris at the place of departure for the afterlife.

According to Michell, in all the numerical manifestations of nature there occur nodal numbers which provide a link between processes and phenomena, and whose proper application exerts an influence on the spirit of place and the people who interact with it. These form a canon of numbers that feature predominantly in traditional cosmologies and religious systems, the entire list being governed by the number 72 and its multiples.[17] The concept is reaffirmed in Plato's *Laws*: "The most important and first study is of numbers in themselves: not of those which are corporeal, but of the whole origin of the odd and the even, and the greatness of their influence on the nature of reality." [18]

Since number is an expression of universal concepts, it was considered very carefully when drawing up the designs of temples. In this the architects sought a correspondence between their work in stone and benevolent cosmic forces. The net effect was to attract those forces, which would enhance the environment for which the structure was built, thereby inviting a numinous state in the people attending the temple. The *Chinese Book of Diagrams* is very specific about this: "By means of the doctrine of numbers, virtuous conduct is brought into contact with invisible things. The diagrams are useful in manifesting the right course of things to men and in bringing the virtuous conduct of men into contact with invisible beings." [19]

Flower of Life. Abydos, Egypt.

Studies into the dimensions of sacred edifices reveal that the numerical and geometric proportions of every room, arch, pillar or nave were calculated to amplify the fundamental principles the individual structure was designed to represent.[20] Simply put, a temple devoted to a masculine principle would be based on a different set of numbers and geometries to one intended to facilitate feminine forces.

Glastonbury Abbey, fusion of the masculine and feminine.

The area of the bluestone circle at Stonehenge is 666, as measured in square megalithic yards, the unit of measure used by ancient architects.[21] Based on the measurement of distance between the surviving stones, the circle may have originally consisted of 59 slender, upright stones marking the passage of two 29.5 lunar months.[22] As such, the original Stonehenge would have represented a feminine circle, the Moon, placed on a solar foundation, thus creating the sacred marriage. The later addition of larger sarsen stones, occupying an area of 1080 square megalithic yards, finally brings together this fusion between masculine and feminine, for in joining the two ground plans of 1080 plus 666 creates 1746, the gematrian number of fusion and the gnostic value of the ideal city, the New Jerusalem.[23]

This concept is incorporated in the design of Glastonbury Abbey. The original temple dedicated St. Mary consisted of a circular temple surrounded by twelve other circular structures.[24] After these burned down, the present structures were constructed over the original site. The numerical value of 1746 is encoded in the measurements of the main axis of the Abbey: 1080, together with that of the adjacent Mary Chapel, 666, thereby revealing the number of fusion as well as the sacred marriage between masculine and feminine.[25]

By looking at information relative to the measures of temples, the buildings reveal themselves to be parables in stone. Like Glastonbury, Chartres Cathedral was designed to represent the cosmic marriage between male and female, thus each of the two front towers is built to different elevations, one representing the numerical value of the Sun, the other the Moon.

When the profile of the Great Pyramid of Giza is placed relative to the *vesica piscis*, magic is unveiled. The vesical shape is formed by the intersection of two equal circles, the circumference of each of which passes through the center of the other; as such it represents the perfect equilibrium between two equal forces, with its

The mother of all oracles. Karnak, Egypt.

interpenetrating center revealing the womb of life, the balance of heaven and earth, spirit and matter. With the height of the *vesica* being the same as the height of the Great Pyramid, 481 feet, the circumference of each circle is 1746 feet – the number of fusion, of the ideal city, and coincidentally, the perimeter length of the Great Pyramid itself.[26]

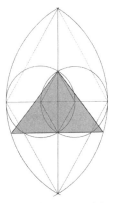

The gematrian number 1746 also represents *hidden spirit, chalice of Jesus, spiritual law,* and *precious pearl of Mary.*[27] All apt descriptions of this glorious edifice.

Inside an environment where the essence of fusion is encapsulated, the inclusion of the human being commences an alchemical process that defines the principal reason why the temples were built. The numerical value of 1746 plus 1, the *alpha* and the upright human, creates the gematrian number 1747 and

Vesical geomety of the Great Pyramid.

its values: *holy spirit and the bride, fruit of the vineyard, knowledge of God,* and *mysteries of Jesus.*[28] The union between temple and human acknowledges the alchemical process that takes place when the two elements become one and indivisible. As the temple exerts its influence, the initiate becomes a recipient of the *chalice of Jesus.* Through immersion in the temple, the initiate receives the *knowledge of God,* and through the subsequent transfiguration of the soul, the individual becomes the fully realized *fruit of the vineyard* – he or she becomes the very embodiment of the city of God.

And at such a moment, the ordinary human becomes extraordinary and *christed.*

Signs of a global pattern.

The adepts recognized that the fate of the soul while residing in the physical body was tied to a cosmos in which geography and the science of the heavens are inextricably interwoven. As the historian Giorgio de Santillana and scientist Hertha von Dechend comment in *Hamlet's Mill,* "Knowledge of cosmic correspondences led up to harmony on an infinite number of levels, and the rigor and absoluteness of number was the instrument with which these correspondences were determined and remembered." [29]

We have already seen how both landscape temples and later constructed temples correspond to the sacred trinity of the triple steps of Vishnu. Given the designers' predilection for engaging in sacred engineering that echoes universal forces, and how such forces are by their very nature geometric, it is not unreasonable to speculate that the temples constructed since the time of the Seven Sages and the Akhu Shemsu Hor may have adhered to an orderly geometric-numeric scheme.

All this began to stir my imagination, particularly after reading myths such as the two doves flying between the navel stones of Delphi and Karnak. It made me realize just how the ancients always left clues in all manner of ways, in all manner of places,

The net on the omphalos of Delphi

just like the unknown stone masons who engraved cryptic symbols on pillars of abbeys and cathedrals. The origin of the Delphi omphalos is in many ways identical to the *Sivalingam* at Arunachela: "it fell from heaven as a mark of god, after Zeus released two golden eagles from the opposite ends of the earth whereupon they flew in an arc and set down at Delphi." This association between birds with navel stones features prominently in the ancient world; an Egyptian *papyrus* depicting Sokar, falcon god of orientation (from which Saqqara is derived), depicts an omphalos topped with an Egyptian measuring ruler and flanked by two birds – the standard symbol in the ancient world for the laying out of meridians and parallels.[30] Not that these are the only connections between Delphi and Egypt, for there are historical accounts and monuments in Delphi indicating the oracle may have been set up by pharaohs of the Ethiopian Dynasty, since even the Greeks portrayed Delphos, the eponymous hero of the site, as a negro.[31] Furthermore, Delphi is strategically situated on a latitude that is 3/7 of the distance from the equator to the north pole, whereas the Egyptian temple of Karnak and its omphalos in the Temple of Amun is precisely 2/7 the distance.[32]

While performing his exhaustive investigation of the Great Pyramid of Giza, the science historian Livio Stecchini began wondering if a relationship exists between these navel stones and lines of latitude and longitude.[33] The surviving omphalos at Delphi is a later Hellenistic reproduction of the original, yet it is still one of the best surviving examples of a 'navel stone'. It is engraved with a net not unlike the

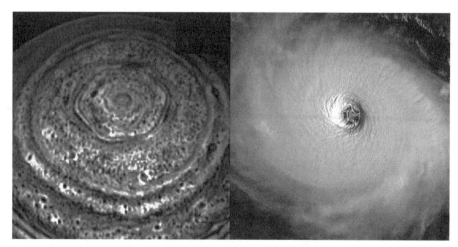
Hexagonal clouds on Jupiter, pentagonal eye of hurricane Isabel on Earth.

geometric 'net' extracted from the parable of Simon Peter, or that unfolding geometry of the universe, the Flower of Life, which is found throughout many temples. But a net can also be interpreted as a grid. If so, why is one carved upon a navel stone?

It was an established practice in the ancient world to mark the descent of the power of divinity with an omphalos. Such a "spot of the fawn" would inevitably identify a place of special electromagnetic interest. Additionally, the geodetic center of ancient cities were often marked by ritual centers, typically a temple or a pillar, as is the case with Persepolis, Susa, Mem-Fer (Memphis), Nimrod, Sardis, even the ancient Chinese capital An-Yang,[34] and as tradition goes, the navels of the earth are interconnected.

Let's see.

Saturn to the rescue.

In 1988, images beamed back of Saturn from Voyager 1 showed the ringed planet's polar vortex flowing in the unmistakable shape of a hexagon.[35] Twenty-five years later we would see another geometric shape from the sky, this time on Earth, in the form of a pentagram staring back from the eye of Hurricane Isabel as it sauntered across the Gulf of Mexico. It was a reminder from Gaia that its living organisms obey pentagonal, geometric values.

It also had me thinking once again about a possible relationship existing between geometry and the positioning of temples, particularly after I came across the writings of the 5th century A.D. Indian astronomer and mathematician Virahamihira who, in quoting much older Indian texts, said "the round ball of the earth, composed of the five elements, abides in space in the midst of the starry sphere, like a piece of iron suspended between magnets." [36] It seemed an unusual departure to ascribe five elements to the Earth when traditionally there have been four: earth, air, fire water. So what was the fifth element? Ether? Perhaps. But I couldn't get my mind away from pentagrams, the Delphi omphalos, Sokar the god of orientation, and the possibility of a temple world grid.

The pentagram of course is the five-sided geometric figure. Like every geometric shape, it can be created by dividing a circle of 360° into five equal parts, yielding a base angle of 72°. This angle is unique to the pentagram, just as 60° is unique to the hexagram, and so forth. When drawn out, the pentagram reveals its other angles: 18, 36, 54, 108 and 144.

With the words of Stecchini ambling across my head, I took a globe, and from the North Pole, divided the circumference and traced the angles common to the pentagram as lines of longitude. But where to begin? Up until the 19th century a number of countries vied for the location of the Earth's Prime Meridian, that arbitrary place that marks 0° longitude and, by definition, sets the position of time and distance for the rest of the world. Then in 1884, at a conference in Washington D.C. it was agreed the honor should go to Greenwich, England, on account of Britain's supremacy in maritime commerce, which at the time was the preferred method of transportation in global trade. Such a commercial basis seemed too superficial with regard to the geodetic placement of temples and would not do for this investigation. A stronger case can be found in Giza/Heliopolis.

One of the most famous ancient maps ever discovered is the seafaring chart of Piri Reis from 1513, for it shows Queen Maud Land in Antarctica free of ice, a condition which existed between 13,000-4000 B.C.[37] How did an admiral in the Mediterranean have known the existence of Antarctica in the 16th century, let alone during a period over 5,000 years before his time? One reasonable possibility is that the map is based on far more remote sources, and clearly from someone with extensive experience of world travel. The clue as to who that someone may have been lies in the map's cartographic projection, which appears to have been centered on the Giza plateau.[38] It may seem unusual at first to base the center of the world at this location, yet the Great Pyramid does lie at the precise geodetic center of the Earth's landmass,[39] and sits on a 'navel of the earth'. Additionally, the building, its angles and dimensions are a perfect representation of the Earth's size and shape, indicating that its designers took an interest in the dimensions of the planet thousands of years before measurements by NASA satellites would prove their calculations to be exact. So, using Giza as the 0° longitude from which to start looking for a pentagonal relationship with temples seemed reasonable. Just as this idea started to intrigue me, research into my first book *Secrets in the Fields* had begun to dominate my entire life, and so I put this quest on the shelf.

72 degrees of wisdom.

The seemingly innocuous pentagonal number 72 carries formidable weight in the universe. In Gematria it bears the value of *the truth*. 72 is also the average number of heart beats per minute for an adult while resting; the percentage of water in the human body; the hours of the life duration of the ovule; the number of names of God

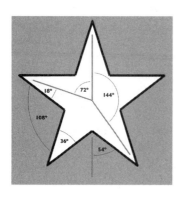

in the Qabalah; the degrees of Jacob's ladder, which took him to heaven; the numerical system of the Druids; the *points* that constitute an inch in typography; the dots per inch of computer screen resolution; the mass of the Moon relative to the Earth's; and the point in sound frequency at which small objects begin to vibrate.

To the antiquarian John Michell (an Aquarian antiquarian, to be exact, since he was born in February), 72 is a kind of keystone, a nodal number from which entire numerical values are deduced, such as the dimensions and distances of the Earth, Sun and Moon, the formula behind the ideal universe, the plan of Stonehenge and other temples, the music scale, the order of planets, and the universal soul. As we saw earlier, it is also the base number from which the canon of traditional cosmologies and religious systems is generated.[40] Michell may well have been on to something, since so many other scholars have made identical observations, particularly with regard to myths and temples:[41] at the Pyramid of Kukulkan there's a room symbolizing the center of the cosmos in which stands a throne in the shape of a red jaguar covered with 72 spots; the dimensions of Teotihuacan are based on multiples of 72; the seven-layered Indonesian temple of Borobudur is crowned with 72 *stupas*, just as the temples of Angkor, Arunachaleswar, and the central courtyard of Luxor with its 72 columns; the angle at which one ascends toward heaven on the staircase of Phnom Bakheng temple at Angkor is estimated at 72°.[42]

The numerical value of 72 is the principal number of the pentagram, others being 108 and 54. These often work in combinations in temples and sacred literature. It occurs repeatedly throughout the *Vedas*, the Babylonian and Chinese traditions, and even the Norse *Valhalla*. 108 beads make up the *mala* prayer beads of the Hindu, while 10,800 Stanzas constitute the Rig Veda, and the number of bricks of the Agnicayana, the Indian fire-altar in Angkor, while its central sanctuary, Phnom Bakheng, is surrounded by exactly 108 towers.[43]

Angkor has five gates. To each of them leads an avenue, each bordered by a row of 108 huge stone figurines, 54 per side, each pulling on a serpent representing the churning of the heavens. In Lebanon, the layered temples of Baalbek rest upon cyclopean retaining walls featuring rectangular blocks of stone five stories high, each weighing 1,100 tons! On this platform stand 54 pillars.

Surely it is more than mere coincidence that one specific canon of numbers features so prominently throughout temples, the writings of Plato, and the initiation practices of the Hung League of China, an archaic secret society akin to the Knights Templar and Free Masons.[44] We could go on indefinitely on the uses and virtues of numbers relating exclusively to the pentagon, specifically its central number 72. But of central importance in our quest for evidence of a geodetic order in temple-building are the following: first, it takes 72 years for the axis of the Earth to move one degree relative to the background of stars; and second, it took the unfeasibly large number of 72 of Set's accomplices to put Osiris into a coffin.

Is there a connection?

One grid, two starting points.

Six years after my first book finally allowed me to have my life back, I resumed the search for a relationship between temple geodesy and the pentagram. Back then, all it took was the identifying of pivotal sacred sites, a massive wall map and several boxes of pins. Then something magical manifested: Google Earth, an annoyingly addictive, not to mention highly accurate computer application. I marked those longitudes relative to the pentagon's unique angles: 18, 36, 54, 72, 108, 144, and 180 degrees, and slowly, an uneasy feeling came over me that I'd seen this pattern somewhere before.

In his excellent book *Heaven's Mirror*, the investigative researcher Graham Hancock had considered the same intriguing possibility, except he approached the idea from a totally different angle – that the geodetic placement of temples was in some way related to the Earth's precession cycle, a concept hit upon in 1969 by Santillana and von Dechend in their opus *Hamlet's Mill*. What's astonishing is that Hancock's numerical system for the relationship of temples on a longitudinal grid are the same as the pentagonal numbers I'd been considering. Like two birds launched from opposite sides of the world and meeting at a navel, we'd approached a similar concept from two different angles and reached similar results. I was actually thankful that Graham got there first because he saved me months of work!

In order to understand Hancock's, Santillana and von Dechen's points of view, it's necessary to take another brief side step and understand how certain factors influence variations in the Earth's otherwise perfect orbital geometry.

A quick lesson on Precession and other celestial mechanics.

The way the Earth's axis behaves allows the two equinoxes and solstice points to creep backwards imperceptibly around its orbital path over a period of 25,920 years. And it works like this:

The equator rotates counter-clockwise, just as the Earth moves counter-clockwise around the Sun, at 18.5 miles per second.

But the Earth's axis of rotation tilts in relation to its plane of orbit, so that over the course of 41,000 years it will tilt between 22.1° and 24.5°, and back again. This axial tilt, also called obliquity, currently stands at 23.5°.

Because the axis is off-center, the natural centrifugal force of the Earth's rotation makes the axis at the poles behave like a spinning top, and move in a clockwise direction that is contra-directional to the counter-clockwise spin of the Earth. Thus, over the course of time, the axis traces an invisible arc backwards relative to the background of stars. In other words the axis is said to precess.

The arc traced by the wobbling axis takes approximately 25,920 years to return to its original point. In so doing, the tip of the axis will aim at a different pole star... today it is Polaris, just as around 3000 B.C. it was *Alpha Draconis* in the constellation Draco; in 13,000 B.C. it would have been *Vega* in Lyre.

Now, if you were to take the circle of the equator and extend it into a greater circle around the Earth and into space, as an observer on the ground you'd gaze upward at this circle and it would be called the plane of the ecliptic. Arranged in almost equal measure around this ring are 12 constellations of the zodiac, each occupying a 30°

segment of that ring (because a 360° circumference divided by 12 equals 30°). And every month, because of the movement of the Earth around the Sun, the Sun will rise against a new zodiacal constellation approximately every 30 days, 12 times a year.

So far, so good. But there's a second phenomenon at work. Because of the relationship between the Earth's axial tilt and its movement backwards along the sky, an observer on the ground will, over the course of a very, very, very long span of time

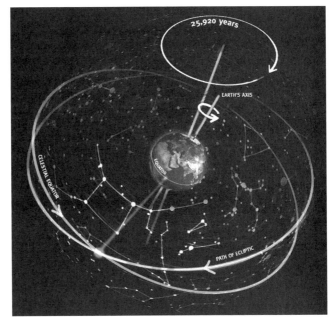

The precessional cycle.

start to see that the Sun, at the moment of the equinox, rises not against the same constellation but a different one, approximately every 2,160 years.

This phenomenon is called the *Precession of the Equinoxes*. Its discovery is attributed to the Greek astronomer and mathematician Hipparchus c.120 B.C., but it was already known to Timocharis of Alexandria c.250 B.C., and recorded by the Babylonians before that. And if Tiwanaku serves as example, as we saw in earlier chapters, the precession of the Earth's cycle was known to adepts even before the great flood.[45]

This is the point where we rejoin the number 72 and its importance in the grand scheme of temple-building:

It takes 72 years (71.6 to be precise) for the equinoctial Sun to move just 1° along the path of the ecliptic.

72° multiplied by 30° for each constellation equals 2,160 years.

12 constellations multiplied by 2,160 years equals the ecliptic cycle of 25,920 years.

Osiris (Slight Return).

Like so many great sagas, the myth of Osiris incorporates specific numbers describing the motion of the heavens into the body of the story by way of allegory. Most prominent of all is 72, the number of Set's co-conspirators that put Osiris into a coffin. Clearly it does not take 72 people to place a body into a coffin, so the myth is asking the reader to interpret the story from a different point of view.

There are several supporting numbers at play in the myth, namely 360, 30 and 12. From these numbers it is simple arithmetic to work out precessional values: 72 multiplied by 30 equals 2160, the years required for the Sun to move along one full constellation; 72 multiplied by 360 equals 25,920, the years of one complete recessional cycle or Great Year.[46]

According to researchers such as Jane Sellers, Graham Hancock and John Michell the pre-eminent number in this code is 72, and the calculus involved in precessional numbers was deliberately encoded into myths to pass along the knowledge to initiates through the ages. After all, it is no accident that the same numbers and correspondences

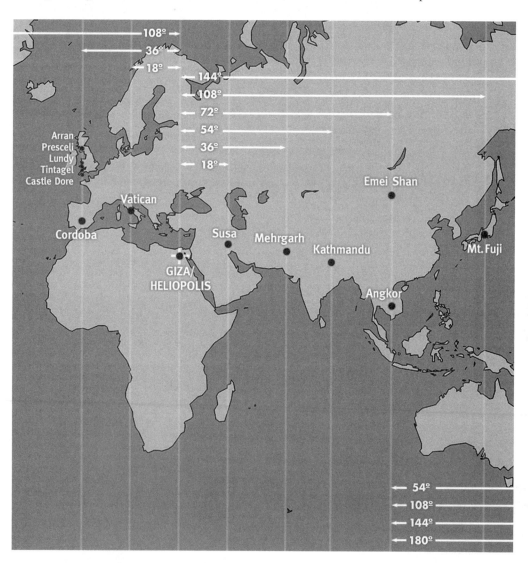

crop up repeatedly in Chinese, Mayan, Nordic and Babylonian myths, as well as the structure of the *Rig Veda* and the Mayan calendar.[47] The symbols used to diffuse these numbers are the millstone and the wheel, along which the heavenly cycles rotate in perpetuity.[48] And although the spokes of the wheel are occasionally damaged by a periodic catastrophe, the cycle is reset and the mill continues to churn.

The Grid below.

Using Giza/Heliopolis as Latitude 0°, Hancock set about looking for relationships between precessional numbers and geodetic temple placement based on the central

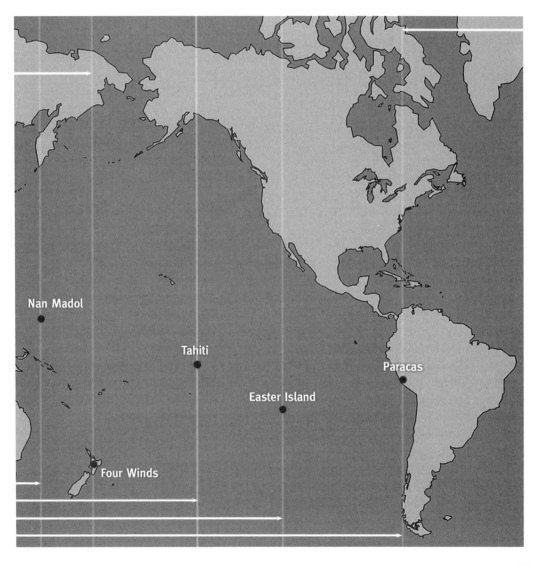

number 72 and its divisibles, 36 and 18; combined, they generate the remaining numbers of the canon: 54, 108, 144 and 180.[49] As strange coincidences go, these precessional numbers are identical to the angles common to the pentagram, the geometry of organic life. Hancock was thus able to link together some of the oldest temple sites to the east of Giza: Angkor, the Micronesian island of Pohnpei ("upon a stone altar") and its pentagonal temple of Nan Madol ("reef of heaven"), Kiribati (also in Micronesia), Tahiti, Easter Island, and the colossal 'tree of knowledge' carved on a hillside at the Bay of Paracas in Peru. [50]

Since I had been compiling my own list, I was curious to see what other landmarks conform to the grid: east of Giza lies Susa (18º), Mehrghar (36º), the Great Stupa and temple complexes of Pashupatinath and Gorakhnath in Kathmandu (54º); Éméi Shan hilltop temple and sacred mountain, as well as the world's largest, hill-carved Buddha at Leshan, China (72º); the sacred mountain Fuji (108º); and the Temple of the Four Winds, New Zealand (144º).

To the west of Giza we find a couple of surprises: the Basilica of St. Peter in Vatican City (18º, minus .5º), one of the holiest Christian sites, is the resting place of Simon Peter, one of the 12 apostles whom we met earlier in this chapter. Conspiracy theorists may read into this what they may however, this site was originally a sacred mound marked by a prominent menhir erected in 204 B.C. to represent the earth mother Cybele. A temple was subsequently erected in her honor, and to the son she bore every year on the 25th December, Attis, a crucified hero-god who rose on the third day, whom the ancient Romans considered a redeemer.[52]

The rest, as they say, is distorted history.

Ironically, the menhir has disappeared from sight, but in its place now stands an *obelisk* removed from its original position at Heliopolis. As to the Basilica, the word is derived from *basilisk*, a serpent, symbol of those telluric lines of force, the spirit roads.

Moving along further west, at 36º we find a long line of sacred sites in Scotland, Wales and England. The stone circles and menhirs of the Scottish Isle of Arran, whose importance as a strategic geodetic marker will be discussed in the next chapter; the Preseli region of Wales – the source of the bluestones of Stonehenge – with Cairn Ingli ("hill of angels") and its attendant dolmen Pentre Ifan; the miniscule Isle of

St. Peter's Basilica and the Innu obelisk.

Lundy and its prehistoric standing stones and giant's graves, populated by people described by the Romans as "a specially holy race of men... who had visions of the future;" Tintagel and Castle Dore, centers of the Arthurian myths.

South of the English Channel the gargantuan menhirs on the tip of Bretagne around Kergadiou, and Carnac (minus 1.6°); in southern Spain, one of the Islamic world's most famous gems, the Mosque of Cordoba, which apparently rests on older foundations. There follows a suspiciously large amount of landmass below the Atlantic Ocean until 108° west of Giza – and 180° east of Angkor – we reach the 650-foot high 'tree of knowledge' etched on the hillside of Paracas on the coast of Peru.[52]

As we shall see, this was just the start of an inspired, global, sacred, engineering project that spanned several thousand years, which sought to restore enchantment and ritual to land, body and soul, and whose legacy sits all around us today.

The mound of Castle Dore, linked with Arthurian lore.
Its entrance aligns directly with Stonehenge 136 miles away.

Pentre Ifan dolmen. Wales

The mosque at Cordoba, Spain.

Borobudur and a few of its 72 stupas. Java.

8

KINGDOMS OF CONSCIENCE.

*"The old stones fossilize a moment in the history of consciousness,
when it seems that the intuitive and intellectual properties of the human
mind hung in a delicate symbiosis."*

~ Paul Devereux

The law of correspondences.

The temple as a representation of the universe is well attested throughout the cultural circles of the ancient Near East, Asia, North Africa and Europe.[1] The sacred places built by the Tamils, Zoroastrians, Khmers, and Egyptians – even up to the early Ptolemaic era – bore a likeness to the cosmos and how each culture interpreted it. Measures and proportions were appropriate to each structure's meaning and function, as were decorative elements, such as the 72 stupas encircling the summit of Borobudur in Java. The courtyards of Islamic mosques are wrapped in thousands of tiny ceramic tiles forming hypnotic, geometric lattices depicting, to Muslims, the image of "God at rest," a statement a physicist might agree with while observing the geometric bonding patterns of molecules under a microscope. In fact, Islamic tile art involves quasicrystalline geometry, a highly-sophisticated math only rediscovered in the late 20th century.[2] At Angkor Wat, courtyards and lakes surround the inner

X-ray fractal pattern of tungsten, and mosque art depicting the "face of Allah."

sanctum, just as the sea surrounds the land; just as the Earth is an island in the solar system, and the solar system an island in a galaxy, *ad infinitum*. Indeed, temples are microcosms of a macrocosm.

Since so much of the foundation of the temple is based on the harnessing of underlying natural forces, maintaining its integrity enables the site to function as a living entity, thus proffering a mediating influence upon the local environment. According to Talmudic studies, ever since a change in climate c.3000 B.C., the Near East was tormented by torrential rains that fell like a monsoon each year, causing widespread damage. Then Solomon built his temple, and the torrents ceased.[3] Maintaining the efficacy of Solomon's Temple appears to have benefited the spiritual comport of the citizenry as well, since a marked improvement was noticed in the relations between the people of that land: "no conflagration ever broke out in Jerusalem, for the fire of the altar kept guard that no alien fire should break out." [4] This led Rabbi Joshua ben Levi to comment, "Had the nations of the world known how beneficial the Temple is to them, they would have surrounded it by camps in order to guard it. For the Temple was more beneficial to them than to Israel." [5]

In so many aspects, the temple represented the embodiment of individual and communal prosperity, and its perpetuation was remembered and reinforced through specific ceremonies. The performance of ritual assured the welfare of the people so long as it adhered to the instructions prescribed by the creator gods, and with an integrity that was true to its origins. Since the temples stood on 'navels of the earth', and their designs represented the harmony of the universe in miniature, the welfare of the surrounding land was to some degree influenced by the proper performance of the service, every event having a determinable effect or correspondence on the functions of nature. According to the Torah, so long as the service to the temple existed, the world was full of blessing for its inhabitants. So if destruction befell the temple, the same fate befell the natural order of things. In China, the abandonment of the rigid and ceremonial cult of Shangte, the heaven-god, was said to lead to "the ruin of states, the destruction of families, and the perishing of individuals." [6]

That the spiritual way of life was preserved for long periods of time was due in great part to groups of pious people maintaining the existence of knowledge through whatever means was available. Since this was also dependent on the quality of leadership, so long as a pharaoh, priest, shaman or king was united spiritually, philosophically and politically, the temple was protected from interference. The problems arose when ego entered the process and when the spiritual caretaker looked upon the ethereal power inherent in the temple as a means of physical power for individual aggrandizement.

Because leaders in ancient times were so closely associated with magic – that is, the practical use of secret knowledge for the manipulation of energy – such matters as the spiritual health of the community, favorable weather for crops, good harvest, and so on, became their responsibility. Hence the pharaoh was hailed as "lord of the flood, plentiful in grain, in whose footsteps is the goddess of harvest." [7] Whenever problems occurred, the blame would fall on the ruler for leading his own life out of balance with the cosmos; in Babylonian tradition, it was not uncommon for the king to be severely punished (a law that would come in useful today). The Chinese Great Law from 1050 B.C. demonstrates this relationship well: "It is the duty of the government at all times to watch carefully the phenomena of nature, which are the echo in the world of nature of the order, or disorder in the world of government. The government is bound to watch the phenomena of nature in order, to be able immediately to amend what is in need of amendment. When the course of nature goes its proper way, it is a sign that the government is good, but when there is some disturbance in nature, it is a sign that there is some sin in the government. With the help of fixed tables it is possible to learn from the disturbance in nature and what is the sin that caused it. Any disturbance in the Sun accuses the emperor. A disturbance around the Sun – the court, the ministers; a disturbance in the Moon – the queen, the harem. Good weather that lasts too long shows that the emperor is too inactive. Days which continue to be cloudy shows that the emperor lacks understanding. Too much rainfall shows that he is unjust. Lack of rain shows that he is careless. Too great a cold shows that he is inconsiderate of others. Stormy wind—that he is lazy. Good harvest proves that everything is alright; bad harvest – that the government is guilty." [8]

Since proper stewardship was by-and-large under the tutelage of a creator god's earthly representation, the success depended on whoever was enthroned. Whenever leaders did look upon the power of the temple for narrow, materialistic gain, everything in the immediate vicinity of the temple became destabilized, including the very kingdom itself, as the history of Solomon's Temple illustrates so well. According to Biblical accounts of words exchanged between God and Solomon, it is clear that Solomon himself lost touch with the laws governing the proper upkeep of the mansion of the gods. Solomon also succumbed to some of the poor habits previously acquired by his father, King David, which further eroded the spiritual governance of the site and precipitated its fall. Consequently, after Solomon's death, the armies of Assyria and

Al-Aqsa mosque above Solomon's Temple.

Egypt ransacked the temple and the land of Israel was split. A thousand years later, Henry VIII would inflict the same upon Glastonbury while seeking, but failing to find, the 'treasure' of the Abbey, for the treasure *was* the Abbey as well as the layers of consecrated soil on which it stood. As the Temple of Solomon fell into disuse and misuse, the old imbalances returned: "Ever since the day that the Temple was destroyed there is no day without a curse… and the fatness of the fruits has been taken away… the ritual purity which ceased caused the taste and smell of the fruit to cease." [9] According to the Torah, so long as the service to the temple existed, the world was full of blessing for its inhabitants. The period of governance under Uzziah restored much-needed balance until the day the king illegally entered the temple in 750 B.C., at which moment a powerful earthquake destroyed the region.[10]

Things did not improve much. Afterwards, Nebuchadnezzar destroyed Solomon's Temple in 586 B.C.; a foundation for a second temple was laid fifty years later and it was not until Herod rebuilt and enlarged on this in 20 B.C. that proper balance returned: "In the days of Herod, when the people were occupied with rebuilding of the Temple, rain fell during the night but in the morning the wind blew and the clouds dispersed and the sun shone… and then they knew that they were engaged in sacred work." [11] That peace was short lived, as simmering tensions between Jews and Romans led Emperor Vespasian to order the burning down of the temple in 70 A.D.

Since then, peace at this 'navel of the earth' has remained elusive.

The symbiotic relationship between the conservation and honoring of the temple and the well-being of people and land – physically, philosophically and spiritually – was emphasized in the original *Building Texts* of the first temples at the time of the builder gods. Naturally, the reverse also applies, and in the Talmudic texts, God clearly states that the lack of correct ritual and improper governance of the temple leads to times of disintegration: "Consider your ways… ye looked for much and, lo, it came to little… Why? Because of mine house that is waste." [12] If only people had read the Talmud, for it is explicit in the correspondence between temple and people: "when the service to the Temple does not exist, the world has no blessings for its inhabitants and the rains do not fall in their season." [13]

Indeed, the instability of the seasons throughout the Near East around the time of the final destruction of the temple in Jerusalem is evidenced by sudden and severe climate change, as the typical south winds which typically brought rains like clockwork suddenly failed and the region became arid.[14]

If there exists a corresponding relationship between the temple and the balance of the land and the spiritual well-being of the people, then creating a vast network of sacred sites benefits everything. The general evidence regarding temple-building throughout Europe and the regions of the Mediterranean suggests a period of uninterrupted progress, from the time of the great flood until around 2500 B.C. With the exception of the odd meteorite strike, volcanic blast or periodic burp of the earth, life was on the up.

The raising of great stones.

What is certain in archaeology is that when it comes to digging up the past, old assumptions are seldom certain for long. With every new lucky turn of the spade, together with improved dating methods, the founding dates of sacred sites continue to roll back with every decade.[15] At 4800 B.C. the Carnac region of north-western France was once considered the oldest temple metropolis in Europe, until the standing stone complexes in Portugal were dated to at least 5000 B.C. The pendulum then swung back to Carnac following the discovery of a partially submerged stone circle on the Isle of Er-Lannic, which would have been wholly above sea level in 7000 B.C.[16] Not to be outdone, the two hundred-or-so sites that ring the massif of Knocknarea on the northwest coast of Ireland are regularly yielding dates of 7490 B.C.[17] In the meantime, the founding of Stonehenge, once established at 1100 B.C., moved to 2600 B.C., but is now accepted as having occurred in 8000 B.C.

Some of the evidence sits under the temple, where the historic foundation is discovered to rest on deeper and deeper origins. Perched on a dramatic pyramid of stone on what would have been dry land 9,000 years ago, the majestic gothic cloister of Mont. St. Michel envelops an older Templar abbey that cradles an earlier Benedictine church, which sits over a neolithic chamber containing a prehistoric rock altar. To the east, Chartres cathedral, the masterpiece in a chain of Gothic creations, stands over a Roman temple that was once a Druid academy that stood on neolithic foundations, resting on a prehistoric mound. Even in northern India there is Sankisa, a monolithic sandstone pillar inscribed with Buddha's teachings. Allegedly created in the 3rd century A.D., the site is layered sequentially with the ruins of a Hindu temple, an Islamic mosque, the tomb of an Islamic saint, and finally, another Hindu temple. This sustained re-enforcing of sacred space

Stone circles on Er-Lannic isle, now partly submerged.

through the ages bears the legacy of Egyptian temple credo, where no site can be considered truly sacred unless it stands on the foundations of previous temples, and specifically, on a mound sourced by the builder gods at *Zep Tepi*. In earlier chapters we learned that these gods survived a flood, were exceptionally tall, and following the consecration of their initial works, bearing the mantle of the Followers of Horus they and their counterparts embarked into the hinterlands to consecrate new sacred mounds – travelers bound to a common cause of rebuilding the former world of the creator gods.[18]

The close resemblance between temple design, construction method, language and local myths around the Pacific Rim, even the Indian Ocean, suggests a common, ostensibly Egyptian origin, whose protagonists were deft navigators of the oceans.[19] Likewise, the fertile crescent of sacred sites along the west coasts of Ireland, Cornwall, France, northern Iberia and Portugal, represent the bulk of the oldest temples in Europe, their stones being tallest nearest the sea and becoming progressively smaller – and of later erection – the further they venture inland, again suggesting a seafaring origin for their creators. The sheer number, scale and concentration of these monuments give the impression of focal points from which other, later sites emerged. And like the pyramids, this 'architecture' just appears overnight and without antecedent, supporting the legends of gods who came from a sinking land, armed with knowledge and considered very advanced by local standards.

This ties-in nicely with the Followers of Horus being equipped with a now-lost brand of esoteric technology. Anyone who has witnessed first-hand the size of the dolmens and menhirs of Roches aux Fées, Kergadiou and Locmariquer in Bretagne, or the uprights and 180-ton capstone of the dolmen at Zambujeiro, Portugal, knows just how ridiculous the assumption is that such sentinels of stone were somehow inched into place by means of wooden rollers. If these adepts did use a form of sound to levitate the stones, as the myths of Tiwanaku, Uxmal and Easter Island declare, then this art survived well into the 1930s, when the Swedish Dr. Jarl was privy to the raising of huge boulders 700-feet up onto a mountain, through the deliberate,

Mont St. Michel. And the original foundation 'navel stone' upon which the whole structure stands.

geometric and mathematical arrangement of musical instruments by a group of monks in Tibet. Using this method, the monks levitated up to six stone blocks per hour on a parabolic flight path. To be certain he had not been the victim of mass-psychosis, Dr, Jarl made two films of the incident, which were promptly confiscated after screening by the English Society sponsoring him, and declared "classified." [20] It would be seventy-five years before scientists at Nottingham University, England, finally revealed an anti-gravity machine capable of floating lumps of metal and heavy stones in mid-air, while in China, scientists did the same to small animals using ultrasound.[21]

Studies into the mathematical and linguistic origins of ancient British temples suggest a heavy Egyptian presence too. The European version of the *obelisk* is the *menhir* ("upright stone"),[22] which represents the temple in its simplest form, the omphalos. Some of the largest examples weigh 400 tons, yet their simplicity makes them no less powerful than their appearance might give. In the northern Celtic lands, their local names reveal Egyptian roots: they were known as *amberics*, and one of the Cornish monoliths is known as *men amber*, meaning "stone obelisk" or "stone of the Sun." [23] The same connection appears at Stonehenge, whose area of approach is the town of Amesbury: *ames* meaning "a place of the sun," and *bury*, "an enclosure"; its earlier name *ambres-bury* derives from the Egyptian *amber*, or "obelisk." [24] Thus, the site of Stonehenge was known as an "enclosure of obelisks, a temple of the Sun."

The Egyptian Karnak and its French namesake Carnac come from *Karn Ac*, "a seat or enclosure of great fire or light." [25] From this is derived *carn* and *cairn* in the Celtic language, the generic names for an earthen or stone enclosure, and Cernunnos, the horned fertility god of nature otherwise known as Pan. Such associations not only suggest a common Egyptian heredity, but the sites of stone are likewise associated with light, wisdom, and fecundity.

In the Iberian Peninsula the names of standing stones also give away their function: *betilo*, from the Semitic *beth-el*, "a house of God." Yet one is hard-pushed to visualize a *menhir* as a type of dwelling, unless, like the *Sivalingam*, it is the spirit of god that resides in the stone. Indeed, in Greece, a *betylo* is a stone of Zeus that

Menhirs at Kergadiou. The oldest sites in Europe (darker grey) emerged around coastal areas.

descended from heaven. Their other name *anta* is a derivative of the Latin *annotare*, meaning "to mark or locate." This leads us to understand that the standing stones are repositories of the effulgent force of a creator god and mark the place where this telluric energy is found on the land. So, in essence, they are 'mansions of the gods'.

The monoliths and the priestly cult that erected them are not ubiquitous to Europe, for they are found far-and-wide throughout the Korean Peninsula, India, Africa and the Middle East.[26] In the harshest part of the Arabian desert there exists a temple similar to Stonehenge at Al Qaseem ("great sunlight"),[27] as a traveler through that land recorded in 1863: "this Arabian monument, erected in the land where the heavenly bodies are known to have once been venerated by the inhabitants... in fact, there is little difference between the stone wonder of Qaseem and that of Wiltshire."[28]

Giant-scale engineering.

While much of the world appears to have been erecting pyramids and citadels, the temple-builders of the British Isles and Bretagne applied their skills on a subtler level with standing stones. But the sheer scale in which they did so is mind-boggling. Sites such as Knowlton and Drewstaignton in southern England, and Callanais in Scotland were in their heyday formidable cities of stone, featuring hundreds of menhirs and stone circles, and avenues stretching for over six miles. They were both ceremonial places as well as cities of knowledge in their own right.

In the small county of Wiltshire, England, hundreds of mounds, giant's graves, long barrows, dolmens, stone circles and conical mounds have somehow managed to dodge all manner of religious, agricultural and commercial bullets. Their primary concentration revolves around the world's largest stone circle, the temple of Avebury and its cluster of preparatory temples. Together they cover an area of roughly 60 square miles, forming one of the most respected and ritualized landscape temples ever known. Some say it is still so today, and having walked it and breathed it for nine years I would have to agree.

Just as Delphi is strategically situated on a latitude 3/7 of the distance from the equator to the North Pole, and Karnak is 2/7, the navel that is Avebury marks the 4/7 spot. In fact, the precise band of latitude runs through the middle of this temple,[29] and specifically where the site's first feature – a giant menhir – originally stood. The geodetic significance of Avebury is therefore global. A connection to Egypt is hinted by the antiquarian William Stukeley: "all the stones of our whole Temple were called Ambres, even by our Phoenician founders, but this [the center stone] particularly. The Egyptians by that name still called theirs obelisks." [30] As late as the 17th century it was suggested that before the Romans named it Avenabury, the name may have been Ambresbury.

To the north and just outside Avebury's formidable chalk embankment, there stood the original stone circle. At the time, it was considered too energetically unstable,

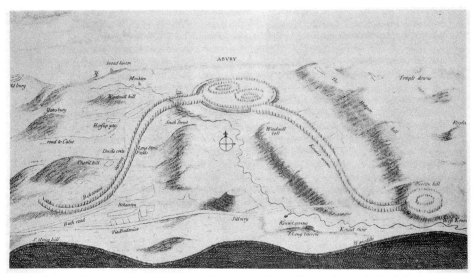

Avebury and its serpentine avenues in their original splendor, as drawn by Stukeley c.1720.

and its stones were taken down and re-used to construct the outer ring of the site as it is marked today.[31]

The study of Avebury is a whole book in itself, so we shall concern ourselves with its example as a ritual metropolis that sustained the delicate trinity of people-land-spirit for some 3,000 years. Many prehistoric pilgrimage tracks lead to this natural sanctuary, and its main thoroughfare, the *Harepath*, is an ancient Saxon name for a spirit road. Avebury's tall embankments originally fully concealed any sight of the stones, and despite the hills that flank its eastern edge, the inner *sanctum* is still completely obscured from view. This was done by design. The ancients saw the temple as the very foundation of life, the physical personification of cosmic forces in perfect equilibrium. If the temple is defiled by any form of impurity, the umbilical connection between earth and heaven is lost, and the tribe disintegrates.[32]

The outer stone circle of Avebury – or what religious fanatics have left of it – once comprised a perimeter boundary of 99 stones (as with Tiwanaku), with a diameter of 1,100-feet; its closest comparison is the Ring of Brogar in the Isles of Orkney, which was erected at the same time, suggesting a link between the two locations. Within this ring of stones are two smaller circles of 27 and 29 stones, resembling two eggs in a frying pan, each respectively calibrated to the sidereal and synodic lunar cycles. Thankfully, William Stukeley spent many years on-site creating accurate drawings and documenting the last orgy of destruction of these circles, his anger barely masked: "And this stupendous fabric, which for some thousands of years, had brav'd the continual assaults of weather, and by the nature of it, when left to itself, like the pyramids of Egypt, would have lasted as long as the globe, hath fallen a sacrifice to the wretched ignorance and avarice of a little village unluckily plac'd within it." [33]

Avebury today. The site houses a village. And since this is Britain, a pub.

Stukeley, a practicing Freemason of his day, went on to describe the destruction of the stones as "an execution," and given the scale of the rampage, which lasted about 200 years, it's no wonder: originally connected to the Avebury henge were two processional stone avenues covering a total of three miles, each consisting of some 200 stones, of which only 32 remain.

The southeastern avenue meandered from an ancillary temple on Overton Hill called the Sanctuary, originally a series of six concentric stone circles that served as a preparatory area for those wishing to enter Avebury. If you recall, these sites were originally built to concentrate and amplify the telluric energy of the land. Since the human body – particularly its brainwaves – emit electromagnetic signals,[34] entering a temple with unstable thoughts or incorrect intent would pollute the site, energetically speaking; such infractions over time would corrupt the temple, leading the surrounding land and its people to fall out of synch. Only when totally prepared were initiates allowed to stroll down the stone avenue and enter Avebury. Stukeley was greatly moved by the final destruction of the Sanctuary between the years 1723-1743, when farmers Green and Griffin removed the stones: "This Overton-hill from time immemorial, the country people have a high notion of. It was (alas, it was!) a very few years ago, crown'd with a most beautiful temple…They still call it the Sanctuary…The loss of this work I did not lament alone; but all the neighbors (except the person that gain'd the little dirty profit), were heartily griev'd for it. It had a beauty that touch'd them far beyond those much greater circles in Avebury town." [35]

Inside Avebury, particular stones served as classrooms for the teaching of specific elements of the Mysteries. There once was a holed stone which stood over a particularly energetic spot (of which only the stump remains) where marriages were conducted by having the couple link hands through the hole; one of the two monoliths forming the entrance has an alcove and a seat and is still used today for healing with sound.

In the northeastern quadrant, the center of one of the lunar circles consisted of three colossal stones (two remain), forming a horseshoe named The Cove.[36] As the name implies, it is the receptacle of telluric forces, where the full energy of the rising sun at midsummer collects into a chalice, just like the horseshoe of bluestones inside Stonehenge. The Cove was the place for shamanic dreaming, where adepts downloaded information from the invisible universe and shared it with the tribe. By 1900 B.C., when a turn of events brought war to the land, warriors would sharpen the blades of their swords on the back of its lozenge stone to carry its protective energy into battle. The marks are still visible today, as is the outline of a large serpent carved on the front, indicating this as the spot where telluric energy is most concentrated.

Over the past 4,000 years the height of Avebury's protective chalk embankment has eroded some 20-feet. Back then, one could barely see the incline of the adjacent hill of Waden, a proto-Germanic derivation of the Norse god Odin who, like so many other creator gods, is associated with wisdom, magic, prophecy, and the leadership of souls. Scandinavians symbolized him with the cube, thereby linking Odin/Wotan with Mt. Meru.[37] From the spot marking the original *menhir* inside Avebury one can

The rising Sun lights Silbury on the winter solstice.

still see the cleft in the chalk where a sightline lines up with the slope of Waden hill as it meets the summit of the artificial hill rising behind it, the breast-shaped mound of Silbury.

Sil-bury takes its name from the Phoenician *sil* meaning "light," thus it is an "enclosure of light." Legend states that around 2650 B.C., local shamans received information from a group of spirit beings named *the Watchers*, who instructed them to erect a six-stepped conical mound as an insurance policy for future times, when humanity would lose its connection to the divine.[38] As word spread of the sacred construction project about to be undertaken, merchants of Light came from all over Europe and as far as Phoenicia to take part in the building of this temple. Traditional historians scoffed at this idea until a shaft dug to the center of the mound revealed a multitude of soils brought in from as far as the Middle East; it also established the date of construction as c2600 B.C.

Exactly at the same time at Saqqara in Egypt, the temple priests were guided to build a six-stepped pyramid by a group of creator gods named the Shining Ones, the equivalent to the Watchers, and the pyramid was subsequently erected by Imhotep, one of the architects of the gods.[39] So again the association with Egypt persists. Avebury, with its two winding avenues of stones, has even been likened to the Egyptian solar disc bearing two serpents, and from the air the resemblance is striking. In fact, the Celts also shared the Egyptian practice of orienting their temples to enhance the correspondence between site and cosmic forces, which we shall deal with in depth later. Simply put, the direction in which the site was aligned played a crucial part in its purpose.

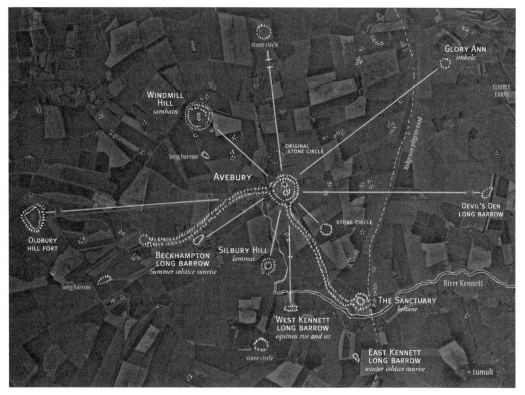

Avebury some of the sites that comprise this ritual landscape.

Avebury, being ringed by processional temples like spokes on a wheel, when seen from above, its ancillary mounds, long barrows, stone circles and dolmens reveal a whole and interconnected complex. In addition to being aligned to each solstice and equinox, the sites are accorded a position on the eight-fold Celtic wheel of life, death and renewal. Occupying the southwestern quadrant lies Silbury, which in the Celtic tradition represents the feast of *Lammas*, a harvest festival that takes place on August 1ˢᵗ. Indeed the shape of the hill resembles that of a pregnant belly or a bosom full of milk, both symbols of the abundance of the land. When archaeologists dug to the center of Silbury they discovered a primordial mound, and under its turf were found small winged insects trapped beneath the first handfuls of building material. These insects are native to the area and still hatch in this part of Britain in the first week of August.[40] The moat on which it stands was engineered to hold the water from the nearby springs when they burst to life every February on the feast of *Imbolc*, the Christian *Candlemas*, day of the Purification of the Virgin.

Speaking of *Imbolc,* the northeastern quadrant is represented by an enclosure locally known as Glory Ann. Now barely recognizable, it once served as a temple of instruction on land owned by the Knights Templar and still called Temple Farm.

Avebury's kingdom of conscience was constructed and dutifully maintained over the course of some 3,000 years before changes in circumstances led to its slow decline. Clearly, the endeavor of engineering a landscape covering 60-square miles required years of forethought and planning, not to mention hard physical labor, and deserves high praise – certainly far more than unenlightened sources at Wikipedia, who state: "The people who built [these large monuments] had to be secure enough to spend time on such non-essential activities." [41] 60-square miles of landscape engineering a *non-essential* activity!? Just goes to show one cannot trust all that is found on the internet. By contrast, the learned earth mysteries author Paul Devereux elucidates: "The old stones fossilize a moment in the history of consciousness, when it seems that the intuitive and intellectual properties of the human mind hung in a delicate symbiosis." [42]

Celtic three-steps.

Avebury and its environs sit on the tip of rolling chalk hills which suddenly give way to steep escarpments and fertile downland. A pilgrim to this sacred land can still imagine these escarpments rising out of some prehistoric sea, which was precisely the case many thousands of years ago, and it is not uncommon to walk these undulating hills and come upon fossils of seashells. On this tip of land there are three artificially-shaped and near-identical escarpments, each standing 11 miles apart like legs of a tripod. In fact, they form an equilateral triangle and Avebury marks its center – a triple step of Vishnu.

Nearby Silbury Hill was also designed as part of an equilateral array of identical mounds, each precisely 5.2 miles apart. Its twin to the east, Merlin's Mound, sits

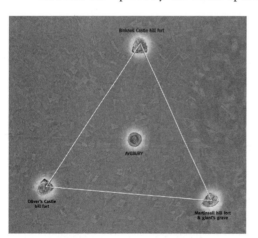

in the town of Marlborough, now with a humiliating water tank plunked on its summit; to the south, the third mound is now a cricket pitch in the hamlet of Wilcot, an unfortunate casualty of the building of the nearby canal during the rush to industrialize England. [43]

But there's more. In esoteric circles, Avebury is said to be part of a 'pyramid of light' that covers a significant portion of the British Isles. It was set up in remote times by a prehistoric priesthood to protect these lands and its thousands of sacred places. [44]

This obscure information was received clairvoyantly by an accomplished and highly-respected local trance medium named Isabelle Kingston. Following the instructions given through her, I pinpointed the other two sites to a high degree of accuracy using satellite images. The second site is a complex of six stone circles in the Moor of Machaire on the Isle of Arran, one the most important temple complexes in Scotland. The Isle is home to several giant's graves and numerous eyewitness accounts of highly luminous flying orbs. Folklore states that the main stone circle itself was built by the giant Fin MacCoul; it is also the one stone circle with a natural radiation count 33% above the background, certainly the highest energy spot of the group, and where researchers have seen tubes of light and other light phenomena. The third site is on one of the wettest and muddiest plots of land I have ever walked, although the

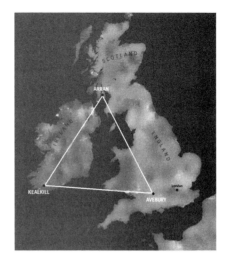

view over Bantry Bay makes up for the ordeal... when the rain *finally* stops. This is the hill temple complex of Kealkill in southwest Ireland, consisting of a stone circle, a radial stone cairn and two attendant standing stones.

In one of those precious moments where science validates psychic phenomena, the form of a flattened pyramid, an equilateral triangle, connects all three sites along a total distance of 960 miles.

The Moor of Machaire. Arran.

The Ways and Leys of the Force.

The temples of the British Isles represent some of the best-studied and well-documented in the world. Firstly, there are thousands of sites still remaining set within relatively compact territory, and secondly, there has been a consistent abundance of scholars and eccentrics who have devoted their time to understanding what they are, why they are where they are, and most importantly, what they are doing.

The Avebury temple complex, along with those at Stonehenge, Stanton Drew, Callanish and Tara, served as major hubs where the sacred arts of astronomy, mathematics and geometry were practiced;[45] as the original priesthood died off – and they too were described as exceptionally tall, and with elongated skulls – the essence of the sites continued as the academies of the Druids. Ceremony and ritual were rigorously maintained according to the temple tradition, where the positions of the Moon and Sun reinforced the relationship between people-land-cosmos and the core values of the temple. By this means, cultures were sustained and maintained. More importantly, the relationship between the temple and its underlying telluric forces was carefully reinforced from season to season, which served the two-way relationship of energizing the place of power, and in return, the temple acted as a mediating influence on the energy grid of the Earth.

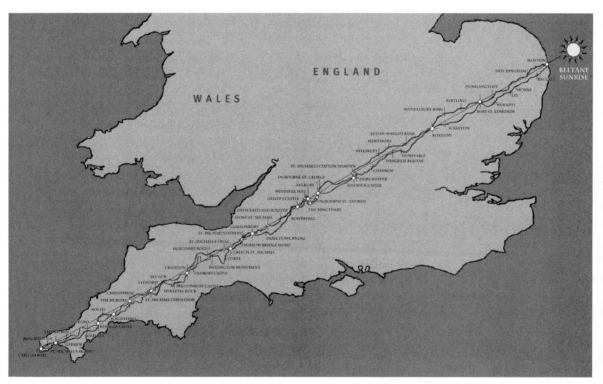

The Michael and Mary telluric alignment and a few of its nodes.

In 1966, John Michell was wandering through southern England visiting its plethora of ancient shrines. His itinerary allowed for a brief stop at Glastonbury Tor and its crowning tower of St. Michael, all that remains of a church that collapsed after an earthquake in 1275. From the summit he could see its mirror image twelve miles to the southwest, the Barrowbridge Mump, also topped with a ruined church and dedicated to the same archangel. There appeared to be some kind of communication between these two identical hills, with identical churches, sharing the same north-eastern trajectory.

As Michell journeyed northeast and towards Avebury, it became apparent that a considerable number of hills, mounds and churches all dedicated to St. Michael or his earthly counterpart St. George were linked by a straight line, what in geodetic studies is called a *ley*. One of the great surviving traditions states that Avebury itself is a great serpent temple marking the geodetic center of a line of consciousness stretching from the south-western tip of England at Land's End – and not far from St. Michel's Mound – to the opposite coast where it meets the North Sea at Hopton.

Michell's hunch of an accurate alignment of sacred sites sharing common purposes and traditions was later confirmed through geodesic calculations by Robert Forrest.[46] This was just the beginning of a major rediscovery of what would turn out to be a deliberately designed archaic system of sacred sites stretching over hundreds of miles. The highly-respected dowser, the late Hamish Miller, together with investigative researcher Paul Broadhurst followed through on Michell's spontaneous revelation and discovered that entwined around the straight pole of the St. Michael ley line is a current of telluric energy, which indeed runs through dozens of sacred locations associated with the famous archangel.[47]

Broadhurst and Miller placed their respective reputations on the line with this discovery, yet their efforts would later be consistently validated by others. Even so, by the time they reached Avebury, they were still unaware that inside the 5,000-year old temple they would find a second telluric current wrapping itself around this invisible axis. It would later become known as the St. Mary line, on account that, just like the St. Michael line, it passes through sanctuaries dedicated to St. Mary or her mother St. Anne. And whereas the St. Michael line carried a positive or masculine charge, the St. Mary line carried a negative or feminine charge. Seen from above southern England the two telluric currents wind their way through hundreds of sanctuaries, joining together at nodes, wrapping around the ley like vertebrae on the back of a mighty spine which itself is directly aligned to the path of the rising Sun on the Celtic solar festival of *Beltane*.[48] At the moment the morning light surfaces from the underworld, it sends a shaft of light to every temple along the axis of southern Britain as though lighting a network of wells imbibing the jubilant energy of the Sun and grounding it into the land.

Extending the Michael and Mary ley as a great circle across the globe, 6,000 miles later it reaches the center of Tiwanaku; on its return journey it bisects the Chinese island of Hainan precisely at its most holiest shrine, the sacred mountain of

Wuzhi, a landscape temple brimming with mythology and dedicated to the five most powerful Li gods.

Essentially, Michell, Broadhurst and Miller tapped into the living memory of the land – just as Aboriginal people have done for millennia – and rediscovered a forgotten territory of natural energies which our ancestors harnessed and used to connect themselves to the bigger picture. To quote Paul Broadhurst, "it leads into a world where everything is truly interdependent, where the Earth is acknowledged as a part of a greater whole, a philosophy which, while rooted in a spiritual understanding, is also pragmatic and practical. The old temples were built to enhance the environment, not to create disharmony, and so a technology of natural forces was employed, the same forces which create life and vitalize the countryside." [49]

Broadhurst and Miller then spent the best part of a decade on a second labor of love: a 2,700-mile linear odyssey across Europe, starting at a lonely hermitage high up on the wind-beaten pyramidal rock of Skellig Michael, off the western coast of Ireland, through the tip of southern Britain and St. Michael's Mount, across the English Channel to Mont St. Michel, along the shrines, mounds and oracles of France, Italy and Greece, finally reaching Israel and the hilltop temples of Mount Tabor – where Jesus experienced his own transfiguration of the soul – to the 9,000-year old temple site of Megiddo. Again, without foreknowledge of where the journey would take them, they discovered a masculine telluric energy line winding its way through St. Michael places, complemented by an interconnecting feminine line traveling through sacred places dedicated to the divine virgin and the earth goddess. As with their English counterparts, these two lines entwined around a central 'pole' stretching diagonally through the axis of Europe. It would be called the Apollo and Athena ley.[50]

Like Michell's revelation whilst connecting with the sacred land and its oracles, the discovery of the Apollo/Athena axis followed from an earlier French scholar's oracular dream during his stay at the sacred hill of Lycabettus, in which it was revealed to him that the sanctuaries dedicated to Apollo lay in a perfect straight line, and intersected with those of the earth goddess Athena.[51]

Skellig Michael, one of the loneliest outposts for a sanctuary, and the start of the Apollo-Athena ley.

The Apollo-Athena ley and a few of the hundreds of temples along its route.

The grid expands.

Studies into the ley lines of the British Isles, the Carnac region, and to a lesser degree the tracks of the Anasazi in New Mexico (for no reason other than the absence of new information), show how the initial temples were augmented across several thousands of years through the addition of new sites such as menhirs, dolmens, tumuli (earthen mounds), early Celtic places of veneration, and with the advent of Christianity, churches and Gothic cathedrals, the majority of which are built over older sites. The alignments were not just random points on a map. They typically were calculated to mark pivotal motions of the Sun and Moon, even to specific stars such as Sirius, the star associated with Isis, Sophia and ancient wisdom, as evidenced by the deliberately aligned axis of the temple of Luxor in Egypt,[52] as well as a prominent mound to the northeast of Avebury. Such extraordinary feats by the ancient surveyors led John Michell to remark, "the surface of Britain is like a palimpsest – an old parchment covered with lines and markings from different periods over thousands of years, linking permanent landmarks and running between opposite ends of the island."[53]

That they also performed an essential service to the well-being of people was hinted at as early as the 7th century B.C. by the biblical prophet Jeremiah: "ask for the old paths, where is the good way, and walk therein, and ye shall find rest for your souls." [54]

The rediscovery of this closely-linked network of temples came during the 1920s in Hereford, England, and as is typical, it occurred as a sudden, mystical revelation when connecting with the land and its temples. The naturalist Alfred Watkins was out horseback riding, and as he stopped to take in the view high up on a hill, the land spoke back and revealed to him a network of lines "standing out like glowing wires all over the surface of the country, intersecting at the sites of churches, old stones, and other spots of traditional sanctity." [55] His years of solitary study and measure revealed a vastly engineered ancient landscape, where prehistoric mounds, spirit roads, ancient tracks, stone markers, Druidic tree groves, beacons, church steeples, and hand-sculpted notches on the summits of hills were purposefully aligned. His findings would later be validated by other pioneers.[56]

Connecting many of the ancient sacred sites throughout Britain is a network of long, straight tracks and stone roads that criss-cross the island from coast-to-coast, sometimes without deviating an inch over the course of a hundred miles. These supernatural feats of surveying were already considered ancient by the 5th century B.C., when King Belinus undertook the task of repairing this old highway system that was falling into ruin. The reason for his work was that the old tracks had wandered off line, and "no one knew just where their boundaries should be." [57] That these paths were considered sacred is evidenced not just by the plethora of ancient places and pilgrimage sites they still bind together to this day, including many prominent cathedrals, but very specific laws codified the rights of travelers on these sacred paths between the sanctuaries: "the temples of the gods… should be so privileged that anyone who escaped to them… must be pardoned by his accuser when he came out… the roads which led to these temples and cities should be included in the same law and that the ploughs of the peasantry should be inalienable." [58] In essence they are spirit roads, with every wayfarer granted immunity from harassment or arrest, even criminals, and any child or foreigner with no knowledge of the language could pass from one end of the country to the other, finding hospitality everywhere. Two of these famous tracks can still be walked today, both crossing to the east of Avebury: the Ridgeway track and the Icknield Way, the latter passing through the heart of the stone circle itself.

While researching potential connections between Rosslyn Chapel in Scotland and Templar sites in France for a separate project, I inadvertently steered onto a road less traveled and found myself sharing that exuberant sense of revelation that Watkins himself must have felt. This road was to take me on a 900-mile ley of sacred sites, beginning just to the north of Rosslyn, in Edinburgh and its 900-year old Holyrood Abbey. Originally built by King David I in an act of thanksgiving, after a flaming cross descended from the sky and saved him from being gorged by the antlers of a hart, the abbey and its en-suite palace would become the seat of power of Kings, Queens and the Scottish Parliament. Just down the road stands St. Giles Cathedral, the High Kirk of Edinburgh, also built in the 12th century. Between these two seats of power is placed the start of the ley, barely 500 yards from the oldest purpose-built

Masonic meeting room in the world, the Chapel of St. John. From there it proceeds to Rosslyn Chapel, site of the Rose Well, symbol of the bloodline of Mary Magdalene and the whole mystery surrounding the location of her final resting place.[59] Its links to the Knights Templar and the mysteries of the Temple of Solomon are extensive, as they were given refuge here by William St. Clair following their bloody purge by King Phillip of France and the Catholic pope Clement V.

The ley then makes its southerly trajectory, passing through eight churches, including one dedicated to Our Lady of Lourdes, which would turn out to be a hint of things to come. It follows to Cirencester Abbey, founded in 1117 as an Augustinian monastery on the site of the oldest-known Saxon church in England, which itself had been built on a Roman sanctuary. It then ambles into Wiltshire, brushing alongside Windmill Hill, and the exact spot where the original western stone avenue of Avebury would have ended. After crossing several tumuli, it reaches the embankments of the hill fort at Rybury before descending into the sinuous Vale of Pewsey and the church of Stanton St. Bernard, followed by Marden Henge, which once contained a stone circle ten times the size of Stonehenge and a mound half the size of Silbury Hill.

The ley line then passes through the heart of Stonehenge.

Having brushed past the front door of Sting's Jacobean residence in the hamlet of Lake and its en-suite tumulus, it continues purposefully through Old Sarum Hill Fort. This gigantic, artificial sacred mound has been in use since at least 3000 B.C., its central conical hill and water-bearing ditch making it the epitome of the primordial mound. In 1075, a cathedral was built on its north western quadrant, but after several calamities and three visitations from the Virgin Mary, the bishop was 'instructed' to move God's church elsewhere, the new location to be chosen by the shot of an arrow. This arrow allegedly was shot by a very muscular individual, for it landed two miles away in a water meadow and, allegedly, on a Neolithic mound. The new church would become one of gothic architecture's finest moments, Salisbury Cathedral. And as luck would have it, the Rosslyn ley passes through its *original* altar.

The location also represents the golden ratio point dividing this ley line.

We now travel southwards once more, through Clearbury Ring hill fort, where-upon the line rises to meet the tip of St. Catherine's Hill at Gods Hill. St. Catherine was the patron saint of the Knights Templar and other esoteric orders that fell outside the favor of the medieval Catholic Church. Passing through the grounds of Highcliffe Castle the ley crosses the English Channel and on to France. However, before departing the shores of Britain, it is worth recalling that this particular quest began as a separate and vague exploration of the Knights Templar. The builder of Highcliffe was Charles Stuart, a baron and a Knight of the Portuguese Order of the Tower and of the Sword of Valour, Loyalty and Merit – a pinnacle of the Portuguese Honors system which bears a passing resemblance to the order of the original Knights Templar. Given how the Order was central to the founding of Portugal as a country only makes the story even more salivating,[60] as does the fact that Queen Elizabeth II shares the same knighthood, and her summer residence in Scotland is Holyrood.

But we digress. Much of the line's journey through France is frustrating in its lack of ancient sites. This is heavily agrarian territory where, through necessity, and often ignorance, the old stones have been broken up for building material; destructive attitudes towards pagan temples by the Catholic Church as well as countless wars have not helped. Still, a number of important connections exist: the ley passes through the ancient churches at Amfreville, Raids, Hambye, and Monthault, before entering the secret world of the Forest de Fougères and the heart of a major Druid temple, and various stone alignments much like those at Carnac to the west. The ley then connects with no less than twelve churches, literally down the nave of La Poitevinière, and the altar of St.-Vivien de Pons; it also meets the hill church of Les Châtelliers-Châteaumur, with its resemblance to Glastonbury Tor.

The Rosslyn ley finally comes to rest 900 miles from its point of origin in Scotland, inside a natural grotto famous for its healing waters and, just as the bishop of Old Sarum experienced, for apparitions of the Virgin Mary to a young woman.

The end of the ley line is the grotto of Lourdes.

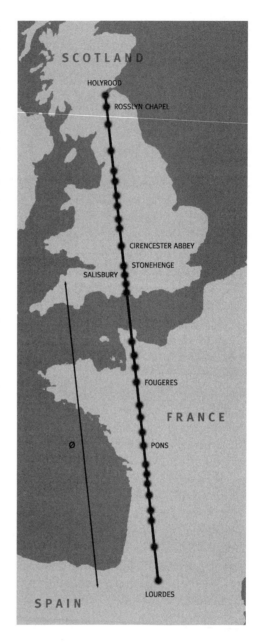

The mystery of the elbow.

Separating England and Wales is the narrow Bristol Channel, whose two distinguishing features are the miniscule island of Caldey, 10,000-feet by 4,000-feet, consisting of a Cistercian Abbey and the time-worn church of Saint Iliud, which is aligned to the northeast and sports a steeple bearing a closer resemblance to a menhir;

then there's the island of Lundy, one mile by three, home to several giant's graves and, according to Celtic mythology, one of the entrances into the Otherworld: "[it] is supposed to be Annwn, or rather a place where mysterious realms can be entered... The most important hill is the Tor of Glastonbury, the most important island is Lundy... [its] inhabitants have human form, but are not strictly human... they are immortals, fairy folk... Gods thinly disguised." [61]

In 1992 the tiny but mysterious Lundy island appeared as a revelation to the mathematician and engineer Robin Heath while staying near Carnac. Robin had already rediscovered that the rectangle formed by the four-station posts at Stonehenge allows the famous monument to resemble the planet Earth in cross-section, while also marking the angles of the midsummer sunrise, the most northerly moonset, and other important events during the year.[62] This rectangle has side ratios of 5:12 units, and a corresponding diagonal of 13. The suggested form is therefore a Pythagorean 5:12:13 triangle, though what it's doing in a monument built nearly 3,000 years before the Greek mathematician is another matter. In essence, this *lunation triangle* allows for the calibration of both solar and lunar cycles; furthermore, with a cord marked at 3:2 the distance on the short side of the triangle, its internal length is equal to the number of lunations in a solar year, 12.369.[63] Robin

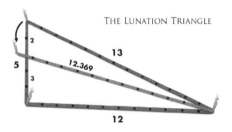

THE LUNATION TRIANGLE

describes the implications of this system of measure inside an ancient monument thus: "[It is] an astonishingly valuable tool for performing a range of astronomically precise tasks, which enable forecasts to be made concerning solar and lunar positions and phases. A Neolithic calendar maker would have given away his entire set of round-bottomed pots for such a technique." [64]

Like Michell's decoding of the aforementioned parable of Peter and the 153 fish, Robin also realized that this strange number of fish, together with Jesus being the 13th person among the 12 disciples, encodes the numerical value of the lunation triangle at Stonehenge, with the square root of 153 equaling 12.369 – the number of lunations in a solar year.

It was at this point that Heath had a vision of the lunation triangle being a reflection of a much larger collection of related points on the landscape, specifically the relationship between Stonehenge and the origin of its bluestones at Preseli, and that speck of rock, Lundy Island, whose Welsh name is Ynys Elen, "the island of the elbow, angle or corner." [65] As it happens, when seen from the air, Lundy actually resembles an elbow or corner. It also lies at the same latitude as Stonehenge. When connecting the three points, Lundy indeed

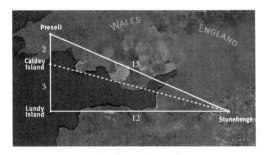

The elbow of Lundy.

forms the elbow or right angle of a large 5:12:13 triangle, its corner occurring on the island at Knights Templar Rock. And just to the north, Caldey Island forms the 3:2 point along the upright.[65]

By drawing a mirror-image of this triangle, the north-point marked by Preseli now becomes the exact location of Castle Dore in the south, and its entrance pointing back to Stonehenge.

To complete this extraordinary lesson in long-distance surveying, consider that the relationship between Caldey Island and Preseli is also mirrored by Stonehenge and a marker two miles north of Avebury,[66] on Monkton Hill, site of nine barrow mounds (and several others destroyed), and beside it, the old Templar academy at Glory Ann.

Heath's theory is that Lundy, not Stonehenge, was the original point of construction, and what's more, as an indication of just how old this ancient metrology is, consider that all three sites have yielded remains dating to 8000 B.C.[67]

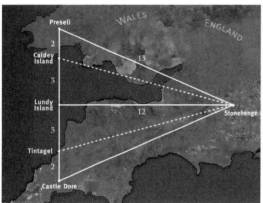 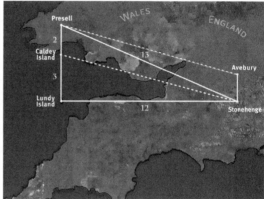

Revelation at Kura Tawhiti.

It's not difficult to find magic at Kura Tawhiti. The landscape temple's mere presence among the untouched Southern Alps of New Zealand is ample compensation for the long journey required to reach it. During my second visit, art was on my mind, particularly the visual resemblance shared between Maori and Celtic sacred art, which at times appear indistinguishable. The site itself precedes the Maori, it is the abode of the Waitaha, the unnaturally tall, fair-skinned mystical race, probably not dissimilar to the giants once witnessed on Easter Island, Aotearoa's bijou neighbor 4,200 miles to the northeast.

It was while standing beside Kura Tawhiti's main power center that strange things began to happen: the spirit of place whispered in my right ear, "Look for what lies opposite, find what's on the other side." Anyone who has experienced this sensation knows just how unsettling it can be, and yet the unease soon gives way to a sense of being totally surrounded by what I can only describe as unconditional love. It took me a couple of days to process the message and understand what exactly I was being asked to find. Since my thoughts had been on the relationship to an equally mysterious culture on the opposite side of the world, I wondered if there may be a connection to another, possibly Celtic, site opposite to Kura Tawhiti.

Once the site's grid coordinates were secured all that was required to find the counterpoint in the northern hemisphere was a good map. When I found it, the quest that followed revealed to me just how the development of these kingdoms of conscience had been conducted not just on a global scale, but how the knowledge was sustained over the course of thousands of years, most likely by adepts who transmitted it from person to person, from brotherhood to brotherhood – individuals who'd persevered to keep a bright light burning even through times of great natural or political turbulence.

Having established the start and end points, I endeavored to discover if any important temples lay along this ley that ran halfway around the world.

Moving north-westward and across Australia, the ley homed-in on the only prominent feature of the endless desert and that nation's most recognizable icon, the sandstone hill of Uluru, which the ley passed to within 9 miles – an acceptable margin given that it is an unmovable mountain and 2,600 miles from the point of origin. The ley continued through the continent and across the Indian Ocean, entering the long island of Java to cross the heart of the temple of Borobudur, a distance of 4,400 miles. Borobudur, with its six-stepped platforms, 2,672 reliefs, 504 statues, and 72 perforated *stupas*, sits on a sacred mound and forms a ley of its own with at least two other temples in Java – Pawon and Mendut – all three sharing a ceremonial route.

The ley continued along the spine of Sumatra, returning to the ocean, and making landfall 7,000 miles away in India, at the sacred hill of Padmanabham – a doppelganger for Glastonbury Tor – its ancillary temple complex being one of the holiest abodes of Vishnu. 300 miles later the ley intersects the temples of Ramtek and Mansar, each perched high up on opposite hills above the level plain like an entrance deliberately created to allow the passage of the ley. In addition to twenty-seven other temples here, there's a university dedicated to *Sanskrit*, one of the oldest forms of writing, and a monument dedicated to the primal sound OM.

Four-hundred miles further along the ley meets another freestanding hill and the ancient site of Meera Mandir, now bearing a temple to Siva and rebuilt in the 14th century. After crossing into Pakistan it passes by the remains of Mehrgarh. It then follows a trajectory through vast desolate plains, arid hills and deserts, the keepers of secrets still waiting to be uncovered. In the mountainous region of Armenia it passes by the north slope of Mt. Ararat

Temple of Pawon.

and Noah's Ark before reaching the monastery of Cokesina in Serbia. Curiously, the ley's passage from Bulgaria to northern Italy closely matches the geographical origin and spread of Bogomilism ("god-loving"), an esoteric order from around 10th century A.D. whose doctrine was closely tied to the Zoroastrians, Manichaeans, Albigensians and Cathars.

In northern Italy, the ley reaches the town of Alba, with its deep Celt and Ligurian roots. Having traveled 10,000 miles I decided to pause briefly and take a look around. The ley passes by the cathedral, but it's the town's name and its heavy Templar presence that are of interest. The name Alba is actually a Latin acronym for the four elements: *Aquarii* (water), *Leone* (Leo, fire), *Bue* (Ox, earth), *Aquila* (eagle, air); these form the sign of a cross. Curious, then, that on the outskirts of town this ley from Kura Tawhiti should cross the Apollo and Athena ley between Ireland and Israel. Did some olden order know of this and memorialized it in the town's name?

In France, the line passes through the 9th century basilica of Vayats, which stands on much earlier foundations. Finally, 12,400 miles later, the journey ends in northern Spain. With just a margin of error of 0.27° of latitude and 0.3° of longitude, we reach one of the oldest sites of pilgrimage in the world, Santiago de Compostela ("field of stars"), an appropriate name in honor of the Celtic stargazers who originally venerated this landscape in Galicia.

So, this is "what lies opposite, what is on the other side." An extraordinary journey of discovery, to say the least.

Esoteric studies always emphasize the balance of opposites, so, not wishing to deny my studies, I was curious as to what might lay on the return leg of the journey. The trip

from New Zealand to Galicia was predominantly over land, and true to the principle of opposites, the return journey was overwhelmingly over water. The only land between Europe and South America is the archipelago of the Açores, a scattering of nine volcanic peaks and rocky fragments insinuating the remains of a larger, but now drowned land. The ley passes through the tip of the island named and dedicated to our old friend São Miguel. Specifically, it crosses the island's most active caldera and the little town nestled inside it named Sete Cidades ("Seven Cities"), although there are no seven cities here, nor have there ever been. However, because of its position in the mid-Atlantic Ridge, the Açores have been central to the legend of Atlantis and its fabled seven cities, and historical records suggest that the name of the town was a deliberate tribute to the location of the ill-fated land given in the accounts by Plato, Pliny, Diodorus and Theopompue.

The ley moves on, passing briefly through Columbia, Venezuela and Ecuador before returning to water and the Pacific Ocean, gliding within fifty-seven miles of the only grain of land between Ecuador and New Zealand: Easter Island and its star-gazing *moai*, before returning home to Kura Tawhiti, 25,000-miles later.

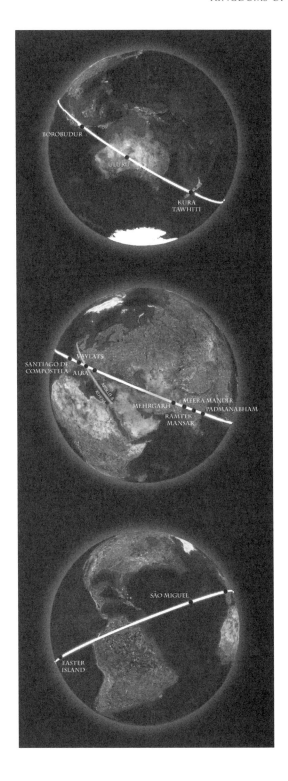

Akhenaten, DNA and that mystical 33.

In our time, the bulldozer of commerce far outruns the spade of archaeology. Whether we shall discover the kingdoms of conscience still buried beneath jungle vines and desert sands remains to be seen. Certainly we have lost tens of thousands of temples to war and ignorance over the last two thousand years, and yet once in a while the earth discloses its ancient secrets. In the dense jungle of Guatemala, forty-seven citadels have recently been discovered and an estimated thirty more await classification. The largest complex, El Mirador, features some of the biggest temples ever built, each internally connected by causeways, and externally to other temples eight miles away.[68] This is a small glimpse into what a global network must have once resembled, a true world-wide web of sacred power places acting as permanent reference points of an archaic library that safeguarded knowledge for the long-term benefit of the human race, where ordinary people were able to plug into the consciousness of a grid whose reach lies far and beyond the confines of this terrestrial sphere.

We saw at the beginning of this chapter how temples were designed as a series of correspondences between the natural world below and the cosmos above. Just how far the builders went in extending this influence to the human body is evidenced by the sourcing of telluric forces, above which the structures were sited, and in turn generated a corresponding effect on the electromagnetic field of the human body. But the ancient architects may have gone a step further in linking together the human body, the temple, and the host planet.

Pour out a container of salt or sand, let it pile slowly on a level surface, and watch it form a conical mound. The angle of the slope will be 32.72°. Why this should be so is a mystery. That enigmatic force called gravity influences the grains to fall just so, and looking around the Earth there are any number of mountains – specifically volcanoes – whose slopes correspond to the very same angle: Mount Fuji, Japan; Chiginagak, Alaska; and Mount Taranaki, New Zealand, are but three examples. All three are sacred mountains.

Oddly, the measurement of the acceleration of gravity, 32.17 feet per second, bears a close relationship.[69]

The mystery of 32.72 is so tantalizingly close to that mystical number 33 that it's worth taking a minute to consider the two.

The Zoroastrian god Ahura Mazda is said to have created the universe with the power of 33 steps. This secret process is reputedly buried within myths and fables and the underlying philosophies of the Tree of Life, typically known as the Qabalah. Through the thorough understanding of its 32 principles, one reaches the 33rd degree or enlightenment. This knowledge would have been a component of the Mystery Schools in Heliopolis, later to become a closely guarded secret within the 33 degrees of Freemasonry, whose roots herald from said academy.

Is 33 just a convenient rounding-off of 32.72? After all, one cannot go around claiming to be a 32.72-degree Mason! Maybe, but why then is the original Scottish

Rite Masonry building in Charleston, South Carolina – the "Mother Supreme Council of the World" – situated at latitude 32.78°? And why did the United States of America, a country founded by Freemasons, establish its border with Mexico at Yuma, where, in the middle of a river, it forms the tip of a pyramid – a Benben – precisely at latitude 32.72°? And why did

the Knights Templar, the precursors of the Freemasons, build a castle at Vadum Iacob in Israel, exactly at latitude 33°, followed by another on the coast at Atlit at 32.71°?

Stranger still, nearby Mount Carmel, 'the vineyard of God' lies at 32.72°; the transfiguration of Jesus on Mount Tabor occurred at 32.69°, while his home in Nazareth is at 32.70°. Like many historical and mythological solar heroes – Alexander the Great, et al – Jesus reaches heaven at the age of 33, which also happens to be the gematrian value of *amen*, the finale of a prayer.

The true fraternity of Freemasonry is an echo of the Followers of Horus, the falcon god of the sky, whose mission was to bring the Light to humanity. The light of the sky is embodied by the Sun. 365 days (the solar year) divided by 11.060606 years (the Sun's cycle) equals 33. Conversely, the Sun defined as a circumference of 360° divided by 11 (the convenient number of the solar cycle) equals 32.72. This numerical value was not lost on the makers of that mansion of transformation, the King's

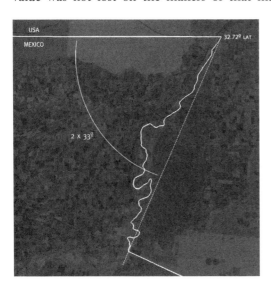

The bizarre behaviour of the U.S. border at Yuma.

Chamber of the Great Pyramid of Giza, whose volume is 327.2 cubic meters;[70] nor on the creator of the Earth when It invented water and chose 32.72° F as the boundary at which this essential ingredient of life transmutates into ice.

Which ultimately brings us to a connection between Stonehenge, Heliopolis, and the referencing of that greatest of temples, the human body. The Edfu *Pyramid Texts* state that after the Followers of Horus set up shop in Heliopolis they wandered far into the hinterland to locate other "mansions of the gods." They did this after a flood, which is now precisely dated to 9703 B.C. Could they have reached the shores of Britain by 8000 B.C. to survey the original location for what would become the grand enclosure of Stonehenge? Earlier in this chapter we saw how temples on these islands share similar linguistic roots, construction techniques and a knowledge of temple practises common with Egyptian culture; we also know that archaeologists now support a date of 8000 B.C. as a probable founding of Stonehenge, and that this temple's connecting points at Lundy Island and Preseli also share a similar date.

There's one further point to consider. The 12th century chronicler Geoffrey of Monmouth does claim this "Giant's Ring" originated from Africa and was brought to the Celtic lands by a race of giants.[71] It's been widely debated that Geoffrey was recounting far older sources when he compiled his work, and undoubtedly the meanings may have been misinterpreted or mistranslated, as they tend to be over long spans of time. It's unlikely the building material for Stonehenge was transported all the way from Africa – the stones are known to have been sourced in Preseli and the Wiltshire Downs. But what *would* have traveled from Africa was the knowledge of surveying and temple-building, and enough giant's graves exist throughout Britain to validate the existence of an older race of people who were physically different to us. Egypt certainly qualifies as a land in Africa, and if you recall, the Akhu Shemsu Hor were described as standing over 12-feet tall.

So, let us now stretch some very long cords.

Measured from the North Pole, the angle subtending Stonehenge and Heliopolis is 33º. Where does the human temple fit in?

Water is made from a mixture of 33 different substances,[72] allowing the human body and its spine of 33 bones to remain alive. But there is a second number that is closely associated with life. Modern research shows that DNA "is a remarkably flexible molecule… and thermal fluctuations can produce bending, stretching and un-pairing in the structure." [73] In its normal state, the angle of rotation of the bDNA helix is 34.61º, but in a dehydrated state it changes into aDNA, as does its angle of rotation, to 32.72º. [74]

In 1346 B.C., the pharaoh Akhenaten broke with tradition and moved the capital of Egypt from Thebes to a site at Til el-Amarna, and named it Akhet-aten ("Horizon of the Aten").[75] The prime motivation for Akhenaten dispensing with Thebes was to wrestle the temple away from the power of an increasingly corrupt priesthood, who had by this time usurped control of the rituals and symbols and come to see the temple as a method of crowd control; the second motivation was to return the focus of worship to a monotheistic cult of the Aten, the Sun, which his father Amenhotep III had commenced in Thebes, but failed due to the prevailing politics. In essence Akhenaten appears to have revitalized the concept upon which Innu/Heliopolis was founded, for Heliopolis was the epitome of the veneration of the Sun, created at *Zep Tepi* as the perfect mound of the gods. There is evidence for this connection at Akhet-aten, for "in the first boundary stele, it is decreed that the sacred bull of Heliopolis was to be buried in the mountain to the east of Akhet-aten… Bringing the bull to

Akhet-aten could show the Heliopolis cult's central importance in Egyptian religion. It could even have been a way of making the new landscape of Akhet-aten sacred, by providing it with a suitable religious monument in the form of the divine bull." [76]

At first glance Akhet-aten seems a ludicrous place to build a city, let alone a capital. It was remote, 120 miles from the nearest complex at Abydos, encircled by desert, and nothing other than the Nile providing an umbilical cord to the rest of the world. Yet two clues suggest a well-conceived plan was at play: first, Akhet-aten is placed precisely at the geodetic center of Egypt; second, although some historians state the area of the city to have been a virgin site, Akhenaten, in his oblation to the Aten, praises the new capital as "the seat of the First Occasion, which he had made for [Aten] that he might rest in it." [77] As we read earlier, to be a 'seat of the First Occasion' the site must be an original primordial mound – in other words, it must stand on ground previously consecrated by the Seven Sages and the builder gods at *Zep Tepi* – that's 8,000 years earlier – as is the case with the sites now occupied by the temples of Philae, Edfu, Kom Ombu, Karnak and Luxor.[78] Thus, when the bull from Innu/Heliopolis was interred, it was to imbue the energy of a primordial mound upon another, perhaps because during that great span of time the site had been left to lie fallow. In any event, it established a symbolic link between the two sites, bestowing upon the new city the beliefs of that older academy to the north.[79] Certainly there were high-ranking people within the court of Akhet-aten who honored the Heliopolitan tradition, one of whom was Hesuefemiunu, "He-gives-praise-in-Innu." [80] There are also suggestions that in preparation for kingship, Akhenaten would have undoubtedly been initiated into the mysteries at Heliopolis, in accordance with the custom.[81]

So, if we act as Akhenaten did: take the 33° location marking the relationship between Stonehenge and Heliopolis and move it south to create a new relationship between Akhet-aten and Stonehenge, the exact angle between the two sites changes, just like our DNA, to 32.72°.

The correspondence between the temple and the land, and ultimately, its influence on people is a grand design that evolved over many thousands of years. It certainly makes one appreciate the ambitious scale of engineering that took place in ancient times, not to mention the role it played in the elevation of the human spirit.

Still, to fully appreciate the interaction between temple and body, the best evidence comes from direct experience.

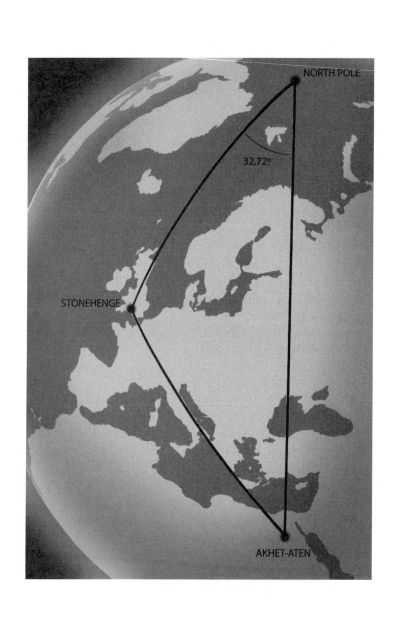

ACT II

1315 Minaret d'El Azhar avec muezzins

9

A VERY PERSONAL JOURNEY.

... And felt the hillside thronged by souls unseen,
Who knew the interest in me, and were keen
That man alive should understand man dead...

~ John Masefield

Once upon a time inside the Great Pyramid.

The call to prayer by the *mu'adhdhin*, his sonorous voice drifting like an ibis across sun-baked mud brick roofs, is the romantic ideal of Egypt. Except when it occurs at six in the morning and you are not genetically equipped to awaken before Ra has risen at least thirty degrees above the horizon. I admit it, I'm one of those people. But once the bedroom curtains were drawn to reveal the towering peaks of the Giza pyramids, I knew this dawn would require a break from my habitual sleeping pattern. Besides, the small group I was with had to reach the plateau by 7 a.m. or risk missing out on the daily allotment of passes into the Great Pyramid.

It was my privilege to be part of this group, under the stewardship of Isabelle Kingston, a former bank liaison officer who took a leap of faith to develop her natural gift as a trance medium under the wing of another psychic luminary, Roger St. John Webster. Since then, her work as an intuitive and healer has earned the respect of even the English police. Over the years Isabelle and I have become great friends, and

Mu'adhdhin, or muezzin, at Mosque d'El Azhar.

by studying alongside her for a decade I can confidently call her one of my mentors. The sign of a great teacher is not in the way they teach, but the way they refine you through subtle guidance while you experience the world of the invisible for yourself. And that, I believe, is Isabelle's great gift.

Once in a while we visit sacred places and quietly go about the business of cleansing subtle energy where it may have been polluted from centuries of neglect or wrong action. Sometimes we are asked to be conduits of light and re-energize the effulgent spirit of place; along with similar groups around the world, we tend the grid. Through these experiences one quickly discovers just how powerful we humans really are, and by developing our sensory perception we are also able to sense and see the invisible universe. Like driving a car, the more you do it the more adept you become. Everyone is born with this ability, but somewhere along the path to adulthood or the towers of statistics or the halls of analysis we lose sight of this gift and become skeptical that other realities can possibly exist. But as our predecessors knew all to well, they do, and they lie but a whisper away.

On any given day the inner passages of the Great Pyramid are a-howling with the refracted echoes of over-excited children and wide-eyed tourists; my first reaction was disappointment, to have traveled this far (and to have risen at the crack of dawn) to stand in a musty, humid tunnel filled with a decibel level I last experienced at a Black Sabbath concert. Nevertheless, along with five members of the group I was probably happier than the rest of our party, who had been unable to secure tickets, and would be experiencing this monument from the outside. For anyone who has never been inside a pyramid, the notion that millions of tons of stone are carefully balanced all around you is disconcerting, to say the least. Claustrophobes need not apply. Breathing can be problematic, the air is laden, the smell of musty stone is everywhere. For someone like me who is 6" 5' tall, some passages are torturous and humiliatingly short. Yet none of this bothered me as we ascended the Grand Gallery in the barren light. I felt very much part of the structure, as though the building and I were one and indivisible.

The six of us reached the voluminous vault of the King's Chamber, it's perfectly bonded, monolithic red granite blocks showcasing the ancient's world's fluent ability to work the hardest stone on earth like pastry. The two women in the group immediately felt uncomfortable in the chamber and exited, along with the hordes of tourists. Within minutes, the three men and I had the whole temple to ourselves, an incredible stroke of luck considering that only a suitcase of *bakshish* can buy you private, quiet time in this wondrous monument. And yet, there we were, alone and silent as gold.

Unusual things began to happen: the pump from the contraption that passed for an air conditioner stopped churning; then the lights turned off. We were immersed in total darkness, in the core of the Great Pyramid. Out of the four, Aaron and I had had more experience in the ways of sacred space, and he suggested we do what we were taught to do, which is honor the spirit of place; one of the others then suggested I lead a toning of the chamber, to which I acquiesced, since I'm generally not comfortable in the limelight. But since there was no light, there was no problem. I tried to find a sweet spot in the coal black chamber, about a third of the way back from the 'sarcophagus'. Again, that sinuous feeling between building and body overcame me, and sounds the likes of which I had never made before, or since, came out from my throat.

As the others joined in, the natural acoustics brewed our voices into an intoxicating melody. It was at this point that my life and my perception of temples changed forever. Emanating out of the granite walls came a group of tall people, all dressed in a type of white silk, and circled the chamber. I still remember turning my head to look at them all (remember, this is in total darkness), there must have been thirty or so. They bowed their heads and I bowed mine. It felt like a reunion with a long lost family, I did not want them to go, my head was filled with many questions to ask. I don't know how many minutes this lasted, it didn't matter… we were in a conclave with magic.

No sooner had we stopped toning when the two dim light bulbs slowly glowed back to life. I looked across at the others, and although no words were exchanged I knew each of these people had also experienced something profound. We took turns lying inside the 'sarcophagus', maybe five minutes at a time. When my turn came I was concerned that, being so tall, I would be a bad fit. But no; the granite, softened by centuries of visitors, embraced my body like a pillow, the flat of my head and the soles of my feet being exactly the length of the receptacle, my shoulders being the precise width. I remember making a mental note that I ought to get a bed made to these specifications on my return home. Further chamber activity was curtailed by the sound of an excited Arab voice hailing from somewhere deep below. We'd probably overstayed our welcome and decided to make haste. In perfect silence.

The bright desert light blinded our exit into the fresh air. Aaron and I exchanged dazed glances, it was obvious we both wanted to say something, so I initiated: "Did you see what I saw up there?"

"You mean the priests, in a circle, all in white!?"

You can't fake moments like this. As the other two came into earshot I remarked on how the 'sarcophagus' had been such a perfect fit for a tall guy like me. To which each of them replied in turn, "It was the same for me." Now, here are four men with different heights – and girths – ranging from 5"5' to 6"5': a variation of one foot. How could a solid stone box be one-size-fits-all? We walked back to meet the rest of the group, probably looking shell-shocked.

"So, how was it?" Isabelle asked. Seeing that I was struggling for words, she told of the rest of the group's morning – how they 'tuned-in' to the origins of the pyramids, among other things, then decided to 'look-in' on us to see if we were behaving ourselves inside the pyramid. "Well, that was a fun experience, wasn't it?" she said, "how you went there with right intent, honoured the site, and the priests came out of the stones."

By now it was obvious Aaron and I had not been hallucinating.

"But what about the thing with the sarcophagus?" I mumbled.

"It's living stone. If you use it for the right reasons, and the site understands this, the stone moulds itself to you. Did you go somewhere nice?"

Indeed I travelled far, visiting several interesting people whose names I do not recall, or for that matter what they told me, except for snippets of information which no doubt would be important in my future work; I also travelled to a number of extraordinary environments I'd never seen before, yet which felt all too familiar. In a matter of a few minutes I had been transported to faraway universes. Makes one marvel at the quality of initiatory experience that could be possible under more favorable conditions.

Needless to say, the experience in the Great Pyramid altered my perception of the world as well as my understanding of why temples were created, and what they can do for you, and *to* you.

Throughout ancient cultures the temple was looked upon as a divine being, and as such, its foundation and construction gave material shape to a divine force who originally had been conceived as a god. In Egypt, the temple was awakened by the Morning Hymns, later adopted by the Cistercians as chants, during which all the parts of the site were addressed as an animate being who is awoken from slumber during the hours of darkness.[1] But it's one thing to be book-smart about these matters and another to have direct validation of the process. For me, the experience in Giza was that more valid because I had not searched for it, I hadn't gone seeking an otherworldly encounter so I could talk (and write) about it later. Such a position serves little purpose other than to validate what you so desperately want, and in the end, it will not be constructive. But walking into a sacred place and allowing yourself to be open to possibility, that's the place where fascinating things occur. It is the thin line between rational and mystical, the abode that painters, musicians and other creatives seek. It is the assembly room of inspiration. The sceptic will never understand this, for by staking a concrete and antagonistic position, the spirit of place will respect that and will never find him. The spirit of place is not there to work for you, it exists to meet you halfway along the bridge, should you make the effort to cross it.

 It would be eight years after my experience when I came across a book by Paul Brunton, an early 20th century journalist who became dissatisfied with the credo of the modern world, and walked the globe meeting philosophers, visiting sacred places and writing about his encounters and experiences along the way, in layman's terms. His philosophical writings alone cover over 20,000 pages. While reading of his travels in Egypt I discovered he also had had a personal experience in the Great Pyramid.

Learning of Brunton's intention to stay the night inside the temple, a local Arab friend warned him, that "every inch of ground is haunted. There is an army of ghosts and *Genni* in that territory." [2] Traditions of the Bedouin going back centuries do tell of lights regularly swirling around the pyramids – specifically the third, smaller pyramid – that they claim are guardian spirits. These lights spiral around the pyramid several times before ascending to the apex, where they discharge like a flame.[3] Unperturbed, Brunton proceeded to stay the night, just as Napoleon had done a century earlier. His experience seems to have been less than favorable at first, but as he relaxed, the energy of the chamber changed in rhythm to his feelings. The following passage from his account took my breath away: "I became conscious of a new presence in the chamber, of someone friendly and benevolent who stood at the entrance and looked down upon me with kind eyes. With his arrival the atmosphere changed completely... He approached my stony seat, and I saw that he was followed by another figure. Both halted at my side and regarded me with grave looks, pregnant with prophetic meaning. I felt that some momentous hour of my life was at hand.

"In my vision the apparition of these two beings presented an unforgettable picture. Their white robes, their sandaled feet, their wise aspect, their tall figures – all these return to the mind's eye... There was a light a-glimmer all around them, which in a most uncanny manner lit up the part of the room. Indeed, they looked more than men, bearing the light mien of demi-gods." [4]

Brunton wrote about his experience in the 1930s, over seventy years before mine, yet the descriptions are identical. With more time and quiet to work with, Brunton was even able to converse with these spirits, who inquired of him, "why dost thou come into this place, seeking to evoke the secret powers? Are not mortal ways enough for thee?" [5] Brunton makes it very clear that the voice was heard inside his head, much like a deaf person might. And he's absolutely correct: anyone who works with subtle forces – such as clairvoyants – will state the communication is heard within, and different in tone to one's mental thoughts; also, the pattern of language is consistent with the recipient's so the conversation can be understood, hence why in many valid trance channellings the syntax is often awkward, just as communication between two vastly different cultures would be. This happens to me the more I work in sacred sites – at Castle Hill, for example, as shared in the previous chapter.

But let's return to the riveting dialogue that ensued: "They are not!" Paul answered. The priest continued: "The stir of many crowds in the cities comforts the trembling heart of man. Go back, mingle with thy fellows, and thou wilt soon forget the light fancy that brings thee here... The way of Dream will draw thee far from the fold of reason. Some have gone upon it – and come back mad. Turn now, whilst there is yet time, and follow the path appointed for mortal feet."

Brunton didn't miss a breath in replying, so sure was he of his chosen path: "I must follow this way. There is none other for me now."

One of the priests bent down and uttered in his ear. "He who gains touch with us loses kin with the world. Art thou able to walk alone?"

"I don't know."

"So be it. Thou hast chosen. Abide by thy choice for there is now no recall.

Farewell." Brunton was then left alone with the second priest: "…the mighty lords of the secret powers have taken thee into their hands. Thou art to be led into the Hall of Learning tonight."

Brunton was instructed to stretch himself in the sarcophagus, which in the old days, he was told, would be lined with papyrus reeds. Brunton wrote that his experience in the sarcophagus was hard to explain – as indeed was mine. He describes being overcome with a sensation like an anesthetic that rendered his muscles taut, like a paralyzing lethargy. Ironically, I experienced an identical sensation not just in the pyramid but several years earlier inside a genuine crop circle, during which I was levitated and taken out of body.[6] After Brunton had gotten past the shock of what was happening – and the experience can be a little discomforting at first – his consciousness went walkabout on a very personal journey.[7]

I was glad not to have read Brunton's notes before my own personal excursion, for no doubt they would have influenced me in some way. The warning made to him – how he would have problems fitting-in with modern life once he had made contact with the invisible – is all too true a statement for people who choose this path into the knowledge, one that super-rational people cannot accept because their minds are closed to the remarkable and the unseen. It is a lonely journey, at best, but one that I, for one, would not exchange for anything, even in spite of the obstacles it has brought. What makes the path tolerable are the experiences, which I sarcastically refer to as 'fringe benefits'. And besides, it's an excuse to indulge in 16-year old Lagavulin, otherwise known in the trade as 'research'.

I was interested in what the second priest-spirit went on to tell Brunton, because there was a ring of truth about it: "In this ancient fane lies the lost record of the early races of man and of the Covenant which they made with their Creator… Know too that chosen men were brought here of old to be shown this Covenant that they might return to their fellows and keep the great secret alive. Take back with thee the warning that when men forsake their Creator and look on their fellows with hate, as with the princes of Atlantis in whose time this Pyramid was built, they are destroyed by the weight of their own iniquity, even as the people of Atlantis were destroyed.

"It was not the Creator who sank Atlantis, but the selfishness, the cruelty, the spiritual blindness of people who dwelt on those doomed lands. The Creator loves all; but the lives of men are governed by invisible laws which He has set over them."

Paul is then told why he has been allowed to experience this crossing of the veil: "because thou art a man versed in these things, and has come among us bearing goodwill and understanding in thy heart, some satisfaction thou shalt have." [8] Still inside the sarcophagus, he is led through passageways and becomes disoriented when looking for the door into a chamber holding the secret records, whereupon the priest offers sagely advice, whose relevance is as important now as it was then: "It matters not whether thou discovered the door or not. Find but the secret passage within the mind that will lead thee to the hidden chamber within thine own soul, and thou shalt have found something worthy indeed. The mystery of the Great Pyramid is the mystery of thine own self. The secret chambers and ancient records are all contained in thine own nature. The lesson of the Pyramid is that man must turn inward, must venture to the unknown centre of his being to find his soul, even as he must venture to the unknown depths of this fane to find its profoundest secret." [9]

A sword of light at Stonehenge.

One person who knew all too well about the importance of connecting with ancient temples was the architect and psychic researcher Frederick Bligh Bond who, in 1908, was appointed by the Church of England as director of excavations at Glastonbury Abbey. Over the course of thirteen years Bond developed a deep connection to the spirit of place, which led him to discover buildings and obelisks buried by layers of silt and time. He did so through a process called automatic writing, in which the spirit of monks who once resided at the abbey instructed, through Bond's writing, where to dig so that the former plan of the abbey may yet see the light of day. What is illuminating about Bond's written notes is how the vernacular of the language is closer to 13th century English than to Bond's own period. Unorthodox his method may have been, but Bond certainly succeeded in unearthing much of the foundations seen today in the abbey grounds. Sadly, for all his gifts, he was fired because the methods were unacceptable to the Church. Which, when you think about it, is strange coming from an institution that supposedly believes in a holy spirit.[10]

Bond's experience is another example of how, in his own words, "connecting with the energy of place often brings about great revelations." Such interactions come in all kinds of ways, and when least expected. In the previous chapter I discussed how an innocent wonder concerning the possible connection between Celtic and Maori art took me to Kura Tawhiti in New Zealand, only to be 'told' at the site to look "for what lies opposite" and discovered a previously unknown global ley line. Or a ley circle, as the case may be. And yet, I had not gone to the temple with the intention of soliciting a response, I merely went with a question in my mind. As my colleagues John Michell, Paul Broadhurst and Hamish Miller have experienced, the assistance comes when one adopts a certain grace, an acceptance and surrender to the temple and to its presiding force. Like a library, these are repositories of very old knowledge, accumulated from millennia of experiences, and as Paul Brunton discovered that night inside the pyramid, when one's heart is true it sets off an energetic chain-reaction. If one is not prepared for the consequences, the interaction can be alarming at first. It's as if your body and its multitude of frequencies[11] carries a PIN number that the temple reads, recognizes, and unlocks the doors to many secret chambers.

In 1987 while living in London with my then wife, I suddenly felt compelled to travel to Stonehenge for the first time. There was absolutely no underlying rationality to this: it was a Friday rush-hour, August, hot, in England, and only a person who is certifiable will get into a car during such a confluence of unfavorable circumstances. But some unyielding magnetic force pulled me. When we finally did reach Stonehenge I was amazed to find the place overrun with rock bands, huge crowds of people wearing painted faces and odd costumes, and an untypical carnival atmosphere. I asked a policeman directing traffic what the commotion was all about, to which he replied, "Harmonic Convergence, mate." Later I would discover just what a momentous occasion this was in the world of esoterica.

On my second visit, many years later, the rigors of professional life had eased somewhat to allow me the luxury of spending quality time researching what really moved my heart: the world of very old and upright stones. I had entered into the spirit of the quest. That evening, another of my mentors and friend, Jane Ross, secured private access into Stonehenge at night, a very rare opportunity, and one in a long string of coincidences which I would later come to understand as the way the invisible world prefers to communicate.

Like Isabelle Kingston, Jane is a gifted sensitive as well as an accountant. Since I was still an initiate, I didn't want to intrude on her work at the site. She suggested I find a stone that 'spoke to me' and we'd reconnect in an hour, which is the time allotted for extra-curricular activity at Stonehenge. I found my stone – or rather, it made its presence known to me – sat down, closed my eyes.

Two hours later I heard the guard whisper somewhere in my vicinity to "come back to the gate when you're ready, sir." Jane and I made our way out humbly, past the monolithic sarsen trilithons, and back to the waiting guard. There was little going on that night and so the three of us sat and exchanged pleasantries while gazing at the rings of stones outlined in the dim twilight. Some of the caretakers at Stonehenge are people who've served in special combat units of the British Military, and although they have seen hard action their demeanor takes on the most peaceful, zen-like quality when talking about the enigmatic stones, particularly about the things they've witnessed: "First it's the large balls of light, incandescent like, which fly through here at incredible speed. Sometimes our boys are following them in helicopters. Then there are the figures dressed in strange, period costume, and we think, 'hallo, some joker's jumped the fence again', and we chase them characters into the stones. We know all the hiding places but we never see them again. They just evaporate. Then there's the fog, real pea-soupers, can't see a blessed thing in front of you. I go check on them stones, it's so dense you can't see them until your nose is right up to them, and you go inside and look up and there's clear sky. Stars. Outside there's fog, inside the weather's perfect.

"The best are the cadets. They come here to get away from the missus, thinking this is an easy job, a few extra quid in the pocket. After their first apparition they run across the field, jump that high fence, get into their cars, they don't even come back for the pay. Did you want sugar with your tea?"

Jane and I retired to a nearby research facility – otherwise known as the pub – to recap the day's events. "So, did anything interesting happen to you?" she asked.

"Not sure, all I remember is closing my eyes for five minutes to take-in the feel of the place, and two hours later I landed back in my body with a thud when I heard this voice whispering our time was up. I had the strangest dream, though. The stone felt like it wrapped me. There was this tall figure of a man, looked as if he had wings, it was hard to see, and he handed me this blazing sword, as though made of light."

Jane stopped drinking. "That happened to *you*!? Oh, boy." I suddenly had the uneasy feeling that life as I knew it was about to change.

Next day we met Isabelle for a long tea and what would be the start of an even longer friendship. The subject of my 'experience' came up in conversation. "You know what," Jane said to Isabelle, "this guy goes into Stonehenge for the first time and he's given a sword of light by Michael."

"Who's Michael?" I wondered.

"That's *archangel* Michael, to you, young man," replied Isabelle. "Well, you certainly have your work cut out for you!"

They laughed. I knew it would be hard work from that point.

It has, and it's been illuminating.

Michael (slight return).

In a perfect world, hindsight would be foresight. As I would discover later, people on the path of the Mysteries are often recipients of the sword of light as a symbol of protection and guidance by the spirit world, as they try to make sense of 'the Knowledge' so it can be learned, taught, and promulgated from age to age. It is one of the highest privileges because in this cynical world it is one of the hardest jobs. It comes with heavy responsibility, and as others have similarly found, life as you know it falls apart. It is not for the weak willed, and had I known any of this, chances are I'd not abandoned my comfortable existence in the modern world. But as I said before, the fringe benefits are amazing.

In the very early days of my desire to understand the reason behind ancient places of power (although I ought to point out that by the age of four I was already drawing pyramids), I learned by helping others who already knew better, and followed by their example. Fortunately, I bumped into people who really knew what they were doing, and over the years I've witnessed wondrous events manifest around them.

One sunny, summer afternoon in Wiltshire, Isabelle's group was called out to clear the energy of a mound which had become tainted through hundreds of years of abuse. Depending on the time of the week and people's disposition, there is never any idea as to how many will show up. Sometimes three; sometimes fifteen, if tea and cake are involved afterwards. At Chisenbury mound, all twenty-eight people showed up and without any promise of culinary delights. That's when you know very serious work is at hand.

Circling the large ring barrow, the group gathered their concentration under a shining sun and calm, azure sky. Following the customary ceremonies, after the third evoking of the words "Archangel Michael" the heavens darkened, the wind whipped up, clouds closed up the sky like a velvet purse and hail and sleet descended upon the group. What I 'saw' floating out of the mound were grotesque and distorted entities doing their utmost to break our concentration and with it the power of the united circle. We persevered for twenty minutes until the site seemed infused with a blinding brightness. Calm returned, the sun shone once more, not a cloud in the blue sky. We were soaked. Two hundred yards away not even the cars were wet.

"Whatever just came out of there, it was pretty ugly," I remarked to Isabelle.

"Yes, and if half the group had seen it, they would've bolted for their lives!"

Oh, the fun we have.

I'd often read accounts of shamans working with the skills taught through the Mysteries Schools to bring rain to parched farmland, but until you experience it, the stories are just abstract experiences that happen to someone else. It taught me much about the power of place, how it becomes corrupted through misuse, and how it can be restored to its correct function by the power of individuals sharing a common and unshakable belief. At some distant point in time, the *Akhu Shemsu Hor* must have engaged in similar work while setting up the primordial mounds of the gods.

Michael. Again.

After years of walking and feeling the energy of place at hundreds of temples around the world, you realize the invisible universe has a very puckish sense of humor. It provides much needed respite on a road that often requires your full concentration, regularly involves heavy reading, and without question, arduous quests to unpronounceable places to look under the strangest of stones. Humor is the key, and the key lies in the word itself: *hu*, an ancient name for god, and *amour*, love. When you engage in *hu-amour* you participate in the act of god-loving, in a non-religious sense.

The late and great dowser Hamish Miller once told me of his adventure to Skellig Michael and the Celtic monastery propped atop this vertiginous, pyramidal island of basalt, nine miles off the coast of Ireland. The madness of a group of monks living there is only eclipsed by the insanity of getting there. Visitors need not be discouraged: eleven months of howling wind, pounding surf, and a thriving colony of gannets, razorbills, guillemots and storm petrels and their descending effluence will do that. But for the sake of research it is worth it, after all, Hamish would discover it to be the starting place of the Apollo and Athena ley.

Nine miles from the Irish coast it may be, but this loneliest of mansions of the archangel Michael, barely 300 acres in size, is impossible to locate in thick fog in the middle of the Atlantic, despite assurances from the fishing captain steering the tiny boat: "Tis over here, sum'where. Or so it was yest'day. 'Tis a wonderful sight, if only you could see it." Miller had no intention of becoming the first Scotsman to reach

America on an oversize skiff, so he took out his iron dowsing rod, connected with the spirit of the island, and sure enough the rods began to point in a specific direction, which the boat captain followed bemusedly. In no time at all, lo and behold, the party arrived at their intended destination, rendering the skipper speechless, a rarity for an Irishman.

Meanwhile in the warm and tame environment of Salisbury cathedral – another home of Michael – I was focusing on locating energy nodes, and unusual deviations from architectural norm that might reveal tidbits of concealed information; the architects of the Gothic were very cunning when it came to hiding knowledge from less benevolent eyes. Having scouted the length of the cathedral I worked out that, like Luxor, Salisbury's floor plan is designed according to the chakras of the human body. By standing at specific places along the nave, the pilgrim stops and feels the gradual upwelling of telluric energy rise from the base of the spine, following through to the heart (the cross of the nave and transept), the throat (choir), third-eye (altar) and finally, the crown (Trinity Chapel).

I returned to the edge of the choir to take stock of the notes, pausing to connect with the inspired mind that created such timeless art. Midway into my reverie I noticed something ambling towards me just above the flagstone floor: an orb of incandescent purple light, about the size of a large fist, hovered past my ankle, with a vapor trail wandering from side to side like the tail of a fish. In my head I could hear it: "Hi, how's the work going?"

"Fine thanks, how about you?" I replied out loud.

"Great. Follow me. Too dee doo…"

Flustered, I looked around at the visitors walking down the choir. "Did you see that? Did anyone see that?" All to no avail. As far as everyone around me was concerned, I was certifiable, with horns growing out of my forehead. I paused and turned to look up at the priest setting down his bible in the pulpit, who gave me the widest grin and several nods of the head. Obviously I was not the first person to experience a conscious being dressed as a ball of light.

I followed the path of the orb and arrived at the rear of the church, and below its outstanding stained glass window, built by a glazier from that other great Gothic mansion, Chartres. There are very few opportune times when the back-light from the sun shines through this window, but when it does, as it did at that moment, it revealed a second design – a large purple pyramid bisected by a serpent, with each node of the chakras rising upwards to the tip of its Benben, where a burst of light radiated in a tribute to revelation.

How all these incidences remind me of the incantation etched on the outer wall of the Pronaos of Edfu: "When you have reached the land of the First Generation… you have awakened the gods on their resting place." [12]

10

THE SEVEN PRINCIPLES
OF SACRED SPACE:

1. WATER.

*Without exception, all temples are surrounded by invisible
yet detectable pathways of underground streams of force.*

~ Merle et Diot, archaeologists, 1935

A landscape temple is created from universal forces by a creator god for humans, and generates a wider spectrum of effect than a human-engineered site. A constructed temple, on the other hand, is built by humans for humans from the distillation of universal forces. It is an extension, a mirror of the undiluted original, even by design – the upright obelisk represents a *Sivalingam*, the *stupa* a sacred mountain, the pyramid a primordial mound, *ad infinitum*.

And just because constructed temples are the product of the observation and rationalization of nature does not make them any poorer, for they allow the architect to specify a degree of control on the effect the site exerts on those who interact with it. Depending on how the elements are combined, the effects vary from temple to temple; the sensory experience at the great pyramid of Giza is far different to that of the Bent Pyramid of Dahshur or the Red Pyramid because all three are designed to

Holy well, St. Clether's church. Cornwall, England.

different specifications and geometries, and different angles illicit different physical and mental responses.[1]

These places of power are alive – living, breathing organisms, environments where the initiate can be "transformed into a god, into a bright star".[2] But how?

It is well known that all temples and places of veneration are strategically sited upon the telluric lines of force that criss-cross the face of the Earth, and whose fluctuations are sufficient to influence the body's electromagnetic field. Since these lines of force are everywhere, it is reasonable to suggest that by consciously standing on one, even in the center of a busy city, is enough to connect you with the Earth's energy grid. This may be so, and if you recall the times you have been drawn to a particular place because it just feels good, that is often an indication your body has sourced the type of energy it requires for its own well-being; animals behave the same way, particularly on farms, where pregnant cows and sheep will seek a vortex upwelling from within the earth to facilitate birthing.[3] But temples go well beyond this because they are a combination of layers of forces at work, creating specific environments that induce a pre-conceived effect on the body's receptive organs.

Every time you stand in a temple the experience differs. The first time, there is the sense of awe; or in the case of pyramids, disbelief *followed* by awe. On the second visit, you adjust to the surroundings and become aware of pockets of subtlety. Beyond that, the site will present itself in a completely different light, revealing to you what is written between the lines. Do this year after year and soon a relationship develops where the site answers you, it reveals its inner secrets. That's when you begin to understand what makes these organisms tick.

That's how the revelation began for many others and myself. And after years of observation, reflection and experience I've noticed how a number of common principles are shared by the vast majority of sacred sites around the world.

Seven principles, to be precise.

These are a blend of forces of nature which were engineered to bring you into intimate contact with worlds unseen, where sacred is distinguished from profane, where one walks in the mansion of the gods.

Depending on cultural conventions there are exceptions to the rule, particularly where people have by-and-large been nomadic, such as the original Aborigines and most North American tribes. Such cultures were immersed with the land; to them every piece of the earth was sacred, they did not feel the need to use geometry or stone to imitate or improve on what they felt was already perfect. For them the landscape temple was sufficient. But for people like the Seven Sages and the Followers of Horus, the constructed temple brought to the rest of us a place where the ideal universe can be experienced. And later, when humanity lost the plot, these same places would serve as an insurance policy to help us remember why we are here, and the opportunity to reconnect with everything we'd forgotten.

Water.

The Edfu *Building Texts* provide one of the most solid records of the processes by which a piece of land, infused with an energetic force, becomes sacred ground, and how the constructed temple takes on the living form of a god who is itself a distillation of the forces of the cosmos. The narrative indicates that after the primordial mound is established, an "enemy snake is overthrown." Since the snake or dragon is the ancient representation of telluric forces that flow through and along the earth, we are told that an energy that is not conducive to the proper function of life is somehow tamed or balanced. This concept is similar to Polynesian philosophy where *tabu* represents an energy that upsets the proper balance of *mana* (magic), what in Africa is known as *baraka*, and to Greeks as *pneuma*.[4] An enclosure is then made on the mound and a channel dug around it containing *mw*, a special type of water consecrated by the protector of the site, the creator god Ptah. The text then makes a specific reference to the *pth-nwyt-mw*, "sanctified water that protects," a kind of energized water with the power to protect the selected piece of land. Only then does *Tanen* (the creative force) emerge from the sacred site and the temple begins its function as the "restoration of the Ancestors." [5]

This consecrated water is of vital importance to the efficacy of the temple, for it contains a power which prevents "the enemy snake from approaching the domain of Horus," [6] inferring that so long as the purity of the water is maintained at the site, the potentially destructive telluric forces of the earth do not interfere with the processes at work inside the sanctuary. This energized water itself behaves as a kind of force field.

The practice of surrounding a temple with an earthen mound and water-retaining ditch is common to hundreds of sacred sites throughout Celtic Britain, such as Knowlton, Arbor Low, Stonehenge and Avebury, as well as the so-called 'hill forts'. Some argue that these sites are nothing more than mere fortifications, although they do not satisfactorily explain why these supposedly defensive ditches lie on the *inside* of the mounds, or why places such as Rybury hill fort sits below higher ground barely a hundred yards outside its earthen walls, rendering such a place useless as a military fortification.

The French archaeologists Merle and Diot published papers to the effect that all prehistoric monuments, without exception, are surrounded by underground streams; the eleven parallel stone rows of Carnac that stretch for almost a mile are aligned to underground streams running parallel to each other.[7] Captain Robert Boothby, who studied sites in Wiltshire in 1935, similarly observed how every long barrow has an underground stream running its full length.[8] Indeed, the prime energy spots in sacred sites tend to be those from which a number of underground streams form a radial pattern: "The constant presence of underground water at the exact centres of these circles and earthworks is a significant feature easily verified by others. If this is allowed to be intentional, then the selection of sites for consecration by the Druids and their

Wells Cathedral sits over several sacred springs, from which its gets its name.

predecessors no longer appears arbitrary, but dictated largely by geological conditions."[9]

Beneath the holiest of Muslim shrines, the Ka'Ba, there exists a well; sacred springs exist below Temple Mount, just as they do beneath Chartres and Glastonbury Tor; the Gothic cathedrals of Wells, Winchester and Salisbury are built on marshland and designed to practically float on such architecturally unsuitable terrain; in fact, so many beautiful pieces of sacred architecture sit on ground wholly unsuitable for heavy structures.[10] The Egyptian pyramids sit above deep fissures of the earth through which flow hundreds of veins of pressurized water. Even stone circles amid the deserts of Nubia and Libya sit on domes of water, as does the Navajo altar in Monument Valley, situated between two voluminous sand dunes out of which bursts a serpentine gush of cold, clear water.

Without exception, every sacred site is located above or beside water. Water is the foundation of every temple.

Like sacred mountains or landscape temples, holy wells and sacred springs are the epitome of the temple in its natural state, and their hypnotic power has been honored since prehistoric times. Many have been integrated within the boundaries of constructed temples, even represented on the inside by the octagonal church font and its holy water. In his delightful discourse on the holy wells of Cornwall, Paul Broadhurst describes how these places were seen by ancient people "as gateways to the Otherworld, where the vital flow of life-force could be used to penetrate the veil of matter to experience a more formative reality. And so they were used to contact unseen realms where communication could take place with the gods and spirits."[11] Celtic Britain – Ireland in particular – still venerates its ancient holy wells and sacred springs, and anyone who visits these remote shrines is often taken aback by the monastic ambience pervading their surroundings. Direct contact with these special waters have provided healing and inspiration for poet and pilgrim since the days of Sumerian Eridu and its temple honoring Ea, the god of the House of Water, where the ritual of baptism was performed as an integral part of temple initiation.

Ea and the Babylonian post-diluvial god Oannes share identical characteristics and attributes thousands of years later with John the Baptist via the linguistic route of the Hebrew *Yohanan*, the Greek *Ioannes*, and finally, the English *John*. Strange how an identical character emerges in the Biblical narrative 9000 years after the god Oannes emerges from the flood, complete with fish symbology, and an aphorism reminiscent of the act of consecration of the Egyptian temple: "Unless one is born of water and the Spirit, he cannot enter the kingdom of God." [12]

Throughout Britain, western France and northern Iberia, holy wells and springs came under the protection of the Celtic church, essentially a reformation of Druidism, which maintained the tradition of honoring the site to the degree that by the Victorian era physicians in London were still sending patients to be cured at such pagan sanctuaries. On my guided excursions to the wells and springs of Cornwall and southern Dorset I have watched groups of excited and inquiring minds develop an immediate languid state of mind as they approach the waters of St. Catherine's well at Cerne, once part of a pagan temple honoring the fertility god Cernunnos. Likewise, the holy well at St. Clether, Cornwall, is a unique sanctuary where a channel of water from the outside well house passes directly through the tiny church and under a rough stone altar resembling one of Stonehenge's trilithons in miniature.

Water at sacred sites is very different in frequency to ordinary water. Tests conducted using infrared spectroscopy show that holy water absorbs light at different frequencies. Holy well water is free from bacteria and contains natural minerals which are known to be beneficial to health and longevity. [13] This extremely pure water also exhibits greater properties of spin, and such vortices create an electrical charge which then generate an electromagnetic field, certainly enough to transform it into something different from ordinary liquid. [14]

Despite the world being covered two-thirds by water, it is still a mysterious element: it grows lighter rather than heavier as it freezes; its surface tension causes it to stick to itself to form a sphere – the shape with the least amount of surface for its volume, requiring the least amount of energy to maintain itself. And yet when its extraneous gases are removed from a drop the size of an inch, it becomes harder than steel. [15] Its potency can be enhanced by the use of crystals, particularly quartz, the prime material found in the stone used in temple-building. This has a marked effect on water's surface tension, and Tibetan physicians have used this combination to make efficacious solutions for their patients. [16] Not surprisingly, enlightened kings and queens of old had water transported from sacred sites to their court by means of rock crystal bowls, which served to maintain the energy of the water during transportation. Anyone who has tried this in recent times knows just how it makes the water taste like liquid air.

In studying ancient settlements, it is surprising how the vast majority evolved around a temple or a singular menhir at their core. Paris grew around a temple dedicated to Isis (hence its original name Par-isis), now beneath the abbey of St. Germain-des-Prés; central London expanded from a mound containing a giant's grave, long since buried beneath the Tower of London. Aside from the obvious desire of people to be close to an earthly embodiment of divinity, in light of

... and indeed it is.

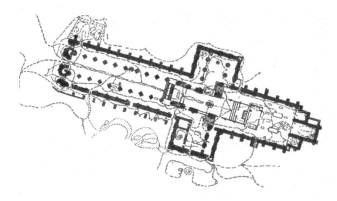

Water veins beneath Winchester Cathedral. England.

the potentized state of water at sacred sites, the practical benefit that derived from the use of such in agriculture requires no further explanation. Indeed, modern efforts to recreate the ancient art of potentized water to enhance plant vitality and growth have proved highly successful.[17]

A life-long study of the relationship between sacred sites, water and energy fields by Guy Underwood reveals how the shape of the temples regularly match underlying forces already at work beneath the soil. Using the early cathedrals as an example – for they were built over ground made sacred thousands of years before – he revealed how the width of walls, the position of fonts and altars, even the placing of doors took underlying veins of water into consideration. Over the course of time, recurring acts of

A holy well honored with offerings and bunting. Trellech, Wales.

prayer and veneration, and the electromagnetic fingerprint left by each person's attendance, has served to enhance the potency of the underlying water, which in turn has magnified the energy of place. Underwood's drawings reveal a distinct relationship between underground veins of water, the electromagnetic lines above them, and the places of the site used most often by congregation and priest. Thus, halos of positive and negative

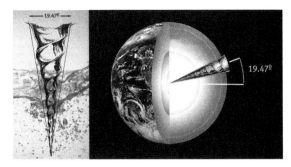

Left: vorticular angle of water. Right: energy upwells from the center of the Earth and emerges at latitude 19.47º, as it does on four other planets.

charges tend to be generated and polarized around original church fonts, wells and altars, the later having been erected over the confluence of several underground springs.[18] This makes energized water, as the primary ingredient of sacred space, a major stimulant of the human body, the element that benefits most from using the temple. Our bodies consist of two-thirds water, just like the Earth, and 90% of the brain is made up of the stuff. Since water retains information,[19] drinking it from a sacred site means one literally imbibes whatever is stored in the memory of place; that is, its natural energy as well as the energy from affirmations and prayers accumulated over hundreds, possibly thousands of years.[20]

The brain generates detectable electromagnetic pulses,[21] meaning that every thought we send emits a small packet of energy. The effects of concentrated thought and its ability to alter the shape of water has been well illustrated in thousands of experiments by the Japanese scientist Masuro Emoto. Seen under a microscope, the directed intent from ordinary people aimed at vials of water shows the ability of even a simple, everyday word such as love, well-intended, to drastically alter the crystalline structure of water. Most revealing of all are the tests conducted on water in Tokyo's main reservoir before and after its blessing by a group of monks, in which the chaotic structure of the capital's drinking supply was radically reorganized into a coherent and geometric shape.[22]

In water we can observe the movement of the vortex, the primary movement in the creation of matter, from galaxies to seashells. The Earth's own vorticular energy discharges from its core at an angle of 19.47º and manifests on the surface as the most active hotspot, the Hawaiian volcano of Mauna Loa, at latitude 19.47º. This angle is reflected in water when a ship creates a wake or when it is spun in a container into a funnel. Spin gives off a magnetic field, and when water is spun, its electromagnetic charge is altered, which in turn adjusts the information stored in its memory.

Since water is a component of blood, and blood requires vorticular motion to move through the veins, it follows that contact with the energetic properties of water at sacred sites will affect the spin ratio of blood, thus altering the information traveling through the body.[23] The body's metabolic processes are dependent on a specific composition of basic elements, fresh water being one of them, and the taking of energized water – even being in contact with it – induces a vitality in the body, just as one feels a clarity of mind after a stroll by a waterfall or by the sea shore.

This is very important when it comes to understanding the interaction between water, the temple and its influence on the human body. Because our sensory organs need to be in a certain condition to be receptive to extra-sensory experiences, stimulating the energy of the water and the blood flow through the body makes us more receptive to the processes taking place inside the temple.

The thermodynamics engineer Pierre Mereaux spent three decades painstakingly studying the megaliths at Carnac. As well he should have, with such an appropriate first name! He discovered that a strong relationship exists between their location and alignment and the fault lines of the region, France's most active earthquake zone.[24] Identical relationships exist between sacred sites in New Mexico and the fault line along the Rio Grande, as well as Anasazi pueblos, and the pyramids of Mesoamerica.[25] We know that the siting of temples over water-bearing fissures is a common feature to sites such as Delphi and Chartres, and given how these fissures cover tens, and sometimes hundreds of miles, it is worth considering how a negative impact on the water of a site would lead to the fall of the temple and, by implication, the fall of the land and the spiritual outlook of its people.

Temples that have fallen into decay have done so through a series of interrelated events, one being a sudden and catastrophic change in the pattern of weather. Whether this is due to a transgression against the temple or natural causes depends on which side of the scientific fence you wish to stand, but from an ancestor's point of view, everything, including the weather, worked like interconnected cogwheels. To some cultures, the imbalances of the people are reflected in the climate; the souls of the Sinagua of Arizona returned to the tribe after death as the elements of rain, heat or wind, or whatever the tribe needed most to maintain its equilibrium. And yet in cases like Jerusalem's Temple Mount, the demise of its sacred springs went hand in hand with the fall of the temple.

One can argue that prevailing arid conditions in the Near East during those times facilitated a fall in the water table, but the same cannot be said for Britain, where it rains incessantly. When a cathedral was built as the Bishop's See on the sacred hill of Old Sarum, no sooner had the last stone been placed when the weather turned violent and blew the structure down. Its replacement also came under a renewed battering from the elements shortly after its consecration, with cracks appearing all over the building. Then the springs dried up, and relations between factions inhabiting the mound went downhill very fast, leading the contemporary observer Peter de Blois to remark, "the church stands as a captive on the hill where it was built, like the ark of God, shut up in the profane house of Baal." [26] Shortly after, Old Sarum fell into total decline and never recovered its original glory.

Water is the blood of the earth and the life-force of the temple, and if that blood should be energized by the numinous quality of the temple's environment, it stands to reason that the same quality is transferred to the initiate or the pilgrim, whether they imbibe it or walk upon it.

The sacred spring at the entrance to Kura Tawhiti. Its curative and recharging waters draw people far and wide. Above the pool stand the stone faces of the two guardians of the site. Before his first ever visit to the site, the dowser Hamish Miller sketched their images (below) following a vivid dream whilst lying in a hospital bed in Sydney.

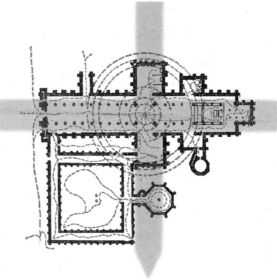

A masterpiece of Gothic architecture, England's Salisbury cathedral sits at the crossroads of two of the earth's telluric lines of energy. It's walls and entrances reference underground veins of water, while beneath its spire, the energy organizes and discharges like ripples in a pond.

11

The Seven Principles of Sacred Space:

2. Electromagnetics.

The Earth is linked to the Sun by a network of magnetic portals which open every eight minutes.
~ NASA, 2008

Snakes whichsoever move along the Earth. Which are in sky and in heaven... which are the arrows of sorcerers.
~ Yajurveda, c.9000 B.C.

Ancient people discerned and marked a place that was energetically different because it empowered them to experience direct contact with subtle realms. Today, the inhabitants of Santa Clara Pueblo in New Mexico still venerate their sacred hill, Tsikumu, which they describe as a place of access to the otherworld, from where their culture is said to have emerged. On this landscape temple the tribespeople work with *Po-wa-ha*, an energy that provides a doorway or conduit between the material world and other realities.[1]

The Aborigines describe such places as *increase centres*, and the use of correct ritual elicits a life force that intensifies the fercundity of people, plants and land. These 'spots of the fawn' are connected to each other by *spirit roads*, pathways of a terrestrial current which Navajo lore describes as tunnels along which the Anasazi once invisibly travelled, and, in a manner of speaking, still do.

The essence of this life force, or *mana*, *baraka*, *prana* or *pneuma*, can be confusing, but energy it certainly is. It has been described as *telluric current*, *earth energy*, and *geomagnetic force*, and it involves the intertwined forces of electricity and magnetism. As the anthropologist William Howells attempted to classify it, "It was the basic force of nature through which everything was done… [its] comparison with electricity, or physical energy, is here inescapable. [It] was believed to be indestructible, although it might be dissipated by improper practices… It flowed continuously from one thing to another and, since the cosmos was built on a dualistic idea, it flowed through heavenly things to earthbound things, just as though from a positive to negative pole." [2]

When NASA discovered magnetic energy spiraling inside tubes linking the Earth to the Sun[3] – even employing the metaphysical word 'portals' – they essentially validated the ancient master geomancers and temple-builders who sourced these very same flux events on the land, because they were all too aware of their connection to territories far and beyond the confines of our terrestrial sphere. The image they chose to represent this elusive telluric force was the serpent or dragon, and in time, this would become a culturally-shared archetype describing the energy's winding behavior along its earthly course as well as the skies; or, as expressed in the *Yajurveda*, "snakes whichsoever move along the Earth, which are in sky and in heaven."[4] The same expression is mirrored in the *Book of What is in the Duat* dating to the times of the creator gods at *Zep Tepi*.

Typically, when a serpent motif is displayed in temples it is an instruction that the telluric current passes through the site, it is the 'X' that marks the spot of the fawn. The Greek and Semitic *omphaloi* typically mark the crossing paths of telluric forces and are sometimes depicted with a serpent wound around them, one of the best-known being the omphalos of Delos, while its sister stone at Delphi even bears the description *tomb of Python*. The main repository of energy at Avebury is marked by a lozenge stone bearing a large carving of a serpent on its outer face; the menhirs of

The serpent stone, Avebury.

the Carnac region and the *betilos* throughout central Portugal often have carved snakes rising from the bottom of these stone sentinels like rays of fire.

The association between the sacred site and winding paths of energy was continued throughout early Christian sites with the depiction of the archangel Michael spearing a dragon, a chore later entrusted to his Catholic equivalent St. George. This negative connotation extends from one of the fundamental doctrines of the Catholic Church, who sought to stamp out all vestiges of so-called pagan traditions (pagan meaning 'a person who lives in the country'), in which the serpent was turned into a representation of evil, and evil was to be eliminated wherever it raised its tail. But to ancient practices the serpent was a natural force to be harnessed for all manner of beneficial purposes, as Richard Wilhelm notes: "In China dragons are not slain; rather their electrical power is kept in the realm, in which it can be made useful. Thus the dragon... is the supreme symbol of temporal power assigned to the Son of Heaven. Only a dragon that kicks over the traces... is dangerous and needs to be subdued." [5]

There are parallels here to the instructions in the Edfu *Pyramid Texts* setting forth the conditions by which a sacred space is established: after the ground is sanctified by the builder gods Djehuti and Seshat, four deities stand at each of the four faces of the site as protectors, while Horus "battles the enemy snake." After this snake is overthrown, the group "settles beside the snake," whereupon it is "pierced." [6] The site is then dedicated to Ra, the solar deity, whereupon it becomes the seat of the mansion of the gods. The fight against the 'enemy snake' is described as an essential pre-condition before a god sanctifies the site as sacred. That the builder gods settled beside the snake implies they were comfortable in the snake's presence; nowhere in the *Pyramid Texts* is it killed.[7] It is true

Small details reveal much about the architect's understanding of subtle forces. In Wells cathedral, a monk piercing a snake and a discharge from a dragon's mouth mark the path of telluric lines inside the building.

that some types of electromagnetic energy are detrimental to the human body; it is a condition known as *geopathic stress*, and given their understanding of subtle forces it is likely the temple builders knew this. So, in 'battling' and 'overthrowing' the snake the builder gods removed such detrimental forces.

Modern physics also understands that this same electromagnetic energy moves – and geomagnetism even more so – as it comes under the influence of the Moon and Sun, not to mention the rotating iron core at the Earth's center. Thus, if telluric currents were fundamental to the establishing of a temple, they required anchoring, they had to be *pierced*.

In the same instructions we are told how the Egyptians were under no illusion that the original sacred temples of the gods were temporary places whose decay merely followed the natural cycle of things in the material world. It is mentioned that the first mansion of the gods perished in a great storm, when a great snake, "the Great Leaping One pierced the feet of the protective entity of the temple, splitting the domain and covering the land in darkness." [8] Since snakes don't leap, we are meant to accept this as a metaphor. Substitute 'snake' for magnetic force, re-read the above paragraph within the context of the period it is describing, and a new insight is revealed. The text refers to the time of the great flood, and it is established in the geological record that, prior to the deluge, the Earth's magnetic field flipped 180°. In the 'Great Leaping snake', it is plausible the Egyptians are describing this catastrophic shift in the earth's magnetic field. Such a disastrous action would have indeed 'pierced the feet of the god', as the force that typically provided the energetic protection of the site now turned against the resident deity. In this manner, the temple was compromised at the hands of the enemy snake.

As mentioned earlier, the re-discovery of the Michael and Mary, and Apollo and Athena telluric lines brought to our attention the existence of the earth's neurological pathways and how these are 'pierced' at the sites through which they flow. Thousands of temples, holy wells, churches, cathedrals, dolmens, menhirs, hill sanctuaries and other special places of veneration are connected to each other like pearls on a string, all behaving like needles of stone and performing acupuncture across the face of the Earth. The majority of early Celtic churches and Gothic cathedrals are situated above pre-existing structures, so the width of aisles and transepts typically conform to the width of the telluric lines flowing through them, with two lines generally meeting beneath the spire – *spire* being a derivation of *spiral* – giving the buildings' cruciform shape a whole different meaning.[9] Together with the underground water veins, they converge at the altar, the spot identified with the original place of shamanic experience, and whose radiations are most likely to 'alter' brainwaves.

In Old English, *altar* used to be spelled *alter*, and together with its Latin derivative *alterar*, it identifies the spot as both a *high place* and a *place of altering*. Which begs one to ask, just who or what is being *altered* and which *high place* are they being transported to?

Since water is also a pre-requisite for the founding of any sacred site, and water generates its own electromagnetic field when spun, it is useful to know that water attracts geomagnetic lines, as NASA has discovered: "when we search for magnetic lines of energy across the face of the Earth, we first locate underground streams of water, because one will attract the other." [10] The combination of these two elements sets up a unique energetic environment, and when a building is placed along its path, the atmosphere inside the structure becomes highly charged. On occasion, light phenomena such as balls of light are witnessed in churches, and more commonly in dolmens, where scientists have watched light beams rising high into the atmosphere. My colleagues and I have witnessed such phenomena over long barrows in southern Britain – the so-called giant's graves; I have also seen an orange orb encompassed within a large green halo, emerging from the top of Silbury Hill, of the most incandescent color - translucent, yet strangely solid; relative to the mound it must have measured 20 feet in diameter, hovering for about thirty seconds above the summit before abruptly evaporating. The phenomenon is part of the folklore of the area.

Obviously these temples are far from being dormant structures.

Castlerigg is a stone circle in the north of England whose 360° unencumbered view of the post-glacial Cumbrian valleys and mountains makes it a sight to behold

A stunning setting for a temple. Castlerigg, England.

at any time of the day or year, in the rain or freezing cold. Energy readings taken of a prominent stone on its eastern flank shows it giving off an ultrasonic signal at sunrise, and when its surrounding area was checked for electrical ground current, the meter went haywire every time it crossed the perimeter of the circle. Eventually the machine ceased to function.[11] The idea that the temples are encircled by a force field has been widely explored. Electrodes planted at henge monuments in southern England reveal how their earthen ditches break the transmission of telluric ground current and conduct its electricity into the ditch, in effect concentrating the energy and releasing it at the entrance to the site, sometimes at double the rate of the surrounding land. This has led to the realization that stone circles, even mounds like Silbury Hill, behave like concentrators of electromagnetic energy.[12] At nearby Avebury, surges in geomagnetic energy have been detected in the remaining stones of the two avenues leading into this massive stone circle, suggesting that, in their original form, these winding causeways were placed on or aligned with areas rich in electromagnetic energy which the stones conducted into the stone circle.[13]

The magnetic readings at Avebury die away at night to a far greater level than can be accounted for under natural circumstances. They charge back at sunrise, with the ground telluric current from the surrounding land attracted to the henge just as magnetic fluctuations of the site reach their maximum.[14] This reveals inasmuch why temple-builders like the Egyptians regarded the temple as a living organism that sleeps at night and awakens at dawn, to the accompaniment of orations from the priests.

The magnetic properties of temples are enhanced by stones containing substantial amounts of magnetite, which makes them behave like weak, albeit huge, magnets. Where granite is used, the inherent magnetic field is strong enough to deflect a compass needle, in some cases by as much as 180° from north to south.[15] One of the scientists who painstakingly took magnetic readings of all remaining sixty-seven stones at Avebury made the following discovery: "The south pole of each stone faces the next stone in line as you move toward the circle. This arrangement means the north poles of the stones generally point south, which are opposing the geomagnetic field. Inside the main and minor stone circles, the south poles of all stones point at the next stone in the circle, in a clockwise direction, with two exceptions: the stones at the two intact causeway entrances have their magnetic poles aligned with those of the avenue, rather than with the clockwise pattern of the circle, up to a ninety-degree difference from their companions in the ring." [16] Those two massive stones happen to

A small portion of Carnac. Impressive, even with many stones removed for building material.

be the entrance stones into the site. The conclusion by physicist John Burke reveals how the design of Avebury and its aligned 'magnets' follows the same principle as a particle collider, such as Fermi Lab, America's largest circular atomic accelerator, in which airborne ions are steered in one direction.

Very similar conditions exist at the megalithic stone metropolis that is Carnac, where 4000 stones arranged in up to thirteen parallel lines, 4300 feet in length, begin and end in egg-shaped stone circles; these stand on deposits of water, where the air is easily ionized. Like Avebury, the height of the stones increases from two feet to as much as thirteen the closer they get to their respective circles. Pierre Mereux's exhaustive study of Carnac shows how the dolmens in the surrounding area amplify and release the telluric energy throughout the day, with the strongest magnetometer readings occurring at dawn. The voltage and magnetic variations are related, and follow the phenomenon known as electric induction: "The dolmen behaves practically as a *bobine* (coil), an electrician would say solenoid, in which currents are induced, provoked by the variations, weaker or stronger, of the surrounding magnetic field. But these phenomena are not produced with any intensity unless the dolmen is constructed with crystalline rocks rich in quartz, such as granite... it is the granite that is important." [17]

His readings of menhirs reveal an energy that pulsates at regular intervals at the base, positively- and negatively-charged, and behaves like ripples in a pond, up to thirty-six feet away from the upright stones; extreme pulsations recycle approximately every

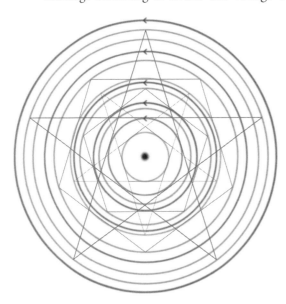

Plan of ripples of energy generated by a menhir. Note how the relationship of the energy conforms to an underlying geometry. Outeiro, Portugal.

70 minutes, showing that the menhirs charge and discharge regularly.[18] Mereux also noticed how the voltage of standing stones in the Grand Ménec alignment diminished the farther away they lay from the stone circle, which itself behaved as a kind of condenser – a concentrator of energy.

Before a violent earthquake toppled it, one of the area's biggest stones, Le Grand Menhir Brisé, stood 64 feet tall, with a volume of 4732 cubic feet. It could theoretically have generated a magnetic field of 134,000 gammas, close to 1/3 of the earth's magnetic field and enough to deflect a compass.[19] It makes one wonder the kind of effects that can be elicited at sacred sites covered by thousands of these menhirs!

Mereux came to the conclusion that a menhir acts like an accumulator, a dolmen like a coil, and a stone circle like a concentrator and accumulator. The composition of the stones and their ability to conduct energy was not lost on Mereux and others either. Being very high in quartz, the specially chosen rocks are piezoelectric, which is to say they generate electricity when compressed or subjected to vibrations. So, Carnac and its 4000-plus stones, being positioned on thirty-one fractures of the most active earthquake zone in France, is in a constant state of vibration, making the stones electromagnetically active. It demonstrates that the menhirs were not planted on this location by chance – particularly as they were transported from 60 miles away – because their presence and orientation is in direct relationship to the terrestrial magnetism.

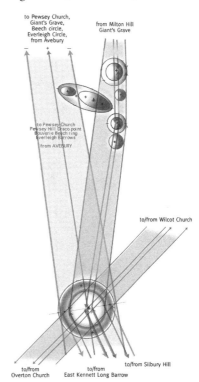

Rising amid the idyllic backdrop of the Usk Valley in Wales, the Llangynidr menhir stands at 14

A group of mounds anchoring and shaping the flow of telluric lines on the land. Wiltshire.

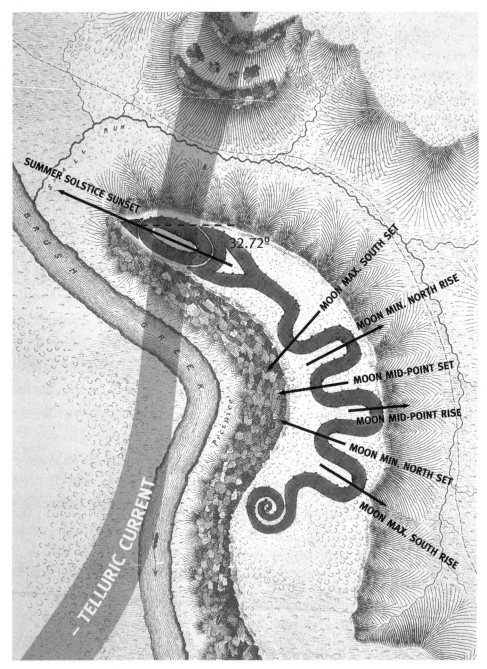

Labels in image:
SUMMER SOLSTICE SUNSET
32.72°
MOON MAX. SOUTH SET
MOON MIN. NORTH RISE
MOON MID-POINT SET
MOON MID-POINT RISE
MOON MIN. NORTH SET
MOON MAX. SOUTH RISE
TELLURIC CURRENT
BRUSH CREEK

Ohio's Serpent Mound. The egg holds a feminine telluric current which connects with other nearby mounds. Each coil references important solar/lunar events over the course of the year. A superb example of a temple whose form follows its function yet does not reveal its true purpose to the uninitiated eye.

feet and has been the subject of careful study for years, principally because one dowser who touched the monolith was sent airborne by the static shock he received. Dowsers have noted how the spiral energy circles up from the ground and around the stone like a cosmic whirlpool. As have scientists measuring its magnetic field strength, who've noted anomalies far beyond normal, leading one to comment, "a water-diviner told

us about it, and we went there and found something measurable. It may be the stone contains, geologically, the reason for the anomaly. Or it may be caused by something we don't yet understand. But I do not personally believe that the stone was accidentally chosen or accidentally placed. The people who put it there knew about its power." [20]

Like their European counterparts, the mounds along the Mississippi River and the Ohio valleys have yielded no skeletal remains, so it stands to reason they were constructed with another purpose in mind. True to form, they have been found to lie at the confluence of telluric energy paths. Where mounds were actually used for ceremonial burials, these too lie along telluric paths, for it was custom to rest the body of a shaman or prominent elder on a spirit road, enabling their soul to journey to the otherworld as quickly as a possible in order that it might convey important information from the world of spirit back to the tribe.

Central Ohio is very rich in such temples, its most famous effigy being the sinuous Serpent Mound. Each of its coils references the rising and setting motions of the Sun and Moon at their extreme positions during the year, as well as the equinox sunrise and sunset;[21] in its mouth, the serpent holds an egg where once stood an omphalos or ritual pole. An alignment through the egg's long axis not only marks the summer solstice sunset, its angle of alignment from east to southeast appears to be 32.72°. It is through this oval feature that the telluric line passes, connecting with a group of ancillary mounds to the northeast, while to the southwest, the energy's path crosses a nearby field and precisely through a genuine crop circle that manifested in 2003. The quarter-mile long serpent sits on a peninsula surrounded by rivers, and to reach it one must first walk past two large mounds that essentially mark the en-trance to the site. Several giant skeletons were exhumed here,[22] and what's more, each of the mounds also mark the nodes of a series of intersecting telluric lines.

During the approach of thunderstorms, magnetometer readings reveal how the site's magnetic field drops dramatically, no doubt helped by the proximity of water as well as the Serpent Mound's position atop a peninsula of dolomite, a particularly electrically-conductive type of limestone.[23] The entire sacred temple even sits in the middle of a massive geological magnetic anomaly caused by a *crypto-explosion* – a type of impact crater.

Still in Ohio, Chillicothe is known for its high concentration of mounds, all of which fall between two large regions of magnetic fields to the north and south. Every mound is placed on a single magnetic anomaly, and where there exists a long straight path of positive magnetic anomalies, a linear mound was erected with its ridge running across them all.[24]

Further west, across the bay from San Francisco stands the hulking mass of Mount Tamalpais. There are at least six native sacred sites here, one of which is a seat large enough for a tall person to sit comfortably. Made from a natural outcrop of serpentine, this green stone has strong magnetic properties that greatly disturb compass needles. It too sits over a fault line, and even today it is a landscape temple used for shamanic journeying.[25]

Carved out of the chalk hillside in Wilmington, England, is a 230-foot tall effigy of a human figure with arms extended and touching two tall poles. In many ways it

The Long Man of Wilmington.

is reminiscent of the Egyptian god Ptah marking the primordial mound with his staffs of life. A feminine telluric current runs through its course, but otherwise, the full explanation behind this odd figure remains elusive. It does, however, remind me of the pairs of isolated *menhirs* I often come across in my travels. These stones have always invited me to stand between them with my arms outstretched, not unlike the pose of the Long Man of Wilmington. Even though I am very tall, the paired stones lie beyond my fingertips; but for someone around nine feet in height they would be an ideal fit. The sensation when standing between them is very pleasant, making you feel recharged and balanced after just a few minutes. It is often the case that one stone emits a positive charge and the other a negative charge, not dissimilar to the way the electrical circuits on the palms of the hands are arranged,[26] suggesting these staffs of stone may once have been used to charge or stimulate the body's electromagnetic circuitry, the Neolithic equivalent of a morning cup of expresso.

Such paired menhirs share three things in common: first, in Ireland, Wales and Portugal they all appear to be spaced equally apart as if measured by the same architect; second, the energy field alternating between them forms an infinity symbol, with its intersecting

'Infinity' movement of energy between menhirs. Preseli, Wales.

loop crossing where a standing person's heart would be (or the base of the spine in a much taller person); and third, the energy originates from an invisible whirlpool about ten feet in front of the stones, what dowsers call *a blind spring*. A small departure from this format is Men-an-Tol in Cornwall ("stone with a hole"). While the same infinity motion of energy is present between its two upright stones, the

Men-an-Tol's energy field. England.

exact crossover sits in the middle of a holed stone. Since remote times people have brought themselves and their children here to be healed. These stones are made of granite, they are magnetic and naturally radioactive, and the obvious comparison to a modern MRI scanner is inescapable.

In 1983 a comprehensive study was finally undertaken to locate magnetism in sacred sites. Using the Rollright stone circle in England as a test subject, the engineer Charles Brooker discovered that "the average intensity of the [geomagnetic] field within the circle was significantly lower than that measured outside, as if the stones acted as a shield." [27] His magnetometer survey shows how bands of magnetic force spiral into the stone circle through a narrow gap of three stones that deviate slightly from the perimeter to create an entrance. These bands then spiral towards the center of the circle as if descending down a hole. To add to the bizarre behavior of the local magnetic field, two of the circle's western stones are magnetically pulsating, tying-in with earlier findings around the Rollrights' outlying menhirs, which pulsate with concentric rings of alternating current and resemble ripples in a pond.[28]

Energy behaving like a force field seems to validate the idea that a protective zone was established around sacred sites following the 'harnessing of the snake', as defined in the Edfu texts. As strange connections go, it brought to my mind another ancient statement, this time from the *Funerary Texts* at Saqqara, and a curious one at that: "Seven degrees of perfection enable passage from earth to heaven." This instruction is widely interpreted as referring to a series of challenges the soul needs to pass before gaining entry into the otherworld. Then again, with Egyptians being so fond of allegory and metaphor, I wondered if the phrase alludes to some doorway or protective barrier the individual crosses when they enter the temple; a passage from earth to heaven suggests a crossing from the profane, material world into a heavenly otherworld, which is precisely the purpose of the temple. But why should there be 'seven degrees of perfection': does the visitor undergo a process of purification? Possibly. If you recall, the temple was considered a mirror of heaven

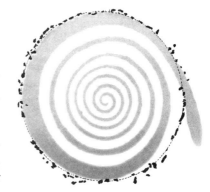

Magnetomer survey of the Rollright stone circle.

on earth, the material dwelling place of a god as well as its physical embodiment. The purity of energy of the temple was everything, and defilement of the *sanctum*, physically or energetically, was seen as a precursor to the downfall of the spirituality of the individual, and hence, the collapse of the tribe.

The more I looked at this extract as an allegory, the more the idea of a protective device made sense. How all this was to be proved was another matter, but the discovery of a force field around stone circles already shows these places do define a threshold from one reality into another.

In support of this possibility, there exists a kind of woven electromagnetic grid over the entire face of the globe. Discovered by the man whose name it bears, Dr. Ernst Hartmann, this network is composed of small rectangular 'nets', and appears as a structure rising from the earth, each line 9 inches thick and spaced at intervals of 6 feet 6 inches by 8 feet, magnetically oriented; the dimensions are very close to the mathematical roots of the Great Pyramid.[29] Hartmann noticed that the intersecting points of the network – the knots – are influenced by underground veins of water as well as magnetic forces emanating naturally from the earth. Consequently, he found that the knots alter in strength from time to time and that a relationship exists between the location of the knots and the adverse health of people who work or sleep on them. Dowsers have been aware of this *geopathic stress* for centuries, and it is not uncommon for them to be hired to alter the location of the Hartmann net on a property, by embedding conductors such as metal rods into the ground, which stretch the electromagnetic net away from desired locations. It is the dowser's equivalent of 'piercing the snake'.

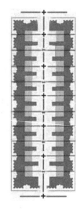

The Field of Reeds entrance with the seven positive 'gates'.

Conversely, the holes of the net are places of neutral space where the weather is perfect. Could a relationship exist between temples and the stretching of this net?

Nothing more came of my musings until I read a fascinating research document by the geobiologist Blanche Merz, in which she conducted readings at temples in Europe, Egypt and India, and found the Hartmann net to be stretched around the temples like a protective membrane. As Merz wrote: "the gigantic Pharaonic structures have this in common: the Hartmann network forms a veritable dam of 18 geomagnetic lines around the perimeter of the buildings." [30] Celebrated temples such as Saqqara, Karnak, Luxor, Kom Ombu, as well as the pyramids, enjoy an immense neutral zone, much in the same way as the henge monuments in Britain circulate electromagnetic forces which concentrate the energy *inside* the temples and in a controlled manner that is beneficial to people. All these places are listed in the Edfu *Building Texts* as the original primordial mounds of the gods. Merz went on to find other energy hotspots at Chartres, Santiago de Compostela, and a plethora of Indian sacred sites; in Tibet she found that *stupas* marked with *nagas* (serpents) identify the position of Hartmann knots, and that telluric energy is transmitted via these upright stones.[31]

After the preparatory entrance at Saqqara, one enters the courtyard of the mansion of the gods.

Naturally, this revived my interest in the 'seven degrees of perfection' and the possibility they might be referring to thresholds of some kind. As it happens, in Egyptian mythology, the passage of the soul into heaven is made through a place called *Sekhet Ianu*, the "Fields of Reeds", a land of paradise where the spirit spends eternity; we simply know it today as the *Elyssian Fields*. Egyptian mythology states that to reach this much-desired land one must pass through a series of gates.[32]

During a visit to Saqqara I had the opportunity to study the passageway leading from the profane world and into the grand courtyard and its evocative stepped pyramid, engineered by Imhotep, an architect of the gods. This passageway is unique in that it is a colonnade of 18 reeds separated by narrow alcoves. Each of the alcoves discharges an alternating field of positive- and negatively-charged force which serves both as a barrier into the temple while at the same time influencing the body's electromagnetic circuitry. In essence, as one walks down this preparatory hallway into Saqqara, one is suitably entranced prior to making contact with the courtyard of the temple and the mansion of the gods. In its time, this was the procedure necessary for dispelling negative thoughts and feelings one may be harboring before entering the sacred abode. Or as the *Funerary Texts* put it, one had "to master oneself before crossing the threshold of each gate." [33]

The numerical relationship between the 18 reeds and the 18 Hartmann lines protecting the perimeter of the temples is unmistakable. But for me, the revelation lay in the readings of the alternating energy field, for they consisted of exactly seven positive-charged currents. Suddenly an answer to the 'seven degrees of wisdom' loomed near. Merz' own research revealed that at the very wide thresholds preceding the initiatory rooms of the temples, the Hartmann net traverses the entrances with *seven tightly-packed grid lines* protecting "the passage from the known to unknown." [34]

I found this engineering isn't reserved just for Egyptian temples. In Ireland, the entrance to the ceremonial chamber at Newgrange is similarly protected by alternating energy currents, with seven positively-charged lines anchored on either side of the chambered passageway before reaching the inner *sanctum*.[35] It seems these precautions were undertaken in different parts of the world, not just for the protection of the site, but also as a preparatory area for the initiate prior to crossing the threshold between visible and invisible, much like the ritual a Muslim pilgrim undertakes as he winds seven times in an ever-decreasing spiral around the Ka'Ba before touching this stone called the "Soul-Body."

Churches erected after the 16th century rarely conform to the underlying telluric pathways of the land. This is not unusual, in fact, it is perfectly consistent with the religious outlook of the times and the move towards scientific rationalism. This did not just happen in Europe, but also in North America. In all the churches I have visited throughout the United States I have been hard-pushed to find a structure referencing telluric forces. I'd thought the earliest churches erected in New England would have maintained a connection to the old ways, but then, given the Puritan background, it wasn't surprising to discover they didn't. After all, these were the very same fun-loving individuals who'd encouraged the destruction of sacred sites in the Old World, and with it the abolition of festivities celebrating the life-affirming cycles of the earth. The closest I found is the cathedral of St. John the Divine in New York. This bizarre conglomerate of Romanesque, Byzantine and Gothic-revival styles is sited beside two telluric lines; one flows through the garden fountain and its statue of, incredibly, the archangel Michael; the other, through the adjacent Senate Hall, once the site of a Masonic meeting place attended by George Washington, a Freemason!

If you look hard enough you'll find exceptions. New Mexico is a place where the spirit of the land is still venerated, and I was pleased to discover that in Santa Fe, the oldest church in America, built of adobe in 1610 and dedicated to our friend San Miguel, stands on the node of two telluric lines. It also stands on top of a Navajo sacred site. Several miles to the north is El Santuario de Chimayo, a contemporary Roman Catholic pilgrimage site with what must be – aside from the sacred mound of Siauliai in Lithuania – a record amount of crucifixes per square inch in the world. The present adobe structure was erected in 1810, yet it is oriented northeast, a feature common to very ancient temples. I was therefore not surprised to find two telluric energy lines forming a node at its center, but referencing only the *inner* part of the building which, I later discovered, had been an Anasazi place of veneration, later honored by the Tewa, who coveted its healing soil and highly mineral waters, just as 300,000 pilgrims do today.

Not far from Santa Fe, the Spanish built a church at Pecos Pueblo in 1621. It is not on a telluric line, but the adjacent native kiva certainly is. Obviously the native tribes followed the traditional practice, which their European overlords sometimes made use of, even if for the most part they were unaware.

Where I did find a virgin and 'modern' church built to old temple specifications was in Pasadena, California, at the Mission San Gabriel Arcangel, constructed in 1791 by Father Cruzado of Cordoba in the Moorish style typical of his original domicile. While dowsing the building I discovered the telluric lines all pass through the doorways of the *original* structure, not the additions, with the node marking the altar. But when one energy line ended at a brick wall I thought my theory was blown, and that the Spanish church builders, too, had probably lost the plot by the 18th century. Until the gardener, who unbeknownst to me had been quietly watching in the shadows, came over to tell me that the wall where my theory apparently failed was one of the original doors of the building, since bricked up and plastered over.

So, honor is due to Father Cruzado.

It is not just the newer religious places that loosely follow the telluric forces, or miss them entirely. Temples along the Nile rescued from rising floodwaters after the building of the Aswan Dam and moved to higher ground, have not retained their relationship to telluric forces either. Philae, while still an exceptionally moving site, has its main telluric current cross diagonally in the courtyard, missing all but the corner of the building; while Abu Simbel, although unquestionably an impressive restoration, has no energy whatsoever. As I later found out, this was independently validated by Blanche Merz: "18 geomagnetic force lines encircle Egyptian temples, except where they have been moved, as with Philae. Even engineers responsible for re-assembling the limestone blocks noted "the temple is no longer the same." [36]

Kiva and en-suite Spanish Mission. Pecos, New Mexico.

Why are these energies fundamental to places of power? The human body, far from being a series of chemical interactions, is now widely accepted as being made of particles of energy. It is a walking electromagnetic edifice sensitive to minute fluctuations in the local geomagnetic field. With electromagnetism playing such a pivotal role in the temple, its influence on the body and its 72% content of water is immediate; not to mention the human skeleton, since bone is a crystalline structure through which flows an electrical charge.

Because the blood that flows through our veins and arteries carries a fair amount of iron, magnetism will work on it like a magnet re-organizes iron filings on a sheet on paper. The same is true for the brain. Substantial amounts of biogenetic particles of magnetite are found in brain tissue and the cerebral cortex. These pyramid-shaped crystals allow humans to detect the Earth's magnetic field. However, under the right conditions, magnetic stimulation of the brain induces dreamlike states, even in waking consciousness.[37]

Lastly, and possibly most importantly, is the effect that telluric energies in temples may have on the pineal gland, a pine cone-shaped protuberance located near the center of the brain. Fluctuations in the geomagnetic field affect the production of chemicals made by the pineal, such as *pinoline*, which interacts with another neurochemical in the brain, *seratonin*, the end result being the creation of *DMT,* a hallucinogen. It is believed that this is the neurochemical trigger for dream states – the hallucinogenic state of consciousness that allows information to be received. In an environment where geomagnetic field intensity is decreased, people are known to experience psychic and shamanic states.[38] It is one of the reasons why the temples were built, and why anyone would wish to attend.

An Egyptian goddess, and Khrishna. The concept of builder gods and archangels
in charge of earth energy is shared across most cultures.

Djehuty, god of wisdom, with his wife Seshat, goddess of buildings.

12

THE SEVEN PRINCIPLES OF SACRED SPACE:

3. SACRED MEASURE.

By means of the doctrine of numbers, virtuous
conduct is brought into contact with invisible things.
~ The Chinese Book of Diagrams

Djehuti arrives at the primordial mound, where a new temple is about to be built, and recites, "I came here in my true form upon the foundation ground of the Great Seat of Ra-Harakhte. I cause its long dimension to be good, its breadth to be exact, all its measurements to be according to the norm, all its sanctuaries to be in the place where they should be, and its halls to resemble the sky." [1] After this declaration of intent, Djehuti and the builder gods establish a unit of measure based on the length of an arm, called the cubit. They are joined by the Seven Sages and Djehuti's wife, Seshat, the goddess of sacred buildings. Seshat then initiates the ceremony of Stretching the Cord, a crucial part in the foundation of the physical temple. Djehuti picks up the thread of the ceremony from here: "I hold the peg. I grasp the handle of the club and grip the measuring cord with Seshat. I turn my eyes to the movements of the stars... I count off time, I watch the clock, I establish the four corners of your temple" [2] In this manner the builder gods establish the four sides of their Enclosure, 'speedy of fashioning', and thus the Great Seat – the mansion of the gods – is born.

This account from the Edfu *Building Texts* describes the process of measuring the temple – the third principle in the creation of a sacred space.

Being sticklers for observing nature's ways and means, it would be astounding if the ancient architects resorted to some plain unit of measure when it came to laying out their temples. As it happens they didn't: they correctly observed the rhythms of the universe, then figured out how to extrapolate important processes via the use of number.

The Egyptians worked with the Cubit, one of the most accurate methods of measure, and commensurate with the principal dimensions of the Earth. Measurements taken by satellite can nowadays establish an accurate picture of the planet's girth to several decimal places, and yet, calculations using the Egyptians' arcane system comes remarkably close. Armed with the Sacred Cubit it is possible to calculate such things as the Earth's polar radius as well as its equatorial circumference.[3] Conversely, the cubit was employed in the layout of the pyramids, from whose measures it is possible to extrapolate all the numbers relating to the size and functions of the planet. It could be said that the Great Pyramid alone is an analog of the planet. The reason was two-fold: one, so that the structure would serve as a reference book for posterity; and two, as the Chinese were well aware, by means of distilling the universe down to number, man-made structures enter into a dialogue with the rest of the universe, and from that conversation, favorable forces come into contact with the structure and the people who enter it.

The cubit system also took into consideration the relationships between the Earth and the Sun, and harmonized weight and time with measure. This timeless and universal appeal meant it was adopted by many other cultures, principally the Babylonians and later, with some alterations, by the Greeks and Romans, before finally becoming the basis of the English Imperial System of Measures.[4]

The engineer Hugh Harleston, Jr. spent a goodly portion of his life studying the 32-square mile metropolis of Teotihuacan. He calculated that the principal unit of measurement used by its creators was the *hunab*, which in the Aztec language means 'unified measure'. Harleston figured out the *hunab* is commensurate with the Egyptian cubit,[5] and its application in both the measurements of the structures and the spatial proportions of the ground plan of the entire ceremonial city revealed the builders' predilection for using the precessional numbers 18, 36, 54, 72, 108 and 144. Just as with Egypt and Angkor, the structures of Teotihuacan employ the same sky-ground dualism, and go a step further in that they are positioned so as to reflect the precise numerical proportions of orbits of planets in the solar system; even the proportional distances between principal structures such as the Sun and Moon pyramids correspond to the ratios of the music scale. With its use as a calendar, and repository of stellar and triangular data, the temple complex of Teotihuacan is nothing short of a cosmic university.[6]

One of the most methodical attempts at revealing a common unit of length employed in ancient temples was conducted by another engineer, Alexander Thom, who surveyed hundreds of stone circles throughout the British Isles and the Carnac region.[7] In old times, surveyors and tradespeople in the Iberian Peninsula used the *vara* ("stick") as a standard unit of measure. It emerged in France as a *verge*, and upon its northern migration to Britain it became the *yard*, which originally meant 'a rod of wood'. Thom noticed how the value of the *vara* averaged 2.75 feet in Iberia, and how this stick was exported during the *Conquista* to the Americas, where it resurfaced in California, Mexico and Peru with an average length of 2.76 feet.[8] Following accurate measurements of stone circles using a theodolite, Thom proved that the sites did follow a common unit of measure, in whole number multiples or fractions thereof. It was based on a specific unit of 2.72 feet. Thom would call it the *Megalithic Yard*.

Only one such comparable unit of measure has existed in recent times, the *pu* of 2.72 miles,[9] last used in the region around Cambodia, home of the Angkor temples.

Thom's hard work was given extensive analysis by top statisticians Broadbent and Hammersley, and his results were later confirmed by the rigorous mathematician David George Kendal.

After thirty-nine years of on-site exploration, the temples must have exerted their influence on the Scottish engineer, albeit subconsciously, because he later became aware of how so many of the stone circles, avenues and stone rows of the ancestors also took important astronomical events into consideration. Thom's surveys of the 5000-year-old complex at Callanais alone is generally accepted as one of the great contributions to the field of archaeoastronomy, and demonstrates just how the ancient builders incorporated metrology,

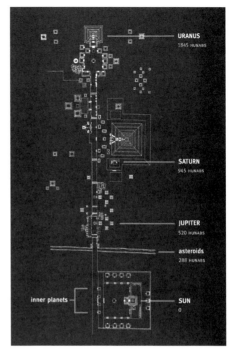

Harlesdon's calculations of Teotihuacan as a reflection of the planets in the solar system.

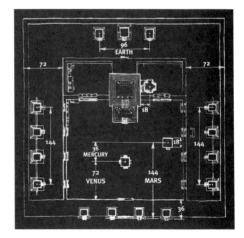

geometry and astronomy into their creations of stone. As he pointed out, "Whatever we do we must avoid approaching the study with the idea that Megalithic man was our inferior in ability to think." [10]

So, there are measures, and then there are sacred measures.

The world of the ancients was all about correspondences. Since the mechanics of the cosmos can be reduced to numerical values, if the blueprint of a temple is based on a unit of measure derived from fundamental universal forces, the temple establishes a resonance and correspondence with all that exists.

God, so the saying goes, is a geometer, and it is not unusual to find numerous murals, illustrations and statues in which It is shown holding a globe in one hand and

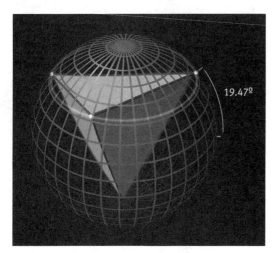

Tetrahedron circumscribed within a sphere.

a compass in the other, as though he/she is measuring the world. Now thanks to Thom's discovery of the exact proportion of the Megalithic Yard, it becomes easier to work out the method by which the master builders arrived at 2.72 as the unit of measure.

The primary geometric building blocks of matter are the tetrahedron and the sphere. The tetrahedron is a triangular pyramid, and its geometry is seen in nature as the lattice that connects the chemical bonds of molecules; in the case of water, the hydrogen bonds

between molecules of water are held in equilibrium by tetrahedral geometry, and the space between H_2O molecules in solid ice measures a uniform 2.72 angstroms.[11]

The geometric solid that is the sphere speaks for itself. When the two come together, an amazing thing happens: when a tetrahedron is circumscribed within a sphere, so that each of its four points touch the surface of the sphere, the ratio of the surface area of these two solids is precisely 2.72.

To go off on a slight tangent, the edges of a circumscribed tetrahedron touch the surface of the sphere at exactly 19.47°.

Transposed onto the Earth, this is equivalent to latitude 19.47° N, where we find the most active hotspot of energy on the planet, the Mauna Loa volcano; the temple complex of Teotihuacan is sited to within 0' 05" of the same latitude. As strange

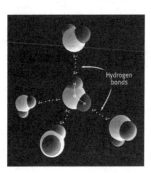

Water molecules and their hydrogen bonds.

coincidences go, 19.47 sq. km marks the area of the parish of São Miguel in the Açores, which we encountered in an earlier chapter as one of the locations along the New Zealand-Santiago de Compostela ley line.

But let us return to 2.72. This numerical value is also found in the orderly motion of heavenly bodies. The Solar Year consists of 365.242 days, whereas the Lunar Year consists of 354.367 days. The difference between the two is 10.875 days.

10.875 days divided by the full lunar month of 29.53 days equals 2.7154, or 2.72 for short.[12]

God the geometer.

It seems this numerical ratio is repeated at many all levels of reality, what is referred to as a *transdimensional constant.* And the linear expression of this value culminates in the Megalithic Yard of 2.72 feet.

Or, if you work in inches, 32.64.

A unit of measure derived from such numerical correspondences becomes an analog of the actions taking place on Earth as well the universe. A temple that is based on such a universal harmonic means that all actions taking place within its space come under the influence of that harmonic.

As does anyone who interacts with it.

The sanctuary of Athena Pronaia at Delphi, a truly feminine temple. Greece.

13

THE SEVEN PRINCIPLES
OF SACRED SPACE:
4. STONE.

Each of us is carving a stone, erecting a column, or cutting a piece of stained glass in the construction of something much bigger than ourselves.

~ Adrienne Clarkson

Wales is dark, brooding territory. In a positive kind of way. Mostly mountainous and composed of some of the oldest and volcanic rocks on the planet, it once provided the sonorous bluestones that make up two circles and a horseshoe of Stonehenge. Many of its sacred sites are associated with Arthurian legends, and dolmens such as Coetan Arthur still bear his name. The farther north one travels the more mysterious and concealed it becomes, especially in Ynis Mon – now the isle of Anglesey – poised on the tip of this proud land, and separated from it by the thin Menai Strait. Its isolation was perhaps why the Druids chose it as the seat of one of their academies, and later served as the last protective barrier against the encroaching Roman legions.

Druids fascinated Julius Caesar. They terrified Nero, and no wonder: a group whose wisdom descended from the Followers of Horus, stories abound of their ability to cast spells and bend the laws of nature to their will. One account by Tacitus describes the moment Roman soldiers finally cornered the Druids on Ynis Mon: "a line of warriors of the opposition was stationed, mainly made up of armed men, amongst them women, with their hair blowing in the wind, while they were carrying torches. Druids were amongst them, shouting terrifying spells, their hands raised towards the heavens, which terrified our soldiers who had never seen such a thing before, so much that their limbs became paralysed. As a result, they remained stationary and were injured." [1]

Two thousand years later and the power inherent in the rocks of Wales has hardly diminished. During a visit to a remote standing stone near Preseli I wandered up a hill with a colleague into what looked like unchartered territory. On a desolate plateau, at the end of a track long overgrown with wild grasses, stood a hulking menhir. "It looks like it hasn't spoken to anyone in hundreds of years," we exclaimed, simultaneously. Indeed, the bulbous stone seemed like it was glad to finally receive visitors. It's strange how such an inanimate object exudes so much personality. I reached out my hand to touch the surface of the stone, whereupon a magnetic force, like an invisible arm, reached out and pulled my hand to its warm surface.

For what felt like an eternity, I could not retract my hand, and all the while marriages, births, ceremonies, duels, festivities, deaths and whole cycles of lives and gossip were downloaded into my head. It was as though I'd watched a hundred centuries of reality shows in seconds. Even stranger, I was later able to recall most of the details. My colleague witnessed the whole episode and asked me if I felt fine, because obviously I didn't, and for the next twenty four hours I was nauseous, drained of energy, as if the 72% of water in my body had just been microwaved.

Given that the stones stand at hotspots of telluric currents soaking up electromagnetic forces, it is not unusual for sensitives, dowsers or lay people to get electric shocks at sacred sites, particularly if the stone's residual energy has not discharged for some time.[2] A researcher at Newgrange in Ireland received a shock from the mound's lintel stone one morning which affected his whole arm. The second time he did it, hesitantly, the charge was gone, as if the stone had discharged itself.[3] The same happened to a retired military officer while touching one of the monoliths of the Rollright stone circle, which left his arm numb for 20 minutes.[4]

The red granite monoliths of the Sphinx temple.

Another person investigating the Rollright stones in 1919 describes how "my landlady was afraid to go as lights had been seen and there were tales of people losing their memory after touching them... I went one evening after work and was fingering one of the group of 'Whispering Knights'... when my hand and arm began to tingle badly and I felt as though I was being pushed away... The tingling lasted throughout the night and the next day."[5] One scientist, coincidentally working at the very same site, reported that "for several nights when there was no moon, I saw a pool of diffuse white light which seemed to be coming out of the ground; it rose a bit above the stones and then tapered off. The whole centre of the circle was generating light."[6]

Such reported and experienced effects are a strong indication of an active, living and breathing, organic temple.

Pierre-Roland Giot, a Breton archaeologist with an international reputation, once asked some engaging questions regarding the role of stones at sacred sites. For example, there seems to be no reason to erect thousands of stones to verify certain risings or settings of the sun or moon. It would have been much simpler for the builders to plant wooden poles; even Professor Alexander Thom realized the sites were far more elaborate than needed.

More questions follow: although they were not built as tombs, the structures were sometimes rediscovered later and used as tombs by people with different views and purposes. And why quarry the stones at a distance when there were plenty available nearby? Was the type of stone important? The architects did not want any old granite but a specific granite. The bluestones of Stonehenge were quarried 140 miles away and transported down a mountain, over rough, undulating terrain, across an estuary, then through marshland, fields, forests and plains. It's the same story in Egypt: the cyclopean red granite blocks of the inner chambers of pyramids, weighing over 50 tons each, came from a quarry in Aswan 625 miles to the south. None of this makes any rational sense unless the stones possess specific properties that make them an integral part of the energetic experience of the temple.

Granite gives off a significant electrostatic charge, and the type used in the Great Pyramid contains 25% quartz and has the ability to enhance sound.[7] The magnetite contained in the granite, often in great quantity, is a natural magnet that creates around it a certain magnetic field. In the Carnac stone avenues, the granite consists of feldspar, quartz, mica, other trace minerals and up to 30% magnetite.[8]

An Egyptian pyramid is a fine example of combining different stone to create a kind of energy storage device. As far as the Giza pyramids are concerned, the core consists of red granite, one of the most conductive rocks on earth due to its high content of quartz, iron, and magnetite. It exudes a natural radioactivity. This core is encased in a rough limestone with a high content of magnesium that acts as an electrical conductor. The limestone was then dressed on the outside by a different type of limestone called *Tura* – finer-grained and highly polished – and because it contains minute traces of magnesium, unlike the inner limestone, it serves as an insulator, keeping the energy *inside* the temple. Naturally, this energy seeks to escape to the top of the structure, so the tips of the pyramids were capped with a Benben stone, often made of dororite and covered with electrum, a two-thirds mix of gold and silver, making it an excellent conductor.

The people entrusted with choosing the correct stone for the temples in Egypt were the Masons, who most likely would have been trained at Heliopolis and certainly would have known the properties of stone, and what stone can do for you, and *to* you. These adepts would much later re-emerge as Free Masons.

In a previous chapter we learned that when the ground for the temple is being prepared, Horus 'overthrows the snake' and the builder gods settle beside it. Once the veins of water and electromagnetism have been manipulated, the measure of the temple is applied, and the fourth principle of sacred space goes into motion, namely the anchoring of the telluric lines of energy. And that's where the correct use of stone is important. In addition to the magnetite, the stones used for sacred sites contain large amounts of quartz, a piezoelectric substance that not only can hold a charge, but like the silica used for computers, it can be instructed to do so.

This may answer the fundamental question of why the stone was needed far-and-above what seemed necessary: it prevented the roving telluric forces from moving, by anchoring them to the spot.

After all, there's nothing more inconvenient than spending years building a fabulous temple only to discover the underlying 'serpent' has slithered elsewhere by the time you've finished!

The ancients did not regard stone as Victorian scientists once did, that it is nothing more than lifeless matter. To them, each stone held specific properties, because, and quite rightly, every stone is made under different conditions. In the world of correspondences, the appropriate type of stone enhances the purpose for which the temple was created.

Being the explosive and expansive personality that it is, the Sun was considered masculine. Its energetic properties are mirrored on Earth by volcanic action.

Thus, volcanic rock vectors masculine energy, and temples where masculine forces are at work are built predominantly with granite, particularly red granite, and basalt, dolorite, greenstone and serpentine.

Conversely, the energy of the Moon was associated with feminine properties, due to the Moon's influence on the fertility cycles of women, animals and crops, as well as the fluid motion of water; plus, the Moon is a reflector of the light from the

Shorter bluestones dwarfed by sarsens in the lunar-solar Stonehenge.

masculine Sun. Thus, rocks borne of the sedimentary action of water were considered feminine, and temples designed to vector feminine qualities are built predominantly with limestone, sandstone, sarsen (a highly compressed sandstone), marble, schist, and on rare occasions such as the floor of the temple of the Sphinx, alabaster.

Masculine and feminine do not imply genders, they are merely types of polarity, much like electricity has its positive and negative currents.

Not all temples favor one quality over another. Some were built with dual-purpose in mind, either because the builders wished to create a balanced environment of forces – the Gothic cathedrals being a good example – or because the nature of the temple itself changed over time due to mitigating circumstances. For these types of temples a combination of volcanic and sedimentary stones were used.

On my travels, I have noted that temples where the lunar or feminine principle has been honored are exclusively built with sedimentary stone; for example, temples along the Mediterranean dedicated to Diana or Aphrodite; Denderah, dedicated to the goddess Hathor; and the lunar circle of Avebury – there's not a pebble of granite anywhere in sight. And yet temples with a solar or masculine history always incorporate one element, no matter how small, of sedimentary stone. Just as positive poles on a magnet repel each other, a masculine temple typically requires one feminine element to function properly.

Boys, it seems, will always need girls.

The sacred sites were created with such conviction, such perfection, that even after thousands of years it is still possible to measure the energy originally established there, still attached to the perimeter of the structures, just as we saw in the previous chapter on electromagnetics. It is a testament to the builders who knew how to harness creative forces that would enable the temples to remain as functioning entities for future generations. Archeologists working at sites such as Avebury have often expressed amazement when dowsers locate missing stones that long ago were toppled into pits and covered with soil. One of the most significant archaeological finds of our age took place at Knowlton henge, a smaller version of Avebury, now minus its entire stone circle. A group of dowsing students located its buried stones by tuning-in to their residual energy, and upon digging, the stones were recovered.[9]

With the addition of stone and its anchoring properties, the temple becomes a kind of condenser. The residual energy of the site is stored in the quartz, iron or magnetite of the stone, its accumulated energy discharging on the visitors who act as grounding rods. It is worth pointing out that nowadays one is forced to walk temples wearing shoes, with their insulating rubber soles, thereby minimizing the grounding of the energy of the site through the soles of the feet. Which makes a visit to a stone circle or a mosque that much more invigorating, since one is able to walk barefoot.

Despite its symplicity, the cubic form of the the Ka'ba represents the symbolic geometry of the material world.

14

THE SEVEN PRINCIPLES
OF SACRED SPACE:

5. SACRED GEOMETRY.

*The true mathematical science is that which measureth the invisible
lines and immortal beams which can pass through clod and turf, hill and
dale. It was for this reason, it was accounted by all ancient priests the
chiefest science; for it gave them power both in their words and works.*

~ John Dee, astrologer and scientist

The universe is a vast energy event of which Galileo once remarked, "it cannot
be understood unless one first learns to comprehend the language and interpret
the characters in which it is written… its characters are triangles, circles and other
geometrical figures, without which it is humanly impossible to understand a single
word of it; without these, one is wandering about in a dark labyrinth." [1]

Galileo's predecessors probably faced the same conundrum, but they also reached
the same conclusion: the universe is geometry. Sky-watchers right up to the era of the
Greek gnostics conferred on each of the planets the status of god, referring to them
as *akousmata*, the 'resonant ones', because rather than being lifeless lumps of matter,
those large atoms floating in space are vibrant and alive. When measuring their mean
orbits, one discovers how an inherent geometric order subtends their places in the
sky: the relative orbits of Mercury and Earth are defined by a pentagram; Earth and
Jupiter by nested hexagons; Jupiter and Neptune by a nine-pointed star, and so on. [2]
Since this geometry reflected the heavenly abode of the gods, it was considered sacred,
and so the concept of sacred geometry entered our lexicon.

207

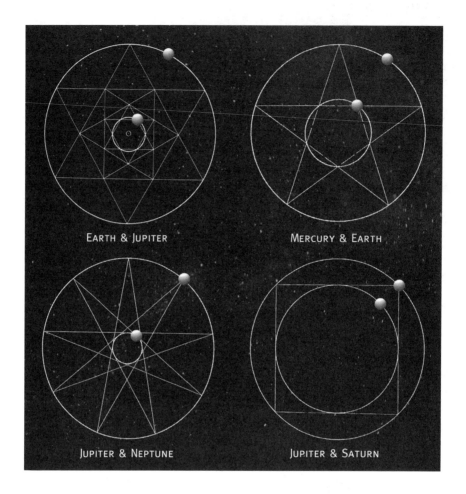

EARTH & JUPITER

MERCURY & EARTH

JUPITER & NEPTUNE

JUPITER & SATURN

The geometric order of the cosmos descends and inhabits our everyday world in the hexagons of a honeycomb, the pentagonal seeds of a dandelion, the octagonal structure of a jellyfish. These harmonics reduce gnomonically into the microscopic world of diatoms, the simplest single-cell life forms, which are resolutely geometric. Smaller still, the molecular bonds that constitute matter are held together by a geometric lattice. Essentially, geometry is a whirlpool of conscious energy manifesting toward solid form. It is the ultimate language of life.

In eastern esoteric and religious philosophy, geometry is seen as an anthropomorphic image of Deity. Its blueprint is reflected in the most essential component of the human body, DNA, where the four base compounds are arranged in bonds of pentagons and hexagons. So like it or not, we are hypnotically drawn to geometric order because, to our biogeometric cells, it is as if we are looking in the mirror. We are a distillation of the universe.

Single-cell diatoms.

The influence of geometric shape on organic substances and metals was most famously demonstrated by Czech patent 91304, in which scaled models of the Great Pyramid were used in Europe to sharpen razor blades and maintain dairy products fresh for up to three weeks.[3] Something about the shape and alignment of this building, even in miniature, has a direct effect on physical, chemical and biological processes. The radio engineer Karel Drbal, who re-discovered the effects of the pyramid shape, reasoned that "by using suitable forms and shapes we should be able to make processes occur faster or delay them." [4] If the environment inside a pyramid is capable of making the crystals in a blade of metal return to their original form, it is highly feasible that the same is possible with human bone, after all, bone is a crystalline structure. The NASA scientist Ottmar Stehle commented that the pyramid shape focuses energy fields, which, he pointed out, is not a far-fetched idea since TV antennas do the same thing.[5] Besides, its shape is a perfect representation of the magnetite crystal, which no doubt played an active part in its design and its influence on the Earth's geomagnetic field.

In his book *Ondes des Formes*, the French engineer and professor of radio Louis Turenne asserts that shapes such as pyramids, spheres and squares act as resonators for telluric and cosmic forces. Just as the shape of a violin improves the quality of tone, shape provides a resonant cavity for crystalline structures.[6] Experiments with geometric shape in Bulgaria and Canada reveal how hospital patients placed in pentagonal shaped rooms have a higher rate of recovery, while schizophrenic patients fare better in trapezoidal rooms; blood placed in spherical shapes coalesces quicker.[7]

It seems that geometric shape can have a corresponding effect on the human body's own geometry. This science was not lost on Czech brewers, who noticed how changing the shape of a barrel has a noticeable effect on the taste of beer.[8]

The geometry of a space influences the way atoms and air interact and move within a given area, just as a vortex in water behaves differently according to the shape through which it flows.[9] Thus, rooms of differing shapes generate different energetic environments that are capable of influencing the senses.

With regard to temples, the geometry of nature was dissected to reveal the inner blueprints of forms and shapes; their cause and effect was measured and

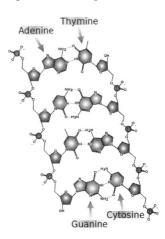

The four base compounds of DNA.

considered. Once it was established that form follows function, specific geometries were applied functionally and strategically to the design of temples so as to induce a corresponding effect on the individual's state of awareness.

The primarily intent was to facilitate growth and transformation of consciousness, the goal being nothing less than the total transmutation of the soul. On a secondary level, the geometric language of nature was used to teach self-understanding in order to accelerate self-development; this was performed, by-and-large, by initiates who understood how to translate shape and symbolism into meditative exercises that led to higher states of consciousness. This practice is found in Buddhist mandalas, the geometric dynamics of which are capable of generating an introspective effect on the minds of their meditators, the idea being to achieve total experience of the source of creation.[10]

There was also a third aim: to surround people with harmony, and in doing so, they in turn would recreate harmony in their world. Like people, nature undergoes continual transformation, yet it ultimately finds balance and whole-iness. If geometry shapes the universe then surely, the ancients posited, the living geometry of a temple can help reshape people.

Geometry and strategic angles were used in temples – inside, outside, overtly or invisibly – to initiate a process of sensory manipulation that begins to open the body's electrical circuits, making it more receptive to finer, more penetrating frequencies and vibrations. Every temple feels different partly because of the type of geometry upon which it is based. Taking the Giza plateau as an example, the consciously-aware pilgrim quickly realizes how each pyramid exerts a different effect on the senses: the Great Pyramid feels different to the Red Pyramid feels different to the Bent Pyramid, and each structure is indeed based on different geometries, just as each was constructed for different purposes. The Giza pyramid's slope angle is based on the

The mathematical formula by which the deliberate geometries of the Bent Pyramid are revealed.

210

seven-sided heptagon; the Red Pyramid is based on the pentagon[11]; and the Bent Pyramid, by using a trigonomic formula, reveals the geometries of both the pentagon and hexagon.[12]

Of all the pyramids I've visited, I can comfortably sit inside or outside the Bent Pyramid for hours and feel very much at home; the same cannot be said of the Great Pyramid which, impressive as it is, can feel unsettling and overwhelming. Many people have expressed the same feeling. The Bent Pyramid is striking, hypnotic, and very grounding, and far from being "a mistake," as most orthodox archaeologists see it, this temple was strategically designed to exert a direct influence on the body while simultaneously working on the functions of the planet.

The effect is due to the combination of its two geometries – the pentagon and hexagon – which are the same as those in human DNA and the Earth. Geometry is the expression of number in space, thus the pentagon is to the hexagon as 5 is to 6, and of all the planets in the solar system, only the Earth incorporates this ratio. It is calculated by taking the 21,600-year period of obliquity (when the Earth's axis tilts between 22.1º – 24.5º) and dividing it by the precessional cycle of 25,920 years (the wobble at the pole). The ratio is 5:6, or geometrically speaking, pentagon : hexagon. Thus, the Bent Pyramid is an analog of the planetary and human bodies, and perhaps a point of fusion between both.

The 5:6 ratio in the clisters of Salisbury Cathedral.

Incidentally, being a metaphor of the balanced relationship between living organisms (which are pentagon-based) and non-living things (hexagon-based), this ratio allows for self-aware human life to evolve on this planet in our solar system and no other, since the 5:6 ratio is unique to the Earth.[13]

This understanding is often encoded in temples. In the Gothic cathedral of Salisbury each archway in the cloisters is composed of alternating pentagrams and hexagrams, the idea being that as one circumambulates in quiet contemplation, the body's sensory organs are opened prior to entering the nave of the cathedral. In many ways, then, Salisbury Cathedral is an analog of the Bent Pyramid.

Sacred geometry is the fourth principle of sacred space, and a very important one at that, since one of the purposes of the temple is to re-establish unity between body and mind and cosmos. When the body is under stress, its geometry is said to become distorted. Under such fragmentary conditions the body seeks to return to a balanced

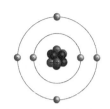

The carbon atom, symbol of humanity. And a Celtic cross.

state, searching for a biogeometric environment in which it can restore compatibility with its surroundings. You will find throughout the course of your life that you are attracted to certain temples at certain times, because your internal geometry is seeking that which it needs to achieve optimum balance, just as it seeks a harmonious, natural setting to revive its soul whenever a disconnection from life occurs. The geometer Michael Schneider states this very well: "The power which we seek is the power with which we seek." [14]

The fundamental proportions of classic temples such as Luxor, Angkor Wat and the Parthenon are based on the harmonics of the Golden Ratio, the spiral that underlies all living organisms. Since the same proportions are inherent in the human body, walking into such temples makes you feel as though you are an integral component of the structure because, in a sense, you are walking inside your self.

There are seven principal sacred geometries used in temples, and each amplifies specific properties:

TRIANGLE

The triangle represents the primary force of creation held in perfect equilibrium. This is represented throughout religious systems as the Holy Trinity, and the Trimurti of the creator gods Siva-Vishnu-Brahma. The triangle is given solid form in the tetrahedron, the primary bond between atoms and molecules, and the strongest and most stable of geometric solids. Such invisible processes are expressed in the human body, which begins life as a microscopic three-part structure; after three weeks, the embryo becomes an enfolded sphere that diversifies into three distinct layers to become the intertwined systems of the body.[15] The cycle outwardly repeats itself in the physical bond between male, female, and their created offspring.

These processes of creation find their way into the modern world, where the threefold division of light – red, green, blue – allows

Square geometry of the pagoda.

212

for a full spectrum of color to be made visible on television screens. The triangle embodies the qualities of strength, stability, and prime creative force. To give strength to communication we often resort to emphasizing commands in threes, just as in the construction industry, beams are fitted in triangles to give maximum strength to weight-bearing structures.

SQUARE

Whereas the triangle reflects actions taking place in the ethereal, its complimentary opposite in the material is the square, which represents the prime elements held in balance on the physical plane: earth, water, fire and air. The square is the essence of harmony in the physical world, the defining of invisible forces on the material realm. The concept is represented in the Celtic cross with its four elements held in equilibrium by a central force, or God. It is often equated with the carbon atom – the symbol of humanity – since carbon is the second most abundant element in the body. A mythopoeic description this may be, yet modern science does acknowledge matter to consist of four states: solids, liquids, gases, and plasma or electronic incandescence. Plato had a very novel way of demonstrating this by filling a jar with soil, water and air, and shaking it. The natural layering into which these settle shows the order of elements: the dense earth on the bottom, followed by water, air, and the light (fire) passing through.

The square is the establishment of coordinates on the physical plane, figuratively represented by the four cardinal directions of north, south, east and west, and embodied in the Hindu *swastika*, a recently stigmatized symbol with origins in the Neolithic period, and meaning 'that which is associated with well being'.

PENTAGRAM

There are pentagrams on flags, logos, five-star hotels, reviews and generals. The pentagram is pervasive in every culture due to its underlying relationship with the Golden Ratio, nature's very own spiral, which is inherent in the mathematical proportions of the pentagram.

The pentagram reflects the harmonics of Earth's living systems, of nature, and it embodies the qualities of life-affirmation, growth, intuition, fertility, and the divine feminine. Lunar temples favor pentagonal geometries due to the Moon's influence on fertility cycles. It also favors temples dedicated to Venus, Ishtar, and Isis. As such, the pentagram was inverted during the Middle Ages during the Catholic

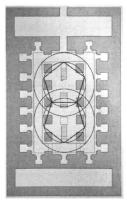

Pentagonal geometry in the Osirion.

213

The Golden Spiral as it relates to the pentagram.

Church's smear campaign against women, depicting the divine feminine as evil, and degrading ancient symbols and their meanings, not unlike the Nazi misuse of the *swastika*.

HEXAGRAM

The pentagram is fluid and feminine, and just as flowing water freezes into ice crystals, its opposite, the hexagram, is rigid and structured. It is therefore considered masculine. The six-pointed star lies behind organizational forms such as the beehive and the microchip. And just as the pentagram is associated with water and the Moon, when the Sun reflects thru glass or water it reveals the six-pointed star, so its properties are solar, logical, and rational. It represents the spiritual warrior, the divine masculine.

HEPTAGRAM

When working with seven we see the forces that shape the universe: the prime notes of sound and the colors of visible light. To the Egyptians, sound and light were primal causes of matter, and they did not necessarily distinguish between either, for in their cosmology Ra was said to have "emitted a cry of light" when the universe came into being.

The seven-sided heptagram represents the mystery of creation, the unknowable, and thus, the source of life. Since the source of the soul is also a mystery, the heptagram equally represents the search for truth, which ultimately leads to enlightenment. And through truth and enlightenment, one is finally liberated from the illusions of the physical world.

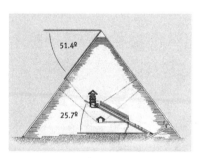

Heptagonal angles define the slopes of the Great Pyramid.

Appropriately, it is the only form in geometry that cannot be bisected to a whole angle: $360° \div 7 = 51.4285714286...$ into infinity, so the heptagon is a mystery unto itself! It's qualities are represented by gods such as Apollo and Seshat, and its numerical symbol is found in the rays emanating from the apply-named Statue of Liberty, which was presented as a gift to the founding American Freemasons by their French counterparts.

OCTAGON

The octagon represents the ultimate balance between material and invisible forces, the fixed male and the mutable female; total balance between material and spiritual, heart and mind: the fully aware, 'christed' human. It is both the inhalation and the exhalation of the breath of creation. Once again we see this creative force reflected in the human body, where the sperm and egg unite to form a whole cell, which doubles to become two, then four, and finally the eighth seamless stage of *mitosis* – a process mirrored in the seven pure notes of sound that make-up the final octave. Science's modern analogy is shown in the *Periodic Table of Elements*, its cosmological model of all naturally-occurring atoms, which chemists discovered are organized in eight main types of elements. In fact, molecular, atomic and subatomic structures are strikingly similar to the geometric patterns of Islamic art and eastern temple architecture, particularly the octagon, since it is said to represent Allah the Compassionate.

A Templar flag.

The octagon symbolizes the ultimate aim of esoteric traditions. Notable, enlightened figures throughout history such as Mohammed, Merlin, the archangel Michael and Jesus have been characterized by either the octagon or its numerical value 8, and the infinity symbol ∞; in gematria, the name *Jesus* carries the value of 888.

Buddha himself prescribed the eightfold path as a cessation of sorrow, by following right views, right intention, right speech, right action, right livelihood, right effort, right mindfulness, right concentration.

Templar influence in the ceiling of the octagonal Founder's Chapel. Batalha, Portugal.

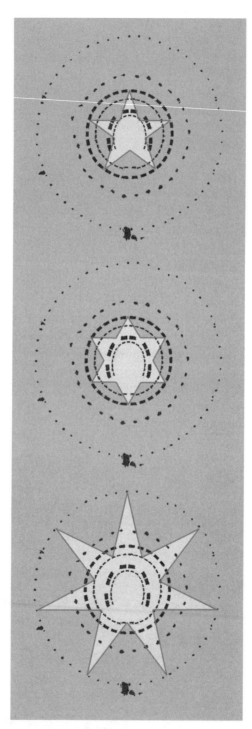

*Just a few of the geometrical relationships
between the arranging of stones at Stonehenge.*

Being the ultimate aim of the human being, the octagon was personified in the Templar flag, as a visible red cross separated by four invisible cross-quarters, over equal areas of black and white, denoting the balance between the forces of darkness and light. Templar churches are also octagonal.

NONAGON

To the ancients, the nine-sided nonagon is the triangle manifested threefold, and given how the triangle represents the prime force of the universe, its threefold expression represents utmost perfection, utmost expression, highest attainment. This is expressed in that creation of the earth, the human body, which evolves in the female womb over the course of nine months. The tail of the sperm half-cell is made of nine twisted threads, and after it unites with the egg, the first step in the doubling process of *mitiosis* is the duplication of a centriole, a set of nine parallel tubes arranged in a ring.

We see this perfection in nature reflected in the Egyptian Ennead of gods, each representing an archetypal principle that regulates the Universe. We also see it reflected in our everyday language expressing the utmost in any endeavor: when we are in love we float on cloud nine; to do our very best is to go the whole nine yards; when we dress up we dress to the nines.

Sacred geometry is bound within us just as it is bound within the walls and stones of temples, be it visibly or occult. Whenever we walk within their perimeter we bring our sacredness into the sacred space that is a material expression of God, and the interaction becomes palpable and inseparable as though the two are one and the same tapestry.

The mystic head of the Cistercian Order, Bernard de Clairvaux, was once asked, "What is God?" He simply replied, "He is length, width, height and depth."

Octagonal fountains are prominent central features of mosques. The same geometry is applied in early Christian and Celtic church fonts.

Stone rows at Kilmartin aligned north-south. Such sites work with magnetic forces. Scotland.

15

THE SEVEN PRINCIPLES OF SACRED SPACE:

6. ORIENTATION.

It is the direction and not the magnitude which is to be taken into consideration.

~ Thomas Paine

After Pierre Mereaux conducted his painstaking survey of Carnac, he considered the orientation of the roof slabs on dolmens could have a significant influence on their purpose, and discovered they did. For one thing, the closer they were oriented magnetic north-south, the stronger the voltage emitted from the stones.[1] Mereaux held steadfast to the concept of science as the only law in the land. For him, 'new age' thinking was anathema. Thus he would not have been aware that his research unknowingly validated an established principle throughout esoteric disciplines: that temples are aligned in accordance to their specific purpose, a similar concept to the Chinese art of *feng shui*.

And so it is that temples sharing similar functions also share the same compass alignments. Pyramids from Giza to Xi'an in China are typically aligned to the four cardinal directions (notable exceptions being in central America), their entrances always pointing north; most of the oldest sites on Earth are aligned to the northeast; temples associated with fertility always face southeast.

Native tribes do not draw any sharp lines of distinction, such as we see, between animals, people and inanimate objects. To them, animate and inanimate forms are considered to be of the same nature and differ only in shape.[2] Even thousands of years ago they considered all elements to be imbued with consciousness; there was no such thing as dead matter, everything was seen as energy in a constant state of transmutation.

Because our visual cortex is capable of detecting only a small fraction of the light spectrum, unless your intuitive abilities are well developed, much of the elemental world cannot be seen. So, to make them tangible and 'visible', each force was given physical form by attributing it a guardian or 'god'. The Celts, Hindus, Egyptians and Sumerians created whole pantheons of gods to represent these life forces and used them as tools to help focus attention on a specific element. Some of them are still with us today, enshrined in the archangels Uri-el, Micha-el, Rapha-el, Gabri-el – *el* meaning "shining one" – each of whom represent the four material forces: earth, fire, air and water.

Never were idols created for the purpose of worship; such a notion developed much later with the fall of culture which ushered the rise of the power of the centralized priesthood, and with it, the descent into idolatry.

Orienting the temple to the energy of specific creative processes enhances the actions taking place inside the sacred space. The orientation is typically defined by the direction in which the entrance faces, for it welcomes the energy into the temple's inner *sanctum*. The earlier discoveries of the way ground energy is directed and channeled through the entrances of monuments leaves little doubt that the concept is not just symbolic but also perfectly functional. So this sixth principle establishes an additional layer of correspondence.

Temple orientation is arranged in two distinct groups, the fixed cardinal directions and the mutable cross-quarters.

NORTH

When the doorway faces north it faces the cold and hardness of the Pole and its bitter winds, making the senses more keenly aware of the physicality of the planet. North-facing temples are therefore associated with the element of earth. They also reference geomagnetism, since magnetism enters the Earth through the Pole.

When rows of standing stones are oriented north-south they are working with this force, since they mimic the path of geomagnetism flowing through the Earth's core; such places make a direct link with the Earth's veins and arteries, they are mediating points between the surface and the inner workings of the planet.

The capstones on dolmens are deliberately oriented to concentrate the effect of telluric energy at the site, much like an antenna. Trevethy Quoit, Cornwall.

In turn, this has a direct influence on humans, for not only do we emanate from the soil, we also are electromagnetic beings. North temples help to achieve a very close bond between people and planet, and may explain why pyramids – already shaped like the mineral magnetite – have such a profound effect on people, both visually and physically.

SOUTH

A temple with an entrance to the south faces the heat of the equator and invokes the element of fire. Symbolically, fire is associated with strength, power and protection, so these are typically solar temples, places that imbue the individual with the power of the Spiritual Warrior. One excellent example is the present temple of Edfu, built by Ramasses II, possibly Egypt's most powerful warrior-pharaoh, and judging by his military record he most certainly used such a place of power to his advantage.

EAST

Entrances in the east symbolically face the light of the reborn Sun. Such temples benefit from the purified morning air, and thus represent that element. Dawn is the awakening from darkness, the Sun emanating out of the underworld, the light returning to the land, hence these are temples associated with enlightenment.

When light shines on something it illuminates, and with illumination comes understanding. Pharaohs and kings and queens who were initiated into the Mysteries would seek to be buried with their heads in the east, so that as their souls entered the spirit world they would find understanding.

It has been discovered that the frequency of light is at its purest at sunrise. Probably for this very reason, seeds are also at their most receptive to growth at this time of day. Since the electrical charge in the air is also at its most formidable, healing temples, such as native American sweat lodges, are oriented east.

WEST

West follows the path of the setting Sun as it descents into the underworld, the location of the spirit. Temples facing west are therefore places of the night horizon, places where one follows the Sun towards communication with the world of spirit; they are halls of introspection, locations for traveling within. This direction references the element of water, which is traditionally associated with communication. In scripture, water and west are presided by the archangel Gabriel, who is always the one entrusted with communication and messages from the world of God; in Christianity, it was he who notified Mary she would be conceiving Jesus. As the Arabic Jibral, he is also said to have delivered the Qu'ran to Muhammad.

Sometimes there are multiple entrances to a temple, indicating the site has a dual purpose. Temples with an east-west alignment are processional sites, for their aisles follow the figurative path of the rising and setting Sun across the sky. Churches and cathedrals tend to be so aligned. Traditionally, baptisms enter via the east door (or are performed in a chamber in the eastern part of the building) so the new-born child may benefit from the pure light and air, whereas funerals enter through the west door so the soul may begin its journey into the world of spirit; traditional church fonts are also placed in the west to reference the element of water.

Where there exist four entrances, such as pagodas and specific central American pyramids, their alignment to the four cardinal points harness each of the material elements, indicating the site is working with all material forces. Interestingly, Mount Kailas – the earthly depiction of Meru – is the central source of four rivers oriented to the four cardinal directions.[3]

These, then, are the fixed, cardinal directions. But to the ancients, the mutable directions – the cross-quarters – were considered the most energetic because they represent points of equilibrium or transition between the fixed, material elements. These are the invisible moments of transition, alchemical and mysterious, and depending on the temple's location on the face of the Earth, they often have the additional value of referencing the solstices and equinoxes. For example, Stonehenge's entrance is reached via a spirit road that begins at the a small stone circle by the River Avon, then follows a three-mile route marked by two earthen ditches. The menhir at the north-eastern entrance into the henge, the *Heel Stone*, in 3100 BC would have aligned with the rising summer solstice Sun, casting a shadow received by the horseshoe of bluestones inside the temple, as though a life force was filling a cup.

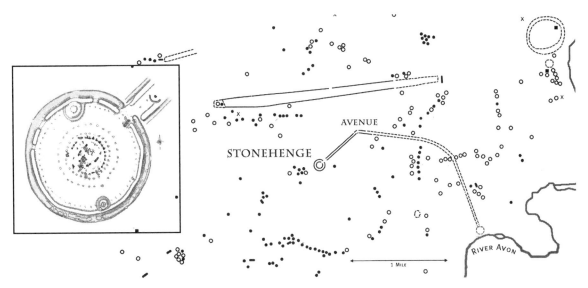

Stonehenge (inset) and its processional spirit road, not dissimilar to the passageways connecting the Nile to the pyramids. Dots represent just some of the mounds and barrows in its vicinity.

SOUTHEAST

Temples oriented to the southeast tend to be precisely aligned to the first emerging rays of the winter solstice, the moment during the solar year when light begins to overcome the dark. In a manner of speaking it is the rebirth of the light, so literally, practically and metaphorically, such sites are associated with fertility, birthing, creativity, even the teaching of sacred sexuality.

One excellent example is the Cradle of Atum, also called Adam's Grave, a long barrow in southern England. Every December 21st this prominent giant's grave, situated on the promontory of the tallest hill in the area, receives into its womb the first rays of the solstice Sun as it breaches the cold, winter horizon.

Adam's Grave long barrow, poised to receive the mid-winter sunrise.

SOUTHWEST

When facing southwest, the temple reflects the August quarter days, when the light that first emerged out of winter has fertilized crops to their full potential and the time of harvest beckons. It is the highest achievement of the light of the Sun. Depending on its latitude, the temple may also reference the Harvest Moon at its most southerly setting – typically the Full Moon closest to the Autumn Equinox – thus honoring the influence that planetary sphere has upon this cycle of fertility. Such temples are places of celebration, they honor the bountiful fruits of the earth, when life is at its most manifest and the fruits of one's labor are exalted. These are temples that celebrate the corn maidens on the feast of *Lughnasadh* and the Celtic solar deity Lugh.

NORTHWEST

Temples facing the northwest represent the time of year when the Sun begins to withdraw, and the long, dark winter nights begin their ascent. At this time, honor is given to the spirit world for the protection of the people through the long darkness of winter and their safe passage into the light of spring. To ancient cultures this was a time when the veil between the worlds was thinnest, the days of *Sammain*, or as it is known today in the West, All Hallows Eve, now Halloween. Such places invoke the feeling of going within, a 'return to the womb' allowing for a process of self-contemplation as one goes deep inside the mystery of life.

NORTHEAST

Temples aligned to the northeast face the rising light of the midsummer Sun, when the solar disc is at its zenith in the northern hemisphere. Metaphorically speaking, this represents the fullest exultation of the ascending light. Such places are associated with ancestral wisdom, with the universal knowledge of the ancient ones. Not surprisingly they are also some of the oldest sites in the world: Stonehenge, Delphi, Luxor; Samarra, Esfahan, Cordoba; the Osirion at Abydos, the stone rows of Carnac, the pyramid of Cholula; the complexes of Teotihuacan, Tula, Chitzen Itza and Tulum; the Aka stone circles off the coast of Okinawa and now underwater; Santo Domingo cathedral on top of the temple of Viracocha in Cuzco. Chartres, once a Druid academy, and possibly a Mesolithic site, is aligned to the northeast and faces the southwest, making it a processional temple for both ancient wisdom and the glory of its fruits.

Temple of the Four Winds, in its last days.
New Zealand.

In the southern hemisphere, the above correspondences appear to be reversed. One of the most sacred of sites in New Zealand is Miringa Te Kakara, the Temple of the Four Winds, a pre-Polynesian Maori crosshouse continuously maintained until 1982, when the last structure became dilapidated and burned down. This *Wharewaenanga* or 'School of Learning' was once an impressive, carved wooden structure in its time, its design underpinned by an octagonal framework and aligned to the four cross-quarters, indicating it as a site of great antiquity; its plan can still be seen on the ground, now marked by two large furrows in the shape of a cross.

Since, like Heliopolis, it was an ancient academy teaching astronomy, genealogy and natural medicine, I was eager to test the theory of orientation at this site, since it is so remote from many of the world's classic temples. True to form it follows the same principles of sacred space: being the source of three sacred rivers, the connection to water is maintained; opposite each entrance there once stood four *niu* poles – the equivalent of the omphalos – each oriented to the solstices and equinoxes The location of the burial mounds (the 'place of going within') sits on the southwest corner, exactly as it would be in the northern hemisphere, because in the southern hemisphere the orientation of sites is switched: north is represented by the South Pole, while south faces the equator; east and west remain constant since the Sun still rises where it should.

Orientation becomes the sixth principle of sacred space. Each principle adds a further level of correspondence between the temple and the natural world around it, making the site as close to a mirror image of the universe as possible.

It took many travels around the world to realize the final principle, but when the epiphany finally occurred, in the true tradition of the temple, it was both a major revelation as well as an obvious one.

Perched inside a natural arch high up on a cliff, this limestone kiva marks the node of two feminine energy lines. Its entrance aligns to the southwest, a tribute to harvest. Inside, two wall niches are carved in the north and southeast, indicating the tribe also honored the earth and the cycle of fertility. Bandelier, New Mexico

Dual-purpose temple. Southeast and southwest entrances at Swinside celebrate fertility and harvest. The two tallest stones are placed on the north and south points, and are the only stones containing large particles of iron; the north stone, in particular, is known to emit high energy readings and deflect compasses. Cumbria.

Devotion. Grande Mosquée de Paris.

16

The Seven Principles of Sacred Space:

7. The Human Key.

The gematrian value of 1746 represents the number of 'fusion' and the 'ideal city'. By adding the alpha, the number of the upright human, it becomes 1747, the adept becomes the embodiment of the 'city of God': they become the 'knowledge of god', the 'fruit of the vineyard'.

Having carried out well-designed experiments over the last decades, a number of respected scientists have reached a conclusion concerning the forces governing the human body and the cosmos: elementally, they are not chemical reactions, they are energetic charges. The human body is an aggregate of an energy field, and that field is interconnected to everything that exists. Energy is the engine that drives everything including our consciousness, and as such, energy can influence us and we can influence it. This energy field is a force and it is full of information, or as Einstein succinctly stated, "the field is the only reality." [1]

In all my meanderings in and around sacred sites I have observed how the principles of water, electromagnetism, measure, stone, sacred geometry and orientation combine like layers on a cake to produce an environment that is tangibly different to its surroundings. Certainly this environment generates a unique effect on the senses of perception. But not every time, and in this lies the mystery behind the last principle of sacred space.

When hordes of tourists circumambulate Stonehenge armed with walkie-talkies, listening to an institutional voice filling their heads with the distorted history of this effulgent monument ("… and hundreds of slaves inched the stones on wooden rollers…"), it seems as though you are looking at a bunch of inert rocks, the site feels shut down, vacant and devoid of soul. It's the same when approaching any sacred site for a purpose other than the one for which it was designed. As the scholar Philip Cousineau observes: "The difference between pilgrim and tourist is the intention of attention, the quality of the curiosity." [2] By shifting the focus of our intent we alter the energetic relationship with the space around us. When that space is a temple, the quality of our intent ignites a symbiotic resonance with the memory of place, as though body and structure become connected by the same tissue, as F.W. Putnam discovered when he surveyed Ohio's Serpent Mound in 1883: "The most singular sensation of awe and admiration overwhelmed me at this sudden realization of my long-cherished desire, for here before me was the mysterious work of an unknown people… I mused on the probabilities of the past; and there seemed to come to me a picture as of a distant time" [3]

The acoustics pioneer and scientist John Reid lives in the vicinity of the majestic stone circles of Castlerigg and Swinside, in one of the most poetic landscapes in the world, the Lake District of northern England. Whenever he has approached temples with the intent of working with them, at those times the spirit of place has opened up to him in a way that differs from general visits: "In visiting Swinside stone circle, on one occasion I approached the site in a very quiet, meditative state. Upon walking into the circle I had a fleeting glimpse into the past: around 100 people were milling around and dancing gaily in simple rustic garb. The flashback lasted only three or four seconds, but the scene was as real as watching a movie." [4] And Swinside, with one of its two entrances facing the southwest, is indeed a temple where harvest was celebrated.

Reid's dedicated research on acoustics in the Great Pyramid of Giza[5] has allowed him to experience that energetic exchange between body and building on numerous occasions: "Some years ago, during an evening research session in the pyramid, I was given a glimpse of a ritual in which the Shem priest, garbed in a leopard skin, conducted a ceremony involving four tonsured priests whose fingertips appeared to be touching the sarcophagus. They were intoning vowel sounds and I even heard their voices, though again only momentarily. It's as though, under certain conditions, a portal to the past opens but it is so transient we have to be alert to have any recall of what we see or hear.

"The vision left me within seconds, so I never knew the purpose of the ritual. In my subsequent textual research I came across a quote by a Greek traveler called Demetrius who wrote 'In Egypt when priests sing hymns to the gods they sing the seven vowels in due succession and the sound of these vowels has such euphony that men listen to it instead of the flute and the lyre.' So it seems that use of chant was part of their devotional practice." [6]

John's experience is uncannily similar to Paul Brunton's as well as my own, as we saw in an earlier chapter. The ancient mysteries author Paul Broadhurst is himself no stranger to the effects of coincidence and the mysterious opening of otherwise closed doors whenever he travels to sacred places, in the spirit of understanding what makes them so. Obstacles are removed as though by magic, clues manifest in the unlikeliest of places, helpful individuals appear at the right juncture pointing to the correct fork in the path of the quest.

As a living entity, a purposefully constructed mansion of the gods is able to read intent like an electric lock reads a PIN number.

It occurred to me that when the individual is aware of the site, even subconsciously, the site becomes aware of the individual. We consecrate a sacred site when we bring our sacred geometry and our intent to the temple. Awareness and intent, both electromagnetic impulses, interact with the forces concentrated at the temple to create a fusion, in essence uniting two temples. Scriptures such as the Talmud often refer to this bond: "Just as God resides in the innermost precincts of the temple, so also the soul dwells in the innermost part of the body." [7] If the temple of God resides within every person, as adepts like Jesus stated,[8] once a sympathetic resonance exists between both, a sacred marriage naturally follows.

Intent, our silent, inner voice, becomes the seventh ingredient of sacred space. It glues the other principles together and brings the structure to life, just as the Followers of Horus once awoke the temple every morning with their orations and oblations. The temple of Man and the temple of the land become one indivisible and mystical whole.

Intent is also the key that allows access into the invisible temple – its subtle energy field. Temple-building cultures such as the Egyptians and Tamils believed in the divinization of the physical form of the original creators, and that their embodiment became divine in the consecrated sacred mounds, Sivalingams and stupas; they became the dwelling places of Siva and Atum, from which the four elements were created and represented as tangible divine beings.[9] Their integrity was protected – from the 'seven gates' of the pharaohs and the seven Hartmann lines guarding the entrances, to the force fields around stone circles. Their immune system is defended from the impurity of thoughts that could lead to the putridity of the zero-point energy field protecting the inner *sanctum*. And once access is granted to the living structure – the physical embodiment of a god – the initiate experiences this kingdom of heaven on Earth.

The skeptic, by contrast, will never feel anything at a temple, for he is already pre-programmed *not* to have an experience, expecting something to be done for him, like a magic trick. To the non-believer, seeing is believing, just as to the initiate, believing *is* seeing. Two faces of the same pillar. Magic aplenty there is, but the temple does not exist as a vending machine dispensing instant energy and self-empowerment; it was deliberately built to be of service, and like any functional partnership, you have to meet it half way.

This subtle difference in the frequency of your intent is what distinguishes you in the presence of a place of divinity, and it will generate an invitation from the site.

Rigorous experiments using directed human thought have shown how our electromagnetic impulses are capable of altering the random movement of machines, even alter the beat of a computerized drumbeat, proving something revolutionary about human consciousness that was once believed limited to the field of mediums and magic.[10]

One experiment relies on the measurement of small changes in the behavior of an electronic device called a Random Event Generator, or REG, designed to produce a random output of + or – pulses, which are converted into binary computer language. The REG is used for the Global Consciousness Project data collection, where the output is measured relative to a mean value. The output of the REG differs from what would be expected without the influence of consciousness. In field studies, a team from Princeton Engineering Anomalies Research found consistent deviations from expected randomicity in data taken in situations where groups become integrated or unified by something of common interest. The evidence infers that a "consciousness field" exists and that intentions or emotional states which structure the field are conveyed as information that is absorbed into the distribution of output of the machine.

Roger Nelson, doctor of Psychology and member of the P.E.A.R. team, conducted several experiments at sacred sites. He was intrigued as to whether the sacredness of these places was due to their collective use over time or because they were imbued with a certain energetic resonance in the first place, or because a combination of forces such as stone, electromagnetism and so forth made it so. During an initial experiment at a Native American landscape temple in Wyoming called Mato Tipila ("Bear's Lodge," now westernized as Devil's Tower), the REG's output was demonstrably affected by a medicine man ceremony. Nelson then decided to see what affect meditation groups would have on the REG when chanting or meditating at interesting sites which were not necessarily sacred. The machine was influenced but only to a small statistical degree.[11]

After trips with meditation groups to Luxor, Karnak and several pyramids, the effects were six times that of ordinary REG trials in the field. In fact they represented the largest effects ever seen. But what astonished Nelson was that the results from twenty seven sites were even higher whenever he walked around the sites in respectful silence, with a portable version of the machine sitting in his pocket. For him it proved that the spirit of place itself registered effects as high as the power emanating from a meditating group.[12]

While temples resonated a high degree of consciousness, the combination of focused group veneration and the temple seemed to create an expanded consciousness that had a marked affect on a machine. Inside the Great Pyramid of Giza the REG veered off its random course with a positive trend during group chants in the Queen's Chamber, and then a strong negative trend in the King's chamber; the same effects also occurred at Karnak. This is consistent with how sensitive people describe the effects in each chamber: the Queen's chamber is uplifting whereas the King's chamber is heavier, making one feel as if dragged into the depths of the earth. It is worth pointing out that the two are lined with different stone – red granite for the King's chamber, limestone for the Queen's. Plotted on a graph, the results from the REG formed a large pyramid, as if the machine had experienced the trip as well.[13]

The focus of intent, especially with a devotion involving a higher, intermediary power, has always been a proven method of achieving the impossible. As the Persian god Ahura Mazda said: "if the due… prayer is offered unto [god] just as it ought to be performed in the perfection of holiness, never again will a hostile horde enter… nor any plague, nor leprosy, nor venomous plants… nor the uplifted spear of a foe." [14]

It's early morning outside Minster church in Cornwall, a Norman structure inclined towards the northeast, built on the site of a Celtic monastery, nestled amid a verdant, atmospheric wood. It was once the site of a rock-cut chapel, the home of a Celtic saint, hence the original name of the site, Talkarn, "rock chapel." [15] It is so piercingly quiet that Isabelle Kingston, Jane Ross and I can hear the mellifluous trickling of water from the nearby sacred spring deep in the moss and trees. We've come to take-in the atmosphere of this ancient place of veneration huddled in the steep valley above the fishing village of Boscastle.

The aroma inside the old church conveys the spirit of quiet contemplation; the musty scent of stone intertwines with the beeswax of candles and the dampness from holy books long thumbed by parishioners here and departed. Isabelle suggests we offer a dedication to the spirit of place by joining our voices in reverence and performing a toning. As usual she dedicates her sound offering to the archangel Michael; Jane offers hers to archangel Gabriel; as for myself, I casually offer my voice to Saint Cecelia.

"Good choice," remarks Isabelle.

"Surely there is no such thing as Saint Cecilia!?" I reply.

"Are you kidding, she's only the patron saint of music," says Jane.

I learn something new every day! We tone for what feels like a good ten minutes, the natural acoustics of the building blending the three voices into an opulent choir. The lights go out by themselves.

The last syllables cascading from our tongues echo into eternity as we stand silently, interspersed in a triangle throughout the nave. As we make our way to the oak front door I glance over at the large, ornate stained glass window. "Would you believe it! The three people we dedicated are represented in the window," I exclaimed. All mouths were ajar.

"Well, well, will you look at that!" Indeed, framed by the gothic arch stand three tall figures, each made of the most colorful stained glass.

We reveled in our glory for the rest of the day. Not only had we communicated with the spirit of place, we even intuited it, and were rightfully pleased with ourselves.

The following year, Jane and I returned with another person, keen to relieve the experience. As we approached the exterior of the church something was amiss. I looked up at the arch where the stained glass window should be, but there was only clear leaded glass. Had something happened? Had the window been damaged, was this a temporary replacement? Quite by chance the priest appeared. We explained the situation. The priest looked at us in disbelief, for "never in the history of the church has there ever been a stained glass window in that wall. Any wall." He walked away to continue his chores, his facial expression implying "crazy tourists." I walked up to the window and inspected the caulking. Indeed he was right. It was extremely old, some of it encrusted with mould; certainly it had not recently been mended. Puzzled, we walked down to the village to seek expert advice and several pints of cider – that is, research.

Paul Broadhurst is Boscastle, in fact he *is* Cornwall. There's little of the history of every sacred place in this wind-beaten corner of Albion he is not aware of. "No, there's never been a record of any stained glass in Minster church," he stated emphatically, "and certainly not in recent times."

The mystery deepened. There was one other witness who could confirm Jane and I were not certifiable. We called on Isabelle at her home in Wiltshire.

"Do you remember that trip we took to Boscastle last year?"

"Indeed, how could I not, that thing with the angels and St. Cecilia in the stained glass window, that was a good laugh, wasn't it?" she glowed.

"There *was* no window. There has *never* been a window."

In the silence, one could hear the mellifluous steam rising from her tea.

Regardless of their shape and size, all temples were built to the same end: to be mirrors of the universe so that ordinary men and women, regardless of culture or creed, may be transformed into gods. These cities of knowledge, once the repository of creator gods, are sacred because of their underlying spiritual technology and the thousands of years of residual energy accumulated from veneration by inquiring minds. The temple is the contact station with the miraculous, the eternal reminder of our own co-creative power, an island of balance on a planet where change is the only constant. Indeed they act "as a magical protector for him in heaven and in earth, unfailingly and regularly and eternally." [16]

The architects designed these heirlooms for our common wealth, an insurance policy for times which they foresaw as cynical and dangerous to the proper conduct of human affairs, when we'd abandon our trust in the divine purpose of life.

They built these places of power so we'd always remember who we really are.

Ascending pilgrim. St. Michael's Tower, Glastonbury Tor.

ACT III

Calanais. Isle of Harris, Scotland.

17

The Rise and Fall of the Temple.

"The mind has lost its cutting edge, we hardly understand the Ancients."
– Gregoire de Tours, 6th Century A.D.

Luck, as they say, favors the prepared.

In contrast to the linear thinking adopted throughout the West, many Eastern philosophies follow the concept of a world governed by circular dynamics in which recurring cycles play a central role. The idea of 'thinking in the round' is found in the oldest of cultures, such as the Aboriginal and the Hopi. They reached this understanding observing the stars and the cycles of nature, from which they distilled the mechanism driving the world down to a few simple concepts, even if from our perspective the symbology used sometimes seems obtuse.

A close examination of the fundamental alignments behind the majority of temples shows a positive obsession with astronomy. From the Chankillo complex in Peru to the stone circle of Calanais in Scotland, the motions of the planets and stars were meticulously tracked and calculated over enormous spans of time, and their corresponding effects predicted. More than 4,000 years ago the Chinese already considered astrology as the basis of an established order. The cosmos in its entirety was considered a living, sacred organism, and its rhythms revealed harmony, permanence and fertility.[1]

It was believed that everything that happens on the material plane is a reflection of recurring actions taking place in the celestial sphere, that the universe is one giant, gnomonic and self-simulating holograph, not unlike the position now considered in quantum physics.[2] As one Confucian moralist advised, "Love everything in the universe, because the sun and the earth are but one body."[3]

The prime device used for calculating cycles was the Precession of the Equinoxes – the wobble of the poles that traces an invisible cone in the sky as seen against the background of 'fixed' constellations. From an earth-bound observer, each constellation is seen to move one degree every 72 years, and that same constellation returns to its original position 25,920 years later – what is known as the Great Platonic Year. Conveniently, there are precisely twelve constellations that circumambulate the equator; each more or less occupies 30° of the sky, the equivalent of a "house" of the zodiac. Elementary multiplication shows that 30° multiplied by 12 equals 360°, the circumference of a circle; and 30° multiplied by 72 years equals 2,160 years, the period of each cycle or 'age'. Twelve constellations multiplied by 2,160 years equals a full 25,920-year cycle.

It seems God, in addition to being a geometer, is also a mathematician.

The cycles do not have strict beginnings and endings, as we in the modern, quantitative world expect. Instead they ebb and flow and overlap over a liquid period of time, influencing and challenging our perception of the world and the pre-conceived notions of ourselves, much like a slow incoming tide wipes away footprints by rearranging the particles of sand. However, the effects of an impending age intensify the closer it approaches, just as water becomes more agitated the closer it reaches boiling point.

Each cycle is governed by the characteristics of its overarching constellation, which in turn influences the course of human affairs.[4] The constellation's symbolism was reinforced throughout temples built or adapted during that cycle, so in the Age of Taurus (c.4420 – 2260 B.C.) effigies of the astrological bull dominate art and sculpture. The traits consistent with Taurus – strength, stability, material forces, earth, great sensual beauty – were therefore the dictum of that period, a time of unusual stability, with the rise of writing, agriculture and social husbandry, and the construction of elegant structures including pyramids and temples, and Mesopotamian, Maltese and Minoan sites of veneration.

As each cycle or age slowly begins to wane, it comes under the influence of the following age, and tied to this almost imperceptible motion there is a gradual increase in natural and celestial phenomena.

Such portents of impending change did not go unnoticed by the temple builders. Around 3100 B.C. there is a sudden rise in construction activity. An entire megalith metropolis is erected at Calanais; in the Boyne Valley region of Ireland, the passage mounds of Newgrange, Knowth and Dowth make their appearance; in England, Stonehenge suddenly inherits its bluestone circles, while the complex around Avebury is given form; in Malta, Haggiar Khem and Mnajdra are either built or expanded, as are temples along the Nile and the fertile crescent of Mesopotamia, while throughout the Mississippi valley there's a sudden proliferation of native American mounds.[5] This noticeable burst in activity may have reflected a number of structures lost to an abrupt rise in sea level which affected sites along coastal regions. Recently discovered stone circles, ceremonial chambers and menhirs in the northern French intertidal regions around Carnac, and the Seine and Somme valleys and estuaries, reveal these sites to have been rapidly inundated by up to fifteen feet of water leading up to 3100 B.C.; several stone circles and menhirs along the Bretagne coast are now only visible at low tide. This coincides with a peak in coastal flooding in the Mississippi delta and the eastern seaboard of America.

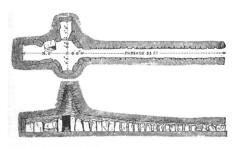

Newgrange passage mound. Ireland.

Several paleoclimatic events appear to have overlapped during this period, because global climate worsened dramatically. Comparative analysis of Greenland ice cores along with tree-ring data identifies land strikes of meteorites in 3150 B.C., one landing in China.[6] Global spikes in sulphate and methane levels indicate such events affected worldwide climate patterns. Throughout Europe and the North Atlantic, a neoglacial period dropped the upper tree line in the Alps by 300 feet, and the effects of this northern cooling period extended as far south as Peru and produced a corresponding drought in the Near East.[7] The Tigris-Euphrates River saw sharp reductions of stream flow, while the Iranian Plateau changed from humid to arid.[8] Most significant of all, what is known today as the Persian Gulf, was then low-lying alluvial land, but in a matter of five hundred years the sea rose so rapidly that the fabled cities of Ur, Eridu, Shuruppak and Sippar suddenly found themselves very close to the sea; silt deposits indicate a complete transgression of the ocean, flooding the cities before lowering to the level it is today.[9]

Significant cooling of the planet was also caused by debris ejected from a 3190 B.C. eruption of the volatile Icelandic volcano Hekla, so it is with good reason

Icelanders refer to this temperamental stratovolcano as "the gateway to Hell." The geologist Robert Schoch summarizes the conditions at this time of overlapping cycles well: "There is evidence that currents in all the major oceans changed, probably in response to shifts in the atmosphere. The surface of the earth itself was moving around a great deal at this time. Every continent was affected by various patterns of uplift, subsidence, tilt, down-warping, earthquakes, and shifting riverbeds." [10]

Some 7,000 years earlier, the changeover from the Age of Leo to Cancer ushered "the time of the First Occasion" – *Zep Tepi* – and with it came a magnetic flip of the poles, followed shortly thereafter by a global flood. That time saw the creation of the primordial mounds, the Sphinx and the sites of the Giza pyramids. So, with the previous change of ages and their effects well carved in myth and memory, the temple-builders no doubt took heed and engaged in a new cycle of construction to preserve the "mansions of the gods." And just like the forces that precipitated the great flood, the events around 3100 B.C. most likely also moved the telluric lines, causing the "enemy snake to churn in the abyss." By anchoring the shifting nodes of these currents with great stone circles, tens of thousands of menhirs worldwide, in addition to expansions of existing temples, the "cities of knowledge" would be protected against potential catastrophe.

Perhaps it is no coincidence that this renewed era in temple-building occurs precisely as Menes (the first pharaoh from a pure human bloodline) is enthroned in Egypt, while in India, the Hindu cycle of *Kali Yuga* is set in motion, and in Central America the last cycle of the Olmec calendar begins its countdown. All these events occurred within a few years of each other, if not at the same time. [11]

Perhaps it is also no coincidence these same cultures recognized the perpetual churning mill of the heavens. [12] In the Tamil/Hindu view, *Yugas* are epochs within a cycle of four ages that wax and wane like the seasons, from creation to destruction, gestation and re-creation. Each *Yuga* exerts an influence upon the Earth and human consciousness, since both are intertwined and integral components of the grand machinery of the solar system, its motion around a central Sun, and the Sun's relationship to the center of our galaxy. During the former cycle of *Satya Yuga*, humanity found itself immersed in a Golden Age, a time of technical and spiritual advancement, grand temples, and the governance by gods, truth, and cities of knowledge. By comparison, this present cycle of *Kali Yuga* is regarded as the cycle of quarrel, war, strife, discord, hypocrisy, spiritual degradation, and a move away from God – essentially the time of unbridled solar/masculine power, an "age of vice."

The ram comes storming in.

Which perfectly describes the characteristics governing the Age of Aries. After the stable world of Taurus came a gradual decline of culture and the increase of blind impulse and bluster, certainly the traits of the ram. The Age of Aries (c.2260–100 B.C.)

marked the demise of established civilizations and the rise in warfare and centralized power. It was no doubt a time of locking horns, noted by a gradual disintegration of responsibility of governorship, and its replacement by ego and the rise of despots and spiritually unqualified kingship.

Severe climate changes again played their part in this scenario. The consequences of the aforementioned neoglacial climate did not go away overnight; instead they persisted for a thousand years, causing inconsistencies in food supplies across much of the third millennium B.C. With weather and the agricultural map becoming unpredictable, temple cultures gradually adopted solar principles (masculine) over lunar (feminine). Tens of thousands of new henges, stone circles, dolmens and passage mounds marked a new round of temple-building c2600 B.C. – especially across Europe – the vast majority, like Gavrinis in France, oriented southeast and towards the rising power of the winter solstice Sun. When crops fail you, the corresponding power of the Sun needs to be exalted. In Egypt, temples are extended, the Giza pyramids are added to and restored;[13] and Stonehenge sees its tall, sarsen trilithons erected, essentially completing the site we know today.

Once again the timing of this renewed construction phase was impeccable, for another meteorite found land in 2345 B.C.[14] And as times move deeper into the Age of the Ram, the empires of Mesopotamia, the Indus Valley and Helmand go into a tailspin, as do those of Celtic Britain, Greece and Anatolia.

During these fluctuating years, temples acted as a bulwark against uncertainty, after all, the transfiguration of the soul never sleeps. In times of inconstancy, when the unknown is your compass, people look to what is certain, and inside a stable and defined environment such as a temple, one can find that balance. Additionally, the temple had proved its worth for thousands of years, it was the place to be close to God because it was built in the image of God, and at times when a climate of fear establishes a bulkhead in the human psyche, the safest place to turn to is where order prevails. Since the temple was a place where one could access information, be it through personal introspection or stones marking celestial transits, the buildings proved an invaluable asset in predicting the arrival of events that may not bode well for the tribe. If the skies indicate a chance of being hit by a piece of it, at least preparations can be made for the certainty that life is going to be impacted very negatively. Luck, after all, favors the prepared.

In this way the temple itself began to accrue a misplaced sense of power, and in an escalating climate of fear, the opportunity was not lost on candidates positioning themselves as potential saviors of the people.

From brotherhood to bother-hood.

Written around 1600 B.C., the Book of Psalms records in its arcane language what seems to be a piece of the sky falling down to earth: "Then the earth shook and trembled, the foundations of the mountains moved and were shaken... There went up a smoke out of his nostrils, and fire out of his mouth devoured: coals were kindled by it... At the brightness that was before him his thick clouds passed, hail stones and coals of fire... he sent out his arrows, and scattered them; and he shot out lightning, and discomfited them. Then the channels of waters were seen and the foundations of the world were laid bare." [15]

Just like the consistencies throughout the flood myths, the midpoint of the Age of Aries is marked by stellar observations from Britain, France, the Levant and China, all similarly describing the unusual behavior of the sky. Even Venus is noted by Babylonian astronomers as being absent from view for nine months – a near impossibility considering it is one of the firmament's brightest objects. Indeed, ice core and tree-ring data from 1628 B.C. identifies land strikes of meteorites, in addition to substantial volcanic activity leading to more volatile weather patterns.[16] This generated further turmoil, particularly in the Near East, where marauding armies overwhelmed Egypt from the north and south and inevitably split the kingdom into a number of fiefdoms.

Between 1200-1150 B.C., Greenland's ice core and tree-ring data match up to reveal high levels of acidity, as weather patterns were flipped across the globe, with normally wet areas becoming dry and freezing, and dry areas becoming unusually wet and warm.[17] This matches a long period of major upheaval, famine, plague and mass movement of people from the British Isles to the Mediterranean, across the Middle East and all the way to China.

Hardly an ancient city was left standing as rulers took advantage of chaos to declare allegiance to a new god: war. All the cities of Anatolia were destroyed; Homer's Troy was plundered and with it fell the golden age of the Greeks; the major centers in Cyprus, Israel, Syria, the Levant, and across the Middle East were burned to the ground. The intimate relationship between nature, gods, temples and people were sorely tested as famine, warfare and social chaos took their toll.

In China, even the Mandate from Heaven was withdrawn from the Shang Dynasty c1122 B.C., because the appointed emperor failed to bring an abundant harvest for the people. An emperor was considered the 'Son of Heaven', and like his Egyptian counterparts, it was his duty to assure good relations between heavenly forces and human affairs.[18] As with all rulers borne from the ideology of the temple, governorship of the people was a highly spiritual responsibility; kingship was a representation of the divine on Earth, and those chosen possessed the knowledge of mediation between the forces of the material and invisible. Now with spiritually-attuned leadership becoming usurped by ever-increasing warlords, good governorship became a hit-and-miss affair as pretenders positioned themselves politically to rule for the sake of acquiring power or prestige. The temple itself was becoming a symbol of acquired power for the individual rather than a steward for the people. Thus, when famine descended upon China, the new emperors were revealed for what they were: impostors. And as failed mediators, their power was stripped. Like so many ancient world-views, the Chinese regarded human corruption as a symptom of the loss of connection with elemental forces.[19] The problem was, just as one corrupt despot was removed, so a whole succession of false gods lined up to take his place.

Understandably there was a marked movement away from a feminine and intuitive sanctity of nature, to a dominant masculine, aggressive, possessive culture. True to the traits of the Age of Aries, humanity was poised to experience the absence of Godliness, as marauding armies desecrated temples and scoured their material wealth. As a final insult, in Britain, the warring between tribes meant the hilltop temples were appropriated and reshaped into fortifications. It took centuries for kingdoms to recover, if they ever did, as the Bronze Age effectively came to an abrupt end.

The politics surrounding the period of Amenhotep III's rule in c1386 B.C. definitively typifies this era, which from the point of view of our inquiry concerns the power struggle for control of the temple away from the pharaoh, and the increasing influence of a corrupt priesthood. Thousands of years of observation would have revealed to the cunning observer that whoever has the pulse of the temple has the potential of manipulating the psyche of the people. Naturally, such a notion runs counter to the purpose and principle of sacred space, but in times of turmoil the unbalanced mind becomes the devil's playground, and apparently noble concepts become a means to an end. Amenhotep III was perhaps one of the last of a line of

Amenhotep and Tiye.

spiritual pharaohs. He presided over a period of unprecedented prosperity and artistic splendor in Egypt, quite a feat considering the chaos ensuing all around; statues of him and his wife Tiye show her hand touching the pharaoh's arm, demonstrating his consideration for the equality of women. Nevertheless, he did inherit an Egypt by now being wedded to a highly political priesthood which had cemented its power and control of the temple, and worse, asserted itself as an intermediary between people and the gods.[20]

By the time of his passing, attempts at removing this bastardized system had fallen short, and the problem was bequeathed to his son Akhenaten, a much misunderstood figure, who attempted to complete the process his father had begun, by reforming the basic assumption: that the pharaoh, as the personalization of a creator god on Earth, should be more powerful than the existing domestic order, as represented by the priests of Amun and their substantial temple estates.[21] He attempted to break their influence by first moving the center of temple culture from Thebes to Amarna, then reigning-in the ever-expanding pantheon of gods into one monotheistic society.

Akhenaten

At Amarna he built the city of Akhet-aten ("the Horizon of the Aten"). Akhenaten's aim was to return the temple to the people, by removing intermediaries, ceasing the blind devotion of idols, and refocusing attention on the original principles on which the temple was founded – namely, self-empowerment through the transfiguration of the soul. In this sense, Akhenaten was way ahead of the game, since monotheism was still but a twinkle in the eye of the Age of Pisces, 1,200 years away in the future. Such a move not surprisingly undermined the employment security of the priestly caste. Needless to say, the reign of Akhenaten came to an abrupt end, his temples, monuments and inscriptions eradicated from the face of the earth at the hands of a vengeful priesthood; even his name was excised from the official lists of Pharaohs, which place Horemheb, the commander-in-chief of the army, as his father's successor!

Akhenaten's son and heir, Tutankhaten, was barely eighteen when he met with an early and highly suspicious death: a blow to the skull, a hasty interment, and a tomb hardly fit for a king of his era. Barely had the boy-king been seated at the throne when the priests forced the young pharaoh to change his name from *aten* to *amun*, and moved the capital back to Thebes, all of which was meant to signal to the people there was no doubt as to who controlled the temple, and hence, the power in the land.[22]

246

Cult of blood.

Historically, in times of chaos, people are likely to give up all manner of freedoms and swear blind allegiance just to afford a little peace at night. And that is precisely how a few abusive people acquire power over many. The rise in idolatry followed the disintegration of knowledge, as more temples around the world fell under the aggrandized power of the priesthood. With so much fear to be spread around, it was easy for the powerful to position themselves as saviors from uncertainty, and any allusions by rulers to rule by divine mandate was nothing more than mere lip service. Indeed, wise leadership became the exception.

By the time the Age of Aries gave way to the Age of Pisces c100 B.C., many temples were being appropriated for purposes different to those for which they'd been built, the most typical being their new use as burial sites. The rich and influential could now be associated with the source of a god's power on Earth by being buried as close as physically possible to the temple. Our modern concept of church graveyards developed from this era, and a casual browse of headstones in old churches reveals that the more status you carried in the community (ie. money), the closer your grave was located to the altar.

Some temples were shut down or closed, physically as well as energetically. The entrance to the Great Pyramid was sealed, and only through much gunpowder was a hole blown on its northern flank by treasure hunters; beneath the sacred mountain of Dehenet, Hatshepsut's temple was shut down energetically following the misuse of sacred sexuality as a means of control rather than education.[23] In Britain, a 90-ton megalith plugged the entrance to the long barrow of West Kennett near Avebury, effectively sealing the passageway and preventing the telluric energy of the site from further misuse.

In the Americas, the Inca, Toltec and Maya appear to have upheld the true concept of the temple right up to the time of Christ, but inevitably even these cultures and their extraordinary works – not to mention all those they inherited – slowly became relics of a bygone era, succumbing to desert sands and jungle vines just as surely as the sites of the Celts were reclaimed by the peat. Like Edfu, they became curiosities of forgotten ages, created by people of such remote antiquity that few understood the original reason why the monuments were built in the first place.

Ancient academies fell under the weight of centralized religious beliefs and political direction, and with the loss of knowledge and its mentors, errors slowly crept into the system, as even the high culture of the Greeks went into decline.[24]

The Romans gained control over ancient temples and draped them in the excesses, misconceptions of the times and the whims of the new solar gods, the Caesars.

These are, of course, very broad strokes in a complex and still-emerging global picture. The culture of the true temple did not vanish entirely during these times, it merely went underground, but its importance as the spiritual compass of people was greatly diminished, because its principles fell into direct conflict with prevailing politics and an aggressive social landscape. In Central America, temple culture actually saw a renaissance, albeit under a veil of ignorance, when the Aztec took the misuse of the temple and the misinterpretation of spiritual knowledge to unprecedented extremes.

During their southerly migration through Mexico, the Aztec inherited the symmetrical metropolis of Tenochtitlan, now Mexico City. By their time, the 32.04 square miles of the "birthplace of gods" to the northeast at Teotihuacan was already an abandoned ruin. To the Aztec, these dilapidated mounds (and by then the Pyramid of the Sun did actually resemble a natural mountain) had been built by a long-lost civilization "at a time when giants and sages inhabited the Earth." [25] The passage of the Pleiades across the meridian of the sky provided the Aztec with an excuse to engage in a bloodbath of human sacrifice, and every fifty-two years this ritual took place to appease the gods: "Deep in their soul the ancient Mexicans could not trust the future. Their world was too fragile, always exposed to a catastrophe. Every fifty-two years the people of the whole empire succumbed to terror, fearing that the last sunset of their "century" would not be followed by a new dawn... terror-stricken crowds thronged to the [Temple of Ul Xochitecatl]. On its summit, the priests were watching the constellation of the Pleiades. The astronomer-priest gave a signal. A prisoner was stretched out on the altar, a stone knife was plunged into his breast with a dull noise, and over the gaping wound a burning stick was waved... The flame would flicker, as if born from the broken breast, and among joyful clamor, messengers lit torches and left to spread fire to the four corners of the central valley. Thus, the world had once more escaped destruction." [26]

According to 17th century accounts by conquistadores, blood sacrifices and cannibalism were widely practiced in temples throughout Central America: "They strike open the wretched Indian's chest with flint knives and hastily tear out the palpitating heart, which with the blood, they present to the idols... They cut off the arms, thighs and head, eating the arms and thighs at ceremonial banquets. The head they hang up on a beam and the body is... given to the beasts of prey." [27]

Even the barbaric Cortez was revulsed: "They have a most horrid and abominable custom, which truly ought to be punished and, which

Aztec use of the temple during the age of fear.

until now we have seen in no other part, and this is that, whenever they wish to ask something of the idols, in order that their plea may find more acceptance, they take many girls and boys and even adults, and in the presence of these idols they open their chests while they are still alive and take out their hearts, and entrails burn them before the idols, offering the smoke as sacrifice. Some of us have seen this, and they say it is the most terrible and frightful thing they have ever witnessed." [28]

When original understanding is lost, all that remains is superstition.

One energy, many masters.

Through the personal and collective stories in earlier chapters, I attempted to give an idea of the power and potential at work in the temples. The experience is difficult to convey in words and only through direct contact can anyone understand what these "mansions of the gods" do *for* you and *to* you. It is an unselfish energy that empowers the self, and the results and experiences are, to a degree, dependent on what the seeker is seeking, and the level of intent and commitment they bring into the premises. So, be careful what you ask for, you may well receive it!

Paradoxically, in this power lies the seed of the downfall of the self. Like great sex, love, food and Alfa Romeos, it has the potential to make one heady and prone to over-indulgence which ultimately gives rise to ego. In essence, this is what occurred to the guardians of the temple during the "age of vice." They got drunk on 'the knowledge', and when you start to believe this power somehow makes you all-powerful and more important than everyone around you, that's when problems arise. Absolute power corrupts without fail.

The human body is a finely-tuned electromagnetic instrument,[29] and the introduction of too much energy too quickly can do strange things. Depending on your disposition, it has the potential to burn out your fuses. Or it can embolden you to become a tyrant. This is why initiates-in-training were never allowed inside pyramids, for the energy in temples of such design – with their specific geometry and insulating stone – is too concentrated; instead, to prevent the body's energy circuits from being overwhelmed, they were trained to raise their residual energy gradually from temple to temple before being allowed loose in those magnificent halls of eternity. Napoleon discovered this for himself after spending a night inside the King's Chamber, only to run for his life the moment the door was flung open in the morning, revealing a pale and visibly shaken man. Napoleon was adamant that no one should ever ask him what took place inside that place. After he became emperor, he hinted that he'd received a presage about his destiny, and even on his death bed, at the point of confiding to the historian Emmanuel las Casas, he instead shook his head and said, "No. What's the use? You'd never believe me." [30]

Temples are repositories of power, designed by master craftsmen possessed of great spirituality and humility. And just as they are capable of altering the individual, so the electromagnetic individual can disrupt the temple, and creation myths and traditions warn of the dangers inherent in this two-way force.

The omphalos is the sacred pillar marking all at once the primeval mound, the umbilical cord with a creator god, and a place where the knowledge can be sourced, hence why adepts who worked with such power places were referred to as *sorcerers*. It was also considered to be a kind of plug that secured "the waters of the abyss from overflowing." Metaphorically speaking, if the omphalos is moved, altered or misused in some way, the power of place can become unstable. In the myths of the Akwasi of British Guyana, the "navel of creation" sits on a watery cavity connected to the bowels of the Earth, and to prevent its overflow, a tightly woven basket is wrapped around the central tree. When a mischievous monkey lifts the basket, the world falls apart.[31] In Central India, the Agaria say "it was the breaking of a large nail of iron that caused our city from the 'golden age' to be flooded." There are identical stories throughout Mongolia and Sumer that link the destruction of the planet by messing with the *lingam* and altering the forces restrained at the site, much like the "stirring of the enemy snake" caused the disintegration of the temples of Egypt.[32]

Glastonbury Tor is a natural hill that 2,000 years ago still resembled a primeval mound as it sat surrounded by shallow inland waters. It stands on fissures that go deep into the land, and its pressurized mineral waters are still a wonder to imbibe today. The legends that surround it and its attendant Abbey also speak of the demise of Britain should the site be desecrated. And that is precisely what happened after 1539 following a rampage by Henry VIII, who'd sought the 'treasure of the abbey', but failing to find it, had the buildings razed to the ground. As with so many legends of sacred sites, the treasure is not so much physical as it is metaphorical. Like the legend of a King Sil buried with a life-size gold statue of himself on a horse beneath Silbury Hill, the metaphor symbolizes the process of spiritual enlightenment through self-realization in the temple; in Glastonbury, the treasure was embedded in the geometric and mathematical values of the structure itself, so when mad Henry destroyed the buildings he wrecked the very treasure he'd been seeking.

Creation myths from Easter Island to Egypt describe how a god creates a "navel on the earth" from which springs a tree bearing fruit, knowledge, and all manner of things that foster civilization. Then, as the Akwasi tradition goes on to state, "in order to diffuse the benefits of the tree all over the world, Sigu [the creator] resolved to cut it down and plant slips and seeds of it everywhere." [33] The task is undertaken by all creatures except that mischievous brown monkey, whom the creator god distracts by sending him off to fetch water while

Solomon's Temple under Temple Mount.

250

the transplanting takes place. This tradition has parallels to the story of Osiris, who gets chopped into fourteen pieces and scattered before being reassembled, and re-emerges as a tree. The same symbolism is used throughout classic Norse, Roman and Greek rites involving creator gods, founders of holy cities, or solar kings whose dismembering into pieces enriches the land and serves to promulgate his status as a bearer of divine influence.

You can also read such stories as allegories: the place where the power of the land meets the descending power of a god serves as a focal point of energy. Groups of adepts, in direct communication with the divine source, travel to the four corners of the Earth and set up new centers of culture, whose focus is a temple occupying other nodes of telluric energy. It is interesting that in the Akwasi story the only mischievous being present is distracted while the sacred work is carried out. The process of temple-building – with its harnessing of telluric forces and encoded astronomy and mathematics – was too important to be tampered with by mischief makers. Certainly there has always been a synergy between 'navels of the earth', telluric energy, and the empowering of the individual. However, since energy is simply energy and it knows not right from wrong, the places of power can equally fall into the wrong hands, and whenever they do, typically the story ends badly for everyone involved. As history bears witness, a corrupt priesthood did figure out how to wrestle power away from the adepts and used the temple as a tool for control rather than the education and empowerment of others.

The focal point of this latent energy sits below every altar or holy of holies, nourishing the land and maintaining the balance of life like blood flowing through veins. And it was the charge of adepts to learn to harness this energy with integrity, as the Babylonian Talmud legend of King David illustrates:

David is digging the foundation for a temple when, at a great depth, he finds the original omphalos. The stone tells David, "I rest upon the abyss," and as the embodiment of the power of God it "lie[s] here to cover-up the abyss." [34] David lifts up the stone to see if this is true and discovers that, yes, removing a stone that is the receptacle of divine energy indeed lets all hell break loose, because suddenly "the Deep arose and threatened to submerge the world." [35]

David then makes us aware he has been instructed in the ways of the sacred knowledge, because he turns to his privy councilor and asks, "Is there anyone who knows whether it is permitted to inscribe the [ineffable] Name upon a sherd, and cast it into the Deep that its waves should subside?" [36] He is addressing Ahithophel, a kind of mentor to David, who decides to play a game of one-upmanship with the King by withholding the information. Meanwhile, the Deep continues to rise. David then issues a command tinged with a curse: "Whoever knows how to stem the tide of the Deep and fails to do it will one day throttle himself." [37] Whereupon Ahithophel tells David, "Yes, by all means inscribe the ineffable name of God [presumably Tetragrammaton] on the sherd," which he does, and casts it into the Deep. Ahithophel's spell works only too well: the waves of the Deep not only subside, they do so to such a degree that

David fears the Earth will be destabilized. So David sings the fifteen Songs of the Ascents as an antidote, whereby the Deep is raised sufficiently and balance is restored to the land.[38]

Later Jewish literature assumes the text is referring to water, but nowhere in the Babylonian myth is water ever mentioned, it just mentions waves. Waves of water below the soil are highly improbable, but not *electromagnetic* waves, and as we saw earlier, telluric currents anchored by stone is indeed part of the technology of sacred space.

The stone holding the energy of David's site is quite possibly the Eben Shetiyah, (the "Stone of Foundation") on Temple Mount, which like so many identical places of power sits on deep fissures. Many world legends identify these 'navels of the earth' as sitting on subterranean channels linking one navel to another like "irrigation channels" that "bear fruit in each country." Thus the legends inform us this network of energy fertilizes the land, on one hand, and on the other is capable of causing global dysfunction whenever the omphalos is tampered with.

In David and Ahithophel we are dealing with two sorcerers – they work with the *source* – the latter engaging in very unethical grandstanding. The Haggadah states that Ahithophel's devotion to the study of the Laws was not founded on worthy motives; that he abused his sacred knowledge in the pursuit of greed and power. Like the prophet and diviner Balaam, he and Ahithophel were the two great sages of that era who, failing to show gratitude to the Source and humility for their wisdom, perished in dishonor – Ahithophel, as David rightly predicted, by hanging himself. Like many notable adepts, Ahithophel was 33-years old when he died. His death was a great loss to David; his wisdom was so great that Scripture itself avoids calling him a man, for his wisdom bordered on that of the angels.[39] A true Darth Vader of his time.

David's dream was to build a temple every bit as good as those made by the creator gods, but he was well aware that only a humble person of right intent and right action is afforded the right to do so, as the words spoken to his son attest: "My son, I had it in my heart to build a house to the name of the Lord my God. But the word of the Lord came to me, saying, you have shed much blood and have waged great wars; you shall not build a house to my name, because you have shed so much blood before me upon the earth. Behold, a son shall be born to you; he shall be a man of peace." [40]

And indeed Solomon (*sol-amun*, a solar hero) goes on to realize his father's dream of building a perfect temple above a 'navel of the earth' at Uru-shalim, the "abode of peace." It is curious that the Dome on this rock, the "Holy Sanctuary" of the Arabs, is also said to have been built by Suleiman ben Daoud (Solomon, Son of David.)[41] And yet despite so many similarities, the abode of peace in Jerusalem has ever since been anything but.

Theater of Pyrrhus at Dodona.

The decapitation of the divine feminine.

Olympia was a high priestess at the Temple of Dodona, the oldest sacred site in Greece, created when Zeus manifested his essence on Earth in the shape of a *betyl*, a navel stone, upon which was built a temple dedicated to Zeus-Amun. Dodona is connected with Karnak-Luxor through a myth of two doves that flew between these sites; the Theban temples also happen to be the principal centers of veneration of Amun. There are great similarities between classic Greek and ancient Egyptian cultures; for one, their gods are interchangeable – Hermes-Djehuti, Dionysus-Osiris, Pan-Min, Aphrodite-Isis/Hathor, and of course Zeus-Amun/Ra. But more so because Greece's most famous luminaries, such as Pythagoras and Plato, had sojourned as students of the Heliopolitan priests, and the wisdom they acquired made Greek culture one of the great wonders of the world. Even Herodotus makes such a claim.[42]

Egypt in 343 B.C. had become a very different place. It found itself under the barbaric rule of Persian despots who desecrated the temples and systematically reduced what was left to rubble. But true to the spirit of great legends, a hero appears in 332 B.C., when Alexander the Great, son of Olympia, defeats the Persians and marches triumphantly into Memphis. The grateful Egyptians immediately make Alexander a pharaoh, whereupon Alexander's first priority is to restore the dual temples of Luxor and Karnak which had fallen into decay. He also amends the Greek calendar by making the New Year fall on July 21st, the traditional heliacal rising of Sirius, the Dog Star – symbol of Isis and the divine feminine and rebirth of knowledge.[43]

Given the thousand years of ascent of the masculine, this sudden interest in resuscitating the temple and the feminine seems almost anomalous, and thus intriguing.

From the age of fourteen, Alexander had been surrounded by tutors of the highest caliber in Greece: Aristotle, who had studied under Plato, and whom Plato described as "the intelligence of the school"; Theophrastus, a scientist and renaissance man whose works on physics, metaphysics, biology and botany greatly influenced later medieval thinkers; and finally, Callisthenes the historian. This brain trust would have molded the young Alexander well, for Aristotle alone taught him the sciences and philosophy, and instilled in the young lad the virtues, the most important being reason. He also would have discussed with his inquiring pupil his most famous work *Politika* in which Aristotle outlined the philosophy of human affairs in what he called the Ideal State.[44]

Did this have an impact on Alexander's enlightened actions in Egypt? Let's consider that another great influence on Alexander was Homer's *Odyssey*, particularly the legend of Jason and the Argonauts, who'd set sail from the island of Pharos, located on the tip of the Nile Delta.[45] All these ideals coalesced into a vision, as Alexander then set into motion a plan for a new city in Egypt dedicated to the resurgence of wisdom which, it was hoped, would re-ignite the world.

Riding out with Ptolemy and Callisthenes, Alexander reached Pharos, where he laid the foundation for the city of Alexandria. Its tutelary goddess would be none other than Isis. On Pharos itself, a lighthouse was erected that would later become one of the seven great wonders of the world, not least because its light was said to shine "as bright as a second sun," a term also attributed to Sirius, the star associated with Isis, Sophia, and wisdom.

Alas, Alexander would not see his dream come true for he dies in Persia, just shy of his 33rd birthday! The city bearing his name was put into motion by his enlightened friend and newly-appointed pharaoh, Ptolemy, and designed as a grid with a cross as its central axis, in the same manner as Saqqara and Akhetaten;[46] its main axis, fixed by Alexander himself, was aligned through the eastern Gate of Helios (the Sun) to the heliacal rising of Sirius.[47] If the alignment is projected into the horizon, it passes the now-submerged portion of the city of Heraklion and its temple dedicated to Isis' consort, Osiris.[48]

In time, Alexandria does blossom as a universal city of wisdom and learning, with the help of Manetho, a priest of Heliopolis, as well as it's most famous institution, the Great Library, a combination of the great temple-library at Heliopolis and the contents of Aristotle's own Lyceum, which Ptolemy had transferred from Athens. The Great Library was charged with accumulating the world's knowledge, and it duly became the spark that revitalized interest in the great arts.

But as with all great tales, there has to be a modicum of tension. This was aptly provided in 307 A.D. during the Roman period of occupation, when Catherine, the daughter of the pagan governor of Alexandria, came to symbolize all that was evil in the world – at least in the Roman way of looking at the world. Catherine was an enlightened woman of the period and a noted scholar who, upon her conversion to Christianity (not to be confused with Catholicism) visited the Roman Emperor Maximinus in an attempt to convince him of the immorality of persecuting Christians. Although unsuccessful, she nevertheless managed to convince his wife, a number of pagan philosophers, as well as many of Maximinus' army. Suitably impressed, the emperor had them all martyred.

However, that would not be the end of it. Catherine was imprisoned, yet all who visited her were also converted. She was subsequently tortured, flayed alive, then condemned to be beaten to death on a spiked wheel. But since the wheel broke when she touched it, she was beheaded instead. Catherine of Alexandria would become a symbol against oppression and tyranny, the inspiration for many emerging esoteric orders such as the Cathars, just as she became the patron saint of the Knights Templar.

Barely five years after her brutal death, the new Emperor Constantine initially accepted Christianity as a faith (humans really are strange, aren't they?). However, during the next seventy years Christianity would not only become the only faith, but Constantine was bullied by the bishops to accept its dominance by militant Christians, and the repercussions of this decision shaped the Catholic Church into what it became: a perversion of the ethics of its central figure, Jesus, much like latter-day Islamist extremists have attempted to dominate the ethics of Islam.[49]

But the Romans were just getting into the downfall of Alexandria, ironically while their own empire was doing the same, and their actions typify the rule of the bully and the ignorant who adamantly despise knowledge and the sacred feminine. This was hardly a propitious era for intellectuals: Neoplatonists were considered heretics alongside Jews (a *heretic* being "someone in possession of facts who is able to choose"); even Christian Gnostics were considered "agents of Satan" and became targets of the militant Christians.[50] In 391 A.D., one-hundred new laws were issued by Emperor Theodosius I depriving Gnostics, Jews, and any order outside the strict confines of Orthodox belief, of property, liberty, temples and books.[51] Then, life in Alexandria reached a state from which it never recovered. According to an account by the Greek Historian Socrates Scholasticus, "At the solicitation of Theophilus, Bishop of

Temple of Luxor in 1870.

Alexandria, the Emperor issued an order at this time for the demolition of the heathen temples in that city… Seizing this opportunity, Theophilus exerted himself to the utmost to expose the pagan mysteries to contempt… he destroyed the Serapeum [part of the Great Library] … he showed full of extravagant superstitions, and he had the [omphalos] carried through the midst of the forum." The rampage through the library and the temples was carried out by Christian fanatics and monks incited by Bishop Theophilus, massacring members of the oppressed sects taking refuge in the Serapeum. Irreplaceable books containing the wisdom of millennia were burned along with their protective buildings.[52] Emperor Theodosius I even held the victims responsible for their own demise.[53]

255

The destruction of temples extended as far as Delphi.[54] During this time the codices of the Nag Hammadi Library were secretly ensconced to avoid destruction; their discovery in 1945 would reveal the hitherto discredited gnostic vision of Jesus, the existence of his brother and potentially a holy bloodline,[55] a gospel banned by the Church and deemed to be older than the four canonical gospels[56] – all of which became a source of huge embarrassment for the Catholic Church.

The embers were still glowing when the mob turned on yet another female intellectual, the accomplished scholar Hypatia. In 400 A.D., in addition to her illustrious career as a mathematician, astronomer, physicist, and inventor, she became the head of the Platonist School of Alexandria. As far as Christian zealots were concerned, science and mathematics were heresies and those who practiced such evil "were to be torn by beasts or else burned alive."[57] Somehow not the kind of ethics Jesus had had in mind. When the fanatical Christian Cyril became Patriarch of Alexandria he began first persecuting Jews, afterward turning his attention to Neoplatonists. Then, as Hypatia returned home one day, "...waylaid her, and dragging her from her carriage, they dragged her into the Church called Caesarium, where they stripped her, and then murdered her by scraping her skin off with tiles and bits of shell. After tearing her body to pieces, they took her mangled limbs to a place called Cinaron and there burnt them."[58]

Cyril was canonized.

Rome collapsed.

The temple and its sages did not altogether die, they just took a sabbatical.

Like Osiris, they were broken up, their parts sown throughout many territories, later to be reborn as tall trees bearing many fruit.

There's a Greek aphorism which states "God without goddess is spiritual insufficiency." It is the same with any temple that thrives on the exclusion of others, as the declaration by God in *Isaiah 56:7* makes evidently clear: "Even them I will bring to my holy mountain, and make them joyful in my house of prayer... My house shall be called a house of prayer for all people."

But sometimes, to appreciate what there is, it is necessary to experience what there is not, and that is true of so many things.

The Parthenon by 1860. Greece.

If you can't convert the people, convert the temple. Pavia dolmen. Portugal.

18

RETURN OF THE INVISIBLES.

It is often joked that suffering is an essential component of art, and the greater the suffering endured by the artist the more important the art.

Even by such standards the keepers of the knowledge have suffered tremendously. Back in 9703 B.C. the Seven Sages were confronted with the problem of a global flood. In the 10th century A.D., gnostics and philosophers were confronted with the Catholic Church and its inquisitors, Christian mob violence, and the burning of their books and bodies.

Our journey has brought us a long way since the "cities of knowledge" of the Tamils and the ancient academy of Innu/Heliopolis, "...the greatest center of magic in Egypt… where the most ancient theology developed. Here were preserved numerous *papyri*, 'magic' in the widest sense of the word, including medical, botanical, zoological and mathematical texts." The focus at these Mystery Schools was intense, for it was a "...sacred science that requires specialists trained for many years to grasp the most secret forces of the universe." [1]

Through the knowledge and energy of the temple, the soul is transfigured, and suitably empowered it reaches into realities the normal senses cannot grasp. In Djehuti's sacred city of Hermopolis there's an inscription in the tomb of Petosiris, a high priest and initiate, that illustrates the feeling of liberation this process brings: "He, who abides in the path of God, passes a whole life in joy, blessed with more wealth than his peers. He grows old in his city, he is a man respected in his province, and all his limbs are young like those of a child. His children are before him of great number and counted among the leaders of their town... at last he comes joyfully to his burial place." [2]

This man seems to be in a state of bliss despite the fact he's about to die.

Through indoctrination into the Mysteries, one was taught the application of *heka*, "magical power," [3] best translated as the control of the forces of nature – the pinnacle of the art of the magi. Knowledge was inseparable from magic because everything was seen as animate.[4] Our modern conventions may scoff at this, and yet if we take the simple observation that the rays of the Sun sustain life, the scientist accepts this is as physics while the ancients called it magic, and yet both are valid inquiries into the same creative force. The ancients did not see the forces sustaining life as beyond the understanding of human intelligence, they merely phrased their understanding in a different language. The art of rationalizing such energies was taught and experienced throughout the academies and temples, and certainly under close supervision of very experienced priests.[5] For them, the big question was this: "Man, like any other speck of life, is the outcome of an interplay of forces. Will he submit to them passively or seek to identify them? The quality of his fate will depend on his answer to these questions." [6] No wonder the sages, philosophers and adepts were prepared to endure great obstacles – the wisdom they kept alive was nothing less than personal illumination that brought about a transfiguration of the self, and through it and inevitably, the liberty of the soul.

The obstacles to self-empowerment in recent times have been formidable. Through a series of edicts, the Catholic Church banned worship at pagan temples, to the point where women who attended standing stones to facilitate childbirth were made to fast for three years.[7] The chances of survival were slim, to say the least. At one point it even became a criminal offense *not* to attend Mass.[8] Along with atrocities and the pogroms of entire sects was the burning of all Gnostic texts, including the irreplaceable works of philosophers and mystics, and with such a degree of bestiality that begs one to ask the question: was the Church merely eradicating the competition (and there were plenty of gentler doctrines to choose from) or erasing evidence that could prove damning to its existence?

Sects and violence.

After the violent events in Alexandria, the sensible thing for anyone working with the old ways was to adopt a clandestine existence so that the transmission of knowledge remained unbroken. Besides, attending sacred sites in and of itself had become a dangerous practice. Still, use of the temple continued surreptitiously until the 11th century,[9] at which point the Church realized its efforts at curbing people's appetite for the old faiths had fallen short, so it applied a new strategy: convert the remaining temples to Catholicism. Throughout Europe there are countless examples of stone circles incorporated into churches, menhirs with their apex recarved into crosses, and massive dolmens refurbished with concrete pillars, conventional church doors, even bell towers!

Various sects promulgating the teachings of the temple existed from at least 200 A.D., one of the most influential being Manichaeism, a sect from Persia whose philosophy precedes some of the early Christian gnostic movements. Led by Mani and twelve disciples, it infiltrated the Roman Empire and reached as far west as the British Isles, and although eventually persecuted throughout the Middle East, it survived in China well into the 16th century.[10]

Like Manichaeism, Christian Gnosticism rivaled the Church's hegemony. It was based on elements of Egyptian and Eastern traditions, and Greek philosophy. There were also the Messalians ("praying people") and Bogomils ("god lovers"), but probably best known of all are the Cathari, also known as Cathars ("pure ones"), who managed to secure a bulkhead throughout southern France, in part because the Church, in believing they had exterminated every possible and perceived contender, fell asleep on the job. Although the Cathari practiced non-violence, their success as a force capable of fighting back lay in its doctrine which, like Manichaeism or Christian Gnosticism, effortlessly converted large sections of the public, even members within the Catholic Church, and local Comtes and the armies at their command.

None of these faiths imposed their doctrine on others, and although each sect had its own idiosyncrasies, they all share much in common: they believed in the state of Duality, a God of Light and a God of Dark, like the Egyptian concept of Horus and Set; they also believed it is the confusion in distinguishing between the contrary principles of spirit and matter during the present cycle of life that causes the

Re-carved Men Marz menhir; stone incorporated into Le Mans cathedral. France.
And a stone circle inside the church of S. Miguel Arrechinaga. Spain.

soul to over-identify with the forces of the material world, thus creating the root of its suffering.[11] In this constant conflict between the soul and the body, 'salvation' is attained through *gnosis*, knowledge of the true nature of things and the universe, the central tenet being the existence of a spiritual realm – essentially a paradise or heaven – as the cherished domain of the soul, of truth, and a loving God. Through gradual self-improvement, and thus self-empowerment, the perfected soul is ultimately liberated. And to this end temples and ancient academies were built and maintained for posterity.

Part of this knowledge was not intellectual, nor was it necessarily written in books. Rather, it was *revealed* knowledge, like a rush of inspiration, when for just a brief moment you see everything with total clarity. Such a revelation can only be discovered through personal experience if one is to understand. And since each soul follows an individual path during incarnation, the credo of these sects, for which they were vehemently persecuted, was to allow individual truth. The *Nag Hammadi Texts* show that Jesus had mastered the liberation of the soul, for after his crucifixion he is stated as saying, "I did not succumb to them as they had planned... I was not afflicted at all. Those who were there punished me, and I did not die in reality but in appearance." [12]

Which brings us to the sects' other fundamental shared belief: the established Church is an impostor, and a diabolical one at that. It is an imitation of the "perfect assembly" it has displaced, since any institution that persecutes the foundation of the true church (ie. the Sons of Light or Gnostic adepts) is tricking its followers into a world of "fear and slavery, worldly cares and abandoned worship... For they did not know the Knowledge of the Greatness, that is from above, and from a fountain of truth, and that it is not from slavery and jealousy, fear and love of worldly matter," as stated in the *Nag Hammadi Texts*.[13]

They further accused the emerging Roman Catholic Church's bishops of being "mere counterfeits," hijacking and twisting the faith of Christ, "having proclaimed a doctrine of a dead man." [14] And they had a point. In 533 A.D., the ecumenical Council deemed the central tenet of spirituality – the resurrection of the soul – a heresy, and warned, "anyone who defends the mystical notion of a soul and the stupendous notion of its return, shall be excommunicated." In other words, persecuted. Later, in what has to be one of the biggest gaffes in history, the Church exposed itself as peddling a myth when Pope Leo X admitted, "All ages can testifie enough how profitable that <u>fable</u> of Christ hath ben to us and our companie." [15]

In essence, the 'organizations' served the spiritual forces of Light, and through initiation into the cult of knowledge they sought to free humans from their enslavement to ignorance, not by physical force but through a wisdom that ultimately exposes "the world rulers of this darkness" so that the souls of men and women are no longer prostitutes to their will.[16]

The Templars return from Jerusalem, with a big secret.

Common sense dictates that nine men did not travel to the Holy Land in 1118 to police hundreds of miles of a pilgrim trail. That task was already the charge of the Hospitallers of St. John. When nine knights departed for Jerusalem under the tutelage of Bernard de Clairvaux, they knew very well what they were to do and where to look for it.

Nine years after selective digging under Temple Mount they packed up and sailed back to Burgundy carrying a big secret, and within months they would be officially recognized as the order of the Knights Templar. A hint as to the magnitude of their find comes from a speech by Bernard himself at their inauguration ceremony: "The work has been accomplished with our help. And the Knights have been sent on the journey through France and Burgundy... under the protection of the Count of Champagne, where all precautions can be taken against all interference by public or ecclesiastical authority; where at this time one can best make sure of a secret, a watch, a hiding place." [17]

When the deciphering of the *Copper Scroll* from Qumran was completed in 1956, it is mentioned that a vast stockpile of gold bullion and valuables had been hidden deep beneath the Temple of Solomon prior to the Roman plunder above ground. Additionally, the scroll mentions the sequestering of an "indeterminable treasure." [18] There is little doubt the Knights Templar unearthed the gold along with a wealth of ancient Hebrew and Syriac manuscripts that had not been edited by the Church.[19] As with the *Nag Hammadi Texts* these included first-hand accounts predating the canonical Gospels, along with proof that the 'virgin birth' and the resurrection had been selectively edited or deliberately falsified to achieve the Church's agenda.[20] Certainly the Knights Templar were well aware of Christianity's more remote origins, for when they were shown a crucifix one knight commented, "Set not much faith in this, for it is too young." [21]

Make no mistake, the Knights Templar were totally dedicated to the ministry of Jesus, as was their benefactor Bernard de Clairvaux and his Cistercian Order, whose ideals of higher education, agriculture, the sacred arts, and the renouncement of violence were far removed from the Roman Church's. The Templar's perceived mission was military yet relatively few of its members were combatants; even their founding motto has unambiguous spiritual overtones: *Not onto us, O Lord, not unto us, but to thy name glory.*

But what of that tantalizing "indeterminable treasure" the knights brought back from Temple Mount? A number of sources make a strong case for it being the Ark of the Covenant,[22] while an equally persuasive argument is made for the physical Ark being absconded from the Temple of Solomon shortly before Nebuchadnezzar ransacked it, and ever since it has rested in the Church of Our Lady of Zion in Aksum, Ethiopia.[23] Either way, such an inquiry falls well outside the scope of this book. Whatever it was they brought back, kings across Western Europe unanimously showered the Knights Templar with pledges of devotional and logistical support. New members swelled the Order and flooded it with hitherto unseen levels of resources. And yet everyone pledging allegiance, including the original Knights, all renounced their wealth and adopted a vow of poverty. The speed with which the landowners handed over their property suggests the Knights had something special to offer in return. We already know that few of the Knights Templar were militants, so we can safely assume that the threat of violence was not one of them. Yet within six weeks of their official founding, they gained a foothold in the tiny kingdom of Portucale, and in as many years were instrumental in the founding of Europe's first country, Portugal.[24] Even by military standards these are remarkable achievements.

Clearly, whatever they brought back from the Near East offered great leverage, because everyone was tripping over themselves to side with nine knights like bees to a hive. Incredibly, the Church granted the Order full immunity, probably because in 1139 the highly influential Bernard facilitated the Cistercian Innocent II to become Pope, creating a rare window of opportunity for Rome to engage in good works.

If you have an indispensable asset, say, your life savings, the smart thing to do is deposit them in separate banks. Let us suppose, then, that the *Ark* was smuggled to Aksum and what the Knights Templar found were some of its *contents*. They did, after all, come home with secret archives full of bundles of ancient scripts and scrolls,[25] and the Temple of Solomon, being a 'navel of the earth', certainly would have been a repository of the knowledge. *Archive* derives from the Greek *arkheia* meaning "magisterial residence," which is a very apt description of the foundation of a temple, a mansion of the god; its root is *arkhe*. If you still swallow the simplistic notion that the Knights Templar were merely seeking physical treasure, then let's examine the etymological fingerprint of that word. *Treasure* derives from the French *trésor*, which eventually migrates into Portuguese as *tesouro*, from which comes *thesauro* or *thesaurus* in Greek, meaning "a storehouse, treasure."

Indeed. But not of gold: a treasure of *words*.

Bernard was a learned man, not to mention a cunning one (from *kunna* meaning "possessing erudition and skill"). He knew that, locked inside Solomon's stables, the Ark of the Covenant held the greatest of all treasures, namely, the words of God: The Tables of Testimony and the Tables of Law.[26] The Ark did not contain Commandments, since God explicitly said to Moses to come up to Sinai and "I will give Thee tables of stone, and a law, <u>and</u> commandments which I have written, that thou mayest teach them." [27] Three separate items. Furthermore, *Exodus 34: 27-28* states that the Tables of Testimony were written by God, and Moses wrote the Ten Commandments separately.

As any good Christian knows, the Ten Commandments are no secret. The same cannot be said for the two Tables, and in Genesis, God offers a hint: "I have made everything with number, measure and weight." The Tables of Law came directly from the fingers of a creator god. They are the Cosmic Equation, the divine law of number, measure, weight, relationship and reason – the recipe for the causes behind the creative forces of the universe. They are a means of power – knowledge so pure that in the wrong hands could prove disastrous; in Solomon's time not even the Levite Guard had access to the Ark. That responsibility was the high priest's alone, and then for someone of the highest integrity. Even so, the numbers in the Laws would most likely have been sealed *within* the actual words of God, exactly like the numerical encryption technique used in *Gematria*, as we saw in earlier chapters; a similar technique for coding alphanumeric knowledge also lies within Qabalah. What was needed in addition to a high priest was a master cryptographer, for example, an adept such as Moses, who had been trained in the initiatory temples of Egypt, and "was learned in all the wisdom of the Egyptians." [28]

Bernard de Clairvaux.

In 12th century Troyes, the Cistercians and Knights Templar also required a cryptographer, and the Court of Champagne was well prepared for the cryptic translation of documents found in the Temple of Solomon, for it had long been a sponsor of an influential school of Cabbalistic and esoteric studies.[29] The focus of their inquiry would most likely have been a document similar to the *Temple Scroll* of Qumran, which contains detailed instructions on how to build a temple. Bernard himself translated the sacred geometry of Solomon's Masons,[30] with further assistance coming from learned Rabbis from nearby Burgundy.[31] And it appears they succeeded in deciphering the code, because when asked "What is God?" Bernard replied, cryptically, "He is length, width, height and depth."

The Great Work.

Bernard's vision for Europe was one more aligned with the true teachings of avatars such as Jesus, not what the Roman Catholic Church had turned them into. His purpose was shared by the central Templar figure Hugues de Payens. And it was a mystical and self-inquiring discovery of God – a principle the practitioners of the ancient Mysteries, all the way to the Seven Sages, would have commended.

During their formative years in Jerusalem the Knights Templar would have rubbed shoulders with Sufism – the gnostic arm of Islam – and soon discovered that Sufis honored Jesus as one of the Seven Sages of Islam, and practiced interfaith pluralism insofar as they believed no single faith possessed all the information of the central cosmic truth. The Knights Templar would also have absorbed local eastern influences, particularly from the descendents of the Sabeans of Harran, the compilers of a great Hermetic book on magic called the *Picatrix*, which was based on 224 manuscripts on Hermeticism, astrology, magic, Qabalah and alchemy, and in which was contained a blueprint for the ideal Hermetic city[32] – the kind of tome one would dedicate nine years in Jerusalem to read and understand.

Sabean comes from the Arabic *saba'ia*, meaning "star people." They were known to have made yearly pilgrimages to the Giza pyramids to conduct astronomical observations, and recognized the pyramids as monuments dedicated to the stars, which proved to be a correct deduction.[33] *Saba'ia* becomes the Portuguese word *sabio*, meaning "scholar," from which is derived *saber* and *sabedoria*, "knowledge" and "wisdom." If the Sabeans of Harran practiced Hermetic wisdom, then its origin would most likely have been Egyptian, for Hermes is the Greek Thoth and the Egyptian Djehuti, the Ibis-headed god of wisdom whose symbol was the Moon, which as it happens, the Sabeans venerated.

As for Harran, it is a Province in modern-day South Eastern Turkey, where Adam and Eve allegedly set foot after their expulsion from the Garden of Eden. It's located a stone's throw from one of the world's oldest sacred sites, Göbekli Tepe.

All this incoming information served to shape Bernard de Clairvaux' undertaking of The Great Work, which like the Islamic practice of *Akbar jihad*, "the greatest effort", would ensure the knowledge rose once more after centuries of repression. Since all parties were by now streetwise from the recent history of ecclesiastically-sponsored butchery, it was decided to engage in a new era of temple-building where not only the knowledge could be taught, but just in case the Roman beast went walkabout once more, the secrets of the knowledge would be protected by encoding them in the very fabric of the new buildings. And since these would be dedicated to the greater glory of God, chances are they would be the last places where the Church would look for heretical information. So began a decades-long construction program that raised Europe's first skyscrapers – the Gothic cathedrals.

Gothic is derived from the Greek *goetia*, meaning "by magic force;" its extension is *goeteuein* meaning "to bewitch." Anyone who has wandered around a Gothic cathedral knows all too well how apt these descriptions are, for these structures indeed bewitch you, since the stone appears to rise and defy gravity as though by some magic force. In 1153, the Gothic style makes its appearance in the new Templar kingdom of Portugal, as the Cistercian monastery of Alcobaça, an astonishing display of levity and subtlety of light, and a present to Bernard before his death from a grateful Portuguese king. Perhaps the most discussed Gothic structure of all is Chartres cathedral, with its "Door of the Initiates" in the north featuring a carved relief of the Ark transported by oxen, and another of a man covering the Ark with a veil, with the accompanying inscription, *Here things take their course; you are to work through the Ark.*[34]

Even before the Druids of Gaul established their main council at the site, Chartres was a sacred mound dedicated to the Divine Mother on which stood a dolmen.[35] After the assembly of the Druidical College was established, it became known as the Place of the Strong Saints. The hill itself served as a focal point for countless menhirs, dolmens, and megalithic structures, few of which remain except in name only.[36]

Armed with the knowledge decoded from the Tables of Laws, Bernard instructed groups of Masons called the Children of Solomon, and construction began on the cathedral.[37] The building is a sermon in stone. Its elevation and proportions are built

Cathedrale de Chartres.

to the same mathematical ratios governing the pure music scale; the choir alone is designed to a 2:1 ratio, the equivalent to the octave in music. Its characteristic ogive arches depict the form of the *vesica piscis*, the divine womb from which all the forms of sacred geometry emerge. The tension created through the balancing of stone on ogive arches gives the building a certain tension, transforming the space into a musical box, while its two slightly different axes create a vibrato effect across the entire building.[38] The cathedral is a tuned resonant cavity, and as modern Russian researchers have found, it stimulates the electromagnetic frequencies of the human brain to such a degree that the capacity for telepathy is increased by 4000%.[39] The choice of material reflects that used in pyramids: limestone on the outside, granite on the inside, specifically the area around the altar, which is balanced over a slab of red granite.

Chartres' positioning strategically follows the course of water veins and telluric currents running through and beneath the building, and pilgrims have sought these vital energies for cures or illumination for thousands of years. The watercourse flowing 120-feet below the nave resembles the curve of a serpent, and several of the cathedral's power points, primarily the altar and the choir, reference this. One hotspot appears notably in front of the statue of the Virgin of the Pillar, which makes one feel as though they're being sucked down a vortex and into the center of the Earth; the afflicted generally feel drawn to leave their burdens here, so to speak. Behind the altar a second vorticular column of energy rises out of the ground to generate a corresponding sense of elation.

After the geobiologist Blanche Merz revealed Egyptian temples to be protected by a telluric network, her attention focused on Chartres, where she discovered the building works along the same principles: an outer protective zone, with a neutral zone around the choir and the original altar,[40] the area formerly occupied by a Gallic temple. This space resides within a horseshoe of columns, precisely as the arrangement

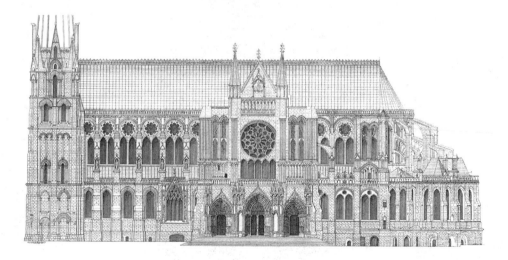

at Stonehenge, which is similarly aligned northeast. As with the passage of reeds in Saqqara, the Hartmann lines are bundled like seven gates that create a protective zone prior to entering this sublime area of personal alteration. At this singular spot, one passes into the Fields of Elysium, and in this unique environment thousands of open-minded pilgrims have entered a state of grace and into a dialogue with the invisible temple.

Merz noted that in two sections around the choir, the energy grid contracts as though reacting to an unnatural impulse. These occur in front of the only clear glass windows in an edifice once noted for the superlative quality of its stained glass. True stained glass is a lost science last seen in Persia around the 11th century, in the hands of alchemists and adepts such as Omar Khayyam.[41] Its use was partly for permeating the interiors of the *Akbar jihad* with a transcendental luminosity, yet its creators claimed the process imbued the glass with certain frequencies of light described to represent "the breath of the universe." The science behind this special glass served to modify the potentially harmful, ultraviolet frequencies of sunlight into the building.[42] Therefore,

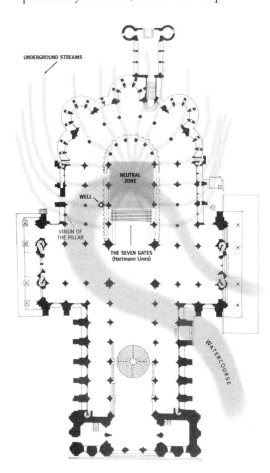

the frequencies received through the skin and the eye were altered, perhaps to further help the religious experience of the initiate. Its effects were witnessed in the 12th century by Robert Grossetête: "its beauty is due to the simplicity with which light is in unison with the music, more harmoniously linked with itself in a relationship of equality." [43] Aside from small fragments in the rose window, Chartres' original stained glass mostly perished through a disastrous fire, as did the recipe. Which brings us to those two sets of clear windows and the distortions in the telluric network: these were destroyed on the orders of Bishop Bridan in the 1770s, so that the congregation could better admire him in full sunlight.[44]

One of the elements that pulls people magnetically to this particular cathedral is the ability to indulge in the meditative practice of walking its labyrinth, much to the annoyance of the present priests who absolutely abhor it and wish it had never been constructed. If they were more

Merz' energy map of Chartres.

spiritually inclined they would discover the eye of the labyrinth is centered on a telluric hotspot with a frequency corresponding to the initiation chambers of the Pharaohs.[45] As one of the first features to be added after the great fire, the labyrinth seems to define this Great Work inasmuch as it is positioned in geometric proportion to the overarching geometry defining the entire building. Since the site is dedicated to the divine feminine, the cathedral is encompassed by a pentagram, as are many of its interior features, including the horseshoe protecting the choir and altar. And nestled within that pentagram is another pentagram, whose point of contact expertly touches the center of the labyrinth.

In honor of the sky-ground dualism of the ancient orders, the Notre Dame cathedrals were placed on the land in the image of the divine virgin, by mirroring the constellation Virgo.[46] They also encapsulate the principle of the divine marriage, the union of the masculine and feminine, and part of this is reflected in the balance of limestone and granite throughout. Naturally, one would expect the correspondence to be continued geometrically. In addition to the pentagram, the architect Gordon Strachan identifies the central features within Chartres as conforming to a series of repeating hexagrams, thereby acknowledging the presence of the geometry of the divine masculine.[47] Yet there is one further mystery to Chartres, and it is how the geometric relationship between the apse and the choir is off-center. This deviation from architectural norm is barely perceptible to the eye, but exists on the cathedral's plan. There are also two irregularly-placed pillars on the south side of the choir which behave at the same time as a code and as a marker, and indeed it is here where the construction of a heptagram – the geometry of the soul and the unknown – references the elements that comprise the apse.[48]

The remarkable thing about the true Gothic era is that never was there any depiction of the crucifixion of Christ. Nor, for that matter, did any part of the interior or the original glass depict images of saints or biblical scenes. This purity conformed to the anagogical journey from the material (the outside of the building) to the immaterial (the interior), a metaphor symbolizing the inward, spiritual path leading to self-realization and the formless realm of God. Bernard himself stated that in the architecture "there should be no decoration, only proportion," since sacred geometry provides a closer representation of the universe and its creator, the irony being that said geometry is invisible to the eye.

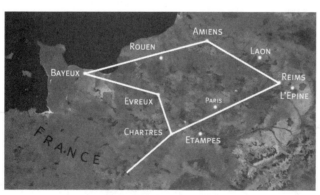

Notre Dame cathedrals referencing Virgo.

The same ideal is found in Islamic mosques, which prohibit iconography, for the pure world of Allah can only be represented by geometry, which they do through the use of mesmerizing tile work.

While the Cistercians and the Knights Templar were busy reasserting the knowledge throughout Europe in alliance with their allies, the Cathari, on the other side of the world, an enlightened priesthood under the protection of Suryavarman II was busy erecting the mighty temple city of Angkor – or re-erecting, if you accept the evidence presented earlier.

Incredible as it may seem, this notable surge in temple-building once again pre-empts global climate changes around the end of the 12th century. Geological records point to a swarm of localized impacts when the Earth crossed the cyclical path of the Taurids meteor stream in 1178 A.D., setting off two generations of bitter cold in Mongolia. China experienced catastrophic flooding, and a series of impact craters in New Zealand accounted for Maori legends of fire falling from the sky that burned forests and wiped out the Moa, the country's large and distinctive flightless birds.[49] Polynesians dispersed en-masse off their islands, while Aztecs moved inland and away from the coast, suggesting some impacts were in the sea and caused devastating tsunamis, prompting the Aztecs to embark on a bloodbath to appease the gods from dishing out further misery from the sky. Likewise, the Inca abandoned coastal pyramids and temples, and moved to the high Andes, while in the southwest of America severe droughts brought down many native cultures such as those at Mesa Verde. Earth was actually spared severe damage, considering the Moon absorbed an impact so large from the same meteor shower that a monk at Canterbury Abbey wrote how it writhed several times "like a wounded serpent," when a torch of flame rose from it, after which the orb turned black from the dust.

Bernard's intuition – to encode for posterity the sacred knowledge of the Ark within the fabric of the Gothic cathedrals – would prove well-founded, for no sooner had the Dominicans reasserted control over the papacy when the persecutions were revived. Under blatantly trumped up charges concocted between the despot Philip IV and Pope Clement V, the Knights Templar were systematically rounded up on Friday, October 13th, 1307. The ones who did not manage to flee to Scotland, Switzerland or Portugal were tortured by the Holy Inquisition to reveal the secrets of the Order, which in spite of the most hideous sadism, not one soul revealed the precious information. Philip IV couldn't care less about the knowledge, he was just after their loot and the annulment of the massive financial debt he owed the Order.

The other perceived threat to the Catholic Church, the Cathari, fared even worse. With zealous help from Philip IV, the Church organized the Albigensian Crusade in what became one of the most horrific genocides in history. I'll attempt to spare all the gruesome details and the vast numbers of men, women and children mercilessly butchered across the Languedoc until "the streets ran in waterfalls of blood." The few

Templars burned alive.

who escaped the savagery enabled the teachings to linger underground throughout the continent; elements of Bogomilism managed to survive in the Balkans until the 15th century until it was also overwhelmed by a militant Islam.

As the flames lapped up the mutilated body of Jacques de Molay, the Grand Master of the Order defiantly predicted the future for his tormentors: "God knows who is wrong and has sinned. Soon a calamity will occur to those who have condemned us to death." In one month Pope Clement V was dead, followed a few months later by Philip IV.

Unless the myths are preserved, the rites performed and the sites maintained as spirit sanctuaries, the living bond is broken, man and nature are separated, and neither man nor nature has any assurance of life in the future. With gnostics of all types wiped out by the Holy Inquisition whenever and wherever they made an appearance, sects adopted the wisdom of invisibility and developed a language of allegory and metaphor with which to communicate to each other, or to promulgate their ideas to the public during their tenure underground. The power of symbol became widespread. One example of the secret communication that appeared sporadically is Francis Bacon's book *New Atlantis*, in which the former Lord Chancellor to James I of England outlines the ideal philosophical utopian state, not unlike Plato's *Timaeus*. Under the patronage of the English monarch, Bacon had already published his landmark work *Advancement of Learning* which set the standard for education and science.

New Atlantis is written with the allegorical coded language and symbolism common to gnostic sects that promotes the knowledge, while at the same time making it obscure enough, and thus safe, from the powers that be. Its protagonists are the Merchants of Light whose quest is for "knowledge of the causes, and secret motions of things." [50] This is accomplished by a group of sages sailing to all countries of the world to "nourish the Light." These disciples are scientists, priests, astronomers and geometers who possess advanced knowledge: "we have some degrees of flying in the air; we have ships and boats for going under water." [51] Not only is this an astonishing vision for its time – 1627 A.D. – but the similarities to the myths of the Seven Sages, and the magician-priests whose advanced knowledge survived the great flood to rebuild the former world of the gods, are uncanny.

Was Bacon consciously bringing these ancient concepts back out of the cupboard? It seems highly probable because the political situation at this time was favorable for wisdom to speak freely – comparatively speaking – for his patron, like himself, appears to have been a Free Mason.[52]

The Gothic marked the last concentrated period of temple-building in recent history, and it would be another seven hundred years before a new momentum manifested. And in the strangest way.

Return of the gods.

It was 1937 when a small boy out walking the English countryside with his uncle witnessed a type of whirlwind incise a meticulous circular shape in the field of barley, with sharply defined edges and plants perfectly spiraled and bent without damage. "A devil's twist," remarked the uncle, a strange force of nature responsible for making the unusual circles as far back as 1830. Certainly these aerial vortices behaved very unusually for a natural force, or the devil, for not only did they make neat shapes without damage, when the farmer lifted the plants up with his pitchfork they sprung back down, as though made molten like glass and re-hardened in their new horizontal positions.[53]

Meanwhile, the same invisible force was responsible for equally baffling markings throughout the North American prairie, and again the eyewitnesses recall a stationary vortex lasting no more than fifteen seconds, swirling and flattening the wheat without damage, accompanied by a high-pitched humming just prior to each event.[54] One by one the reports got stranger. A couple saw "a huge yellow-white circular object standing on end, like a funfair wheel," barely 200 yards away, and on that very spot the next morning lay a perfect circular shape, again with plants left hovering an inch above the soil.[55] The elusive force was better defined in 1966, when a driver pulling over to the side of a road during a rain shower came face-to-face with it: a vertical blue tube appeared in the adjacent field, accompanied by a loud hissing noise. He watched as the rain ran down the sides of this 'tube' as if it were solid, while underneath, a circle with perfect sides manifested in less than thirty seconds.[56]

There are some 300 reports and eyewitness accounts of crop circles dating to 1590, with a sudden and exponential surge starting around 1980.[57] If you happen to be a keen television viewer – and if you're still reading this book, chances are you probably are not – you will no doubt have come across 'official' explanations on National Geographic, Discovery Channel or The History Channel that the entire phenomenon of crop circles is an elaborate hoax perpetrated by two elderly pub chums called Doug and Dave. Their story goes like this: because they were bored, they went out one night in 1978 and made a crop circle using a plank of wood tied to a length of string. Next morning, there was so much interest in what they had done, they decided to keep going, to "fool the pompous experts." After 'making' some 5,000 crop circles – worldwide – they decided to call *Today* newspaper in 1991, hold a press conference and admit they did it all because – and this is straight from the horses' mouths – after thirteen years of nocturnal movements away from the marital bed, their wives finally got suspicious, so they decided to come clean.

They took the collected press corps out to a field to recreate a circle and show just how "so-called" scientists are so easily fooled. The next day, quality newspapers such as *The Independent* reported, "After the demonstration by Doug and Dave I find it easier to believe in little green men than in this story by Bower and Chorley."[58] Another quality paper in Switzerland was equally skeptical. What sparked some the press' curiosity was, during the press conference, the attending researchers cross-examined Doug Bower and Dave Chorley and found they'd merely regurgitated published information, yet when confronted with the vast data of *unpublished* evidence, they began to back-pedal, and in some cases, retract their statements. How was it possible they had created two 600-foot long pictograms in separate counties during the same night? How did they manage to do it in separate *countries* at the same time? If they began hoaxing in 1978, who made the other crop circles dating back four centuries? They claimed never to have been active in the Avebury area, yet the majority of activity in Britain had been Avebury and its megaliths; they claimed to have made a design in the natural ampitheater of Cheesefoot Head for fourteen consecutive years, yet records indicate the claim to be completely false. In the end, even Doug and Dave seemed uncertain as to what they had made and where.[59] The *Today*-sponsored PR field trip was turning into a nightmare, especially when the host farmer Peter Renwick remarked on Doug and Dave's showcase that afternoon: "You can see from the corn's lying that something mechanical has actually caused that, it's been caused by people trampling it. The ones I've seen are not like that; they're much flatter, flat as a pancake. This may be some of the answer but not all of it." [60]

Of course, none of this has ever been aired by the media.

Farmer Renwick was right, it wasn't the answer. But ever since, millions have fallen for the crude deception, including the editors at Wikipedia, which proves one also cannot trust everything on the Internet. Conspiracy theorists may snigger at all this, but earlier that summer a CBS reporter was warned by a French government scientist that the British government would soon be presenting two people to the press as the makers of all crop circles.[61] Furthermore, the story that finally appeared in *Today* was traced to a fictitious press agency created by the British Ministry of Defense.[62] The story gets more sinister. After Doug and Dave's 'retirement', the baton was allegedly passed on to a group of hoaxers called Team Satan, then changed to Circlemakers just to confuse the public. Recent investigations indicate its ringleader was recruited in London by MI5 (British Military Intelligence).[63] If so, the debunking of crop circles by well-funded skeptical groups and their media allies smacks of a kinder, gentler Inquisition. The investigative reporter Armen Victorian infiltrated a key hoaxing gang by posing as a business interest and revealed the disinformation is being carried out by elements within three governments, and most surprising of all, the Vatican.[64] In my book *Secrets in the Fields* I set out the full body of evidence clearly proving the hoax theory is itself a hoax.

The evidence also proves the existence of a real phenomenon, and the reason for bringing up crop circles in this work is because there exists a tangible connection to telluric energy, temples, the creator gods mentioned at the start of this work, and most importantly, the subtle forces involved in the transfiguration of the soul. As I mentioned earlier, they are quite possibly the first concentrated period of temple-making since the Gothic cathedrals, and the timing appears to be deliberate.

But first, allow me to briefly outline the scientific evidence. The first researcher of crop circles was the late Pat Delgado, a former NASA engineer whose elegant statement summarizes the argument well: "It is perfectly natural to ask if the circles are hoaxes, but very difficult to explain why they cannot be hoaxed satisfactorily." [65] Indeed, laboratory analysis of plants and soil reveal how their crystalline structures have been visibly altered by an intense, yet short burst of heat; the affected stems show burn marks on the outside, while inside, the water is boiled in a fraction of a second, whereupon it expands and creates a hole in the plant's softest tissue, the node, before escaping as steam. Farmers who've witnessed the effect do describe steam coming

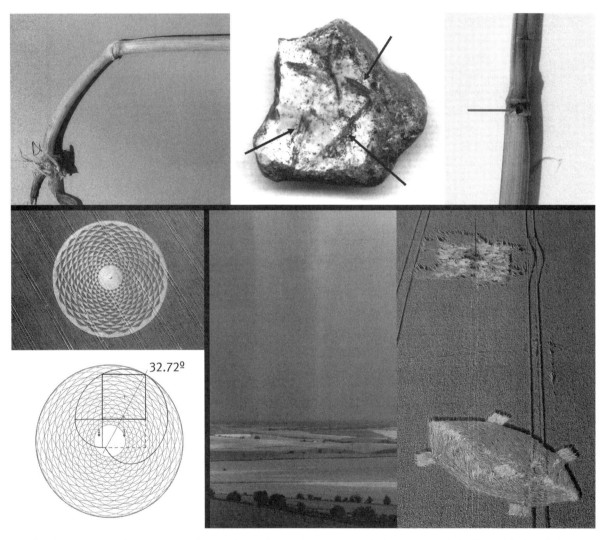

Top: the anomalous bend; plant stalks flash-burned onto a lump of flint; hole created by the boiling of the interior liquid. Below: encoded Golden Ratio spiral and the angle of manifestation; beams of light creating crop circle; glyph with nearby discharge caused by descending tube of energy touching the overhead wire and grounding at the electricity pole.

out of the crop circles, which is precisely what happens to water when boiled by high-pressure infrasound. Both ultrasound and infrasound are major causative forces behind crop circles, but incredibly, these frequencies cause no damage, indicating a non-destructive phenomenon at work which has complete cooperation from the materials with which it interacts.[66] And there are many: wheat, barley, canola, potatoes, corn, snow and trees.

One of the big mysteries surrounding the thousands of genuine crop circles is, no matter in which of the twenty-nine countries they've appeared, they always reference local sacred sites – either by a symbolic link to their history, by ley alignment, or by the fact that every genuine crop circle always appears on nodes of the earth's telluric pathways, and these electromagnetic conveyor belts connect to the nearby temples.[67]

Scientific measurements show the crop circles contain residual electromagnetic frequencies which are statistically higher inside than outside the design, and around their perimeter there exists a type of force field, identical in principle to the 'seven gates' or the seven Hartmann lines protecting the thresholds of temples. As you'd expect, the veil between worlds is perceptibly thin inside a crop circle, and hundreds of reports attest to people experiencing changes in consciousness, a goodly number coming from skeptical visitors. Healings are also common; in one extreme case a young man who ingested the affected seeds saw the disappearance of a 99% malignant eye tumor.[68]

We could just as well be describing the forces at work inside a temple. For one thing, like stone circles, the crop circles emit ultrasound, whose high frequencies

Nine spirals crop glyph. Wiltshire, England.

276

stimulate the brain's electromagnetic frequencies and the pineal gland, a major component in the alteration of awareness.[69] Ultrasound is also known to work magic on human tissue and bone hence its increasing use in today's hospitals.

Since crop circles possess an electromagnetic fingerprint, and their placement along the Earth's telluric lines connects to nearby temples, it suggests the former may be influencing the latter. You may recall how sacred sites were deliberately shut down centuries ago as a precaution against their misuse. Is it therefore a coincidence how the surge in crop circle activity in the latter part of the 20th century (and there have been some 10,000 reports so far) neatly coincides with a surge in interest in ancient temples, as though something has awoken in the land – as though a window has been flung open, allowing people a glimpse into their sacred inheritance, the window into that "walled enclosure" called *pairi-daeza* – paradise?

In 1998, a Wiltshire resident described seeing a tube descend "like a cookie cutter" from the clouds, barely 100-yards away, and swirl the heads of wheat for about fifteen seconds before retracting skywards; her dog barked incessantly and tugged at the leash towards this column of light. The timing of her experience corroborated the photo I had taken at the same moment from a hill five miles away, which shows the field in question being touched by a vertical beam. However, the actual crop circle only appeared the following day. This is where such eyewitness accounts are valuable, because they split into two distinctive groups: those who see the design appear right in front of them and those where the design materializes later.

Crop circles come in two swirl motions: clockwise or counter-clockwise. Russian engineers studying the motion of bio-dynamic fluids have noted how counter-clockwise rotation inputs energy into a solution, whereas clockwise rotation releases energy. In other words, energy descends or ascends depending on the direction of its vortex.[70] With regard to crop circles, when a column of light descends and creates an image simultaneously, the indication is of information being imprinted on the Earth's telluric lines, much like one used to record a person's voice on a strip of magnetic cassette tape. But if the pattern *appears* much later, it suggests the beam has triggered a response from the living planet.

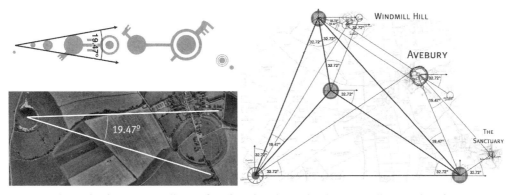

The angle of energy upwelling is found in the relationship between Silbury and Avebury, as well as crop circles, and their relationship to nearby sites.

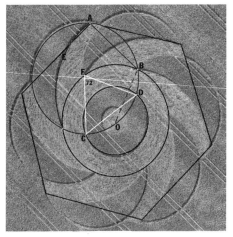

Encoded. Ptolemi's Theorem of Chords.

This concept is not so far-fetched when you recall how and why the original primordial mounds and *Sivalingams* were created. Those sites mark the descent of a radiant, effulgent column of light, said to be the essence of a creator god materializing on our physical plane. On these sites, future "mansions of the gods" would be constructed in their image, and that image is based on geometric form, and there is no doubt that the majority of temples around the world are predominantly geometric, as are crop circles. There is one further, tantalizing connection. As the Egyptologist Eve Reymond discovered during her deciphering of the Edfu texts, the earliest temples were founded near, and even enshrined the piece of earth in which the *symbols* of the creative powers were believed to have been concealed.[71] Is it possible some of these concealed symbols are being activated as though put there for future use – an insurance policy for humanity?

This detail made me recall a vital piece of information channeled under trance by the respected English sensitive Isabelle Kingston.

During one of her group meetings back in 1982, in the days when crop circles were rare and unreported events, Isabelle inadvertently vectored a universal consciousness who instructed her on the emergence of symbols that would be helping to raise the consciousness of humanity. The focal point of the transmission, it said, would be Silbury Hill, the tall, conical mound named for a collective of creator gods named the Shining Ones.[72] The source identified itself as the Watchers. This group appears throughout myths and legends either as gods or creational forces of light, often by that very same name, and typically described as very tall, ethereal beings. They're also referenced in the Egyptian *Book of Coming Forth by Day*: "Behold, oh ye shining ones, ye men and gods," [73] where they also go by the name *Neters* – the original creator gods who vanished after a flood consumed the Earth.

Could it be possible these 'crop churches' mark the return of the creator gods? Native American cultures and Aboriginal tribes react very emotionally to the glyphs, not least because the early designs are etched as petroglyphs in their own landscape temples. For them, the crop glyphs are signs of the return of the 'star people', representing for many a fulfillment of prophecy and the close of an age. Certainly the knowledge is prevalent in the

Invisible matrix of sacred geometry of a crop circle

crop circles, typically veiled within their visual designs, much like it is in temples. Five new mathematical theorems have been decoded by the late Professor Gerald Hawkins, whose own published work on Stonehenge opened the door on that site as a complex astronomical marker.[74] The designs regularly reference 19.47º, the angle of energy upwelling, just as they do 32.72º, the angle of material manifestation.[75] These angles are also used to define the location of the crop circle relative to the local sacred site, indicating the glyphs and the temples are communicating with each other using angles associated with the transfer of energy, and therefore, information.[76]

These temples are created by master craftsmen with a high intellectual profile.

Just as the Gothic has its Chartres and the Khmer has its Angkor, so crop circles have the Barbury Castle *Tetrahedron*. Named after the field where it made its magical appearance in 1991 following a night of incandescent flying objects making improbable maneuvers in the sky above, the *Tetrahedron* single-handedly caught the imagination of the world and its press. *"Now Fake This!"* screamed one newspaper headline. A few months later the British government responded to the surge in world-wide interest, which by that point had taken on a religious fervor, by concocting the ridiculous story of Doug and Dave.

From the evidence on the ground, the Barbury *Tetrahedron* has no earthly origin, and it's proved a source of great scholarship, as one morsel of encoded information after another is revealed. For a start, the design bears an uncanny similarity to the alchemical blueprint explaining the process behind matter.[77] From the measure of its flattened crop, the sum of its circular areas is 31,680 square feet, which in ancient cosmology represents the number of measure, in miles, of an imaginary perimeter square around the Earth, with 3,168 being the gematrian value of the phrase *Lord Jesus Christ*, and 316.8 the circumference in feet of the lintel ring at Stonehenge, as well as the perimeter square of St. Mary's Chapel in Glastonbury.[78]

The *Tetrahedron* crop glyph, like Chartres, encodes the ratio 5:6:7, expressed by three geometric lattices generating the various features of the design as it appears to the eye. What is presented in this glyph is nothing less than the sacred marriage of masculine and feminine, and the transfiguration of the soul. Hardly surprising, then, that of all crop glyphs this one received front-page exposure around the world, and to this day remains the one crop circle that brought an awakening to millions of people.

And just like a temple, the physical beauty of these new landscape temples bides us to enter a place of power where the soul once again remembers to find its home.

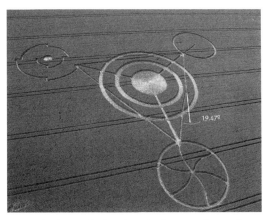

Tetrahedron. The bend in the line encodes 19.47º.

Tetrahedron crop glyph's concealed 5:6:7 geometry.

Sitting in the shade of her mellow garden, through which the St. Michael telluric line quietly goes about its business, Isabelle Kingston and I discussed the Watchers' primary motive: to awaken humanity, so it responds to its responsibility.

"They came before in human form," Isabelle said, "they were the ones who were the ancient teachers and the tall beings that are in every culture. They said that in order for them to communicate with us, they needed to set up the right frequency."

Because their frequency is considerably faster to our world of matter, the Watchers laid down places of power eons ago to be used as communication points. These would be made available at a time in the future when it would be necessary to communicate with us again. There are now groups of adepts and initiates around the world reopening these places of power so that contact can once again take place.

Isabelle added, "They set up the blueprint of much information, both technical and spiritual. They would give signs of their intervention [via crop circles] but these signs would also unlock the potential within humanity, for whatever they chose that would be released within them. If they chose to go with ego, domination, that would affect them. Or compassion. It would amplify whatever was within, positive or negative. They said that at some level within us we have the knowledge of the Universe; the truths are there but we've become blind to them. They are reminding us to be responsible, to bring people back to the land, back into sync with the Earth, because we lost our link."

As the statement from God in the *Gospel of John* says, "And, (it shall come to pass in the last days) I will show wonders in the heavens above, and signs in the earth below." [79] As with previous phases in temple-building, the timing of these modern temples is uncanny, not least because we find ourselves once more on the threshold of significant climate changes. This generation is witnessing the rising of seas and shifting weather patterns; *Asteroid 1999 RQ36* has NASA concerned it will make landfall in 2182,[80] while the magnetic poles that have been rapidly moving for the past 2,000 years are expected to reverse before the year 2300,[81] just as they did back in 10,400 B.C. These events are predicted to occur during the time-frame when the Age of Pisces acquiesces to the already emerging Age of Aquarius. Should they come to pass, we now have the understanding with which to be suitably prepared.

At the start of our quest we learned how the descending light of creator gods established primordial mounds upon which "mansions of the gods" would be built, to help transform the human into a god and to act as an insurance policy for times when we'd forget our divine potential. This brings us to the most important revelation in the transcripts of the Watchers, and it concerns the physical locations of their effulgent columns of light: that the sites of crop glyphs are intended to be marked as places of reference for future temples.[82] Indeed, long after the visible signs of crop circles have been harvested and reconfigured into bread, their invisible energy signatures do linger for years, allowing these new primordial mounds to be detected and noted.[83]

These are not temporary temples, but lasting pools of energy, metaphors of the universe where, long after the material body has vanished, the soul lives forever.

And so new mansions of the gods shall be built.

The knowledge will be preserved.

The Great Work will reverberate until eternity.

A new home in Paris for the Luxor obelisk. To the northeast, the Church of Mary Magdalene looks on.

19

108 Degrees of Wisdom.

"Is it not written in your law...I said You are gods?"
~ Jesus, in *John 10:33-34*

Pilgrim and scholar Phil Cousineau once wrote, "We need to renew ourselves in territories that are fresh and wild. We need to come home through the body of alien lands." [1] People have on occasion gone to extreme lengths to experience for themselves the places of power. Taktsang is a 17th century monastery in Bhutan, built on a vertiginous rock outcrop beside an 8th century vision quest cave that was the sacred residence of a monk who 'flew' there several hundred miles from Tibet. Considering the geologically inhospitable location, it seems a lot of effort to go to, unless there was already a numinous quality about the place which inspired such a valiant quest.

In *The Way of the Sacred*, Francis Huxley points out it is precisely through the sharing of sacred territory that people have come not only to discover the idea of their origins and their destiny, but to have experiences of it that reveal the meaning in their lives: "The sacred itself is plainly a mystery of consciousness using the word 'mystery' to signify not a problem that can be intellectually solved, but a process of awakening and transformation that must be acted out in order to be experienced, and experienced if one is to make it one's own." [2]

The experiences our predecessors once lived have much to teach us, because for them a sacred place was "...not just a physical location, but a psychic touchstone from which to better understand the cosmos without and the self within. To assume that in a few generations the human species could evolve into not needing special places to affirm self-identity implies an evolutionary leap of unprecedented dimensions in human history." [3]

Temples fire the imagination so that the soul may follow. Darkness becomes understood without falling prey to it. And should you allow it, a renewal takes place that stokes a special energy necessary for your work in life. Ultimately, temples are living intermediaries designed for self-empowerment, and through the culture of knowledge, the individual can understand the immortality of the soul and discover his or her purpose for being. As Jesus made evidently clear: "The Kingdom is in your center, and is about you, and when you know yourselves, you will be aware that you are the sons of the Living Father. And you shall know that you are in the city of God, and that you are the city." [4]

Samarra, "a joy for all who see."

Some see such empowerment as a threat, or an opportunity for personal aggrandizement – Nero ordered the cutting down of the sacred grove of the Celtic queen Boudicca, whereupon her power dissolved and her tribe was conquered. Charlemagne felled the sacred tree Irminsul, the omphalos of Saxony within the national sanctuary, so as to impose his new order. William the Conqueror, one of the last kings to understand the manipulation of subtle energies, imposed his intent on the sacred mound of the city of London – upon which now stands the infamous Tower of London – and through his will at this and other navels of Britain he subdued the land. As is the case when cycles change, cultures once founded on spiritual inheritances were betrayed and their places of power inevitably used for the domination of others. Like the Aztec, travesties were made of subtle symbolic rituals and spiritual icons, which then were used to prop up false cultures and gods. [5]

Earth will always be a place of light, dark and various shades in-between, a sand-box where we come to play, experiment and refine. And despite obstacles in the upward spiral of our human condition, the ancient systems of knowledge are still with us and all around: obelisks that once graced Luxor and Heliopolis now stand patiently amid the noise and chaos in the heart of Paris, London and New York. In Western Europe alone, some 6,000 pilgrimage routes still beckon the intrepid seeker, while in the east 1,800 Hindu shrines stoically accommodate 20 million pilgrims each year. [6]

The triple steps of Vishnu continue to be emphasized with newer temples: the 'stairway to heaven' at Sammara from 5500 B.C., rebuilt in 847 A.D., is now connected with the Shah Mosque of Isfahan, a superlative masterpiece of Persian architecture.

Together with Eridu, home to the temple of the Sumerian water god Enki, and its first ruler Apkallu ("big man from the water") who brought civilization to Mesopotamia, they form a perfect right-angle triangle covering 1,100 miles.

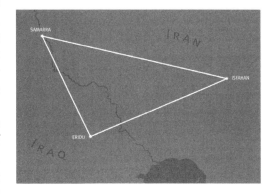

As for the invisible colleges of the adepts and the Followers of Horus, they live on in various forms, names and guises, quietly upholding the knowledge right in front of your very eyes, for the principles of temple-making do not just cover one building: when conceived on a grand scale they transform a whole city into a temple, and with it the capacity to influence an entire nation of people. This has been quietly taking place in the center of Paris for over three centuries, where adepts have shaped this city founded around the cult of Isis, by strategically placing prominent buildings and boulevards in deliberate alignment with the rising of the star of wisdom, Sirius, in a manner identical to the temples of Karnak and Luxor.[7]

This homage to the ancient knowledge also finds itself 4,000 miles farther west. In the 18th century, a group of visionaries seized the moment and created a city-temple on virgin soil, dedicated to the resuscitation of liberty and the enlightenment of the individual.

On October 13th, 1307, the Order of the Knights Templar was met with violent suppression. On the same day in 1792, a ceremony took place to lay the cornerstone of the mansion of the United States' President, the White House. The timing could not have been more symbolic. The following year saw another inauguration ceremony, the laying of the cornerstone of the U.S. Capitol on September 18th, 1793, presided by George Washington, a Grand Master Freemason. Far beyond an ordinary government building, this was to be "the first temple dedicated to the sovereignty of the people," as wrote Thomas Jefferson.[8] The timing

The Washington Monument

of the ceremony of this "Temple of Liberty" was planned to coincide with another significant event, this time in the heavens, when the Sun entered the constellation Virgo, a symbol of the exaltation of the Divine Virgin. As the Masonic author David Ovason points out: "The Virgoan connection has also been emphasized in a number of foundation charts, which are of fundamental importance to Washington D.C. The foundation of the city itself, and the three corners of the triangle, which L'Enfant had marked out for its center (the Capitol, the White House and the Washington Monument) were each set down on the earth at a time when the constellation Virgo had a particular importance in the skies." [9]

A city was raised around the Capitol, designed by the French Architect Pierre-Charles L'Enfant, with the participation of Washington, Jefferson and another architect, Andrew Ellicott; all four were Freemasons. The ambitious plan conceals sacred geometries, a Cabbalistic *Tree of Life*, and a number of octagonal relationships centered on the Capitol and the White House.[10] A more cunning feature is the manner in which L'Enfant designed the city plan to appear as though the main axis is fixed to the equinox sunrise and sunset,[11] when in fact the principal route of this city-temple is the ceremonial avenue of the 'king', Pennsylvania Avenue, which joins the Capitol to the White House. The alignment between the two is both significant and deliberate, for at dawn on September 18th, 1793, Sirius would have been seen rising directly above Jenkins Hill, the future site of the Capitol.[12] As authors Robert Bauval and Graham Hancock observed, "If you were both a land surveyor, as well as a Freemason (like Ellicott and Washington) it would have been difficult under these circumstances not to associate the event of the helical rising of Sirius viewed from Washington in 1793 with the 'birth' of a new federal city and capital of the world's first true republic since Rome." [13]

L'Enfant and Ellicott's symbolic trinity of the Capitol, the White House and the Washington Monument forms the shape of a perfect right-angle triangle, a triple step of Vishnu.

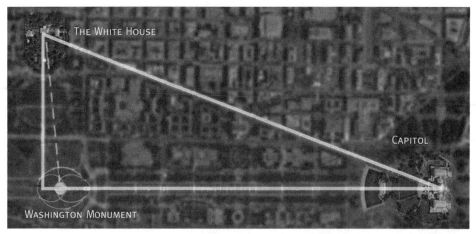

Washington Monument was moved 414 ft. east due to unsuitable terrain.

Directly to the south and gazing over Washington from the highest hill in Alexandria, Virginia, stands Masonic Lodge 22, with a tower modeled on the lighthouse at Pharos, drawing new pilgrims up the Potomac river and into the city of knowledge, just as Alexander the Great once intended with his Egyptian namesake.

The Alexandria Lodge, where George Washington practiced his craft, is aligned 19.47º to the White House, just as the Lincoln Memorial is aligned to it at the pyramidal angle of 51.42º.

Precisely north of the White House is the Mother Supreme Council of the Ancient and Accepted Scottish Rite of Freemasonry, also known as the House of the Temple, its distance to the White House and Washington's obelisk being in the ratio of 2:1, an octave in music.

56 years after the final dedication ceremony of Washington's obelisk, a ground-breaking ceremony took place for a building shaped in the symbolic geometry of Sirius: the Pentagon. The ceremony took place on September 11th, 1941, on the heliacal rising of this star of Isis above the site.[14] From the center of the Pentagon, the White House and the Capitol lie at precisely 32.72º, the angle of manifestation.

It seems the stellar magic practiced thousands of years ago in the pre-diluvial world of the creator gods is still at play in one of the world's newest capitals.

But why choose this particular location upon which to build the future capital of the United States?

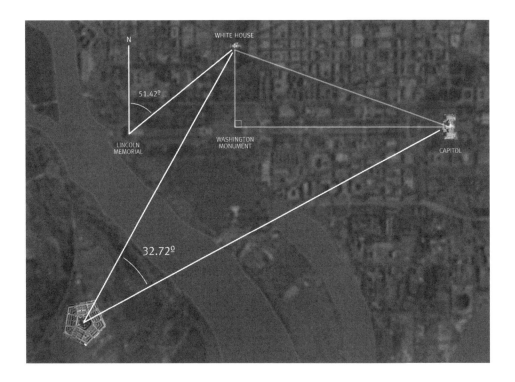

Earlier in this work we saw how great places of power are positioned on longitudes according to a pentagonal-precessional grid. That so many Freemasons played prominent roles in this recent historical push for the liberty of humanity and the design of a new 'city of knowledge' is no accident.

The roots of the knowledge of the Freemasons lie in the original city of knowledge, Heliopolis, the zero-point longitude of the ancient world.

One of the principal pentagonal numbers is 108.

108° west of Heliopolis sits the dome of the Capitol of Washington D.C.

A site becomes sacred through the accumulation of universal forces and the quality of veneration over time. Its compounded energy is neither right nor wrong, it is simply energy. The *quality* of integrity and intent will ultimately define its purpose and the direction of its power.

When you decide to claim your legacy in the places of power, which direction will you choose?

Washington D.C., originally planned as a modern city-temple.

REFERENCES

OUR LEGACY BEQUEATHED BY GODS.

1. E.R.E. Reymond, The Mythological Origin of the Egyptian Temple, Manchester University Press, 1969. pp.112-126, p.180
2. From Fragments of Chaldean History, Berossus, by Alexander Polyhist, in Ancient Fragments, by I.P. Cory, Forgotten Books, 2007, p.43; and Gerald Verbrugghe and John Wickersham, Berossos and Matheno, University of Michigan Press, 1999, p44
3. John Michener, Traditions of the Seven Rishis, Montilal, Banarsidass, Delhi 1982
4. R.O. Faulkner, The Ancient Pyramid Texts, Oxford University Press, 1969, p.159
5. E.A. Wallis-Budge, The Egyptian Heaven and Hell (The Book of What is in the Duat), Marin Hopkinson Co, London 1925, p 240
6. E.J. Brill, The Nag Hammadi Library, Leiden, New York, 1988, p85

CHAPTER 1. A LONG MEMORY OF PLACES OF POWER.

1. Delia Goetz and Sylvannus Morley, Popol Vuh: The Sacred Book of the Ancient Quiche Maya, University of Oklahoma Press, 1991, p168
2. Lauren van der Post, The Lost World of the Kalahari, Hogarth Press, London, 1980
3. Frank Waters, Book of the Hopi, Viking Press, New York, 1965
4. 'Dreamtime' stories of stars 'crashing to earth with a noise like thunder', along with their names, have led to exact locations of meteorite impact craters which occurred millions of years ago. See "Aboriginal Folklore Leads to Meteorite Impact Crater", Cosmos Online, January 7, 2010
5. Helen Watson cited in David Turnbull, Maps Are Territories, University Of Chicago Press, 1989. p28
6. Bruce Chatwin, The Songlines, Viking, Markham, 1987
7. Paul Devereux, Fairy Paths and Spirit Roads, Vega, London, 2003. p23
8. Chatwin, op. cit., p108
9. Personal communication from Isabelle Kingston. One fact which has led to the understanding of hill forts as non-military fortifications is their protective ditches lie inside the mounds, not outside, rendering them useless as fortifications.

10. Dr. Tony Scott-Morley, cited in David Elkington and Paul Ellson, In The Name of the Gods, Green Man Press, Sherbourne, 2001. p144
11. Maurice Hertzog, Annapurna, E.P. Dutton, New York, 1953
12. John Burke and Kaj Halberg, Seed of Knowledge, Stone of Plenty, Council Oak Books, San Francisco, 2005
13. Grizzlybear Lake, Power Centers, The Quest magazine, Winter 1989
14. The New Testament, Matthew 17
15. James Swan, Sacred Places In Nature: Is There A Significant Difference?, Psi Research, 4 (1), 1985. p108-117
16. Burke and Halberg, op. cit.
17. J. Halifax, Shaman: The Wounded Healer, Crossroads, New York, 1982
18. See for example, Becker and Selden, The Body Electric; Lawrence Blair, Rhythms of Vision; Valerie Hunt, Infinite Mind; Lynne McTaggart, The Field; et al.
19. Sir E.A. Wallis-Budge, Legends of Our Lady Mary, Oxford University Press, 1933
20. Giorgio de Santillana and Hertha von Dechend, Hamlet's Mill, David R. Godine, New York, p221
21. Skanda Purana, 12, chapter 2, verse 52; M.C. Subramanian, Glory Of Arunachela, Sri Ramanasramam, Tiruvannamalai, 1998, p100
22. Skandananda, Arunachela Holy Hill, Sri Ramanasramam, Tiruvannamalai, 1995, xi-xl
23. Barry Brailsford, Song of Waitaha, Wharariki Publishing Co, Castle Hill, 2006
24. From the dowsing work of Hamish Miller, and written in In Search of the Southern Serpent, Penwith Press and StonePrint Press, 2006
25. Joseph Campbell, The Mythic Image, Princeton University Press, Princeton, 1974

CHAPTER TWO. THE MYSTERY OF THE THREE STEPS OF VISHNU

1. M. Sundarraj, Rig Vedic Studies, International Society for the Investigation of Ancient Civilization, Chenai, 1997, p83
2. Ralph Griffith, Hymns of the Rgveda, 1.154, Munisharam Manoharlal, Delhi, 1987, p.1-3
3. ibid, 1.155.4
4. Elaine Pagels, The Gnostic Gospels, Penguin, London, 1990, pp.15-16
5. James Robinson, The Nag Hammadi Library, E.J. Bill, New York, 1988, p.165, p.184

6. Griffith, op. cit., 1.155.6. The same line of inquiry was followed by Graham Hancock in Underworld, op.cit, p.240

7. Jonathan Edward Kidder, Himiko and Japan's elusive chiefdom of Yamatai: archaeology, history, and mythology. Honolulu: University of Hawaii Press, 2007.

8. Graham Hancock reached a parallel conclusion in Underworld, op.cit., p240, although he validates another probable line of inquiry.

9. Graham Hancock and Santha Faiia, Heaven's Mirror, Crown Pub., NewYork, 1998, p96-98

10. David Elkington and Paul Ellson, op.cit, pp.264-5

11. Isabelle Kingston, personal communication. This has been one of the secrets throughout esoteric orders.

12. Laurence Gardner, Lost Secrets of the Ark, Barnes and Noble, New York, 2005

13. Julian Cope, The Megalithic European, Element, London, 2004, p.279

14. John Anthony West, Serpent in the Sky, Quest Books, Wheaton, 1993, p35

15. Discussion on triangles and the ideology of Zen Buddhism, in Mitchell Bring and Josse Wayemberg, Japanese Garden: Design and Meaning, McGraw Hill, New York, 1981

16. D'Arcy Wentworth Thompson, On Growth and Form, Cambridge University Press, Cambridge, 1961

17. Fritjof Capra, The Tao of Physics, Fontana, London, 1985, p.193

18. From a 1972 interview, cited in Power Centers by Grizzlybear Lake, The Quest Magazine, Winter 1989.

19. Joseph Pearce, The Magical Child, E.P. Dutton, New York, 1977

CHAPTER THREE. NAVELS OF THE EARTH, PLACES OF THE GODS.

1. John Mitchener, Traditions of the Seven Rishis, Motilal Banersidass, Delhi, 1982, p206

2. Samuel Noah Kramer, History Begins at Sumer, University of Pennsylvania Press, 1991, p.149-151

3. Skandananda, Arunachela HolyHill, Sre Ramanasraram, Tiruvannamalai, 1995, xi-xix

4. Einar Palsson, The Dome of Heaven, Reykiavik, 1992.

5. Liv Kjørsvik Schei and Connie Moberg, The Faroe Islands, London 1991; and referenced in Michell, The Sacred Centre, p. 64 op. cit

6. John Michell, The Sacred Center, Thames and Hudson, London, 1994, p.77

7. The original calculation by John Michell, takes the alignment from the southern tip of present-day England, which makes the overall geometry slightly asymmetrical. However, at the time of writing John did not have access to inundation maps which would have shown a larger landmass exposed c9700 BC. The new graphic enhances his original work and makes the geometry symmetrical. See The Sacred Centre, op. cit.

8. Giraldus Cambrensis, T. Wright, trans. Topographia Hiberniae, London, 1905, p.117

9. Michell, The Sacred Center, op.cit, p129

10. E.R.E. Reymond, op.cit., pp.257-262, p.327.

11. G. Maspero, The Dawn of Civilization, SPCK, London, 1894, p.134

12. ibid

13. The Ancient Egyptian Pyramid Texts, utterance 1587. E.A. Wallis Budge, Egyptian Heaven and Hell (Book of What is in the Duat), Martin Hopkinson Co., London, 1925, p.196

14. Reymond, op.cit., p.90

15. ibid, p.59

16. E.A. Wallis Budge, op. cit., p.196

17. Matthew 16, 13-19

18. Utterance 600, Budge, op. cit.

19. Henri Frankfort, Kingship and the Gods, University of Chicago Press, Chicago, 1978, p.153; and cited in Graham Hancock and Santha Faiia, Heaven's Mirror, Crown Pub., New York, 1998, p.105

20. Budge, op. cit.

21. See for example, Aubrey Burl, Stones of Brittany, et al.

22. The main thesis by Graham Hancock in Sign And The Seal.

23. Steven Fischer in the Journal of Pacific History, 29 (1), 3-18; also Father Sebastian Englert, Island at the Centre of the World, Robert Hale and Co., London, 1972, p30.

24. Thor Heyerdahl, Kon Tiki, Skyhorse Publishing, 2010, p.140

25. Steven Fischer, op.cit.

26. David Hatcher Childress, Lost Cities of Ancient Lemuria and the Pacific, Adventures Unlimited Press, Stelle, 1988.

27. Mircea Eliade (tr. Philip Mairet). 'Symbolism of the Centre' in Images and Symbols." Princeton, 1991, pp.48-51

28. John Michell, The Sacred Center, op. cit., p.6

29. As discussed in my previous book Secrets In

The Fields, Hampton Roads, Charlottesville, 2002, pp.235-237

30. Charles Brooker, Magnetism and the Standing Stones, New Scientist, 13 January 1983, p.105

31. John Michell, op.cit.

32. ibid

33. Edwin Bernbaum, Sacred Mountains of the World, Sierra Club books, San Francisco, 1990, p.32

34. Persians: Masters of Empire, Time-Life Medical, New York, 1995, pp. 7-8

35. Josephus, Jewish Antiquities, Loeb Classics, 1930

36. Lewis Ginzberg, The Legends of the Jews, Jewish Publication Society of America, Philadelphia, 1988, Vol. 1, p.12

37. See the works of John Michell, in which this student of Plato dissects the philosopher's words and reveals coded information and whole numerical cosmologies; in particular The View Over Atlantis and The Dimensions of Paradise.

38. Mircea Eliade, The Sacred and the Profane, New York, 1959, 32-36

39. Joseph Campbell, The Mythic Image, Princeton University Press, Princeton, 1974

CHAPTER FOUR. CITIES OF KNOWLEDGE

1. Pedro Cieza de Leon, Chronicle of Peru, Hakluyk Society, London, 1864 and 1883, Pt. 1, Ch. 87.

2. Professor Arthur Posnansky, Tiahuanacu: The Cradle of American Man, J.J Augustin, New York, 1945, vol. II, p.89; Samuel Noah Kramer, History Begins at Sumer, University of Pennsylvania Press, 1991, p.149-151

3. H.S. Bellamy and P. Allan, The Calendar of Tiahuanaco: The Measuring System of the Oldest Civilization, Faber & Faber, London, 1956, p.16

4. Referenced in Graham Hancock, Underworld, Crown Publishing, New York, p.32

5. Clive Ruggles in Current Studies in Archaeoastronomy: Conversations Across Time and Space, J. Fountain & R. Sinclair, eds., Carolina Academy Press, Durham, 2005

6. See Hancock and Faiia, Heaven's Mirror, p.304

7. See Hancock, Fingerprints of the Gods, Crown, New York, 1995, p.85

8. See the main thesis by Graham Hancock in Heaven's Mirror, Fingerprints of the Gods; also Gerald Hawkins, Stonehenge Decoded; Alexander Thom, Megalithic Sites in Britain.

9. Robin Heath & John Michell, The Measure of Albion, Bluestone Press, St. Dogmaels, 2004, p.31

10. Posnansky, op. cit. p.49, 88

11. ibid p.47, and referenced in Graham Hancock, Fingerprints of the Gods, op. cit., p.79

12. Gerald Hawkins, Stonehenge Decoded, Doubleday, New York, 1965

13. Harold Osborne, Indians of the Andes: Aymaras and Quechuas, K. Paul & Routledge, London, 1952, p.54

14. William Sullivan, The Secret of the Incas, Three Rivers Press, New York, 1997, p.119

15. Hancock and Faiia, Heaven's Mirror, op. cit., p.275

16. Sullivan, op.cit, p.118

17. Hancock and Faiia, Heaven's Mirror, op.cit, p.275

18. The Pyramid Texts, utterance 600

19. Hancock, op.cit, p.178

20. Hancock, in Keeper of Genesis, p.185

21. Reymond, op.cit., p.43, pp.47-51, p.316

22. R. T. Rundle Clark, Myth and Symbol in Ancient Egypt, Thames & Hudson, London, 1978, p.27

23. ibid, pp.263-5

24. Translation of the Shabaka stone by Miriam Lichtheim, Ancient Egyptian Literature, Vol. I, University of California Press, Los Angeles, 1975, pp.3-57

25. As proposed in the thesis by Robert Bauval and Graham Hancock in The Message of the Sphinx, p.133-145

26. ibid, pp.58-72

27. ibid, p.77

28. Reymond, op.cit., p.316; and Hancock and Faiia, Heaven's Mirror, op.cit., p.64

29. ibid

30. The oldest date was made using the most refined of all the methods by the astronomer F.S. Richards in 1921. Sir Norman Lockyer established a date of 3700 B.C.

31. See for example the works of Hancock and Bauval, Robin Heath, Giorgio de Santillana, et al.

32. Hancock and Faiia, Heaven's Mirror, op.cit., p.126; from George Coedes, Angkor: An Introduction, Oxford University Press, London, 1966, p.87

33. Hancock and Faiia, Heaven's Mirror, op.cit., p.133

34. R.O. Faulkner, The Ancient Pyramid Texts, Aris & Phillips, Warminster. p.159

35. Bellamy and Allan, op. cit., p.16

36. ibid, p.18

37. Hancock and Faiia, Heaven's Mirror, op. cit., p.258

38. ibid

39. Reymond, op. cit., p.49, p.300

40. ibid, p.47

41. Bauval and Hancock, Message of the Sphinx, op. cit.

42. See for example Bauval and Hancock, The Message of the Sphinx; also Robert Bauval, The Orion Mystery, et al.

43. E. Naville, Excavations at Abydos, Journal of Egyptian Archaeology, vol. 1, 1914, pp.160-165

44. Reymond, op. cit., p.93

45. ibid, p.316

46. ibid, p.255, p.306

47. John Grigsby, as referenced in Hancock and Faiia, Heaven's Mirror, op. cit, p.169

48. D. Evans et al, A comprehensive archaeological map of the world's largest pre-industrial settlement complex at Angkor, Cambodia, Proceedings of the National Academy of Sciences of the USA, August 23, 2007.

49. Charles Higham, The Civilization of Angkor, University of California Press, 2004, pp. 1-2.

50. Quoted in Brief Presentation by Venerable Vodano Sophan Seng, Khmer-Canadian Buddhist Cultural Center, 2005, p.2

CHAPTER FIVE. HERE COMES THE FLOOD

1. Michael Hoffman, Egypt Before the Pharaohs, Michael O'Mara Books, London, 1991, p.12

2. E.A. Wallis Budge, The Egyptian Heaven and Hell, Volume II, op. cit., pp.4-5. Digs at mounds called Giants Graves throughout the British Isles yielded skeletons of 12 feet in height, some with six fingers. In fact there exists overwhelming physical proof for a race of tall people. See for example, History And Antiquities Of Allerdale Ward; Forbidden Land by Robert Lyman; Strange Relics from the Depths of the Earth by Joseph Jochmans; The Timeless Earth, et al

3. The main thesis by Graham Hancock and Robert Bauval in The Message of the Sphinx, op.cit.

4. Labib Habachi, The Obelisks of Egypt, The American University Press, Cairo, 1988, pp.39-40

5. N. Mahalingam, Kumari Kandam: The Lost Continent, Proceedings of the Fifth International Conference/Seminar of Tamil Studies, Madras, 1981, pp.2-54. Geological evidence is found in inundation maps provided by Glenn Milne and referenced throughout Graham Hancock, Underworld, op.cit.

6. ibid

7. Graham Hancock, Underworld, op. cit., p.250

8. N. Mahalingam, op.cit

9. Skanda Purana, 12, chapter 2, verse 52

10. S.R. Rao, Dawn and Devolution of the Indus Civilization, Aditya Prakashan, New Delhi, 1991, pp.126-142

11. Graham Hancock, Underworld, op.cit., p.284

12. ibid

13. ibid, p.203

14. Anton and Simon Mifsud, Dossier Malta: Evidence for the Magdalenian, Malta 1997, p.128; and Graham Hancock, Underworld, op.cit., chapter 15 and 17.

15. Samuel Noah Kramer, History Begins at Sumer, University of Pennsylvania Press, 1991, pp.149-151

16. C.E. Brasseur de Bourbourg abbé, Manuscrit Troano, Imprimerie Impériale, Paris, 1869. Cited in Peter Tompkins, Mysteries of the Mexican Pyramids, p.114

17. C.E. Brasseur de Bourbourg abbé, Chronologie Historique des Mexicains, cited in Tompkins, ibid p. 116

18. Paulina Zelitsky's report to Reuters, December 7, 2001; also on the BBC, Lost City Found Beneath Cuban Waters; et al

19. ibid

20. Graham Hancock, Underworld, op.cit. p.212, pp.596-624

21. Professor Masaki Kimura, Yonaguni Japan, in New Scientist, 27 Nov. 2009. And referenced in Graham Hancock, Underworld, op.cit., Ch.27

22. New Scientist, 6.1.1972, p. 7

23. G.R.S. Mead, Thrice Great Hermes: Studies in Hellenistic Theosophy and Gnosis, Book III, p.59

24. Prof. Arthur Posnansky, Tiahuanacu: The Cradle of American Man, Ministry of Education, La Paz, 1957, vol. I, pp. 39-55

25. Charles Hapgood, Path of the Pole, Adventures Unlimited Press, 1999, p.255

26. S.Yu. Sokolov, 2008, published in Doklady Akademii Nauk, 2008, Vol. 418, No. 5, pp.655–659; IPCC, 2001. Climate Change 2001: The Scientific Basis. Contribution of

Working Group I to the Third Assessment Report of the Intergovernmental Panel on Climate Change. J.T. Houghton, Y. Ding, D.J. Griggs, M. Noguer, P.J. van der Linden, X. Dai, K. Maskell and C.A. Johnson (eds.). Cambridge University Press, 881pp. et. al.

27. Prof. Arthur Posnansky, op. cit., pp.39-55

28. See for example the Popol Vuh

29. Charles Hapgood, op.cit., p.137

30. Epic of Gilgamesh - Penguin Classics, London, 1988, pp.109-11

31. ibid

32. As stated throughout Frederick Filby, The Flood Reconsidered, Pickering and Inglis Ltd., London 1970. Or 175 myths, according to W. Bruce Masse, P. Bobrowsky, H. Rickman eds., Comet/Asteroid Impacts and Human Society, Springer, Berlin, 2007, p.48

33. J.T. Milik, The Book of Enoch, Oxford University Press, London, 1976, et al.

34. For example; J.J. Collins, The Sibylline Oracles of Egyptian Judaism, Missoula, 1974, et al.

35. A. Tollman, and E. Kristan-Tollman, The youngest big impact on Earth deduced from geological and historical evidence. Terra Nova. v. 6, no. 2, 1994, pp. 209-217

36. W. Bruce Masse, P. Bobrowsky, H. Rickman eds., Comet/Asteroid Impacts and Human Society, Springer, Berlin, 2007, p.55

37. Popol Vuh, p.93

38. Immanuel Velikovsky, Earth in Upheaval, Dell Pub., 1968, pp.42-44

39. Jorgen Peder Steffensen, N.I.B. Center For Ice and Climate, University of Copenhagen, 11 Dec. 2008

40. William Fix: Pyramid Odyssey - Mercury Media, Urbanna, Virginia 1978, p. 52-53

41. Glenn Milne, Dept. of Geology, University of Durham, reference in Graham Hancock: Underworld, p. 53; also Christopher Knight and Robert Lomas: Uriel's Machine - Fair Winds Press, 2001, p56-59

42. Klaus Schmidt: Göbekli Tepe - Southeastern Turkey. A preliminary Report on the 1995–1999 Excavations. In: Palèorient CNRS Ed., Paris 2000: 26.1, pp. 45–54

CHAPTER SIX. SEVEN SAGES

1. William Sullivan, The Secret of the Incas, 219; and Graham Hancock, Fingerprints of the Gods, op. cit., p.52

2. Quoted in Anthony Roberts, Sowers of Thunder, Ryder and Co., London, 1978, p.182

3. Guinness Book of World Records

4. J.E. Thompson, Maya History and Religion, University of Oklahoma Press, 1970, p.240; and referenced in Graham Hancock and Faiia, Heaven's Mirror, op. cit., p.235

5. Graham Hancock, ibid; and Harold Osborne, Indians of the Andes, Routledge and Kegan Paul, London, 1954, p.64

6. E.A.E. Reymond, The Mythical Origin of the Egyptian Temple, op. cit., p.38

7. F. W. Christian, The Caroline Islands, p.81

8. Graham Hancock and Faiia, Heaven's Mirror, op. cit., p.201-203; and Dr. Arthur Saxe, The Nan Madol Area of Pohnpei, Office of the High Commissioner, Trust Territory of the Pacific, Saipan, 1980

9. Reymond, op.cit., p.122, 316

10. ibid

11. E.A. Wallis Budge The Egyptian Heaven and Hell, op. cit.,, p. 462

12. Francis Maziere, Mysteries of Easter Island, Collins, London, 1969, p.41-122; and John Flenley, Easter Island, Earth Island, Thames & Hudson, London, 1992, p.56-148; also referenced in Graham Hancock and Faiia, Heaven's Mirror, op. cit., p.226-235.

13. ibid

14. William Sullivan, The Secret of the Incas, op. cit., p.219; and Graham Hancock, Fingerprints of the Gods, p.52

15. Alfred Metreux, ref. in Heaven's Mirror, p.235

16. Maziere, op.cit

17. Alexander Polyhistor, Und Der Platoniker Albinos Und Der Falsche Alkinoos, Jacob Freudenthal, Kessinger Publishing, 1875

18. King James Bible version; 4 the First Book of Enoch, scrolls of Qumran.

19. Roberts, op.cit., p.186-187; also noted in Hancock and Faiia, Heaven's Mirror, op. cit.

20. Barry Brailsford, Song of the Waitaha: Histories of a Nation, Wharariki Publishing, Castle Hill, 1999; and Hamish Miller, In Search Of The Southern Serpent, op. cit.

21. See for example Anthony Roberts, op. cit.,; and John Michell, Megalithomania: Artists, Antiquarians and Archaeologists at the Old Stone Monuments; et al

22. Roberts, ibid.

23. ibid, p.31
24. Copious excavations of these skeletons can be found in Memoirs of the Historical Society of Pennsylvania, vol. 12; Ohio Historical and Archaeological Society, vol. 2; Minnesota Geological Survey, vol. 1; Aborigines of Minnesota; Gods, Demons and UFOs, by Eric Norman; et al
25. Robert, op. cit.
26. Selim Hassan, The Sphinx, Cairo, 1949; and Gaston Maspero, The Dawn of Civilization, SPCK, London, 1894, p.247; see also Graham Hancock, Fingerprints of the Gods, et al.
27. R.A. Schwaller de Lubicz, Sacred Science: The King of Pharaonic Theocracy, Inner Traditions, Vermont, 1982, p. 111
28. Reymond, op.cit.
29. ibid, p.8, referenced in Hancock, Fingerprints of the Gods, p.200
30. For example, The Book of Sothis, attributed to Menetho
31. Reymond, op.cit,
32. Andrew Tomas, From Atlantis to Discovery, Robert Hale, London, 1972, p. 109
33. For example, Hapgood, Maps of the Ancient Sea Kings, et al.
34. Referenced in Hancock and Bauval, The Message of the Sphinx, op.cit., p. 92
35. See Robert Bauval, The Orion Mystery; Bauval and Hancock, ibid; et al
36. De Bello Gallico, E.C Kennedy ed., book VI, p.8-9, Duckworth Publishing, 1992
37. E.A. Wallis Budge, The Book of the Dead, Gramercy, New York, 1999, p.6
38. John Cooper (ed.), Plato: Complete Works, Hackett Publishing Company, Indianapolis, 1997, p. 551-2
39. John Michell, The Sacred Center, Thames and Hudson, London, 1994, p. 14
40. Matsya Purana, Pt. 1, 635
41. See Robert Bauval, The Orion Mystery; Bauval and Hancock, The Mystery of the Sphinx, et al
42. For example, see Paul Broadhurst, Green Man and the Dragon, et al.
43. Plato, Parmenides, trans. R.E. Allen, Yale University, New Haven, 1997, 342e-343b
44. Giorgio de Santillana and Hertha von Dechend, Hamlets Mill, Gambit, Boston, 1969, p.73
45. Samuel Noah Kramer, History Begins at Sumer, University of Pennsylvania Press, 1991, p.151-152
46. Ralph Griffith (trans.), Hymns of the Rigveda,

Munisharam Manoharlal Publishers, Delhi, 1987, vol. 1, p.99
47. The ground-penetrating radar scans clearly show the fossilized ribs of timber belonging to a massive ship on the slopes of Mount Ararat. Evidence was found of man-made alloys. Aerial images and ground photos also show a definitive shape of a massive hull whose dimensions accord with biblical measurements. See Rene Noorbergen, The Ark File; and the accounts by Flavius Josephus, c. 90 A.D., the famous Jewish historian who stated, "Its remains are shown there by the inhabitants to this day." He quotes Berosi the Chaldean, c. 290 B.C
48. John Michell, The Sacred Center, op. cit., p. 14
49. E.A. Wallis Budge, Hieroglyphic Dictionary, p.11b
50. Cited in Hancock, Fingerprints of the Gods, p.202
51. Santillana and Dechend, op. cit., p.73
52. The Nag Hammadi Library, ed. J.M. Robertson, Leiden, New York, 1988, p.122

CHAPTER SEVEN. BUILDERS OF THE GRID

1. Reymond, op. cit., p.112-114
2. ibid
3. ibid, p.180-190
4. Klaus-Dieter Linsmeier and Klaus Schmidt: Ein anatolisches Stonehenge. In: Moderne Archäologie. Spektrum-der-Wissenschaft-Verlag, Heidelberg 2003
5. See for example R.O. Faulkner, The Ancient Pyramid Texts, Aris & Phillips, Warminster. p.159; and traditions at Teotihuacan.
6. Kenneth Pelletier, Mind As Healer, Mind As Slayer, Dell Publishing, New York, 1977
7. For example, see Rand and Rose Flem-Ath, When the Sky Fell; Roland Dixon, Ahasta Myths; et al.
8. NASA JPL press release March 2, 2010
9. Raphael Patai, Man and Temple, Ktav Publishing House, New York, 1967
10. John Michell, The Dimensions of Paradise, Thames and Hudson, London, 1988, p.185-193
11. John Michell, New View Over Atlantis, Thames & Hudson, London, 1983, p.187-188
12. Michell, Dimensions of Paradise, op. cit., p.180
13. ibid, p174-6

14. ibid; and commented by David Fideler in Jesus Christ, Son of God, Quest Books, 1993

15. See for example Drunvalo Melchisedek, The Ancient Secret of the Flower of Life; Richard Wilhelm and C.G. Jung, The Secret of the Golden Flower: The Chinese Book of Life, et al.

16. See for example, Drunvalo Melchisedek, The Ancient Secret of the flower of Life, Light Technology Publishing, Clear Light Trust, 1999; et al

17. Michell, Dimensions of Paradise, op. cit., p.54-55

18. In the Epinomis of Plato's Laws.

19. Referenced in Michell, op. cit., p.46

20. Such as the work of Michell and Louis Chapentier on Chartres, Lawlor on the Osirion; and Keith Chritchlow, Tons Brunes, et al

21. Michell, The Dimensions of Paradise, op. cit., p. 185; and Alexander Thom, Megalithic Measures, op. cit.

22. Robin Heath, Sun, Moon & Stonehenge, Bluestone Press, Cardigan, 1998, p.13-15

23. Michell, City of Revelation, op. cit.

24. John Michell, The New View Over Atlantis, op. cit., p.170-180

25. ibid

26. ibid

27. ibid, p.194

28. ibid

29. Giorgio de Santillana and Hertha von Dechend, Hamlet's Mill, Gambit, Boston, 1969, p.74.

30. Peter Tompkins, Secrets of the Great Pyramid, Penguin Books, London, 1978, p.298, 349

31. ibid, p.349

32. ibid, p.350

33. ibid

34. ibid; and Michell, At the Center of the World, Thames and Hudson, London, 1994

35. A hexagonal feature around Saturn's North Pole, D.A. Godfrey, AA (National Optical Astronomy Observatories, Tucson, AZ), Icarus, vol. 76, Nov. 1988, p. 335-356.

36. Pancasiddhantika, XII, Thibaut trans., p.69

37. Charles Hapgood, Maps of the Ancient Sea Kings, Chilton Book Co., Philadelphia, 1966, p.93-98, 235

38. ibid

39. Piazzi Smyth, On an Equal Surface Projection for Maps of the World, Edmonton & Douglas, Edinburgh, 1870

40. Michell, The Dimensions of Paradise, op. cit., p.54-55

41. For example, Giorgio de Santillana, Graham Hancock, Robert Bauval, Jane Sellers, et al

42. Hancock and Faiia, Heaven's Mirror, op.cit., p.164

43. J. Filliozat, L'Inde et les Echanges Scientifiques dans L'antiquite, Chiers d'Histoire Mondiale, 1953, p358

44. Leon Comber, Traditional Mysteries of the Chinese Secret Societies of Malaysia, Eastern Universities Press, Singapore, 1961, p.52; referenced in Hancock, Fingerprints of the Gods, p.262

45. See also Robert Bauval, Graham Hancock, Giorgio de Santillana, et al

46. Jane Sellers, The Death of the Gods in Ancient Egypt, Penguin, London, 1992; also Hancock, Fingerprints of the Gods; Santillana, Hamlet's Mill, et al.

47. Anthony Aveni, Skywatchers of Ancient Mexico, University of Texas Press, Dallas, p.143

48. Hamlet's Mill, op. cit.

49. Heaven's Mirror, op. cit., p.254

50. ibid

51. ibid

52. ibid

CHAPTER EIGHT. KINGDOMS OF CONSCIENCE

1. Raphael Patai, Man and Temple, 1967, p.105; also M. Hocart, Kings and Councillors, Cairo, 1936, p.220

2. Peter Lu, in Advanced Geometry of Islamic Art, BBC News, February 23, 2007

3. Patai, op. cit., p.126

4. ibid

5. ibid, p.127

6. Edvard Westermarck, The Origin and Development of the Moral Ideas, London, 1906, vol. II, p.713

7. Ivan Engnell, Studies in Divine Kingship in the Ancient Near East, 2nd ed., 1967, p13

8. L. Wieger, Histoire des Croyances Religiueses et des Opinions Philosophiques en Chine, Hien Hien, 1922, p.64

9. Patai, op. cit., p.125

10. Steve Austin, The Extraordinary Middle East Earthquake of 750 BC, Institute of Creation Research, San Diego, 1989

11. Patai, op. cit.

12. ibid

13. ibid

14. ibid
15. "British and American scientists have found radio carbon dating, used to give a rough guide to the age of an object, can be wrong by thousands of years. It means humans may have been on earth for a lot longer than previously thought and accepted versions of early history could need a radical rethink. Experts have known for years that carbon dating is inexact but until researchers from Bristol and Harvard completed their study no one knew by how much." As quoted in Dating study 'means human history rethink', BBC News June 29, 2001. And in Carbon Dating May be Wrong by 10,000 Years, Roger Highfield, London Daily Telegraph, June 30, 2001: "Scientists say their key tool for dating ancient artefacts might be wrong by 10,000 years, which could push back the timing of key events in history and improve understanding of climate change."
16. Aubrey Burl, Megalithic Britanny, Thames & Hudson, London, 1985, p.14; Michael Poynder, Pi In The Sky, Rider, London, 1992, p.173
17. Goran Burenhult, The Megalithic Cemetery of Carrowmore, Co. Sligo, Goran Burenhult Publications, 2001; and Stephan Bergh, Knocknarea, the Ultimate Monument, in Monuments and Landscape in Atlantic Europe, ed. Chris Scarre, Routledge, 2002
18. As mentioned in earlier chapters by E.R.E. Reymond,op. cit.
19. See for example, Thor Heyerdahl, Kon Tiki: Voyages Across The Pacific by Raft, Simon & Schuster, New York, 1990
20. Bruce Cathie, The Bridge to Infinity, Quark Enterprises/Brookfield Press, Auckland, 1995, pp.139-146
21. Peter King in the New Journal of Physics, and quoted in How To Float Like A Stone, David Adam, The Guardian, May 11, 2005; and Scientists Levitate Small Animals, Charles Choi, LiveScience.com, November 29, 2006, reporting on article in the Journal of Applied Physics, Nov. 20, 2006.
22. For example, Robin Heath and John Michell, The Measure of Albion, Bluestone Press, St. Dogmaels, 2004; et al.
23. Harold Bailey, The Lost Language of Symbolism, Benn, London 1912, vol. 2, p.191
24. William Stukeley, Abury, 1743
25. Bailey, op. cit
26. See for example, Ferguson Rude Stone Monuments, et al.
27. Harold Bailey, op.cit., vol. 2, p.180
28. William Gifford Palgrave, Narrative of a Year's Journey Through Ventral and Eastern Arabia, 1862-63, vol. 1, MacMillan And Co., London, 1865, p.250
29. Heath and Michell, The Measure of Albion, op.cit., p.21
30. William Stukeley, Abury, a Temple of the British Druids, 1743, p.24
31. From Stuart Piggott's findings, discussed in Aubrey Burl, Prehistoric Avebury, p.298
32. Reymond, op cit
33. Stukeley, op cit, p.15
34. For example, Becker and Selden, The Body Electric; Valerie Hunt, Infinite Mind; et al
35. Stukeley, op. cit.
36. Personal communication from Isabelle Kingston; and located by Broadhurst and Miller in The Sun and the Serpent, Pendragon Press, Pendragon Press, Launceston, 1989
37. Harold Bailey, op. cit., p.181
38. Personal communication from Isabelle Kingston.
39. ibid
40. R.J.C. Atkinson, Antiquity 41, 1967
41. Wikipedia, Avebury, en.wikipedia.org/wiki/Avebury#Before_the_henge
42. Paul Devereux, Earth Memory, Ll ewellyn, 1992, p.21
43. Personal communication from Isabelle Kingston, originally described in her trance channeling. I was able to validate the reference to the forgotten mound in the 17th century history of Wiltshire's county records.
44. Personal communication from Isabelle Kingston.
45. See for example the work of Alexander Thom in Megalith Sites, et al.
46. Paul Broadhurst and Hamish Miller, The Sun and the Serpent, op. cit., p.13
47. ibid
48. ibid
49. ibid, p.20
50. Paul Broadhurst and Hamish Miller, Dance of the Dragon, Pendragon Press, Launceston, 2000
51. ibid, p.1
52. Robert Bauval and Graham Hancock, Talisman, Element, London, 2004, p.414; et al
53. Quoted by John Michell in The Measure of Albion, Bluestone Press, St. Dogmaels, 2004, p.87
54. Jeremiah xxxi, 21
55. Alfred Watkins, the Old Straight Track,

Abacus, London, 1974, pp.xv-xvi

56. For example, the work of Alexander Thom, Sir Norman Lockyer, John Michell, Paul Broadhurst and Hamish Miller, et al

57. From Geoffrey of Monmouth, The History of the Kings and Queens of Britain, trans. Lewis Thorpe, Penguin, London, 1966, and quoted in The Measure of Albion, ibid, p.88

58. From the Molmutine Laws, in the Geoffrey of Monmouth, The History of the Kings and Queens of Britain, op.cit., p.89

59. Tim Wallace-Murphy and Marilyn Hopkins, Rosslyn: Guardian of the Secrets of the Holy Grail, 1999; Beigent, Lee, Holy Blood Holy Grail, Delacorte Press, 2005; et al

60. But you'll have to wait until my next book to find out.

61. Geoffrey Ashe, Mithology of the British Isles, Methuen, 2000

62. Robin Heath, Sun, Moon & Stonehenge, Bluestone Press, St. Dogmaels, 1998, pp.64-70

63. ibid

64. ibid

65. ibid. p.77, and as in the Modern Welsh Dictionary

66. Heath, ibid

67. ibid p.78; see also reference 15

68. See Publications and Papers of the Mirador Basin Project, Foundation for Anthropological Research and Environmental Studies and Idaho State University.

69. As per the General Conference on Weights and Measures.

70. From the measurements taken by acoustics researcher John Reid. Private communication.

71. Geoffrey of Monmouth, The History of the Kings and Queens of Britain, ed. Lewis Thorpe, Penguin, London, 1977, p.72, 65, 196, 364

72. Richa Arora, The Encyclopedia of Evolutionary Biology, Anmol Pubs., 2004, p.52

73. Lehninger, Nelson and Cox, as quoted in Fundamentals of Biochemistry, Daniel Nelson and Michael Cox, W.H. Freeman, 5th edition, 2008, p.310

74. ibid

75. Norman de Garis Davis and Seymour Ricci, The Rock Tombs of El Amarna, Egypt Exploration Society, Part 1, London, 1903, p.1

76. Dominic Montserrat, Akhenaten: history, fantasy, and ancient Egypt, Routledge, New York, 2000, p.37

77. Anthony Mercatante, Who's Who In Egyptian Mythology, Clarkson N. Porter, New York, 1978, p.18; Frank Joseph and Laura Beaudoin, Opening the Ark of the Covenant, The Career Press, Franklin Lakes, 2007, p.100

78. E.R.E. Reymond, op.cit., pp.43-51

79. ibid, p.19

80. ibid

81. B Lohr, Ahanjati in Heliopolis, GM 11, 1974, pp.33-38; Cyril Aldred, Akhenaten: King of Egypt, Thames & Hudson, 1991

CHAPTER NINE. A VERY PERSONAL ODYSSEY

1. E.R.E. Reymond, Mystical Origins of the Egyptian Temple, University of Manchester Press, op.cit., p.294

2. Paul Brunton, A Search in Secret Egypt, E.P. Dutton, 1936, p.69

3. From a report by Dr. Abbate Pacha, V.P. of the Institut Egyptien, quoted in Brunton, p.76

4. ibid, p.70

5. ibid, p.73

6. Freddy Silva, Secrets in the Fields: The Science and Mysticism of Crop Circles, Hampton Roads, Charlottesville, 2002, pp.290-292

7. ibid, p.75.

8. ibid, p.77

9. ibid

10. Tim Robinson-Ball, The Rediscovery of Glastonbury, Sutton Publishing, 2007; and John Michell, The Dimensions of Paradise, op. cit.

11. See for example, Valerie Hunt, Infinite Mind; Becker and Selden, The Body Electric, et al

12. E.R.E. Reymond, op. cit., p.132

CHAPTER TEN. WATER

1. For example, the effects of geometries on the human body, as discussed in Sheila Ostrander and Lynn Schroeder's Psychic Discoveries Behind The Iron Curtain., Marlowe and Co., New York, 1977

2. R.O. Faulkner, The Ancient Pyramid Texts, Aris & Phillips, Warminster. p.159

3. Guy Underwood, The Pattern of the Past, Abacus, London, 1974, pp.60-62

4. William Howells, The Heathens, Doubleday, New York, 1962

5. E.R.E. Reymond, op.cit., pp.20-22

6. ibid, pp.141-142

7. Louis Merle, Radiesthesie et Prehistoire, 1933; Charles Diot, Les Sourciers et les Monuments

Megalithiques, 1935

8. Robert Boothby, Journal of the British Society of Dowsers, volume 2, 1935, p.115
9. Reginald Smith, Journal of the British Society of Dowsers, volume 2, 1939
10. Guy Underwood, op. cit., p.162.
11. Paul Broadhurst, Secret Shrines, Mythos Press, Launceston, 1988, p.3
12. Gospel of John 3:5
13. Peter Tompkins & Christopher Bird, Secrets of the Soil, Arkana, London, 1989, pp.99-105
14. Richard Gerber, Vibrational Medicine, Bear and Co, Santa Fe, 2001; Daily Telegraph, July 1, 2009
15. Tompkins & Bird, op. cit.
16. ibid
17. ibid
18. As in Tom Graves, Needles of Stone; Guy Underwood, op. cit; Blanche Merz, Cosmic Points of Energy; et al
19. As proved by the work of Jacques Benveniste, published in Nature 1988; Paul Devereux, Earthmind, Destiny Books, 1992, p.170; Daily Telegraph, December 1988. Also, see notes pp.103-4 Tompkins & Bird Secrets of the Soil, op. cit.; Benveniste's work was reproduced and validated by seven independent laboratories. See author's letter www.telegraph.co.uk/comment/letters/3585045/water-memory
20. Paul Devereux, Places of Power, Blandford Press, Blandford, 1999
21. Pierre Mereux, Carnac: Des Pierres Pour Les Vivants, Net et Bretagne, Kerwangwenn, 1992, Ch XIII
22. Throughout the various books by Masuro Emoto, such as Hidden Messages in Water, Love Thyself, Healing Power of Water.
23. Robert Becker and Gary Selden, The Body Electric, as referenced in Elkington and Ellson, In The Name of the Gods, op. cit., p.171
24. Pierre Mereux, op. cit., Ch. XV
25. John Burke and Kaj Halberg, Seed of Knowledge, Stone of Plenty, Council Oak Books, San Francisco, 2005
26. Petrus Blesensis, Epist. 105

**CHAPTER ELEVEN.
ELECTROMAGNETICS**

1. Communication from Pueblo native Rina Swentzell; and cited Devereux, Places of Power, op.cit.
2. William Howells, The Heathens, Doubleday, New York, 1948
3. www.jpl.nasa.gov: Magnetic Portals Connect Sun and Earth. October 30, 2008
4. J. Vogel, Indian Serpent Lore or The Nagas in Hindu Legend and Art, Kessinger Publishing, 2005, p.7
5. Richard Wilhelm, I Ching, Book of Changes, Princeton University Press, 1967, p.39
6. E.R.E Reymond, op. cit., p.35
7. ibid, p.252
8. ibid, pp.112-114
9. See for example Hamish Miller, The Sun and the Serpent, op. cit.; Freddy Silva, Secrets In the Fields, op. cit.; David Cowan and Chris Arnold, Ley Lines and Earth Energies, Adventures Unlimited Press, Kempton, 2003; et al
10. www.jpl.nasa.gov. The reference was removed from the website barely two weeks after its publication. No explanation has ever been given.
11. Paul Devereux, Earth Memory, Llewellyn, St. Paul, 1992, p.168
12. John Burke and Kaj Halberg, op.cit., p.126
13. ibid, p.129
14. ibid
15. Devereux, op.cit.; Burke and Halberg, p.130; et al
16. Burke and Helberg, op.cit., p.130
17. Pierre Mereaux, Carnac: Des Pierres Pour Les Vivants, Kerwangwenn, Nature & Bretagne,1992, p.138
18. ibid, pp.139-142
19. ibid
20. Eduardo Balanovski, quoted in Francis Hitching, Earth Magic, Cassell, London, 1976
21. Clark and Marjorie Hardman, Ohio Archaeologist, 37(3):34-40, 1987
22. Historical Collections of Noble County, Ohio, 1872, pp.350-351; Susan Woodward and Jerry McDonald, Indian Mounds of the Middle Ohio Valley, The McDonald & Woodward Publishing Company, Blacksburg, 1986; et al
23. John Burke and Kaj, op.cit., p.86
24. ibid, p.80
25. Paul Devereux, The Power of Place, Blandford, London, 1990, p.185
26. Gregg Braden, Awakening To Zero Point, Seven Directions Media, Seattle, 1997
27. Charles Brooker, Magnetism and Standing Stones, New Scientist, January 13, 1983
28. Tom Graves, Needles of Stone, Harper Collins, London, 1986
29. Robert Hartmann, Wetter, Boden, Mensch,

brochure no. 13, 1983, Eberbach am Necktar

30. Blanche Merz, Points of Cosmic Energy, C.W. Daniel and Co., Saffron Walden, 1985, pp.32-33
31. ibid, p.83
32. E.A. Wallis-Budge, The Egyptian Heaven and Hell, Keagan Paul, London, 1937, p.37
33. ibid
34. Merz, op.cit., pp.33-34
35. Michael Poynder, Pi In The Sky, Rider, London, 1992, p.88
36. ibid, p.72
37. M.A. Persinger and L.A. Ruttan and S. Koren, Enhancement of temporal lobe-related experiences during brief exposures to milligauss intensity ELF magnetic field, Journal of Biochemistry, 9, 1990, pp.33-45: Robert Becker and Gary Selden, The Body Electric: Electromagnetism and the Foundation of Life, Quill, William Morrow, New York, 1985; A.P. Dubrov, The Geomagnetic Field and Life: Geo-magnetobiology, Plenum Press, New York, 1978; J.L. Kirschvink, et al. "Magnetite biomineralization in the human brain." Proceedings of the National Academy of Sciences, 89 (1992):7683-7687. Synopsis originally published in Future History, Vol. 8, by H. Coetzee, Ph.D
38. Serena Roney-Dougal, The Faery Faith, Green Magic, London, 2002, pp.10-14; and E.C. May et al, Review of the psychoenergetic research conducted at SRI International, SRI International Technical Report, March 1988

CHAPTER TWELVE. SACRED MEASURE

1. E.R.E. Reymond, op.cit, p.309
2. ibid, p.310
3. Robin Heath and John Michell, The Measure of Albion, Bluestone Press, St. Dogmaels, 2004, p.9
4. Peter Tompkins and Christopher Bird, Secrets of the Great Pyramid, op. cit., p.304; John Michell, City of Revelation, op. cit., p.108; and Heath and Michell, et al.
5. Peter Tompkins, Mysteries of the Mexican Pyramids, Thames & Hudson, London, 1987, pp.241-266
6. Tompkins, ibid
7. Alexander Thom, Megalithic Sites in Britain, Oxford University Press, 1967; and with A.S. Thom in Megalithic Remains in Britain and Brittany, Oxford University Press, 1978

8. ibid, p.34
9. Lowis D'A. Jackson, Modern Metrology, Crosby Lockwood, London, 1882, p.358
10. Thom, ibid, p.166
11. Guy Murchie, The Seven Mysteries of Life, Mariner Books, New York,1999, p.465
12. Heath and Michell, op.cit, pp.30-31

CHAPTER THIRTEEN. STONE

1. Tacitus, Annals, 14:30
2. For example see Devereux, Places of Power, et al
3. Martin Brennan, The Stars and the Stones, Thames & Hudson, London, 1983
4. Devereux, Places of Power, op.cit., p.49
5. L. Chapman, The Ley Hunter, no. 94, 1982
6. John Steele, Internal Dragon Project report, 1982, quoted Devereux, Places of Power, p. 75
7. John Reid, personal communication.
8. Pierre Mereaux, Carnac: Des Pierres Pour Les Vivants, Kerwangwenn, Nature & Bretagne,1992
9. Paul Craddock, Dowsers Discover Concealed Megalith, British Society of Dowsers Journal, December 2005

CHAPTER FOURTEEN. SACRED GEOMETRY

1. Maurice Finnochiaro, The Essential Galileo, Hackett Publishing, Indianapolis, 2008, p.183
2. John Martineau, A Book of Coincidence, Wooden Books, Powys, 1995; and Ofmil. C. Haynes, The Harmony of the Spheres, Wooden Books, Powys, 1997
3. Sheila Ostrander and Lynn Schroeder, Psychic Discoveries Behind the Iron Curtain, Bantam, New York, 1971, pp.366-372
4. V. Safonov, Razor Blades and the Cheops Pyramid, Moscow Komsomolets, May 26, 1968
5. Ostrander & Schroeder, op. cit., p.370
6. L. Turenne: De La Baguette de Coudrier aux Oetecteurs du prospeeteur, Les minereaux, Les ondes des formes geornetriques, La Lecture sur plans, La evolution de la matiere, Les ondes nocives, Paris, 1935
7. Ostrander & Schroeder, op. cit., p.370
8. ibid
9. Theodor Schwenck, Sensitive Chaos, Rudolf Steiner Press, Forest Row, 1976

10. Madhu Khanna, Yantra, Thames & Hudson, London, 1979, pp.9-12
11. My thanks to Alex Sokolowski, editor, www. World Mysteries.com, for his original calculations on the Bent and Red Pyramids.
12. ibid
13. Mary Bennett and David Percy, Dark Moon, Aulis, London, p.391
14. Michael Schneider, The Beginner's Guide to Constructing the Universe, Harper Perennial, New York, 1994, p. xxiv
15. ibid, p.54

CHAPTER FIFTEEN. ORIENTATION

1. Pierre Mereaux, Carnac: Des Pierres Pour Les Vivants, Kerwangwenn, Nature & Bretagne,1992 p.141
2. Everard Ferdinand Thurn, Among the Indians of Guiana, 1883, p.350
3. Edwin Bernbaum, op. cit., p.8

CHAPTER SIXTEEN. THE HUMAN KEY

1. M. Capek, The Philosophical Impact of Contemporary Physics, Van Nostrand, Princeton, 1961, p.319
2. Phil Cousineau, The Art of Pilgrimage, Conari Press, Berkeley, 1998, p.99
3. F.W. Putnam at the Serpent Mound, American Association for the Advancement of Science, 1883
4. John Reid, personal communication.
5. John Stuart Reid, Egyptian Sonics: a Preliminary Investigation Concerning the Hypothesis That the Ancient Egyptians Had Developed a Sonic Science by the fourth Dynasty, Sonic Age Limited, 42nd Edition, 2001
6. John Reid, personal communication.
7. Talmut, Berakot 10a
8. Bible, 1 Corinthians 3.16-17
9. E.R.E. Reymond, op. cit., p.59
10. Outlined in Lynne McTaggart, The Field, HarperCollins, New York, 2008, pp.109-122; and Dean Radin and Roger Nelson, Evidence for consciousness-related anomalies; and 'When immovable objections meet irresistible evidence, Behavioral and Brain Sciences, 1987, 10: 600-1
11. Roger Nelson, FieldREG measurements in Egypt: resonant consciousness at sacred sites, Princeton Engineering Anomalies Research, School of Engineering/Applied Science, PEAR Technical Note 97002, July 1997; and Nelson et al, FieldREGH: consciousness field effects: replications and explorations, Journal of Scientific Exploration, 1998, 12 (3), 425-54; and McTaggart, The Field, pp.205-7
12. ibid
13. ibid
14. Edward Westermarck, The Origin and Development of the Moral Ideas, MacMillan and Co., London, 1908, vol.II, p.661
15. Paul Broadhurst, The Secret Land, Mythos Press, Launceston, 2010, p.61
16. E.A. Wallis-Budge, The Egyptian Heaven and Hell, op. cit., p.240

CHAPTER SEVENTEEN. THE RISE AND FALL OF THE TEMPLE

1. Mircea Eliade, The Sacred and the Profane, Harper & Row, New York, 1961
2. See for example Michael Talbot, The Holographic Universe; and the work of David Bohm and Karl Pribram.
3. Mike Bzillie, Exodus to Arthur: Catastrophic Encounters with Comets, B.T. Batsford, London, 1999; Robert Schoch Voyages of the Pyramid Builders, Tarcher, New York, 2004; Fisher et al, The Holocene 5, 1, 19, 1995; M.G.L. Baillie, and M.A.R. Munro, Nature, 332 345, 1988
4. The sceptical statistician Michel Gauquelin tried to prove that astrological signs bore no influence on the course of individual, yet after 20,000 cases he was proved wrong, these forces indeed have an effect. See The Cosmic Clocks, Paladin, St. Albans, 1969.
5. Climate, Culture, and Catastrophe in the Ancient World, Richard Meehan, ed., Stanford University, www.stanford.edu/~meehan/donnellyr/summary.html
6. Baillie, op.cit; Schoch; Fisher et al, ibid.
7. Thompson et al Late Glacial Stage and Holocene Tropical Ice Core Records from Huascaran, Peru. Science v 269 7 July 1995
8. Kay Johnson and Kay Johnstone, Climatic Change, 3, 1981, p 251
9. Graham Hancock, Underworld, op. cit., pp.29-33; David Oppenheimer, Eden in the East, Weidenfeld and Nicholson, London, 1998, p.57; Georges Roux, Ancient Iraq, Penguin Books, London, p.4; et al
10. Baillie, op.cit; Robert Schoch, op.cit., p.222

11. The accepted date for the Olmec calendar found at Tres Zapotes is 3114 BC, the commencement of the Kali Yuga is 3003 BC, and the enthronement of Menes is 3100 BC. Given the discrepancies in dating systems and the inconsistencies in Carbon-14 dating it is quite feasible all these events took place at the same time.

12. Giorgio de Santillana and Hertha von Dechend, Hamlet's Mill, op. cit

13. Schoch, ibid; Robert Bauval's research also shows that the Great Pyramid was built over many stages and aligned to the stars of the age. See The Orion Mystery; et al

14. Baillie, op.cit; Schoch, ibid.

15. Psalms 18

16. Baillie, op.cit; Schoch, ibid

17. Baillie, op.cit; Schoch, ibid, p 217

18. A. Migot, Cinq Millenaires d'Astrologie, Janus, no.8, 1965, ref. Gauquelin, The Cosmic Clocks, p.33

19. Wing Tsit Chan, A Sourcebook of Chinese Philosophy, Princeton University Press, 1963, pp.286-8; quoted in Schoch p.198

20. Nicholas Grimmal, A History of Ancient Egypt, Blackwell Books, Oxford, 1992, pp.223-225

21. Joann Fletcher, Chronicle of a Pharaoh: The Intimate Life of Amenhotep III, Oxford University Press, 2000, pp.161-162

22. Christine El Mahdy, Tutankhamun: The Life and Death of the Boy-King, St. Martin's Press, London, 2000 ; Andrew Collins and Chris Ogilvie-Herald, Tutankhamun: The Exodus Conspiracy, Virgin Books 2010; Bob Brier, The Murder of Tutankhamun, Berkley Books, New York,1998; et al

23. From my own dowsing results, later confirmed by personal communication from Isabelle Kingston.

24. According to Rabbinical Literature, Num. R. xxii; Tosef., Sohah, iv. 19; II Sam. xvi. 23, Yer. Sanh. x. 2 and 29a, Suk. 53a et seq. See also www.jewishencyclopedia.com

25. Peter Tompkins, Mysteries of the Mexican Pyramids, Thames & Hudson, London, 1987, pp.12-14; et al.

26. Jacques Soustelle, The Daily Life of the Aztecs on the Eve of the Spanish Conquest, trans. P. O'Brian, Weidenfeld & Nicholson, New York, 1961

27. Bernal Diaz, Historia verdadera de la Conquista de Nueva España, 1632

28. Hernán Cortés, Cartas de Relación, 1523.

29. Editorial Porrúa. 2005, p.26

29. See for example Becker and Selden's The Body Electric, Valerie Hunt's Infinite Mind, et al

30. Cited in Tompkins, Secrets of the Great Pyramid, op. cit., p.50

31. W.H. Brett, The Indian Tribes of Guiana, Robert Carter and Bros., New York, 1853, pp.378-84

32. Verrier Elwin, The Agaria, 1942, Oxford University Press edition, 1992, p.96; G.M. Potanin, et al.

33. Giorgio de Santillana and Hertha von Dechend, op.cit., p.217

34. Louis Ginzberg, The Legends of the Jews, The Jewish Publication Society of America, Philadelphia, 1954, vol. 4, p.96

35. ibid; and Raphael Patai, op.cit., p.56

36. ibid

37. Ginzberg, ibid; Patai, ibid

38. ibid

39. Rabbinical Literature, op.cit.

40. Chronicles. Ch 22

41. David Elkington and Paul Ellson, op. cit., pp.109-110

42. Herodotus, The Histories, II, pp.55-56

43. Jean-Michel Augebert, Les Mysteres du Soleil, Robert Laffont, Paris, 1971, p.144; John Anthony West, Serpent in the Sky, Quest Books, Wheaton, 1993, et al

44. Aristotle, Politics, III, 1283b

45. Homer, The Odyssey, Book 4

46. Andre Bernard, Alexandrie la Grande, Hachette, Paris, 1998, p.66

47. Robert Bauval in Talisman, op. cit., p.208

48. Bauval, ibid; temple referenced in Herodotus.

49. H. A. Drake, Constantine and the Bishops: The Politics of Intolerance, Johns Hopkins University Press, 1999, pp.349-403

50. Iraneus, cited in Elaine Pagels, The Gnostic Gospels, Penguin, London, 1990, p.68

51. Timothy Freke and Peter Gandy, The Jesus Mysteries, Thorsons-Element, London, 2000, p.300

52. E. M. Forster, Alexandria: A History and a Guide, Peter Smith, Gloucester, 1968, p.5, 160

53. Drake, op. cit., p.404

54. Edward Gibbon, David Wormsley, ed., The History of the Decline and Fall of the Roman Empire, Penguin Books, London, 2009, ch28

55. For example, Baigent and Leigh, Holy Blood Holy Grail, op. cit.; et al

56. Elaine Pagels, op. cit., pp.13-15

57. Margaret Alic, Hypatia's Heritage: A History of Women in Science from antiquity Through

the Nineteenth Century, Beacon Press,
Boston, 1986
58. Socrates Scholasticus, Ecclesiastical History,
book VI, Ch. 15

CHAPTER EIGHTEEN. RETURN OF THE INVISIBLES

1. Christian Jacq, Magic and Mystery in Ancient Egypt, Souvenir Press, London, 1998, pp.15-19
2. Cited in ibid p.13
3. Alan Gardiner, Egyptian Grammar, Griffith Institute, 1957; and cited in Talisman, p.81
4. ibid, p.14
5. ibid
6. ibid
7. Keith Thomas, Religion and the Decline of Magic, Wiedenfield & Nicholson, London 1971; et al
8. Thomas, ibid
9. ibid
10. Andrew Wellburn, Mani, the Angel and the Column of Glory, Floris Books, Edinburgh, 1998, pp.36-68
11. Yuri Stoyanov, The Other God, Yale University Press, New Haven, 2000, pp.108-110
12. James Robinson, ed., The Nag Hammadi Library, Second Treatise of the Great Seth, E.J. Bill, New York, p.365
13. ibid, pp.362-367
14. ibid
15. John Bale, Acta Romanorum Pontificum, translated from Latin into English as The Pageant of the Popes in 1574; and quoted as "This myth of Christ has served us well", in Michael Baigent, Richard Leigh and Henry Lincoln, The Messianic Legacy, Dell, London, 1989
16. Robinson, op.cit., p.194
17. Louis Charpentier, The Mysteries of Chartres Cathedral, Avon, New York, 1975, pp.74-75
18. Albert Wolters, The Copper Scroll: Overview, Text and Translation, Sheffield Academic Press, Sheffield, 1996
19. Laurence Gardner, The Bloodline of the Holy Grail, Element Books, Shaftsbury, 1996, p 265
20. ibid
21. Elkington and Ellson, op. cit., p99
22. For example Laurence Gardiner, Bloodline of the Holy Grail; Charpentier, Mysteries of Chartres Cathedral; et al
23. Graham Hancock, The Sign and the Seal, Crown, New York, 1992

24. Author's own research, the subject of the next book.
25. Gardner, op.cit., p.102
26. Charpentier, op.cit., p.60
27. Exodus 24:12
28. The Bible, Acts VII, 22; Gardner, Lost Secrets of the Sacred Ark; et al
29. Gardner, op.cit., p.260
30. ibid p.103
31. Charpentier, op.cit., p.62
32. Albert Hourani, A History of the Arab Peoples, Faber and Faber, London 1991. And cited in Hancock & Bauval Talisman, pp.165-6
33. Robert Bauval, The Orion Mystery; Hancock and Bauval, The Message of the Sphinx; et al.
34. Charpentier, op.cit., p.75
35. ibid, p.79
36. ibid, pp.287-29
37. Gardner, op.cit., p.110
38. Gordon Strachan, Chartres: Sacred Geometry, Sacred Space, Floris, Edinburgh, 2003, p.12
39. Elkington and Ellson, op.cit.
40. Merz, op. cit., pp.105-121
41. Regine Pernoud, Les Grandes Epoques de l'Aet en Occident, Ed. Du Cheine; and Charpentier, op. cit., p.149
42. Laurence Gardner, Genesis of the Grail Kings, Fair Winds Press, 2002, p.183
43. Charpentier, op.cit., p.147
44. Merz, op.cit., p.108
45. ibid, p.112
46. Charpentier, op.cit., p.30
47. Strachan, op.cit., p.82
48. Charpentier, op.cit., pp.112-113
49. Schoch, op.cit., pp.210-11
50. Francis Bacon, New Atlantis, Kessinger Pub. Co., Kila, 1992
51. ibid, p.329
52. Robert Lomas, The Invisible College, Headline, London, pp.71-86
53. Freddy Silva, Secrets In The Fields: The Science and Mysticism of Crop Circles, Hampton Roads, Charlottesville, 2002, pp. 4-5
54. ibid, p.6
55. Ibid, p.8
56. Terry Wilson, The Secret History of Crop Circles, CCCS, Paignton, 1998, p.59
57. For example, Terry Wilson, op. cit.; Jeffrey Wilson, ICCRA: Colin Andrews CPR International database.
58. Silva, op.cit., p.37
59. ibid, pp.36-39
60. Interview with John MacNish, Crop Circle Communique, UFO Central Home Video,

1991

61. Silva, op.cit., p.39

62. Personal communication from George Wingfield, cited in Silva, ibid, pp.39-40

63. Crop Circles: The Hidden Truth, DVD, Richard Hall, Executive Producer, www.richplanet.net

64. Silva, ibid, p.54

65. Silva, op.cit., p.117

66. ibid, pp117-139, 204-227

67. ibid, pp.220-248; and John Michell, ed., Dowsing the Crop Circles, Gothic Image, Glastonbury, 1991

68. Silva, op.cit., pp.249-261

69. Lucy Pringle, Crop Circles, Thorsons, London,1999; Harry Wiener, External Chemical Messengers, New York State Journal of Medicine, 1968; et al

70. Silva, op.cit., p.233; Tompkins and Bird, Secrets of the Soil, 1992

71. Reymond, op.cit., p.103

72. See the full transcripts, Silva, op.cit., pp.272-276

73. Egyptian Book of Coming Forth By Day, Ch. 134, 15-17

74. Silva, op.cit., pp.194-200

75. ibid, pp.130-131

76. ibid, pp.179-190; John Martineau, Crop Circle Geometry, Wooden Books, Powys, 1996

77. Michespacher, Qabbalah in Alchymia, 1616

78. John Michell, Geometry and Symbolism at Barbury Castle, cited in Silva, op.cit., pp.153-154

79. Acts of the Apostles 2:19

80. Report in the Daily Telegraph, Space, July 29, 2010

81. Nature, 12 February, 1976

82. Isabelle Kingston, personal communication

83. Richard Andrews, in Dowsing the Crop Circles, John Michell, ed., op. cit., pp.33-39; and Silva, op. cit., p.242

CHAPTER NINETEEN. 108 DEGREES OF WISDOM

1. Phil Cousineau, The Art of Pilgrimage, Conari Press, Berkeley, 1998, p. 104

2. Francis Huxley, The Way of the Sacred, Doubleday, New York, 1974, cited in Cousineau, op. cit., p.96

3. James Swan, The Power of Place & Human Environments, Gateway Books, Bath, 1991, p73

4. James Robinson, ed., the Nag Hamadi Library, Brill, 1996, p.153; William Birks and Robert Gilbert, The Treasure of Montsegur, Crucible, 1987, p.140

5. Laurette Sejourne, Burning Water: Thought and Religion in Ancient Mexico, Shambhala, Berkeley, 1976, p.28

6. Cousineau, op. cit., p.96

7. The central thesis of Graham Hancock and Robert Bauval in Talisman, op. cit.

8. Andrew Lipscomb and Albert Ellery Bergh, eds., The Writings of Thomas Jefferson, Washington, DC, 1903, p.179

9. David Ovason, The Secret Zodiac of Washington DC, Century, London, 1999, p.379

10. Michael Baigent and Richard Leigh, The Temple and the Lodge, Jonathan Cape, London, 1989, pp.261-262

11. Ovason, ibid, p.83

12. Graham Hancock and Robert Bauval, Talisman, op. cit., pp.471-472

13. ibid, p.473

14. Robert Bauval and Graham Hancock, ibid, p478

IMAGE CREDITS

Freddy Silva (www.invisibletemple.com and www.freddysilva.com)
i, 10, 14, 16, 21, 26 top left (top right, bottom left), 26 bottom, 27, 29, 30, 31, 36, 38-41, 46 (after on John Michell's diagram in *The Sacred Centre*), 47, 49, 51, 55, 60-62, 64 (based on USC survey, Henry Mitchell and the French Commission, 1798), 65-68, 70, 74 (based on Hancock & Milne in *Talisman*), 77, 83, 88, 91 (left), 93, 97, 99, 106 (based on John Michell's diagram in *The Dimensions of Paradise*), 107, 108, 109 (based on John Michell's diagram in *The Dimensions of Paradise*), 110, 112, 115, 117 (part based on Graham Hancock's original calculations and diagram in *Heaven's Mirror*), 118, 122, 125, 126 (right), 127, 130, 132-135, 136 (after Broadhurst & Miller in *The Sun and the Serpent*), 142, 143-144 (based on Robin Heath's diagrams in *Sun, Moon & Stonehenge*), 146-149, 152, 167, 170-173, 175 (top), 176 (adapted from Guy Underwood in *The Pattern of the Past*), 178-179, 181, 182 (bottom); 183 (bottom), 184 (composite based on Squier & Davis' original map, and data from Clark Hardman, Jr. & Marjorie Hardman, William Romain, Robert Fletcher, Terry Cameron, Jeffrey Wilson, and the author), 186, 187 (top), 187 (bottom, after Charles Brooker), 188-191, 194, 197 (adapted from Hugh Harlesden's drawings in *Secrets of the Mexican Pyramids*, 198, 202, 204, 208 (based on John Martineau and Ofmil C. Haynes, *A Little Book of Coincidence*, and *The Harmony of the Spheres* (Wooden Books), 210 (geometry based on Alex Sokoloski, www.WorldMysteries.com), 211, 212 (top), 213 (adapted from Robert Lawlor in *Sacred Geometry*, 214-215, 216 (after John Michell), 218, 221, 223, 224, 226-228, 235, 241, 245, 258, 269 (based on Blanche Merz in *Points of Cosmic Energy*), 270 (based on Louis Charpentier in *The Mysteries of Chartres Cathedral*), 276-278, 277 (adapted from John Martineau in *Crop Circle Geometry* (Wooden Books), 280, 282, 285 (top), 286-287.

Martin Page (www.sacredsites.com)
25, 28, 42, 44, 50, 70 (top), 80, 84, 87, 100, 120, 126 (left), 138, 201.

Santha Faiia (www.grahamhancock.com/gallery/) : 72

Dr. Masaaki Kimura: 78; **Paul Broadhurst**: 139; **Guy Underwood**: 172, 176 (adapted); **Hamish Miller**: 175 (bottom); **Kevin Ruane**: 246; **Richard Wintle**: 279

Library of Congress: p.119 (top) 1909; p.119 (bottom) J. Laurent, c.1860; p.124 Matson Photo Service c.1924; p.145 unknown; p.154 Maison Bonfils c1867; p.185 Ohio State Archaeological & Historical Society; p.207 G. Eric or Edith Matson, for American Colony Jerusalem, 1910; p.217 Maison Bonfils c.1867; p.250 American Colony (Jerusalem) Photo Dept. 1900-1920; p.285 (bottom) Detroit Pub. co. c1890; p.289 Carol Highsmith.

Other sources: p.ix 19th Century German engraving; p.24 Bhuttanese 19th Century thanka; p.26 top left, The Two Babylons, Alexander Hislop; p.26 top left - bottom right, Kitto's *Illustrated Commentary, 1840*; p.48, *La vie et les Paysages en Égypte : études en héliotypies tirées d'après nature* 1870; p.56 from Arthur Posnanski *Tihuanacu: Cradle of American Man*; p.58-59 from *Peru Incidents of Travel*, 1877; p.91 (right) Strand Magazine 1895; p.108 (bottom) NASA; p.129 William Stukeley c.1720 from *Abury*; p.158 Cornelis de Bruijn (c.1652-1727); p.193 from *Two Babylons*, Alexander Hislop, 1898; p.199 from *Bible Moralisé* of Blanche of Castile, 1220; p.209 from Ernst Haekel's *Kunstformen der Natur*, 1904; p.225 H.T. Ferrar, 1930; p.241 (top) *Wakeman's handbook of Irish antiquities*, 1903; p.248 *Codex Magliabechiano*, 16th century; p.255 *La vie et les paysages en Égypte : études en héliotypies tirées d'après nature*, 1870; p.257 unknown c.1850; p.261 authors unknown; p.265 From *A Short History of Monks and Monasteries* by Alfred Wesley Wishart (1865-1933); p.268 from G. Dehio and G. von Bezold, *Die Kirchliche Baukunst des abendlandes*, Stuttgart, 1887; p.272 unknown, 13th Century; p.288 Philip Crocker 1812.

Creative Commons: p.18, Jack Hynes; 22, Gisling; 69, Bjørn Christian Tørrissen; 103, Zunkir; 212, (btm) wicki; 238, Marta Gutowska; 253, Onno Zweers; 267, Félix Potuit; 23, Douglas J. McLaughlin; 182-3 (t), Kamel15; 284, Magnus Manske.

Freddy Silva is one of the world's leading experts on sacred sites, and a researcher into the interaction between temples and consciousness. He is the best-selling author of Secrets in the Fields, director of several documentaries, and a fine art photographer.

He lectures worldwide and has made keynote presentations at the International Science and Consciousness Conference, and the International Society For The Study Of Subtle Energies & Energy Medicine, in addition to appearances on television, video documentaries and radio shows.

Described by the CEO of Universal Light Expo as "perhaps the best metaphysical speaker in the world right now."

Visit Freddy at www.invisibletemple. com

INDEX

NUMBERS

19.47º 173, 198, 279, 287
32.72º 148, 149, 150, 151,
    185, 279, 287
51.42º 287
666º 104, 105, 107
1746 fusion 107, 109

A

Aborigines 19, 177, 278
Abraxas 104
Abu Simbel 191
Abydos 66, 67, 68, 106, 151
Açores 75, 146, 198
Adam and Eve 34, 266
Aeschylus 96
Agaria 250
Age of Aquarius 281
Age of Aries 242
Age of Leo 242
Age of Pisces 246, 247, 281
Ahau 73
Ahithophel 251, 252
ahu 89
Ahura Mazda 148, 233
Ahu Te Pito Kura 89
Ail na Mírenn 48
Akbar jihad 266, 269
Akhenaten ix, 53, 150, 246
Akhetaten 150, 246, 254
akhu 89, 98
Akhu Shemsu Hor 92, 98,
    109, 150, 164
Aksum 51, 263
Aku-Aku 89
Akwasi, myths of 250
Al-Aqsa Mosque 54
Alba 146
Albigensian Crusade 271
Alcobaça monastery 266
Alexander the Great 253
Alexandria 96, 254
Alexandria, Virginia 287
Allah 271
Allegewi 91
Alpha Draconis 114
altar, meaning of 180

Al Qaseem 128
Amarna 246
Amarnath 45
Amenhotep III 150, 245
Amesbury 127
Amun-Ra 49, 96, 253
An-Yang 111
Ana 54, 80
Anasazi 19, 28, 38, 139, 174,
    190
Anatolia 243
Angkor 59, 61, 62, 68, 69,
    71, 76, 113, 116, 271
Anglesey 201
ankh hor 68
Annapurna 20
Anne 38
anta 128
Antarctica 94, 112
anti-gravity 127
Anu 80
Aphrodite 253
Apkallu 92
Apollo 138, 214
Apollo and Athena ley lines
    138, 146, 164, 180
apron 40
Arabia 128
Arbor Low 48, 169
Archaeoastronomy 197
archangels 220
Archangel Gabriel 222, 233
Archangel Michael 163, 164,
    178, 190, 215, 233
archeoastronomy 60
archive, etymology of 264
Aristotle 253, 254
Ark of the Covenant 51, 263,
    264, 266
Arran 135
Arthurian legends 201
Arunachala 27, 29, 37, 43,
    48, 55, 75, 86
Arunachaleswar 27, 113
Arunta 54
Aryas 97
Asteroid 1999 RQ36 280
astral alignments 59
Aswan 203
As Above, So Below 41

As Without, So Within 41
Aten 150
Athena 138
Atlantis 75, 82, 146, 160
Atlit 149
Attis 117
Atum 27, 49, 50, 63, 231
Atu Motua 52
Australia 20
Avebury 128, 131, 137, 139,
    141, 169, 178, 181,
    241
axial tilt 60, 61
Aztecs 248, 271
Aztlán 76

B

Baalbek 113
Babylonian 123
Bacon, Francis 272
Bahamas 77
Balaam 252
balls of light 180
Bandelier 226
baraka 169
Barbury Castle Tetrahedron
    279
Barrowbridge Mump 137
basilisk 117
Bedouin 37
Belinus 140
Bell Rock 38
Beltane 38, 137
Benben 49, 50, 51, 54, 63,
    64, 103, 165, 203
Bent Pyramid 167, 211
Bernard de Clairvaux 217,
    263, 264, 265, 266,
    270
betilo 127, 178
Bhagavad Gita 35
Bible 50, 104
bio-dynamic fluids 277
blind spring. 187
blood 173, 192
bloodline of Christ 256
bluestones 203
Bogomils 98, 146, 261
Bolivia 19, 22, 56, 57
Bond, Frederick Bligh 161

bone 209
Book of Psalms 243
Book of What is in the Duat
        178
Borobudur 113, 145
Boudicca 284
Brahma 27, 33, 40
brain 192
brainwaves 25, 131, 180
Brighid 48
Britain 22
British Ministry of Defense
        274
Brittany 47, 51
Brunton, Paul 158, 159, 160,
        161
Buddha 215
builder gods 12
Building Texts 101, 169, 188,
        195
burial direction 222

C

Caesars 247
Cairn Ingli 31
Calanais 128, 197, 239, 241
Caldey island 142
Callisthenes 254
Canterbury Abbey 271
carbon atom 104, 212, 213
cardinal directions 219
Carnac 16, 51, 125, 127,
        139, 169, 174, 178,
        182, 183, 196, 203,
        219, 241
Castlerigg 48, 180
Castle Dore 144
Castle Hill 29
Cathari 255, 261, 271
Catherine of Alexandria 254
Catholic Church 34, 104,
        178, 213, 255, 259,
        260, 262, 265, 271
Celtic 38
Celtic wheel 133
centriole 217
cerebral cortex 192
Cerne 171
Cernunnos 127, 171
Cessair 48

Chaco Canyon 19
channelling 278
Charlemagne 284
Chartres cathedral 98, 103,
        107, 125, 165, 170,
        174, 188, 266, 269
Cherokee 91
Chichen Itza 77
Chiginagak 148
Chilean earthquake 103
Chillicothe 186
China 19, 21, 23, 29, 35, 37
China's five sacred mountains
        21
Chinese Book of Diagrams
        106, 195
Chinese Great Law 123
Cholula 86
Christianity 255
Christian Gnosticism 255,
        261
Church of Our Lady of Zion
        263
Cirencester Abbey 141
Cistercians 158, 265, 271
Cistercian Order 263
city of God 284
city of knowledge 12, 43
Clearbury Ring Hill Fort 141
climate change 45, 79, 82,
        271, 280
Codex Tro-Cortesianus 76
Codex Vaticanus 86
Cokesina 146
comet 79, 81, 82
concealed symbols 278
conductivity discontinuity 21
Confucian Board of Rites 98
consciousness 210, 229, 232,
        278
Constantine, Emperor 255
constellations 115, 240
Copper Scroll 263
Cornwall 47, 126
Cosmic Equation 264
creator gods 11, 278
Creek nation 91
crop circles 185, 273, 274,
        277, 278, 281
crop circle eyewitness 273,

277
Cruach Phadraig 25, 38
crucifix 263
crucifixion 262
crystalline structure of bone
        209
Cuba 77
cube 26
Cubit 196
Cuzco 61, 63
Cybele 116
Cyril of Alexandria 256

D

Daghdha 38
Dalai Lama 29
dance of Siva 41
Dead Sea Scrolls 81
Dehenet 26, 37
Delgado, Pat 275
Delos 178
Delphi 96, 109, 110, 128,
        174, 178, 256
Dendera 63, 99, 205
Deneb 71
diatoms 208
Dionysus 253
divine virgin 270
Djehuti 33, 64, 73, 78, 93,
        94, 95, 179, 195, 253,
        266
Djinn 24
DMT 192
DNA 150, 208
Dodona 253
dod lanes 19
Dol-de-Bretagne 51, 126
dolmens 221
dolorite 204
Dominicans 271
Doug and Dave 273
doves 68, 80, 81, 96, 109
dowsers 205
Dowsing 185
Dowth 241
Dr. Jarl 126
Draco 71, 114
dragons 178, 179
Dravidian culture 43
Druidic Mysteries Schools 47

Druids 18, 20, 94, 95, 98,
    112, 125, 142, 169,
    171, 201, 202, 266
Dwarka 62, 76

E

Ea 80, 170
Earth's magnetic field 183
earth energy 178
Easter Island 12, 51, 52, 70,
    73, 85, 88, 89, 93,
    116, 146
Eben Shetiyah 54, 252
Edfu 11, 63, 64, 66, 73, 93,
    151
Edfu Building Texts 11
Edfu Pyramid Texts 278
Egyptian creation myth 82
Eire 38, 48
electric induction 182
electric shocks, from stone
    202
electromagnetic energy 21,
    25, 40, 102, 103, 131,
    148, 168, 171, 173,
    179, 180, 181, 183,
    189, 192, 231, 232,
    252, 268, 276
electromagnetic grid 188
electrostatic charge 203
electrum 51, 203
Ellicott, Andrew 286
Elyssian Fields 189
El Deir monastery 44
El Mirador 148
El Santuario de Chimayo 190
Éméi Shan 35, 116
endocrine glands 102
enemy snake 169, 179, 180
Enki 58, 76
enlightenment 222
Enlil/Ninlil/Ninurta 44
Ennead 217
Enoch 81
Epic of Gilgamesh 80
Er-Lannic 125
Eridu 58, 76, 170, 241, 285
Ériu 48
Er Grah 51
evil 178

F

fairy paths 19
Faroe Islands 45, 46
Father-Son-Holy Spirit 33
feng shui 219
Fermi Lab 182
Fields of Elysium 269
First Occasion vii, 37, 242
flood vii, 11, 12, 18, 27, 48,
    73, 80, 81, 82
flood myths vii, 81
Flower of Life 106, 111
Followers of Horus 73, 92,
    95, 99, 102, 126, 149,
    168, 201, 231
fonts 170, 173
Forbidden City 106
force field 169, 181, 188, 231
Forest de Fougères 142
four material forces 220
Freemasons 113, 148, 149,
    190, 214, 272, 285
Fuji 116, 148
Funerary Texts 187, 189
fusion 104, 107, 109, 211

G

Gabbar 35
Galicia 146
Galileo 207
Garden of Eden 266
Gavrinis 243
Gematria 104, 112, 215, 265,
    279
Genesis 34
Genni 159
Geoffrey of Monmouth 150
geomagnetic anomalies 22
geomagnetism 21, 179, 181,
    187, 192, 209
geometry, influence of 209
geopathic stress 179, 188
George Washington 190, 285
Gerald Hawkins 62
giant 12, 135, 186
giant's grave 135, 143, 150,
    171, 180
giants 86, 89, 90, 91, 144,
    150, 157, 159, 185,

    248, 278
Gibborim 90
Giza vii, 28, 37, 49, 52, 59,
    61, 62, 63, 64, 65, 66,
    71, 76, 112
Giza/Heliopolis 112
Giza pyramids 266
Glastonbury 279
Glastonbury Abbey 107, 124,
    161
Glastonbury Tor 137, 170,
    250
Global Consciousness Project
    232
Glory Ann 133, 144
gnosis 28
Gnostics 98
Gnostic Gospels 34, 99
Gnostic texts 18
Göbekli Tepe 82, 102, 103,
    266
God, as geometer 198
gods 11
Golden Age 17, 55, 74, 75,
    242, 250
golden ratio 141
Gorakhnath 116
Gospel of John 280
Gothic cathedrals 139, 266,
    271
Graham Hancock 57, 63
Grand Ménec 183
granite 94, 157, 181, 203
gravity 21, 148
gravity anomalies 22
Great Platonic Year 240
Great Pyramid of Giza 89, 93,
    103, 107, 110, 112,
    149, 158, 167, 203,
    209, 210, 230, 232,
    247
Greenland ice cores 82, 241,
    244
Guatemala 148

H

Haggadah 252
Haggiar Khem 241
Hainan 137
Halloween 224

Hall of Learning 160
Hall of Records 94
hands, electrical circuit 186
Harmonic Convergence 162
Hartmann Grid 188
Hartmann lines 231, 269, 276
Hathor 99, 253
healing 21
heka 260
hekau 52, 86
Hekla volcano 241
Heliopolis (also see Innu) vii, 48, 49, 51, 53, 55, 63, 64, 71, 73, 74, 78, 117, 148, 150, 254, 259, 284, 288
henge 181, 188
Heng Shān 23, 37, 45
Henry VIII 124, 250
heptagram 214, 270
Heraklion 254
Hermes 253, 266
Hermeticism 265
Hermopolis 260
Herod 124
Herodotus 253
hexagon 111, 207, 211
hexagram 214
Highcliffe Castle 141
High Kirk of Edinburgh 140
hill forts 20
hill of Hor 44
Hill of Uisneach 38, 48
hill of Uisneach 38, 48
Hinduism 21
Hiva 52, 89
Hoi Sophoí 96
Holyrood Abbey 140
Holy Inquisition 271
Holy of Holies 27
holy wells 170, 171
Homer 254
Hopi 17, 18
Hopi creation myth 18
Horemheb 246
Horus 25, 26, 44, 63, 169, 179
House of Sokar 64
Hsuan-k'ung Ssu 23

Hu 164
Huari 86
Huà Shan 37
Hugues de Payens 265
human body, energy field 229
human sacrifice 248
hunab 196
hydrogen bonds 198
Hypatia 256

I

Iberia 126, 197
Iceland 45
Icknield Way 140
ideal city 265
Ideal State 254
Imhotep 55, 98, 132, 189
Imperial System of Measures 196
Inca 57, 247, 271
increase centres 177
India 27, 28, 35, 48, 52
Indus Valley 243
Innocent II 264
Innu/Heliopolis vii, 48, 49, 51, 104
intent 230, 231, 232, 233
Ireland 14, 19, 25, 38, 46, 47, 48, 86, 90, 126, 164, 170, 186, 189, 202
Irminsul 284
Isfahan 285
Isis 25, 26, 37, 64, 78, 82, 83, 139, 253, 254
Islamic art 121, 215
Islamic mosques 271
Isles of Scilly 47
Isle of Man 46, 47, 48

J

Jacob's ladder 112
Jacob Roggeveen 88
Jainism 24
Japan 29, 30, 37, 45
Jason and the Argonauts 96, 254
Jeremiah 139
Jericho 90
Jerusalem 13, 54, 174, 252

Jesus Christ 22, 25, 26, 37, 50, 96, 104, 105, 109, 138, 143, 149, 215, 231, 255, 262, 279, 284
Jnana puri 12, 55
John the Baptist 170
July 21 253
Jupiter 79, 207

K

Ka'ba 25, 98, 170, 190
Kabbalah (also Qabalah) 265
Kahnimweiso Namkhet 62, 76, 87
Kalahari 18
Kalakh 44
Kalasasaya 58, 60, 61, 62
Kali Yuga 242
Karnak 63, 66, 67, 96, 109, 110, 127, 128, 151, 188, 232
Kathmandu 116
Kealkill 135
Kergadiou 126
King's Chamber 149, 156, 249
kings 53
King David 54, 123, 251
King Sil 250
Kiribati 116
Kirk Michael 47
kiva 190, 226
Knights Templar 13, 95, 98, 113, 133, 141, 144, 146, 149, 255, 263, 265, 271, 285
Knocknarea 38, 125
Knowlton henge 128, 169, 205
Knowth 241
Kolossi 98
Kom Ombu 63, 151, 188
Kon-Tiki Viracocha 61, 62, 63
Kore Kosmou 73, 78, 85, 101, 121, 155
Krishna 76
Kumari Kandam 74, 75
Kura Tawhiti 29, 144, 161,

175
Kushasthali 76

L

L'Enfant, Pierre 286
labyrinth, Chartres 25, 269
Lake Titicaca 63, 79
Languedoc 271
Laptev Sea 79
last glacial maximum 74
Law Rock 45
La Conquista 17
levitate 126
ley line 137, 138, 139, 140,
    141, 145, 146, 276
Le Grand Menhir Brisé 183
light frequencies 269
limestone 37, 203, 205
Lincoln Memorial 287
lingam, also Sivalingam 43,
    44, 52, 53, 54
Llangynidr menhir 183
Locmariquer 126
Lompock Rancho 91
London 171
London obelisk 284
longitude 110, 111, 112
long barrows 90, 169, 180
Long Man of Wilmington
    186
lords of Light 12, 93
Loughcrew 93
Lourdes 142
Lugh 38, 47, 224
Lughnasadh 224
lunations 143
lunation triangle 143
Lundy island 143
Lung Mei 19
Luxor 37, 59, 63, 113, 139,
    151, 165, 188, 232,
    284
Lyonesse 47

M

Maa Sharda 35
Machu Picchu 78
magician-priests 52
magnetism 19, 20, 21, 22, 52

magnetic field 78, 187, 203
magnetic field, reversal of
    180, 242, 280
magnetism 178, 186, 188,
    192, 219
magnetite 181, 192, 203,
    204, 205, 209
Mahabalipuram 62, 76
Maldives 75, 76
Malta 76, 77, 240
mana 52, 169
Mandate from Heaven 244
Manetho 254
Manichaeism 98, 261
Mansar 145
Manu 81, 86, 97
Maori 88, 144, 225, 271
marae 89
Marden Henge 141
Marotini 30
Mary 25, 26, 37, 74, 105,
    107, 109, 180, 222
Mary Magdalene 105, 141
Masuro Emoto 173
Mata-Ki-Te- Rani 51
Mato Tipila 232
Matsya Purana 95
Mauna Loa 173
Maya 17, 18, 43, 76, 81, 247
Meera Mandir 145
Megalithic Yard 107
Megiddo 138
Mehrgarh 116, 145
memory 94
Memphis 111, 253
Men-an-Tol 187
menhir 51, 117, 127, 171,
    178, 183
Menec 51
Menes, pharaoh 73, 242
Menkaure 94
Men of High Degree 20
Merchants of Light 98, 272
Merlin 215
Merlin's Mound 134
Mesa Verde 271
Mesopotamia 240, 241, 243,
    285
Messalians 261
meteorites 241, 243, 271

Metonic Cycle 60
MI5 274
Michael 137
Michael and Mary lines 180
Micronesia 62
Min 253
Minoan 240
Minster church 233
Miringa Te Kakara 225
Mission San Gabriel Arcangel
    190
Mnajdra 241
moai 85, 88, 89
Mohammed 215
Mont St. Michel 125, 138
Monument Valley 170
Moses 29, 37, 264
mosque 121, 205
Mount Ararat 97, 145
Mount Carmel 149
Mount Fuji 30, 37, 45
Mount Haku 37
Mount Kailas 25, 35, 45
Mount Katherine 37
Mount Meru 24, 25, 26, 35,
    131
Mount Miwa 29, 37
Mount Olympus 28
Mount Sinai 29
Mount Tabor 138, 149
Mount Tamalpais 186
Mount Taylor 28
music scale 196, 268
mw 169
Mysteries Schools 13, 39, 47,
    51, 53, 95, 104, 148,
    164, 259

N

Nabu 44
nagas 188
Nag Hammadi 13, 34
Nag Hammadi Library 256
Nag Hammadi Texts 262
Nanda Devi 28
Nan Madol 76, 87, 116
NASA 79, 112, 177, 178,
    180, 209, 280
native American mounds 241
Navajo 38, 177, 190

navels of the earth 122
navel stone 61, 98, 111
Neak Pean 71
Nebuchadnezzar 124
Neoplatonists 255
Neters/Neteru 73, 92, 101, 278
Newgrange 189, 202, 241
New Atlantis 272
New England 190
New Mexico 19, 27, 30, 38, 174, 177
New Testament 25, 105
New York obelisk 284
New Zealand 29, 30, 77, 89, 90, 161, 198, 271
Nimrod 111
niu pole 226
Noah 48, 81, 82
Noah's Ark 146
node 23, 102, 165, 190, 191
nonagon 217
northeast 225
North Pole 128, 150
number of the beast 104

O

Oannes 170
obelisk 49, 50, 51, 117, 284
obliquity, period of 211
octagon 215, 286
Odin 131
Odyssey 254
Ohio 185
Old Sarum 141, 174
Olmec calendar 242
Olympia 253
OM 145
Omar Khayyam 269
omphalos 110, 178, 185, 250, 284
orbits of planets 196
Organization of Nag Hammadi 98
Orion 37
Orkney 45
Osirion 66, 67, 106, 213
Osiris 26, 64, 65, 66, 68, 69, 73, 78, 82, 83, 113, 115, 251, 253, 254

Otherworld 143, 185, 187

P

Padmanabham 145
Padmasambhava 23
pagan, meaning of 178
Palenque 77
Pan 96, 253
Paracas, Bay of 61, 62, 116
paradise/pairi-daeza vii, 24, 25, 26, 27, 28, 30, 34, 37, 40, 45, 47, 50, 53, 102, 189, 262, 277
Paris 171, 284
Pasadena 190
Pashupatinath 116
path of the ecliptic 115
Pawon temple 145
Pennsylvania Avenue 286
pentagon 211
Pentagon, The 287
pentagram 105, 111, 113, 116, 207, 213, 214
Periodic Table of Elements 215
Persepolis 111
Peter and the 153 fish 105, 143
Petra 44, 50
petroglyphs 20
pharaoh 40, 123
Pharos 254, 287
Philae 63, 151, 191
Philip IV 141, 271
Phnom Bakheng 113
Picatrix 265
piezoelectric 183
pineal gland 192, 277
Piri Reis 112
Place of the Strong Saints 266
planets 207
Plato 40, 54, 74, 75, 82, 113, 146, 213, 253
Platonist School of Alexandria 256
Pleiades 248
pneuma 169
Po-wa-ha 177
Pohnpei 76, 87, 116
Pope Clement V 271

Pope Gregory 141
Pope Leo X 262
Popul Vuh 17
Portugal 28, 38, 125, 126, 178, 264, 266, 271
Portuguese 94
Portuguese Honors system 141
Posnansky, Arthur 60, 61, 62
potentized water 172
Precessional Cycle 12, 65, 66, 114, 211
precessional numbers 116, 196
Precession of the Equinoxes 115, 240
Preseli 202
priests of Amun 246
Primeval Mound 49
Prime Meridian 111
primordial mounds 35, 37, 53, 63, 64, 66, 141, 278
Pronaos of Edfu 165
Ptah 49, 50, 169, 186
pth-nwyt-mw 169
Ptolemy 254
pu 197
Puranas 86
Purification of the Virgin 133
Puritan 190
Putuó Shan 35
Pyramids 26, 76, 167, 174, 188, 196, 203, 219, 232, 249, 271
Pyramid of Kukulkan 113
Pyramid Texts, see also Edfu 43, 49, 64, 65, 67, 69, 71, 93, 149, 179
Pythagoras 39, 253
Pythagorean triangle 143

Q

Qabalah (also Kabbalah) 104, 112, 148
Qu'ran 222
quartz 21, 92, 171, 182, 183, 203, 204, 205
Quechua Maya 43, 94
Quiche Maya 17, 18

Qumran 263
Qumran Scrolls 90, 102

R

Ra 89, 179, 195, 214, 253
radioactivity 187, 203
Ramtek 145
Random Event Generator 232
red granite 49, 203, 204, 268
Red Pyramid 211
Ridgeway track 140
Rig Veda 33, 34
Ring of Brogar 129
ritual 122
Robin Hood 96
Roches aux Fées 126
Rollright stone circle 187,
    202
Romans 94
root of suffering 262
Rosslyn Chapel 140
Rostau 37
Rybury 141, 169

S

Sabeans of Harran 265, 266
sacred geometry 207, 268,
    270
sacred measure 197
sacred mound 26
sacred mountains 22
sacred number 104
Sacsayhuamán 63, 67, 78
Sagas 45, 52
sages 11, 272
Sages of Mehweret 94
Saint Cecelia 233
Saint Iliud 142
Salisbury Cathedral 141, 165,
    211
Sammain 224
Sammara 285
sandstone 205
Sangams 75
Sanskrit 145
Santa Clara Pueblo 177
Santa Fe 190
Santiago de Compostela 146,
    188

São Miguel 198
Saqqara 98, 110, 132, 188,
    189, 254, 269
Sardis 111
sarsen 205
Saturn 111
Satya Yuga, 242
Scotland 271
Scottish Rite Masonry build-
    ing 148
sea level 77
sects 272
sects, religious 261
sedimentary stone 205
Sekhet Ianu 189
serpent 34, 113, 117, 178,
    185, 268
Serpent Mound 91, 185, 230
Serra de Estrela 28
Seshat 179, 195, 214
Set 82, 113, 115
Seven degrees of perfection
    187, 189
seven gates 231, 276
Seven principles 168
Seven sages vii, 12, 85, 86,
    87, 89, 91, 93, 95, 96,
    97, 98, 99, 102, 109,
    151, 168, 195, 259,
    272
Seven Sages of Islam 265
Shakaba Texts 64
Shangte 122
Shemsu Hor 73
Shesep Ankh 63
Shetland 45
Shining Ones 38, 86, 90, 96,
    132, 278
Shinto shrines 37
Shiprock 27
Shuruppak 241
Siauliai 190
Sibylline Oracles 81
Silbury Hill 132, 134, 180,
    181, 250, 278
Simon Peter 116
Sinagua 38, 174
Sinai 37
Sinhalese people 26
Sioux 21, 45

Sioux legends 91
Sippar 241
Sirius 139, 253, 254, 286
Siva vii, 12, 25, 27, 28, 30,
    32, 33, 34, 35, 37, 40,
    41, 43, 44, 48, 49,
    55, 231
Sivalingam, also lingam 27,
    44, 45, 48, 49, 71,
    110
Skanda Purana 17, 75, 78
Skellig Michael 138, 164
sky-ground dualism 41, 50,
    65, 69, 104, 196
Socrates Scholasticus 255
Sokar 110
Solomon 252
Solomon's Masons 265
Solomon's Temple 13, 54,
    122, 123, 124, 263,
    265
Songs of the Ascents 252
Sons of Light 81, 262
sorcerer, meaning 250
sound 63, 86, 126, 157, 203,
    214, 215, 230
Specifications of the Mounds
    of the Early Primeval
    Age 94
Sphinx 63, 65, 66, 71, 242
spire 180
spirit roads 19, 20, 117, 129,
    177, 185
spots of the fawn 18, 44, 111
square 213
Sri Lanka 26
St. Catherine 141
St. Catherine's Hill 141
St. Catherine's well 171
St. Clether 171
St. Germain-des-Pres 171
St. John's Gospel 105
St. John the Divine 190
St. Luke 47
St. Mary 137
St. Mary's Chapel 279
St. Michael 138, 146
St. Michael telluric line
    (see also Michael and Mary
    ley) 280

stained glass 269
stepped pyramids 44
stone 202
Stonehenge viii, 11, 14, 31,
        58, 59, 60, 62, 78, 86,
        102, 107, 113, 117,
        118, 141, 143, 161,
        162, 163, 169, 171,
        201, 203, 204, 216,
        223, 241, 279
Stretching the Cord 195
stupa 26, 188
subatomic particle 40
Sufi 265
Suleiman ben Daoud 252
Sumer 12, 44, 250
superstition 249
Suryavarman II 68, 271
Susa 54, 111, 116
swastika 213
sweat lodges 222
Swinside stone circle 227, 230
Switzerland 271
symbols 278

T

Ta-Mery 74, 92
Tables of Laws 264, 266
tabu 169
Tacitus 201
Tahiti 116
Tài Shan 37, 45
Taktsang Dzong 23, 283
tall, see also giants 29
Talmud 122, 231, 251
Tamil culture 43
Tamil Nadu 27, 43, 74, 75
Tanen 169
Taoist 21, 37
Tara 48
Taranaki 30, 148
Tarxien 76
Taurids 271
Taurus, age of 240
Ta Mery 26
Te-Pito-O-Te-Henua 51
telepathic communication 96
telepathy 18, 20, 268
telluric currents 21, 23, 34,
        117, 131, 137, 138,

169, 176, 178, 180,
        181, 182, 185, 186,
        190, 191, 204, 268,
        270, 276
Templar, see also Knights
        Templar 38
Temple Mount 86, 170, 174,
        252, 263
Temple of the Four Winds
        116, 225
Temple of the Seven Pagodas
        76
Tenochtitlan 248
Ten Commandments 264
Teotihuacan 19, 113, 196,
        198, 248
Tetragrammaton 251
tetrahedron 40, 41, 198
Tewa people 23, 190
Theodosius I 255
Theophrastus 253
The Baphuon 71
the Field 229
The Great Work 98, 265,
        266, 270, 281
the Sanctuary, stone circle 131
The Tables of Testimony 264
Thingvellir 45
Thom, Alexander 196
Thomas Jefferson 285
Thoth, see also Djehuti 266
Tibet 127, 171, 188
Tigris-Euphrates River 241
Tikal 77
Til el-Amarna 150
Timaeus 272
Tirupati 45
Tiwanaku vii, 56, 57, 59, 60,
        61, 62, 63, 71, 73, 74,
        76, 78, 79, 126, 129,
        137
Tiye 246
Tolkappiyam 43
Toltec 76, 247
toning 233
Torah 122
Tower of Babel 44
Tower of London 171, 284
transfiguration of the soul
        246, 260, 274, 279

travelling gods 12
Treasure, etymology of 264
Tree of Knowledge 34, 52, 61,
        62, 116
Tree of Life 148, 286
triangle 33, 35, 37, 38, 39,
        40, 41, 47, 48, 50,
        212
Trimurti 33, 34
triple steps of Vishnu 37, 78,
        109, 134, 285
Triskele 47
Troy 244
Tse Bit'ai, see also Shiprock
        27, 29, 38
Tsoodzil 28, 38
Tuatha Dé Danaan 38, 48, 80
Tulum 77
Tura limestone 203
Tutankamun 246

U

U.S. Capitol 285
Uanna 89
ultrasound 127, 181
Uluru 45, 145
underground springs 173
Ur 241
Ursa Major 95
Ursa Minor 71
Uru-shalim 252
Utnapishtim 80
Uxmal 77, 86, 87, 93, 126
Uzziah 124

V

Vadum Iacob 149
Valley of the Kings and
        Queens 26, 37
vara 197
Vatican 116, 274
Vayats 146
Vedas 12, 29, 75
Vega 114
Venus, missing 244
vesica piscis 268
Vespasian 124
vineyard of God 149
Viracocha 61, 62, 63, 86, 90

Virahamihira 111
Virgin Mary, see also Mary
    141, 142
Virgo, constellation 270, 285
Vishnu vii, 27, 32, 33, 34,
    35, 36, 37, 38, 39, 40,
    41, 44, 62, 68, 76, 78,
    80, 145
Vishnu Purana 35
visions 21
vision quests 20
Visvakarma 27, 44, 55, 98
vortex 173
vortex, of energy 268

W

Waitaha 29, 90, 144
Washington D.C 111, 286
Washington Monument 286
Watchers 81, 132, 278, 280
water 150, 169, 170, 171,
    172, 173, 174, 176,
    180, 182, 185, 188,
    192, 198, 202, 204,
    205, 209, 213, 214,
    268
Watkins, Alfred 140
Wells 170
White House 285, 286
William St. Clair 141
William the Conqueror 284
Wilmington 186
Winchester 170
Windmill Hill 141
wise men 31
Wotan 131
Wutái Shan 35
Wuzhi 138
Wyoming 232

X

Xi' an pyramids 219

Y

Yajurveda 178
Yggdrasil Tree 52
Ynis Mon 201
Ynys Elen 143
Yonaguni 73, 77, 78

Yucatan 76, 77
Yugas 75, 242
Yuma 149

Z

Zambujeiro 126
Zazen meditation 40
Zep Tepi 37, 63, 64, 65, 71,
    74, 76, 78, 126, 242
Zeus 96, 110, 127, 253
ziggurats 44
Ziusudra 96
zodiac 105, 114, 240
Zoroastrians 102

Hampton Roads Publishing Company
....for the evolving human spirit

Hampton Roads Publishing Company publishes books on a variety
of subjects, including spirituality, health, and other related topics.

For a copy of our latest trade catalog, call 978-465-0504 or visit
our website at *www.redwheelweiser.com*